I0083759

Civic Discourse
and Cultural Politics
in Canada

Recent Titles in
Civic Discourse for the Third Millennium
Michael H. Prosser, Series Editor

Civic Discourse and Cultural Politics in Canada

A Cacophony of Voices

EDITED BY
Sherry Devereaux Ferguson
AND Leslie Regan Shade

Civic Discourse for the Third Millennium
MICHAEL H. PROSSER, *Series Editor*

ABLEX PUBLISHING
Westport, Connecticut • London

Library of Congress Cataloging-in-Publication Data

Civic discourse and cultural politics in Canada : a cacophony of voices / edited by Sherry
Devereaux Ferguson and Leslie Regan Shade.
    p.   cm.—(Civic discourse for the third millennium)
    Includes bibliographical references and index.
    ISBN 1–56750–596–1 (alk. paper)—ISBN 1–56750–597–X (pbk. : alk. paper)
    1. Civil society—Canada. 2. Political planning—Canada. 3. Information
technology—Political aspects—Canada. 4. Canada—Politics and government—1980–
5. Canada—Social conditions—1991– I. Ferguson, Sherry Devereaux. II. Shade,
Leslie Regan, 1957– III. Series.
JL186.5.C58 2002
300'971—dc21   2002016338

British Library Cataloguing in Publication Data is available.

Copyright © 2002 by Sherry Devereaux Ferguson and Leslie Regan Shade

All rights reserved. No portion of this book may be
reproduced, by any process or technique, without the
express written consent of the publisher.

Library of Congress Catalog Card Number: 2002016338
ISBN: 1–56750–596–1
      1–56750–597–X (pbk.)

First published in 2002

Ablex Publishing, 88 Post Road West, Westport, CT 06881
An imprint of Greenwood Publishing Group, Inc.
www.ablexbooks.com

Printed in the United States of America

The paper used in this book complies with the
Permanent Paper Standard issued by the National
Information Standards Organization (Z39.48–1984).

10 9 8 7 6 5 4 3 2 1

Copyright Acknowledgments

The authors and publisher are grateful for permission to reproduce material from the following:

R. Caplan (Ed.), *Cape Breton Works: More Lives from Cape Breton's Magazine* (Wreck Cove, NS: Breton Books, 1996). Reprinted with permission.

G. Ingram, A. Bouthillette, & Y. Retter (Eds.), *Queers in Space: Communities/ Public Places/Sites of Resistance* (Seattle, WA: Bay Press, 1997). Reprinted with permission.

Benjamin West, *The Death of General Wolfe*; François-Louis-Joseph Watteau, *The Death of Montcalm*; Robert Harris, *Cartoon for "Meeting of the Delegates of British North America to Settle the Terms of Confederation, Quebec, October 1864"*; and Robert Houle, *Kanata*, National Gallery of Canada, Ottawa. Reprinted with permission.

Charles Huot, *Esquisse de la première séance de la Chambre d'Assemblée* and Napoléon Bourassa, The *Apotheosis of Christopher Columbus*. Musée du Québec. Reprinted with permission.

In memory of my grandfather,
John Solon Gunn, M.D.
Member of first graduating class, Memphis Hospital Medical College,
University of Tennessee, April 25, 1902

Who bequeathed me his library and his passion for learning

Sherry Devereaux Ferguson

Contents

Part I

Introduction

Chapter 1

A Cacophony of Voices: Competing for the Future

Sherry Devereaux Ferguson

Canadians in the twenty-first century face a number of challenges: the threat to cultural identities posed by new information and communication technologies, feminist voices raised against a system that neglects older and single women and leaves many children in poverty, an aging society, and questions related to social cohesion as the country grows more racially and ethnically diverse. Calls for sovereignty echo from francophone Québec to the western provinces, where many people feel more connected to western Americans than to eastern Canadians. The uneasy relationship between center and periphery threatens not to hold, and quietly, in the shadows, a large Native community moves slowly but relentlessly toward self-government.

In the meantime, governments grapple to make large, unwieldy, bureaucratic structures responsive to the demands of a wired and networked society. They ask civil society organizations to participate in flexible and cooperative relationships, but the systems within which they sculpt their relationships are hard and archaic, ill suited to supporting the new operational models. A new paradigm is required, but who is to offer the model when governments around the world struggle to implement the paradigm that Canadians now question?

This introductory chapter discusses the dominant threads in Canadian civic discourse. One thread relates to competing voices (cultural and political) and a second to issues of governance, globalization, and civil society. A third and final thread involves Canada's quest for national identity and cultural sovereignty. The theme of new information and communication technologies appears throughout this discussion and book, an insistent presence that cannot be ignored.

THE MANY VOICES OF CANADA

Canada prides itself on its mosaic (as opposed to melting pot) character. A 1997 study found that "multiculturalism/tolerance" ranked seventh among the values important to Canadians (Dasko, 2000). Unlike the deteriorating situation in many countries, marked by ethnic and religious conflicts, trends in Canada show an increasingly tolerant population, with 76 percent of Canadians agreeing in 1997 that immigration has a positive impact on our economy (as opposed to 35 percent in 1993). Whereas 61 percent of Canadians (polled in 1997) believed that Canada admits too many immigrants, the figure had dropped to 44 percent by 2000. Approval of our country's multicultural policy remains high at 62 percent, up from 51 percent in 1991 (Dasko, 2000).

Canadians are a smorgasbord of people from all over the world—the Bahamas, Hong Kong, China, Japan, Kenya, Portugal, Sri Lanka, Sweden, Italy, France, Great Britain, and others too numerous to mention. Canadians speak 15 languages other than French or English as their mother tongues (Statistics Canada, 1996 census). This does not include a very large number of languages that are spoken by relatively small percentages of Canadians. Many children of first- and second-generation Canadians attend Saturday classes to learn a second or third language. Our country is a prime hunting ground for international models such as Shalom and Linda Evangelista because the country is a mixture of exotic ethnic types and blonde Scandinavians, whose ethnicity is valued and protected by Canadian laws. It would be difficult to find a country that celebrates cultural diversity more than Canada.

Demographics other than ethnicity are also transforming the country, and the face of Canada is growing older. In recognition of changing global demographics, the United Nations established 1999 as the Year of Older Persons. Almost one out of eight Canadians is over 65 years of age. By the year 2020, one out of every five Canadians will be a senior. The numbers will increase to almost one out of four by 2041. These figures stand in stark opposition to earlier periods in time. In 1921, for example, only one out of 20 Canadians was a senior (Statistics Canada, 2001).

The majority of seniors live in private households. Most live alone, and a large percentage of older Canadians own their own homes. Surveys confirm that, above all else, seniors value their independence (Bess, 1999). Moreover, they ask to be recognized as individuals, not members of a homogeneous demographic group. They resent the old stereotypes ("Growing Older," 1994). Not unlike other Canadians, their key issues are health, housing, income, and transportation (Canadian Council on Social Development, 1998; Seniors Secretariat, 1990).

Traditionally, seniors have been a group left on the sidelines of society, retiring from an active role in life at the same time that they retire from their jobs. However, current trends show large numbers continuing their participation in political, economic, and social life after they reach 65. For example, one group of seniors in Victoria, British Columbia, called the "Raging Grannies," first captured headlines in 1988. The movement soon spread to the islands off British Columbia, including the Gabriola and Saltspring Islands; and representatives from Victoria, Vancouver, Gabriola, Comox, and Saltspring attended the founding conference. When they first got together in 1988, they thought they would be a "one-day stand at an anti-uranium rally in front of the BC legislature" (Raging Grannies, 2001), but now they cannot fulfill all the requests for appearances. As one writer said, "They're street theatre, they're funny, they're dead serious, they're angry, they're raging, they want nuclear weapons and everything that contributes to their manufacture out of Canada, they want a clean world for their children and their children's children, they're Raging Grannies" (Raging Grannies, 2001). Activities include the following:

They sing outrageous songs to familiar tunes, dress in outlandish costumes and relentlessly protest the presence of American warships and submarines armed with nuclear weapons in our waters, the presence of a nuclear weapons guidance system on Winchelsea Island off Nanoose, the continuing and intensifying involvement of Canada in a military strategy they believe is wrong. And they have more work than they can handle. (Raging Grannies, 2001)

More seniors run for political offices at all levels of government than in past years. Inputting key words such as *advocacy* and *protest* into web searches brings up a surprising number of sites dedicated to seniors' issues and efforts. Whatever their orientation, seniors are not the bland, colorless group that we once thought we knew and understood, and advertising and marketing executives have learned that they cannot address this target group with one strategy. Government departments that publish telephone numbers for inquiries and complaints know that the largest number of calls typically come from seniors, who have the time, energy, and money to become involved. A recently dismantled Canadian Internet activist web site for seniors was called "Fax the Feds" (2001).

At the same time that studies suggest that seniors have become more engaged in civic life, other surveys demonstrate that young people have become increasingly disengaged. Recent news accounts label Canadian youth as *apathetic, disinterested,* and even *antisocial* (Harvey, 2000). Alain Giguere presented the conclusions of his company's most recent polling efforts at the annual meeting of the Canadian Conference of Catholic Bishops. The Montreal-based public opinion firm CROP has been surveying Canadians on key values since 1983. The firm conducts three-hour interviews with 2,700 Canadians, including 442 in the 15–24 age group. The

surveys identify respondents' views on 100 key values. Harvey (2000) summarized these views in the following way:

Mr. Giguere said he was reluctant to bring the bishops the results of public opinion
surveys . . . because of the shocking findings about today's youth. Today's youth
love violence, are sexually permissive, get high on risk-taking, are weak on ethics
and social concern and low on religion and the importance of family. . . . They are
more individualistic, more thrill-seeking, more consumer-oriented, more pleasure-
seeking, and more impatient of social restraints than any recent generation. . . . And
there is no sign they will change as they grow older, because the 15–24-year-olds
of 1990 still hold much the same values today as they did then. . . . Only 15 per
cent of today's youth share values similar to those of their parents: a strong moral
sense, an emphasis on the importance of family, an interest in religion, and a concern for society as a whole. It's a real culture shock. (p. A7)

The majority of respondents in the 15–24 age group said that, in varying
degrees, they "get a kick out of violence" (Harvey, 2000, p. A7). Giguere
told the bishops: "We are dealing with a generation that has grown up on
Hollywood. They are bombarded with sex and violence and have no sense
of responsibility. I tremble to see what kind of society they are going to
produce in 20–25 years" (p. A7). The only contrary trend surfaced in Canadians over 35, who had "begun to feel the void in our community values" (p. A7).

A recent conference at McGill University in Montreal (2000) addressed
issues of citizenship, with a particular focus on youth. University graduates
who had entered the teaching profession spoke to some of the criticisms
leveled against youth. They argued that the old educational systems are
outdated—that they tell the stories of "dead white men" to which contemporary youth cannot relate. They urged that young people should be
allowed to bring their own multicultural stories and heritage into the class-
rooms and to learn about citizenship by becoming active in political rallies
and institutions (rather than just reading about the civic rights of Canadians). They said that civic educators should put more emphasis on engagement outside the classroom ("Can Canadian Civics," 2000). Others argue
that young people may be less engaged as citizens of Canada, but they are
becoming more involved than their parents as citizens of a global society.
Defying the idea that Canada's youth are apathetic and listless observers
of civic life, the recent protests against free trade in Seattle and Québec
City included a large representation of university students.

Taking these arguments to a broader level, Potter (Chapter 8 in this
volume) refers to the results of the World Values Survey. He says that this
survey reveals "a post-materialist citizenry in Canada, who are less deferential and more willing to engage in protest behavior." In fact, citing Nevitte's (1996) work, Potter points out that Canadians are the "most

protest-oriented of all the national samples." He says that government leaders had the feeling that Canadians were leading the anti-MAI protests. So the depiction of Canadians (particularly youth) as an apathetic lot may be deceiving. In addition, Canada has strong critical traditions in academia and a thriving popular theater community that draws its inspiration from Boal's (1985) theater of the oppressed. Representative performing groups include Catalyst Theatre and Peace Theatre (Alberta), Headlines Theatre (Vancouver), Theatre Sans Détour (Québec), and Mixed Company and KYTES (Ontario).

This engagement in civic life and commitment to social justice are also evident in other spheres. In October 2000, women staged marches in Québec and elsewhere in Canada against poverty and violence against women. In the same month, the Supreme Court of Canada passed a new ruling that the courts and those responsible for child welfare should weigh the safety and well-being of children over the rights of parents. There was only one dissenting vote. At the same time that women have organized to gain a louder and more powerful voice, fathers' rights groups have issued a call to arms, demanding greater access to children; and grandparents lobby for the right to maintain contact with estranged grandchildren. The movements are international. Lesbians and gays have stepped to the forefront to demand equal status under the law, social benefits, and the right to marry. In February 2000, the federal government passed Bill C-23, which extended the status of common law partners to same-sex couples. The legislation affected more than 60 federal statutes, although a later amendment specified that marriage was not one of the rights covered by the bill.

The above references to cacophonous voices in Canada are certainly not exhaustive; they do not even include all of the groups covered in this book. But they do suggest the diversity and power of competing groups, each with its own issues and cargo of cultural, social, and political values.

CIVIL SOCIETY, GLOBALIZATION, AND GOVERNANCE

Some argue that Canada's celebration of cultural and regional diversity and political plurality creates a situation whereby citizens may lack "the minimum levels of shared awareness and values that are preconditions for building national public judgment" (Rosell, 1999, p. 104). Differences in worldview, cultural backgrounds, languages, and political ideologies make it difficult to engage in the kind of dialogue that is required to sustain and nurture democratic society. Our official language policy mandates that all Canadians become bilingual and bicultural, and our multicultural policy seeks to ensure that Canadians do not lose touch with their diverse cultural roots. For these reasons, nationalists argue that governments have a responsibility to define a vision and create a framework wherein people can discover or construct shared values through dialogue. The essential venue for such discourse, proponents say, must be civil society—a third sphere "composed of individuals, groups, and organizations who seek to act in the public interest on a voluntary basis," as opposed to the spheres of commerce and government (Barber, cited in Rosell, p. 106). Some define civil society as "anti-state" or "anti-hegemony" (Van Rooy, cited in Sawatsky, 2000, p. 2), a situation in which the people exercise power.

According to these definitions, religious organizations, educational institutions, professional groups, and environmental organizations are all part of civil society. Such organizations "mediate" between government and the market (Kettering Foundation, p. 6, cited in Torjman, 1997). Terms associated with civil society include the *public interest, social capital, voluntary, non-profit, civility,* and *nation-building.* When members of a community attend church, join a social club, volunteer for a United Way campaign, help a neighbor, or even have coffee with a friend, they create social capital (Shah, 1997). All of these terms imply a grassroots involvement, people working at the community level to build connections and trust and interpersonal relationships. According to Torjman (1997), civil society is "a search for civility" whereby "all citizens—individual, corporate and government—assume responsibility for promoting economic, social and environmental well-being" (p. 1). Al Etmanski, of the Planned Lifetime Advocacy Network (PLAN), says that Canada has managed to create innovative models that "take the best from American and British activity and thought and create a way of building community that's much different from elsewhere" (cited in Sawatsky, 2000, p. 4).

Some argue that the term *civil society* is too ill-defined, confusing, ambiguous, and broad to be meaningful. Al Hatton (quoted in Sawatsky, 2000), director of the National Voluntary Organization, says that we should talk instead about "precepts of justice and citizenship and sustainability and caring" if we want people to know what we mean (p. 9). And in Canada, some 175,000 voluntary, non-profit organizations bring these principles to life: "[They] provide community services; organize cultural, educational, and sporting activities; and lobby for change on the political front" (North-South Institute, 1999). They have achieved many positive changes on a national and global front.

Torjman (1997) sets out three objectives for civil society: to build and strengthen "caring communities," to ensure economic security through "job creation and the equitable distribution of existing work," and to promote social investment by "directing resources towards the well-being and positive development of people" (p. 1). According to this view, governments have a responsibility to encourage and support problem-solving efforts by citizens, communities, and local economies. Like Torjman, the Caledon Institute (a Canadian think tank on social policy) sees the roles of government and business as sustaining and supporting the activities of civil society. Not all agree with this principle. Some believe that governments are too involved in regulating, funding, and creating policies for civil society. Others believe that governments are abdicating their responsibilities when they expect too much from this third sector, and they fear that civil society may falter under the heavy load. As one civil society group noted, "Despite the pivotal role that civil society plays within our democratic society, it is under attack by a myriad of social, political, economic and technological shifts—government cutbacks, government offloading, donor fatigue, decline in public engagement, increased cultural atomization, erosion of standards" (Civil Society Project, 2000, p. 1).

While the trend toward civil society has gained in momentum, a contrary trend toward globalization and internationalization has concomitantly developed. The idea of what constitutes a community has been stretched to its limits as electronic communities proliferate and individuals and groups bond with remote others who share similar interests and values. Concepts of citizenship become watery and ill-defined in such a milieu, and civil society loses much of its potential for bringing people together in a real—not virtual—town hall. Governments flounder as they attempt to legislate and regulate in areas that lie outside national boundaries. Issues related to cultural and economic sovereignty permeate the millennial debate over control of the Internet, much as they punctuated the debate over the direct broadcast satellite in the 1970s. But there is a new edge and urgency to the debate as economic power moves from governments to multinational corporations. In an environment of contradictions, governments seek to balance the competing interests of many different constituencies, ideologies, and principles. They confront the demand to achieve a balance between individual and collective rights, cultural pluralism and social cohesion, free trade and cultural protectionism, economic prosperity and protection of the environment, linguistic duality and multiculturalism, and community values and globalization.

In an age of relativity when almost every Canadian value is on the table for negotiation, governments must find workable definitions for *private* versus *public space*, *free speech*, and *human rights*. In an age when knowledge spreads itself like a thin vapor around the world, and no one contains all of it, Canadians expect their politicians and bureaucrats to be omniscient. But the number and complexity of questions exceeds individual capacity to answer them. Perhaps in the hope that new labels will bring new ideas, political philosophers coin new words to discuss old concepts. The term *civil society* replaces the *voluntary sector*. People talk about *neoliberalism* in an effort to avoid confusing the old *liberalism* and the new *conservatism*. The critical school splits itself into radical critical theorists and (not-so-radical?) critical theorists, who are really more like Lockean liberals.

QUEST FOR THE HOLY GRAIL: NATIONAL IDENTITY

The "looking glass" or reflected appraisal theory of interpersonal communication says that people define themselves, in large part, by how others view them (Adler & Towne, 1987). If this academic precept is true, then Canada may be in trouble. The nearest entity to our country is the United States, and few Americans have any knowledge of Canada beyond the stereotypes perpetuated in the media and the kinds of pictures that adorn our postcards: a land of ice and snow; Inuit dwellers; lumberjacks in plaid shirts; and mounted police, suited out in red uniforms.

The fact is that most Americans know only the myth of Canada. When I taught at the University of Windsor, across the river from Detroit, students who worked for Customs and Revenue Canada often recounted humorous stories of Americans who crossed the border in mid-July with snow equipment strapped aboard their cars, looking for the nearest ski resort. In early 2000, comedian Rick Mercer (associated with the political satire "This Hour has 22 Minutes," a production of the Canadian Broadcasting Corporation) attended a Michigan fund-raising event for presidential hopeful George W. Bush. Posing as a reporter, Mercer (2000) asked Bush if he was pleased to have the support of Prime Minister Jean "Poutine" (see also CBC, 2000). Mercer pronounced the word *poutine* several times in a loud, clear voice, leaving little room for misunderstanding. (For those who live outside of Canada, *poutine* is the name of a popular Québec junk food made from french fries, cheese curds, and beef gravy.) The *Washington Post* (2000) recounted the event as follows:

"A question from Canada, governor?" the "reporter" asked. "A question from Canada?"

"Yeah? What about it," Bush snapped as he walked along, signing autographs. "The prime minister of Canada, Jean Putin [Poutine]," the reporter said, "has said you look like the man who should lead the free world into the 21st century."

Bush stopped and visibly brightened. "Well, I appreciate his strong statement," Bush said enthusiastically. "He understands I believe in free trade . . . that I want to make sure our relations with our most important neighbor to the north of us, the Canadians, is strong." (Kamen, 2000, p. A15)

The *Washington Post* went on to say that, if you go too much further north, you end up in Russia, the home of Vladimir Putin.

Bush's failure to recognize the name of the current prime minister of Canada derives, in part, from the local nature of much newspaper coverage in the United States and the failure of its national media to report Canadian news. When former Prime Minister Pierre Trudeau died in September 2000, few American television stations or newspapers noted his death or carried the story. Yet Trudeau was a Canadian icon—flamboyant, intellectual, and controversial, well-known in other parts of the world. Many international dignitaries attended his funeral. Yet few Americans knew his name—then or now.

A recent article by Elmer (2000) talks about the process by which the American film industry alters even the landscape of Canada when it moves into cities such as Vancouver, Toronto, and Montreal. Using computer technologies, American filmmakers erase and alter features of the landscape that could identify the location of programs such as *The X-Files* and *Millennium*: "American programmes shot in Canada efface all signs of Canadianess, be they national icons, license plates—even mountains (as is often the case with Fox programmes shot in Vancouver)." Americans would be surprised to learn how many of their movies are shot in these three cities and even more surprised to learn how many of their film and television stars come from Canada. Comic sensations Jim Carrey and Tom Green are both Canadian products, as are singers Alanis Morrissette, Bryan Adams, Sarah McLaughlin, and Celine Dion; *Titanic* director James Cameron; and actor Michael J. Fox. It has been said that Canada's biggest cultural export is people.

As a consequence of this schizophrenic relationship with Americans, a relationship whereby Canadians morph into the American landscape and performance scene, the country engages in an ongoing quest for its Holy Grail, national identity. Canadians are adamant in asserting that they differ from their American cousins with respect to social values and ideologies, and they engage in a near-national pastime of searching for self-definition— which usually translates into defining themselves in terms of what they *are not* rather than what they *are*; and, to the average Canadian, what they *are not* is American. As Innis (1972) observed: "So conscious are we of the presence and power of our big neighbour that the nationalism of Canadian people often seems anti-American rather than pro-Canadian" (p. 1).

Coupled with concerns about finding our national identity are fears about losing our cultural sovereignty, and Canada's proximity to the United States poses one of the strongest threats. Seventy-five percent of Canadians live within one hour (by automobile) of the American border. Thousands of Canadian seniors or "snowbirds" migrate each fall or winter to Florida and other southern locations. English Canadians and Americans share a common language and compatible political and cultural histories. When Americans go to war, Canadians join them. When the American dollar drops, the Canadian economy suffers a decline. Like "Siamese twins . . . who cannot separate and live" (cited in Innis, 1972, p. 1), the two systems depend on each other for life support.

Canadians participate actively in American culture, in the sense that satellite television and radio signals ignore national boundaries. Seventy percent of Canadian households have cable television, which allows them to watch such American artifacts as *Friends, Who Wants to Be a Millionaire?*, and *Survivor*. They follow *Days of Our Lives*, NFL football, NBA basketball, and presidential campaigns. Aggravating the situation is the fact that Canadian media stress individualism over nationalism (Lorimer & Gasher, 2000). The mandate of the Canadian Broadcast Corporation (CBC) is to encourage the production and airing of Canadian products, but the task is difficult. Whenever money becomes tight, the cuts often hit this organization, and the CBC becomes a political football. Yet many believe that the CBC is the vehicle that will transport Canadians in our quest for national identity. Nationalists also believe that, if Canada hopes to be more than a distribution center for American films and television programs, the CBC may be its best hope.

No book on Canadian issues would be complete without raising the debate over our health care system—a debate that reaches into the most sacred corners of our value trove. When asked to define the differences between Canada and the United States, the discussion always turns to health care. Whatever their political persuasion or economic status, Canadians unite in the belief that the principle of universal health care is inviolable, and no politician to date has been bold or rash enough to advocate a serious dismantling of the system. Still, some worry that "incrementalism" could destroy the universality of the system. They fear the initiation of a two-tiered system similar to that in the United States. Thus, while Americans worry about the *absence* of health care reform, Canadians worry about the *possibility* of reform.

Although concerned about the issue of universality, health care providers themselves accept that Canada's health care system needs to be updated. Many believe in the viability of a new population health model that recognizes the significance of many different variables (social, economic, genetic, and other) on the health of an individual. Following the steps of the United Nations, federal, provincial, and territorial governments in Canada have advocated the adoption of this model. A true commitment to this model, however, requires a large-scale financial commitment to eliminating poverty, emphasizing preventive health care, and investing heavily in medical research and genomics. Canada ranks consistently at the top of the United Nations Human Development Index (a composite measure of life expectancy at birth) and ranks often as the best country in the world in which to live. Staying at the top of this list will be a challenge as governments are pressed to eliminate the national debt and to lower individual and corporate taxes. It is believed that those most at risk are older Canadians, women, and children.

CONCLUSION

Canadians face critical future decisions on how best to accommodate the many voices that clamor for recognition: how to maintain a national identity, while still remaining competitive and open to outside influences; how to allow Canadians access to a full range of choices in cable, television, and cinema, while maintaining a viable Canadian film and television industry; how to keep Canadian artists and performers at home when the lure of American markets is so strong; how to give an audible voice to seniors and marginalized communities, to engage youth, to ensure a strong and accessible health care system, to nurture our bilingual character, to foster cultural pluralism while encouraging close knit communities; and how to mobilize the Internet in support of society's most noble objectives. Canadians speak hopefully of the promise in the new information and communication technologies for fostering a more dynamic civic dialogue and encouraging civil society, even while they express fears about globalization and new world economies that could exclude all but the most powerful nations.

REFERENCES

Adler, R. B., & Towne, N. (1987). *Looking out/looking in: Interpersonal communication* (5th ed.). New York: Holt, Rinehart and Winston.

Bess, I. (1999, Autumn). Seniors behind the wheel. In *Canadian Social Trends.* Ottawa: Statistics Canada, catalogue no. 11–008.

Boal, A. (1985). *Theater of the oppressed.* New York: Urizen Books.

Can Canadian civics education succeed? A debate. (2000, October). Plenary session, Citizenship Conference, Montreal, Quebec.

Canada Council on Social Development (for the Division of Aging and Seniors, Health Canada). (1998). Canada's seniors. http://www.hc-gc.ca/seniors-aines.

CBC Radio ("The Arts Report"). (2000, March 2). Rick Mercer catches George W. Bush off guard. http://www.infoculture.cbc.ca/archives/cultpol/cultpol_03022000.

Civil Society Project. (2000, October). Civil society in Canada: Overview. http://www.impacs.org/civilsociety/main.htm, pp. 1–2.

Dasko, D. (2000, October). A survey of Canadian values and attitudes. Environics research poll. Presented at Citizenship Conference, Montreal, Quebec.

Elmer, G. (1997). *The X-Files* and profiles of Canadian landscape. *Borderlines 44,* 6–9.

Fax the feds. (2001). http://www.web.net/faxfeds/1296link.htm.

Growing older, growing bolder: Looking at seniors' rights and ageism. (1994). *The Moment 21.* http://www.mbnet.mb.ca/crm/lifestyl/advoc/moment.html.

Harvey, B. (2000, October 14). Attitude of today's youth shocking, bishops told. *The Ottawa Citizen,* p. A7.

Innis, H. (Ed.). (1972). *Issues for the seventies: Americanization.* Toronto: McGraw-Hill Ryerson Limited.

Kamen, A. (2000, March 1). A nose ring and Burns says hello. . . . http://www.washingtonpost.com/wp-srv/WPlate/2000–03/01/1931–030/00-idx.html, p. 15.

Lorimer, R., & Gasher, M. (2001). *Mass communication in Canada* (4th ed). Don Mills, ON: Oxford University Press.

Mercer, R. (2000). Shop talk. *TV Guide.* http://www.tvguidelive.com/shop-talk/rick-mercer.html.

Nevitte, N. (1996). *The decline of deference.* Peterborough, ON: Broadview Press.

North-South Institute. (1999). Overview. Civil society and global change (Canadian Development Report). www.nsi-ins.ca/ensi/publications/cdr/98/.

Putnam, R. D. (1993). *Making democracy work: Civic traditions in modern Italy.* Princeton, NJ: Princeton University Press.

Raging Grannies. (2001, April). http://library.usask.ca/herstory/granni.html.

Rosell, S. A. (1999). *Renewing governance: Governing by learning in the information age.* Don Mills, ON: Oxford University Press.

Sawatsky, K. (2000, January). Civil society in Canada: An overview. http://www.IMPACS.BC.CA/civilsociety/karens.htm.

Seniors Secretariat (Health Canada). (1990). Canada's seniors: Active, dynamic and involved. Ottawa, ON: Minister of Supply and Services, Government of Canada, catalogue no. H88–3/8–1990.

Shah, D. (1997, May). Civic participation, interpersonal trust. Paper presented to the Political Communication Division, International Communication Association annual conference, Montreal, Quebec.

Statistics Canada web site. Accessed in April 2001. http://www.statcan.ca/start.html.

Torjman, S. (1997, March). Civil society: Reclaiming our humanity. http://www.caledonist.org/full72htm, pp. 1–13.

Chapter 2

Who's Afraid of Canadian Culture?

Leslie Regan Shade

This chapter examines current debates on cultural globalization, with particular emphasis on the implications for Canada in culture and trade debates. First, I look briefly at arguments about the importance of cultural sovereignty for Canada and at regulatory and legislative measures enacted by government to promote Canadian culture. Canadian nationalists, as well as a number of critical communication scholars (not all Canadian), have expressed the fear that American "monoculture" will overtake Canada. Second, I use a case study of the World Trade Organization's (WTO) decision on split-run magazines to situate the debates within the larger global economic scenario. Finally, I examine the likely fate of culture, as predicted in current trade debates, including the Free Trade Area of the Americas (FTAA) and General Agreement on Trade in Services (GATS) deliberations.

THIS CANADA HAS 10 PROVINCES AND THREE TERRITORIES

Anderson's (1983) reflection that nationhood is "an imagined political community" (p. 6) rings true with Canada. For almost a century, Canadian nationalists have attempted to assert Canadian cultural sovereignty, in order to control the effects of American newspapers, films, television, magazines, comic books, videotapes, and music flooding across the borders. Although American cultural products continually flood the borders of other countries—both First World and Third World—Canada's situation is somewhat unique in that its exposure is mediated by its geographical proximity to the U.S. border (approximately 80% of the Canadian population resides within 100 kilometers of the U.S. border) and the large size of the country, resulting in distances between communities (Thompson, 1992, p. 189). In Europe, the metaphor of "Canadianization" refers to the "anticipated changes that will follow new broadcasting technologies" (Collins, 1990, p. ix), alluding to the rapid Americanization of content.

As early as the 1920s, Graham Spry and members of the Canadian Radio League recognized and advocated the importance of establishing a public broadcasting system distinct from its commercial counterpart to the south. "It is a choice between the State and the United States," Spry said, calling for government support of communications policy in order to foster "Canada as a nation, as a community, as a social organism" (Babe, 2000, p. 41). This sense of broadcasting as a social and non-commercial utility (related to and encompassing the concerns of the community) is one of the strengths of the Canadian "identity" (Raboy, 1990). Unlike the situation in the United States, public broadcasting in Canada (under the guise of the (CBC) has been and remains a stalwart institution (Ledbetter, 1998).

Canada can brag that it is one of the most technologically advanced countries in the world, with "major infrastructure advantages, including the world's highest combined penetration of telephones, cable TV and home electronics like the VCR" (Ellis, 1994, p. 11). Nonetheless, schizophrenia exists between the race to implement diverse communications technologies and the fact that often these technologies carry more non-Canadian cultural material than Canadian cultural material. Two recurring viewpoints have surfaced with respect to the new technological developments and media convergence: first, the idea that culture can colonize minds and, second, that cultural sovereignty is a necessary condition for political sovereignty. The twist now is that culture has less to do with proximity and more to do with "technology, information, and the diffusion of texts" (Acland, 1994, p. 235).

Some Canadians fear that the global sweep of networked technologies, amidst an increasing climate of open competition, could result in the Americanization of Canada (Menzies, 1996; Raboy, 1997). Will Canadians have the same access to the channels of production and distribution as their southern neighbors? Culture and trade debates have exacerbated these concerns. The Multilateral Agreement on Investment (MAI) debate in 1997 raised new questions on cultural rights. MAI followed in the wake of other global agreements such as the North American Free Trade Agreement (NAFTA), which gave a cultural exemption for Canada; the General Agreement on Tariffs and Trade (GATT); and the World Trade Organization (Clarke & Barlow, 1997). With the current FTAA and GATS deliberations, the debates on trade and culture have become even murkier and more controversial.

Cultural sovereignty can be defined as the ability of a country to enact laws and policies that protect and promote its culture and cultural industries. In Canada, cultural policies on heritage, film, television, and now multimedia policy are brought to life through legislation, regulation, program support, or taxation measures. Legislation by the federal government created and modified cultural institutions such as the CBC and established cultural rights through the *Copyright Act*. Regulations established the governance of Canada's broadcasting, cable, and telecommunications sectors. For instance, the *Broadcasting Act* requires that TV and radio stations play or air a certain amount of Canadian content, and the Canadian Radio-Television and Telecommunications Commission (CRTC) reinforces this regulation. Program support includes a variety of grants and contributions for Canada's cultural industries; agencies such as the Canada Council, Telefilm, and the National Film Board administer many of these programs. Specific programs for targeted cultural industries include the Feature Film Fund and the Book Publishing Industry Development Program. Taxation measures include tax credits for corporations that support Canadian cultural industries. The *Income Tax Act*, for instance, allows Canadian advertisers to claim expenses on advertising placed in periodicals and on television stations that are Canadian owned (75% and 80%, respectively).

TOWARD AN AMERICAN MONOCULTURE?

> What we view as culture, the U.S. views as business. What we view as encouraging choice, the U.S. views as erecting barriers. (Neil, 1998)

Debates over Canadian content have centered on the cultural imperialism thesis: Are Canadians swamped by an intrusion of American monoculture? Will the Canadian identity be eroded if Canadians are not able to consume and produce their own media products?

International sales of U.S. software and entertainment products were estimated at $60.2 billion (USD) in 1996 alone, "more than any other U.S. industry" (Farhi & Rosenfeld, 1998, p. 6). American media critics such as Barber (1998), McChesney (2000), and Schiller (2000) have documented the strength and power of the American cultural and media industries. All are concerned with the erosion of democracy in light of huge media consolidation, technological convergence, and the decline of public broadcasting. Schiller critiques the American "free flow of information" doctrine as an attempt to establish a new world information and communication order. Barber coins the phenomenon "McWorld," which he contends "represents an American push into the future animated by onrushing economic, technological, and ecological forces that demand integration and uniformity and that mesmerize people everywhere with fast music, fast computers, and fast food, MTV, Macintosh, and McDonald's" (1998, p. 1). McChesney has plotted the connections between the global media system and the global capitalist political economy. He argues that neoliberalism is the culprit: "The centrepiece of neoliberal policies is invariably a call for commercial media and communication markets to be deregulated. What this means in practice is that they are 're-regulated' to serve corporate interests" (p. 2).

Some Canadian critics, who deride the notion that American culture is a threat to Canadian sovereignty, ridicule the establishment of Canadian content (CanCon) requirements for radio and television broadcasting:

[The regulations] have become intolerable. They restrict the choices of viewers/ listeners and raise the price of cable TV services. Worst of all, the Cancon policy involves the coercion of the many (including taxation) to provide benefits to a few, notably the producers of Cancon and the few people who enjoy consuming it. (Stanbury, 1996)

Taras (1999) argues the opposite; he advocates stronger CanCon regulation, contending, "The result of an unregulated market would be even greater control by the Hollywood entertainment conglomerates. Ted Turner and Rupert Murdoch have no interest in telling Canadian stories or reflecting Canadian realities" (p. 223).

Minister of Canadian Heritage Sheila Copps (1998) has taken an international role in the debates on cultural globalization. Arguing that "world institutions must see culture as more than merely entertainment or merely an afterthought of decision-making" (p. 17), Copps has enlisted the support of other ministers of culture to form the International Network on Cultural Policy. This network builds on the work initiated at the UNESCO Intergovernmental Conference on Cultural Policies for Development in Stockholm. Currently, 46 countries are members of the International Network on Cultural Policy, whose purpose is "to build increased awareness and support for cultural diversity in an era of globalization and technological change" (see www.pch.gc.ca/network-reseau/eng.htm). Other network objectives include strengthening cultural and linguistic diversity, supporting local and national cultures, and ensuring that culture is accounted for in international negotiations. The network has two working groups: one involved with cultural diversity and globalization and the other with diversity and broadcasting. The Canadian Council for the Arts is one of the active groups in the debate. States Council Chair Jean-Louis Roux commented on the relationship of culture to trade: "[Culture] cannot be treated like just another thing to be bought and sold, subject to the vagaries of market demand. American pop culture is so pervasive. . . . Obviously, we can't prevent that, but we need to make certain our own culture has a chance" (Gauthier, 2000, p. E4).

THE CASE OF SPLIT-RUN MAGAZINES

"A devastating blow" (Magder, 1999, p. 12) was dealt to Canada's cultural industries when the WTO overturned legislation designed to block the sale in Canada of U.S. split-run magazines through the imposition of an 80 percent excise tax on the accrual of Canadian advertising revenues. Split-run magazines are Canadian editions of magazines originally published in another country (in this case, the United States). The magazines contain the basic content of the original, but ads targeted at Canadians replace more than 5 percent of the original advertisements. Sales and advertising in Canada cover the cost of producing split-run magazines. Split-run magazines and Canadian-produced magazines compete for advertising revenue needed to cover production costs.

The dispute over split-run magazines arose when *Sports Illustrated* (owned by Time Warner) began, in the 1990s, to electronically transmit the magazine in order to evade physical borders. The Canadian government's response was to impose an 80 percent excise tax on advertising in split-run magazines and to provide lower postal rates and subsidies to Canadian magazines.

The WTO ruling, settled through the WTO Dispute Settlement Body (DSB), made clear that Canadian cultural policies are not sacrosanct. *Canada-Certain Measures Concerning Periodicals* challenged the cultural aspect of a "good" and failed to acknowledge the cultural distinction of "goods." A clear victory for the United States, this ruling exemplifies how the free-flow doctrine of information (first enunciated in new world information and communication order debates of the 1970s) has become "the doctrine of free trade" (Magder, 1999, p. 14).

Carmody (1999) contends that the "dominant gaze of WTO decision-making is so fixedly economic that it is in some ways blind to context" (p. 25). In this instance, the WTO did not recognize or accept cultural justifications for regulation and legislation. A cultural waiver under WTO agreements is one remedy that could ameliorate future cultural disputes. However, because of the WTO ruling, the Canadian government has opened its market to U.S. split-run magazines, relaxed foreign ownership controls in the Canadian publishing industry, and abolished the postal subsidy. In compensation, the government has promised more subsidies to the Canadian publishing industry.

WHOSE FREE TRADE?

The challenge is how to establish internationally trade rules that create spaces in which citizens (more than just sheer consumers) are able to create cultural goods and services, express themselves through them, and choose the ones they wish to buy, in fair and equitable conditions. At stake is the capacity to create, to express oneself publicly and to have the ability to choose. (UNESCO, 2000)

Will current negotiations of FTAA further undermine the role of cultural sovereignty? FTAA, considered by government leaders at the Summit of the Americas in Québec City in April 2001, had as its goal the integration of GATS with the powers of the defunct MAI (Lee, 2001). Critics fear that such integration would "create a new trade powerhouse with sweeping new authority over every aspect of life in Canada and the Americas" (Barlow, 2001).

How would this agreement affect culture? Barlow (2001), speaking for the Council of Canadians, believes culture will either be fully included in the pact or will be *exempted* (using language similar to that used in NAFTA Annex 2106). There, articles dealing with the cultural industry (Art. 2005: 2) give the United States "the right to retaliate against Canada with measures 'of equivalent commercial effect' and to do so using sectors unrelated to culture" (Barlow, 2001, p. 36). In effect, this agreement allows the United States to decide if Canadian cultural measures are "inconsistent" with NAFTA and to retaliate against Canada, who would have no legal recourse in the event of an unfavorable ruling.

The fear is that cultural services will be included in the definition of services under GATS. GATS is "a multilateral agreement that restricts government actions affecting services through legally enforceable constraints backed up by trade sanctions" (Sinclair, 2000, p. 29). Services commercialized and regulated could include broadcasting (even public broadcasting) and telecommunications. If GATS is put into place, then the principles of national treatment and most favored nation will apply to cultural services. The national treatment principle accords the same status to imported goods and foreign services as to locally produced goods, domestic services, and local trademarks, copyrights, and patents. The most-favored-nation principle states that countries are to grant equal treatment (never favorable or discriminatory) to goods and services produced by all WTO members (UNESCO, 2000).

These principles challenge government subsidies to cultural industries, including those to the CBC and Canadian book publishers. The principles also call into question legislation limiting foreign investment in broadcasting, telecommunications, and cable companies, as well as regulations governing Canadian content. The Canadian government would not be able to restrict its arts and culture subsidies and grants to Canadian individuals and organizations but would also have to award funds to American and other corporations within the FTAA hemisphere. The threat here, according to the Council of Canadians, would be that "Canada's domination by the U.S. entertainment industry would be written into international law" (Council of Canadians, 2001).

Bhagwati (2000), who asks whether protectionist policies are the ideal way to deal with cultural concerns, suggests the creation of alternative policy options. Through the Cultural Industries Sectoral Advisory Group on International Trade (SAGIT), Canada has proposed a New International

Instrument on Cultural Diversity (NIICD). Rather than using the cultural exemption strategy in NAFTA (this exemption takes culture "off the table"), SAGIT suggests that a new instrument on cultural diversity would recognize not only the importance of cultural diversity, but also "acknowledge that goods and services are significantly different from other products, acknowledge that domestic measures and policies intended to ensure access to a variety of indigenous cultural products are significantly different from other policies, set out rules on the kind of domestic regulatory and other measures that countries can and cannot use to enhance cultural and linguistic diversity, and establish how trade disciplines would apply or not apply to cultural measures that meet the agreed upon rules" (DFAIT, 1999). The instrument would also "indicate where trade disciplines would or would not apply" and "state explicitly when domestic cultural measures would be permitted and not subject to trade retaliation" (DFAIT, 1999, p. 31). Proponents of the instrument would seek international consensus on the responsibility to encourage indigenous cultural expression and to develop regulatory and other measures for the protection of cultural and linguistic diversity.

It is inevitable that the debates over the role of trade in culture will continue, unabated, in the coming years. Divergent voices have struggled to be heard, and as has been seen in the Québec City Summit of the Americas protest, civil society groups and citizens have perhaps impacted public opinion. In terms of culture and trade issues, it is necessary to recognize that culture is a human right and forms an essential basis of human relations (Carmody, 1999). How to reconcile this sentiment with the economic imperative of trade discourse and to open the trade question to such debate will be a genuine challenge.

REFERENCES

Acland, C. (1994). Cultural survival: Sleeping with the elephant. In D. Glenday & A. Duffy (Eds.), Canadian society: Understanding and surviving in the 1990s (pp. 223–251). Toronto: McClelland and Stewart.

Anderson, B. (1983). Imagined communities: Reflections on the origins and spread of nationalism. London: Verso.

Babe, R. (2000). Canadian communication thought: Ten foundational writers. Toronto: University of Toronto Press.

Barber, B. (1998). Democracy at risk: American culture in a global world. World Policy Journal 29 (13), 1–9.

Barlow, M. (2001). The Free Trade Area of the Americas and the threat to social programs, environmental sustainability and social justice in Canada and the Americas. Ottawa: Council of Canadians.

Barlow, M., & Clarke, T. (2001). Global showdown: How the new activists are fighting global corporate rule. Toronto: Stoddart.

Bhagwati, J. (2000). Trade and culture: America's blind spot. In J. Bhagwati, The

   wind of the hundred days: How Washington mismanaged globalization
   (pp. 209–213). Cambridge, MA: MIT Press.

Carmody, C. C. (1999). When "cultural identity was not an issue": Thinking about
   Canada—Certain measures concerning periodicals. *Law and Policy in In-*
   ternational Business 231 (1), 1–62.

Clarke, T., & Barlow, M. (1997). *The Multilateral Agreement on Investment (MAI)*
   and the threat to Canadian sovereignty. Toronto: Stoddart.

Collins, R. (1990). *Culture, communication & national identity: The case of Ca-*
   nadian television. Toronto: University of Toronto Press.

Copps, S. (1998). Celine Dion: Made in Canada. *New Perspectives Quarterly 15*
   (5), 17–18.

Council of Canadians. (2001). *Stop the FTAA! Democracy before trade/Non à la*
   ZLEA: La démocratie d'abord! (Pamphlet).

Department of Foreign Affairs and International Trade, The Cultural Industries
   Sectoral Advisory Group on International Trade (DFAIT). (1999, February).
   Canadian culture in a global world: New strategies for culture and trade.
   Ottawa: DFAIT.

Ellis, D. (1994). *Culture & the information highway: New roles for carriers &*
   content providers. Ottawa: Stentor Telecom Policy, Inc.

Farhi, P. & Rosenfeld, M. (1998, November 30). Exporting America. *The Wash-*
   ington Post National Weekly Edition, pp. 6–7.

Gauthier, N. (2000, November 30). Ottawa, the world's cultural stage. *Ottawa*
   Citizen, p. E1.

Ledbetter, J. (1998). *Made possible by . . . : The death of public broadcasting in*
   the United States. London: Verso.

Lee, M. (2001, April). *Inside the fortress: What's going on at the FTAA negotia-*
   tions. Ottawa: Canadian Centre for Policy Alternatives.

Magder, T. (1999, August). Going global. *The Canadian Forum,* 11–16.

McChesney, R. W. (2000). *Rich media, poor democracy: Communication politics*
   in dubious times. New York: The New Press.

McChesney, R. W. (2001, March). Global media, neoliberalism, and imperialism.
   Monthly Review 52, 1–19.

Menzies, H. (1996). *Whose brave new world? The information highway and the*
   new economy. Toronto: Between the Lines.

Neil, G. T. (1998). The MAI and culture. In *Dismantling democracy: The Multi-*
   lateral Agreement on Investment (MAI) and its impact. Ottawa: James Lorimer.

Raboy, M. (1990). *Missed opportunities: The story of Canada's broadcasting pol-*
   icy. Toronto: University of Toronto Press.

Raboy, M. (1997). Cultural sovereignty, public participation, and democratization
   of the public sphere: The Canadian debate on the new information infrastructure. In B. Kahin & E. Wilson (Eds.), *National information infrastruc-*
   ture initiatives: Vision and policy design (pp. 190–216). Cambridge, MA:
   MIT Press.

Schiller, H. I. (2000). *Living in the number one country: Reflections from a critic*
   of American empire. New York: Seven Stories Press.

Sinclair, S. (2000). *GATS: How the World Trade Organization's new "services" negotiations threaten democracy*. Ottawa: Canadian Centre for Policy Alternatives.

Stanbury, W. T. (1996, October). Cancon rules should be canned. *Policy Options*. www.media-awareness.ca.

Taras, D. (1999). *Power & betrayal in the Canadian media*. Peterborough, ON: Broadview Press.

Thompson, J. H. (1992). Canada's quest for cultural sovereignty: Protection, promotion, and popular culture. In H. Holmes & D. Taras (Eds)., *Seeing ourselves: Media power and policy in Canada* (pp. 188–201). Toronto: Harcourt Brace Jovanovich Canada.

UNESCO. (2000). *Culture, trade and globalization: Questions and answers*. www.unesco.org/culture/industries/trade.html.

Chapter 3

Principles, Politics, Human Rights

Scott Streiner

Human rights have become the *lingua franca* of Canadian politics over the past 20 years. Once the preserve of cloistered political philosophers and lonely activists, human rights has become the rallying cry for a range of agendas that would have baffled John Locke and Jean-Jacques Rousseau, the progenitors of natural rights and social contract theory. Conventional analysis of human rights issues tends to rely on an implicit—and simplistic—understanding of rights as "givens." Meanwhile, in the arena of social competition, individuals and organizations apply the language of fundamental rights to an ever-expanding set of disputes that involve allocation of resources. Theory needs to catch up with practice, in part so that practice may be better framed.

This chapter begins with the argument that the prevailing, abstract conceptualization of human rights pays too little attention to their political dimension. It then examines struggles around pay equity in Canada's federal jurisdiction, showing how the view of pay equity as a human right (or not) relates to issues of resource distribution. The chapter concludes with reflections on the implications, for both the activist and scholar, of the wide use of a human rights discourse.

THE NATURE OF RIGHTS

The idea of human rights is grounded in the ethical assertion that, by virtue of their shared humanity, all people deserve certain minimum protections and benefits. This assertion dates back to the seventeenth century, when a traditional hierarchy (which fixed every person's station in life) began to give way to a more fluid society. In this society, social position was not the exclusive determinant of treatment of the individual.

Natural rights theorists believe that individuals are innately free, a condition that preceded (and thus supercedes) social arrangements. To respect this natural order, social rules must respect and defend individual desires, not the opposite (Locke, 1967; Rousseau, 1994). Although such propositions underpinned the American and French Revolutions, the notion of natural rights was disputed from the outset. Utilitarians such as Bentham (cited in Waldron, 1987) ridiculed such discourse as metaphysical "mumbo-jumbo," and conservatives such as Burke (cited in Waldron, 1987) warned that adherence to such ideas would produce violent social chaos. Marxists, on the other hand, argued that natural rights reinforced the ability of the bourgeoisie to exploit the proletariat (Waldron, 1987). Such critiques attacked the very foundation of natural rights; and from the mid-nineteenth to the mid-twentieth century, natural rights theory took a place on the sidelines.

The idea of natural rights was revived in the wake of World War II. Reeling from revelations about the scope and barbarism of the Holocaust, international representatives led by Eleanor Roosevelt and Canadian diplomat John Humphrey crafted the *Universal Declaration of Human Rights* (Morsink, 1993). Adopted on December 10, 1948, the *Universal Declaration* describes itself as "a common standard of achievement for all peoples and all nations" and asserts in its first article, "All human beings are born free and equal in dignity and rights."

The framers of the *Universal Declaration* believed it would provide a solid safeguard against any repetition of the horrors of the 1940s. No longer could governments argue that sovereign power gave them the prerogative to behave as they chose toward those under their control. Supporters hoped that concern for the preservation and promotion of equal human dignity, rather than the whims of the powerful, would dictate new social structures and policies.

This view of the role of public authority has gained wide acceptance in recent decades. Conventional theory takes for granted that just social arrangements will advance equal rights—rights that flow from unassailable first principles. Liberal philosopher/lawyer Dworkin (2000), whose work has influenced the jurisprudence of the Supreme Court of Canada, captures the spirit of this belief when he writes, "No government is legitimate that does not show equal concern for the fate of all those citizens over whom it claims dominion and from whom it claims allegiance. Equal concern is the sovereign virtue of political community—without it government is only tyranny" (p. 1).

Fundamental challenges to the emphasis on human rights have come from both postmodern thinkers and relativists. Postmodern philosophers contest the existence of defensible foundations for any normative theory, and relativists see human rights as predicated on distinctly Western—rather than universal—premises (Evans, 1998). Such challenges inject important caveats and caution into the debate about rights, but in the extreme, do not cohere into a persuasive alternative. Can we imagine a society without some guiding principles? Evidently not, since postmodern philosophers themselves have begun to label notions such as "justice" as immune from deconstruction. Can we imagine a world in which no cross-cultural, ethnic-based judgments are permitted? Evidently not, since even the most radical relativist agrees that certain acts of extreme brutality should be condemned wherever they occur.

That being said, the dominant philosophical/legal conceptualization of human rights remains problematic. Contemporary discussions of rights tend to reify them—to think about them as if they already exist "out there," requiring only to be elucidated and implemented by human beings. Thus, Dworkin (1986) can conceive of the processes of litigation and jurisprudence as the quest for the "right answer." This sense of rights as imminent infuses them with substantial potency; indeed, some see them as a sort of religion for a secularized world. But this conception of rights also masks the extent to which their definition is a product of social negotiation, and their use a function of political calculation.

Comparing lists of human rights reveals the lack of any consistent or obvious standard for including one right over another one. The process of hammering out the *Universal Declaration*, which took almost two years, was at times marked by acrimonious disagreement (Humphrey, 1984). Similar debates have characterized the drafting of human rights clauses for national constitutions and the development of human rights statutes. Beyond a general consensus that people should not, for example, be arbitrarily killed or tortured, one often runs into intense controversy over what qualifies as a human right. The United States has still not ratified the 1966 *International Covenant on Social, Economic and Cultural Rights*—a document that is one of the three components of the *International Bill of Rights* (the other two are the *Universal Declaration* and *International Covenant on Civil and Political Rights*).

If human rights were really "givens" to the degree that the prevailing image suggests, one would not expect the degree of controversy that has accompanied their enshrinement. Such controversy does not necessarily lend support to the postmodern/relativist denial of any common ground for notions of rights. People may share a certain inspiration regarding the intrinsic value of a human life well lived, without seeing eye to eye on the implications of this inspiration in terms of social norms. The ongoing debate *does* imply that the establishment of rights-based boundaries of behavior is achieved as much through gritty social competition as abstract discovery and deduction.

Disputes over what should be deemed a human right are intensely political, because that designation raises a benefit or program above day-to-day politics. Those whose agendas are defined as human rights have an inherent advantage in the contest over collective priorities and resources. Once deemed a human right, the right moves to the front of the political queue. Because basic rights supercede positive law, they are shielded from the give-and-take that usually accompanies political decisions about funding and the application of social authority.

This does not mean that human rights are *only* political tools, empty of philosophically defensible substance or genuine vision. It does mean, however, that if our conceptualization is excessively abstract and ignores the political component in the definition of human rights, we run the risk of analytical impoverishment. As the next section on pay equity in Canada's federal jurisdiction shows, the process of establishing and implementing a human right is simultaneously a matter of principle and politics.

DEFINING AND PURSUING PAY EQUITY

Pay equity is a public policy aimed at reducing wage discrimination against "women's work." This policy resulted from the belief that part of the earnings gap between men and women is due to a traditional tendency to undervalue jobs done mainly by women. It seeks to rectify this problem by requiring a reexamination of the relative worth and wages of male- and female-predominant work performed in the same establishment.

Today in Canada, full-time working women take home 72 cents for every dollar earned by their male counterparts (Statistics Canada, 2000). Factors such as education and years of experience only partly explain the difference. The remaining gap is often attributed to biases about the value of jobs done mostly by women. The fact that relative wage rates have remained fairly stable over time, despite major changes in the economy, also suggests that something more than supply and demand affects salaries.

Pay equity proponents trace the undervaluation of "women's work" to an era when working women's income was secondary to that of men, who were considered to be the breadwinners. Women's jobs, which often built on women's domestic roles, were seen as easy and dispensable. This undervaluation also reflects the greater historical assertiveness of male workers and a general social inclination to deprecate that which is associated with "femaleness." Although attitudes have changed over time, critics argue that biased patterns of compensation are ingrained.

These patterns cannot be changed by long-standing equal pay for equal work laws, since these laws require comparison of identical jobs. Pay equity responds to this dilemma by requiring equal pay for *work of equal value*—in other words, by permitting the comparison of dissimilar male- and female-predominant work. It is the notion of "equal value" that provokes controversy (Weiner & Gunderson, 1990).

Pay equity programs use job evaluation systems to determine the relative value of male- and female-predominant jobs. Employers have applied these systems for years in setting relative wage rates. They rate jobs against a common set of factors such as interpersonal skills, analytical abilities, accountability for budgets, responsibility for people's health, physical or emotional effort, and unpleasant working conditions. The effectiveness of job evaluation systems in ensuring pay equity depends upon their ability to fully recognize the range of work done by women and men and ongoing monitoring to ensure consistency in applications.

Pay equity has been part of Canadian legislation since the mid-1970s. Pressure for its enactment began with the 1970 report of the Royal Commission on the Status of Women, which recommended that the federal government ratify the International Labour Organization's *Convention concerning Equal Remuneration for Men and Women Workers for Work of Equal Value* and follow up with legislative action (*Royal Commission Report*, 1970). Ottawa ratified the convention in 1972 and, five years later, included an equal pay for work of equal value section in the new *Canadian Human Rights Act*. About the same time, the Québec government incorporated an equal value clause into its *Charter of Human Rights and Freedoms*. In both cases, enforcement depended on complaint investigations by human rights commissions.

During the 1980s and 1990s, many provinces also adopted pay equity statutes or policies. Most policies were proactive, meaning that they relied on mandatory measures and deadlines rather than complaints to achieve compliance. They also vested authority to oversee compliance in a specialized body or unit. The most sweeping statutes were Ontario's 1987 and Québec's 1997 laws, both of which detail a series of steps that must be taken by both public and private sector employers to ensure non-discriminatory wage-setting practices (Gallant & Streiner, 1998).

The battle over pay equity has been fought on several levels. Radical critics argue that, despite its good intentions, pay equity fails to make much of a difference. They also say that pay equity laws divide and demoralize workers (Brenner, 1990; Cuneo, 1990; Lewis, 1988). Conservative opponents dispute the assumptions that underlie pay equity, contending that wages result from supply and demand and that any attempt to adjudge the relative value of dissimilar jobs is artificial and bound to distort the economy (Flanagan, 1986; Killingsworth, 1990; Rhoads, 1993). A number of critics of varying ideological stripes (mostly conservative) have also contended that, whatever the factors shaping salaries, it is a mistake to think of pay equity as a human right. In the context of this discussion, this last argument holds the most interest.

An excellent illustration of the debate over whether pay equity should be treated as a human right occurred in February 2001, when the Canadian Human Rights Commission (2001) submitted a report to Parliament entitled *Time for Action*.[1] The report advocated replacement of the complaints-based pay equity regime at the federal level with a proactive statute. The report began by asserting that pay equity is a human right:

Human rights are about respect for the equality and dignity of all people. They require that we treat others fairly and avoid actions which disadvantage people because of personal characteristics such as their sex, age, colour, disability, or religion. When the value of work done mainly by women is not appropriately recognized, the people performing it are not paid and treated equitably. This is a form of sex discrimination. If your income is low because you're in a job performed mostly by women, your fundamental rights to equality and dignity are not being respected. Pay equity is a way of identifying and eliminating such discrimination.

In its lead recommendation, the report stressed the importance of legislation in recognizing pay equity as a human right and the necessity to establish neutral bodies to administer and oversee implementation of the policy:

Practically speaking, this means vesting the authority for overseeing implementation of the law with an independent agency. . . . Programs to protect and promote fundamental rights are most effective, and most credible, when they are handled by bodies operating at arms-length from government and from any political considerations.

The right-wing *National Post* ("Equity Zealotry," 2001) found the report's reasoning to be both dubious and dangerous, branding it the work of "empire-building bureaucrats" and attacking the "absurdity of treating pay parity as an issue of fundamental rights." In order to advance "leftist egalitarianism," fumed the *Post*, the Commission was willing to pillage the human rights tradition and negate that most fundamental of rights, freedom of contract, by denying men and women the liberty to work for whatever wages they please. Pay equity's emphasis on results, the *Post* warned, would leave "values that Canadians take for granted—to own property, to seek and make one's fortune, to enjoy the fruits of success . . . vulnerable to statist attack."

The *Post*'s agitation was obviously not due solely to philosophical differences regarding the precise definition of a human right. The writer's concern also related to the practical implications of what gets counted as a human right. The editorial in question did not claim that there is no such thing as a human right; so it was not postmodern or relativist in spirit. It simply wished to preserve that hallowed status for negotiated contracts, property ownership, personal enrichment, and the like. These are, of course, the sorts of rights historically favored by those who oppose any impediment to the continued affluence and influence of the powerful.

The editorial correctly argued that treating pay equity as a human right (which is how it has been viewed at the federal level since first being leg-islated) could place limits on other rights (such as amassing property). For example, an employer who must raise wages for female-predominant work (after job evaluation shows it to be underpaid) may not be able to accumulate the same fortune as would otherwise have been possible. In other words, the *Post* objected to the possibility that a form of redistribution or "leftist egalitarianism" would achieve the same inviolable plane as the prerogative to acquire and keep wealth. This objection highlights the political dimension of the debate. To a certain extent, the argument about whether pay equity is a human right boils down to the question of whether society should promote a transfer of wealth to poorly paid, female-predominant jobs. When pay equity is treated as a human right, the probability of that transfer taking place is greater.

The largest and most widely discussed case ever launched under the *Canadian Human Rights Act*'s pay equity provisions demonstrated that this probability was not merely theoretical. The case pitted the Public Service Alliance of Canada (PSAC) against the federal Treasury Board. In 1984, the PSAC filed a pay equity complaint on behalf of clerks working for the federal government. The next year the government and its unions, including the PSAC, undertook an expansive study in which joint committees evaluated thousands of jobs. By 1989, the parties had managed to agree on evaluation scores for all the jobs. However, they had reached a deadlock on the wage adjustments required to correct the differentials they had identified. The Treasury Board proceeded to pay unilateral increases based on its own calculation method, and two unions (one of them the PSAC) complained to the Canadian Human Rights Commission that those increases had failed to address all the wage discrimination found by the joint study. After examining the evidence, the Commission referred the unions' complaints to the Canadian Human Rights Tribunal, a separate body, for a binding decision.

Consideration of the case by the Tribunal took seven years. Over that period, the PSAC was under tremendous pressure to settle, especially after the other union involved in the litigation reached a resolution with the government. At one stage, the Treasury Board retained the services of a high-profile feminist lawyer to try to negotiate a deal with the PSAC and publicly put over $1 billion on the table. To the surprise (and chagrin) of many, the PSAC refused to settle, arguing that pay equity was a fundamental human right and that the union would rather wait for a Tribunal decision than compromise. More than a few observers believed that this position was naive and overstated the status of pay equity.

In July 1998, the Tribunal issued a decision that appeared to belie such criticisms. The decision's most important component was endorsement of a wage adjustment calculation formula suggested by the Commission—a formula that would result in payouts of several billion dollars. (Canadian Human Rights Tribunal, 1998).

Distressed by this potential liability, the government applied to the federal court for judicial review of the decision, arguing that the Tribunal's understanding of the pay equity provisions of the *Canadian Human Rights Act* had been unduly generous. In October 1999, the Court rejected the government's application, stating that the Tribunal decision was reasonable. The judgment implied that too much delay had already occurred. Moreover, the Court unambiguously endorsed the view of pay equity as a human right, applying to it the "living tree" principle of interpretation used for constitutional questions. Pay equity, it stated, was intended to correct a "social injustice . . . systemic wage discrimination for work of equal value resulting from the historical segregation of the labour world by gender, and the undervaluation of women's work" (Federal Court of Canada, 1999). Left with few options—and prodded even by conservative commentators and opposition politicians to cut its losses—the government negotiated an agreement with the PSAC for application of the July 1998 Tribunal decision. The cost of the agreement has been estimated at $3.5 billion.

The unfolding of this case illustrates how the conceptualization of pay equity (or any other benefit or program) as a human right can have major implications for real-world allocation of resources. Reliance on pay equity's status as a human right helped the PSAC to win a high-stakes struggle with a government that saw pay equity in less absolute terms. Had pay equity been left to the give-and-take of the regular political game, it is inconceivable that the PSAC's members would have received wage increases on the same scale; indeed, it is questionable whether the valuation of female-predominant work would have even made it onto the Treasury Board's agenda.

The designation of pay equity as a human right, then, is contentious not merely because of differences over the correct exegesis of first principles, but also (perhaps primarily) because it affects the political question of who gets what. The *National Post* knows that if pay equity is kept on the list of recognized human rights, and if the mechanisms for implementing it are improved, the existing distribution of wealth will be somewhat less secure. The PSAC knows this as well. The difference between them, to no small degree, turns on whether they want to preserve or change that distribution.

IMPLICATIONS

The political struggles of disadvantaged groups, such as workers performing low-paid "women's work," are largely about obtaining a larger share of resources. Framing demands in terms of human rights can be, as the federal pay equity case shows, a very effective strategy. In the face of formidable opponents who have little difficulty prevailing in the normal political process, the less powerful can take advantage of "rights talk" to place social contests on a different level and force changes in the status quo.

The potency of rights-based claims has led to their proliferation. This is especially true in countries such as Canada, where the protection of basic rights has supplanted more traditional types of common culture at the core of national identity. Increases in the heterogeneity of Canadian society over the past three decades (due largely to substantial Third World immigration) and the desire to distinguish the northern mouse from the elephant to the south have meant a growing association between "Canadianess" and values such as tolerance, respect, and fairness. In such a climate, the language of rights is particularly resonant.

In some respects, the increasing usage of a rights discourse is welcome, since it often reflects the assertion of claims by long-silenced sectors. Whether it is Aboriginal communities seeking access to natural resources, gay and lesbian couples seeking employment benefits comparable to those of heterosexual colleagues, or people with disabilities seeking accommodations that enable them to find and keep decent jobs, the human rights strategy undoubtedly plays an important role in addressing historical disadvantage that might otherwise be ignored—or at least downplayed—by the majority.

On the other hand, expansive use of rights talk also carries a number of risks. The first is the potential for trivialization. Like Weimar Republic tender, the currency of human rights may become devalued if overused. The second is the potential for demobilization. As Mandel (1989) has stated with respect to the *Canadian Charter of Rights and Freedoms*, an emphasis on rights-based litigation may legalize inherently political disputes and so alienate the very people who have the greatest stake in their outcome. The third is the potential for fragmentation. If struggles over social priorities are articulated solely in the vocabulary of fundamental rights, the capacity of competing groups to feel empathy and achieve compromise may be reduced.

For activists, one implication is that human rights claims may be conducive to success in the search for resources, but they need to be employed with a degree of caution and grounded in something more than expediency. For scholars, the implication is that assessments of human rights battles need to be sophisticated enough to capture those battles' multiple dimensions. An analytical dichotomy between human rights as products of principle and politics is a false dichotomy. Both dimensions underlie the definition and deployment of human rights, and any examination that neglects one of them will underrepresent the richness of the social processes at work.

The future of human rights talk in Canada cannot easily be predicted. An undeniable tension exists between the effectiveness of rights claims and the erosion that accompanies their ubiquitousness. A key question is whether this tension will lead to the gradual abandonment of the discourse or a clearer conceptualization, which reinforces the vitality of the discourse. The answer, which will shape Canadian society for many years, will depend on the actions of everyone from anti-globalization protesters marching in the streets to human rights officials meeting in office towers to academics "beavering away" in university libraries.

NOTES

At the time of writing, the author was a doctoral candidate in the Department of Political Science, Carleton University, and a senior manager with the Canadian Human Rights Commission. Written by the author in his academic capacity, the views expressed herein are exclusively personal in nature.

1. In the interests of intellectual honesty, I feel obliged to mention that I was the report's main wordsmith. That being said, it is also worth noting that such reports are rarely individual products; rather, they reflect an organization's shared views, arrived at through internal discussions and direction from those at the top. In addition, I hope that reflexivity regarding my role allows me to achieve a degree of detachment about the product.

REFERENCES

Brenner, J. (1990). Radical versus liberal approaches to the feminization of poverty and comparable worth. In K. V. Hansen & I. J. Philipson (Eds.), *Women, class, and the feminist imagination: A socialist-feminist reader* (pp. 491–507). Philadelphia: Temple University Press.

Canadian Human Rights Commission. (2001). *Time for action: A special report to Parliament on pay equity.* www.chrc-ccdp.ca.

Canadian Human Rights Tribunal. (1998). *Public Service Alliance of Canada v. Treasury Board of Canada.* http://www.chrt-tcdp.gc.ca/decisions/docs/psac2-e.htm.

Cuneo, C. J. (1990). *Pay equity: The labour-feminist challenge.* Toronto: Oxford University Press.

Dworkin, R. M. (1986). *Law's empire.* Cambridge, MA: Belknap Press.

Dworkin, R. M. (2000). *Sovereign virtue.* Cambridge, MA: Harvard University Press.

Equity zealotry. (2001, February 16). *National Post.* www.nationalpost.com.

Evans, T. (Ed.). (1998). *Human rights fifty years on: A reappraisal.* Manchester: Manchester University Press.

Federal Court of Canada. (1999). *Canada (Attorney General) v. Public Service Alliance of Canada (T.D.).* http://www.fja.gc.ca/en/cf/2000/vol1/html/2000fca25356.p.en.html.

Flanagan, T. (1986). Equal pay for work of equal value: Some theoretical criticisms. *Canadian Public Policy 13,* 434–459.

Gallant, C., & Streiner, S. (1998). Pay equity in Canada: Lessons learned and future directions. In Institute for Women's Policy Research, *Women's progress: Perspectives on the past, blueprint for the future* (pp. 93–101). Washington, DC: George Washington University.

Humphrey, J. P. (1984). *Human rights and the United Nations: A great adventure.* Dobbs Ferry, NY: University Press of America.

Killingsworth, M. R. (1990). *The economics of comparable worth.* Kalamazoo, MI: W. E. Upjohn Institute for Employment Research.

Lewis, D. J. (1988). *Just give us the money.* Vancouver, BC: Women's Research Centre.

Locke, J. (1967). *Two treatises on government.* Cambridge, MA: Cambridge University Press.

Mandel, M. (1989). *The Charter of Rights and the legalization of politics in Canada.* Toronto: Wall and Thompson.

Morsink, J. (1993). World War Two and the *Universal Declaration. Human Rights Quarterly 15*, 357–405.

Rhoads, S. E. (1993). *Incomparable worth: Pay equity meets the market.* Cambridge, MA: Cambridge University Press.

Rousseau, Jean-Jacques. (1994). *Discourse of political economy and the social contract.* Trans., Intro., and Notes by Christopher Betts. Oxford: Oxford University Press.

Royal Commission report on the status of women. (1970). Ottawa: Supply and Services Canada.

Statistics Canada. (2000). *Average earnings by sex and work pattern.* http://www.statcan.gc.ca/english/Pgdb/People/Labour/labor01b.htm.

Waldron, J. (1987). *Nonsense upon stilts.* London: Methuen.

Weiner, N., & Gunderson, M. (1990). *Pay equity: Issues, options and experiences.* Markham, ON: Butterworths.

Part II

Quiet Voices, Marginalized and At-Risk Communities

Chapter 4

Cleaning Up the City: Squeegee Kids and the Social Purification of Urban Canada

Derek Foster

On January 31, 2000, the Ontario government passed the controversial *Safe Streets Act*. This act outlawed aggressive begging and so-called "squeegee kids." The Ontario Progressive Conservative Party introduced this "get-tough" tactic as one of their top three legislative priorities for their second parliamentary session. Indeed, many credit the Ontario Progressive Conservative Party's 1999 electoral victory to the prioritization of themes of law and order. These themes fit well with Premier Mike Harris' "common sense revolution," a plan to restore Ontario's economic vitality and quality of life through more efficient government, lower taxes, more jobs, and safer streets. While the meaning of "economic vitality" was generally clear to everyone, "quality of life" assumed a more amorphous shape, depending on who interpreted the term. To the conservative government, "quality of life" implied a commitment to "cleaning up the streets"—getting the squeegee kids off the corners and returning them to the back alleys. Not everyone agreed with this philosophy, but the government did not ask for—or encourage—a dialogue.

If the primary point of civic discourse is to enable citizens to become more active and effective participants in democratic culture, then the recent controversy over squeegee kids reveals much about perceptions of who merits inclusion in this culture and whose voices should be silenced. Squeegee kids are those (mostly younger) individuals who approach stopped cars at urban intersections and offer (or as some say, threaten) to clean windshields. Opinion on whether or not this arguably disruptive practice should be allowed to continue has been quite divisive. The issue has served as a lightning rod for the debate over who deserves to partake of public space and who merits disciplinary measures for refusing to conform to a regimented vision of public behavior. The squeegee kids, however, have been notably absent from this debate, and their supporters and defenders have lacked the power to compete successfully with those who exercise power in Ontario society.

This chapter seeks to identify the social actors in the debate and their positions, the process by which squeegee kids were defined as "a problem," the ideologies behind the debate, the social meaning of the discourse over squeegee kids, and the possibilities for a mutually beneficial dialogue. The chapter does not seek to reveal who was "right" or "wrong," but to elaborate how the issue came to be framed in such a manner in the first place. While Harris' *Safe Streets Act* effectively brought the public debate over squeegee kids to an abrupt conclusion, the academic debate over the rights of all members of society to access and use public space continues unabated.

WHO ARE THE SOCIAL ACTORS AND WHAT DO THEY REPRESENT?

The notion of "cacophonous" voices is decidedly apropos for this project, for the discourse over squeegee kids involves social actors of seemingly mutually exclusive life worlds—the conservative government of Mike Harris (and the constituents who gave Harris a sound majority) versus the street kids of Ontario. In other words, a group on the margins of society confronted the dominant social order. The two lined up on opposite sides, in the manner of a debate, negating any notion that a true dialogue could develop. Clark (1996) asserts that discourse should take the form of "conversation or dialogue—literally, a running back and forth" (p. 29). However, there was no evidence of a conversation or dialogue in the case of the squeegee kids, only a heated debate. Therefore, this chapter uses the term *discourse* in a fashion different from Clarke's definition, referring at different times to "dominant discourse," "strong discourse," or just "discourse."

Distinguishing between legislators and "interpreters" is relevant to a definition of ideologies and positions reflected in the debate over the squeegee kids. Referring to legislators, Bauman (1987) notes that they represent "the typically modern view of the world . . . [as] one of an essentially orderly totality" (p. 3). In the discourse over squeegee kids, governments at all levels are literally legislators. They make authoritative statements and select opinions that become correct and binding.

With no access to the system, squeegee kids and those who support their cause are automatically cast in the role of the disempowered when arbitrating between "valid" opinions and "less legitimate" ones. They are akin to "postmodern interpreters," and the typical postmodern view of the world is "one of an unlimited number of models of order, each one generated by a relatively autonomous set of practices" (Bauman, 1987, p. 4).

Postmodern interpreters do not seek to select the best social order, but to facilitate communication among autonomous participants.

In the debate over the squeegee kids, these conflicting worldviews manifest themselves in attitudes toward the use of public space. The first (the legislators and sympathetic constituents) see the city as open but restricted to use by "legitimate" publics, who practice accepted behaviors. The City of Ottawa anti-panhandling bylaw, for example, states that its purpose is "to provide for an environment free from certain public nuisances which may degrade the quality and tranquility of life" (No. 117–91). Legislators see public space as something that must be planned and made orderly and safe. They oppose those who are prepared to tolerate the risks of disorder, and they see unsolicited activity (of the sort undertaken by squeegee kids and their defenders) as an illegitimate expression of public life.

The interpreters (community activists, members of anti-poverty coalitions, and squeegee kids), on the other hand, hold an unconstrained vision of city life, perceiving that such public spaces should exclude no one. The National Anti-Poverty Organization (NAPO), for example, believes that panhandlers and other members of the lower socioeconomic class have every right to be in public spaces. They do not believe that the act of asking another person for money is, by itself, a threatening activity. They also represent the belief that the city should welcome the unknown. They see risk not as disorder and threat, but as potential. In a position paper on anti-panhandling bylaws, the NAPO (1999) highlights the growing tendency of governments in Canada to treat the poorest Canadians as a class of "untouchables." The position paper asserts that these attempts exemplify "discriminatory legislation . . . [and that] 'poor bashing' does not and should not remain an acceptable public attitude or the dominant public discourse" (p. 16).

HOW ARE SQUEEGEE KIDS CONSTRUCTED AS A PROBLEM?

Critics claim that debate over squeegee kids is about more than legislative priorities of the Ontario government. It is also about ideology, about who belongs and who does not, and about how the powerful construct social problems:

Problems come into discourse as reinforcements of ideologies. . . . They signify who are virtuous and useful and who are dangerous or inadequate, which actions will be rewarded and which penalized. . . . They create beliefs about the relative importance of events and objects. They are critical in determining who exercise[s] authority and who accept[s] it. (Edelman, 1988, p. 12)

For example, spokesperson for the NAPO Laurie Rektor says that laws such as the *Safe Streets Act* "foster a climate of intolerance and divisiveness.

Their underlying message is one of hatred against poor people" (Dawson, 1999, p. 8). The social construction of squeegee kids occurs stepwise through reification, in which the enemy must be recognized in order to be exterminated (Aho, 1994; Berger & Luckman, 1966).

The first step in this process of social construction is *naming*. Persons, acts, or situations are not inherently good or evil. However, society may perceive them as problems if discussion and the everyday circulation of meanings so defines them. And though the term *squeegee kid* is a fairly literal description of the activity in the streets, some think it is not sufficiently evocative. After the court appearance of five squeegee kids (the youngest 18, the oldest 22), the writer of one letter to an editor exclaimed, "They aren't in juvenile court; these are not young offenders—they are highwaymen—one who practices robbery on the highway. Why not call them for what they really are?" (Cofell, 1998, p. A15). Bureaucrats at every level of government have been similarly concerned with finding apt terms for the threat. Toronto Councilor Kyle Rae referred to squeegee kids as "gangs" (Maloney, 1997, p. A1); Toronto Mayor Lastman termed them "thugs" and "beggars"; and Federal Transport Minister David Collenette branded "squeegeers" as misfits when he said that they constitute a "hazard" (Demian, 1998, p. C2). Mayor Lastman's references also labeled squeegee kids as "pests" and "intimidators" (Rankin, 1998, p. A6). As a subject of civic discourse, squeegee kids demonstrate that defamatory language rarely, if ever, simply describes things; it also rhetorically constructs an enemy, which must be destroyed.

The second step in the process of social construction is *legitimation*. The labels established through naming must "stick"; and if they are to adhere, the system must validate the labels. Placing the issue of squeegee kids on the legislative agenda clearly achieved this end. In the summer of 1998, Ontario Premier Mike Harris asked the province's Crime Control Commission to address the issue, and subsequently the *Safe Streets Act* turned a moral issue into a legal one.

Although every government report on homelessness has acknowledged the plight of the squeegee kid, public opinion polls have reinforced and legitimized the notion of squeegee kids as a safety hazard and a nuisance that must be eliminated. These surveys also provide evidence that the government and the media may have "primed" the public to care about issues of law and order and crime. In 1999, for example, crime ranked high (third place) on a list of voter concerns (Frum & Duffy, 1999, p. A6). Ontario residents were worried about threats of civic disorder, especially "petty" crimes such as panhandling, vandalism, and public drunkenness. Yet these fears expressed themselves in the face of a downward trend in serious crimes; and a Toronto poll, taken a year earlier, found squeegee kids did not rank as a significant issue, even though two-thirds of respondents believed they were a safety hazard and should not be allowed on city streets

(Botchford, 1998, p. 4). Similarly, a 1998 Ottawa survey reported that 45 percent of respondents thought that squeegee kids should definitely not be allowed to continue their practice, but the poll also found that people did not get "excited" over the issue (Ebner & Spears, 1998, p. B1). These polls demonstrate that, even though many people wanted this nuisance removed from the streets, the social construction of squeegee kids as an enemy had not yet been completed.

The third stage in social construction is *myth making*, a process that validates defamatory labels. In the case of the squeegee kids, society has constructed the myth of depraved (rather than deprived) youth, who are a scourge on law-abiding society. The myth also paints the squeegee kid as "lazy," "dirty," and foul-smelling (Rankin, 1998, p. A6), as well as "abusive . . . and spaced on drugs" (Marshall, 1997, p. A22). The myth of the squeegee kid is alternative, "different from us": "Their lips, cheeks, tongue and nose may be pierced, their heads randomly adorned with shocks of hair, tinted a smorgasbord of colors found in a crayon box" (Rankin, 1998, p. A6). What is the impact of this myth building?

When the dominant culture defines some groups as different, as the "other", the members of these groups are imprisoned in their bodies. Dominant discourse defines them in terms of bodily characteristics and constructs these bodies as ugly, dirty, defiled, impure, contaminated or sick. (Young, 1990)

An attempt by Naomi Klein to defend the leader of Ontario's coalition against poverty illustrated that the defenders of the poor and squeegee kids also run the risk of being labeled as dangerous threats to law and order. Klein's column in *The Globe and Mail* ran under the following title: "Would you invite John Clarke to your riot?" (Palmer, 2000, p. 29).

This myth—or captivating fiction—of the squeegee kids as a blight on law-abiding society may or may not be valid. As philosopher Alasdair MacIntyre (1970) concludes, myths are neither true nor false, but living or dead. A myth is alive if it continues to give meaning to human life. In this tradition, it is less important to show who is "right" and who is "wronged" than to explain why the issue of the squeegee kids has gained such prominence and what it means for the contemporary social fabric.

The fourth stage in the social construction of the squeegee kids as threat is that of *sedimentation*. This term refers to the transmission of experience from one person to the next so that the experience becomes available to those who have never had it. Eventually, a discourse of demeaning labels becomes, with each retelling, "common sense" so that everybody begins to recognize squeegee kids as disorderly and dangerous. Members of the public reiterate the government discourse, which argues for protection of public space. They proclaim that squeegee kids and other unsightly—if not dangerous—youth pose a danger to their persons, businesses, and commerce.

Tales of encounters with squeegee kids, retold in the media, also contribute to this end.

The fifth and final stage of social construction is *ritual*. The ongoing squeegee encounters vividly dramatize these processes. One reporter describes this ritual in typical fashion: "Some horrified motorists put their hands in front of their faces, as if the teens were vampires and the looming squeegees crucifixes. Others merely nodded no. A small percentage, motivated by benevolence, intimidation or obligation, paid for the service" (Freeze, 1997, p. D1).

The preceding discussion describes how those in authority construct squeegee kids as threatening figures who must be dealt with decisively. In this way, they ensure an environment devoid of potentially menacing others, who do not fit comfortably within the dominant ideology. While not "politically correct," Premier Harris' government discourse is nonetheless "economically correct"; and the force of the rhetoric gains in strength as competing political institutions (e.g., anti-poverty associations such as OCAP and NAPO) lose ground. Bauman (1999) says that "strong discourse" of the variety used in the debate over squeegee kids is almost impossible to combat. The "realism" of the strong discourse is unquestioned because it orients "the economic choices of all those who dominate economic relations and adds its own, properly symbolic, force" (p. 28).

WHAT IS THE SOCIAL MEANING OF THIS DISCOURSE?

This debate reveals not only alternative views of public life, but also potentially irreconcilable ones. This discourse of risk avoidance and of "cleaning up the city" largely responds to squeegee kids' public presence— they are all too visible. Like the homeless, squeegee kids become indicators of how much disorder society can withstand. The proposed solution is to legislate them out of existence. With the rejection of who "we" are *not* and a repudiation of worlds in which "we" do *not* want to live, the mobilization of an ideology of social purification has become the order of the day. In Douglas' (1966) terms, the administrative, disciplinary logic sees squeegee kids as human refuse: "Dirt is essentially disorder. Dirt offends against order. Eliminating it is not a negative movement, but a positive effort to organize the environment" (p. 2). In simple terms, the government wishes to "clean up the city." Much of this debate about how to establish order relates indirectly to definitions of *risk* and *fear*, whose alleviation demands the expulsion of visible signs of disorder and disruption.

Furedi (1997) notes that safety has become a fundamental value in the 1990s. In his 1999 Throne Speech, Premier Harris tapped into this "climate of fear" when he suggested that "people have a right to go about their business, walk through their communities, send their children to school, and go to bed at night, free from the fear of violence against their person, their families or their property" (n.p.). In tabling the safe streets bill, Ontario Attorney General Jim Flaherty used similar fear appeals. He stated that "all people in Ontario have the right to drive on the roads, walk down the street or go to public places without being or feeling intimidated" (McCarten, 1999, p. A9).

Both the government and the media reinforce a sense of the urban scene in which citizens continually confront issues of risk and insecurity in the places where they live. Through her analysis of purity, Douglas (1966) expresses the ideological nature of this discourse of risk avoidance that has become central to the framing of both political debate and social action: "I believe that ideas about separating, purifying, demarcating and punishing transgressions have as their main function to impose system on an inherently untidy experience" (p. 4). In an elaboration of this purification impulse, Bauman (1997) suggests the appropriateness of applying these concepts to the discourse over squeegee kids:

Purity is a vision of things put in places different from those they would occupy if not prompted to move elsewhere. . . . There is no way of thinking about purity without having an image of "order" . . . the opposite of "purity"—the dirt, the filth, "polluting agents"—are things "out of place." It is not the intrinsic quality of things which makes them into "dirt," but solely their location; more precisely, their location in the order of things envisaged by the purity-seekers. (p. 6)

This characterization of a world that is easily divided between the defiling and the desirous is evocative. It explains why, just as there is a vocal call for the extermination of squeegee kids, there is a similarly vociferous defense of them: "Although this kind of differentiation is dependent on disgust, the very features which are reviled are also desired because they represent those features of the civilized self which are repressed" (Sibley, 1995, p. 51). Political and civic discourse thrives on conflict of this nature. Forestalling even the possibility of dialogue, this conflict spawns further divisive rhetoric that damns the party that refuses to see things on your terms. The possibility for an amicable solution becomes remote.

WHAT IS THE POSSIBILITY OF ACHIEVING A MUTUALLY BENEFICIAL DIALOGUE?

A true dialogue, grounded in mutual respect for all participants, is not easy or comfortable to achieve: "To enact dialogue, the parties must fuse their perspectives, while maintaining the uniqueness of their perspectives. The parties form a unity in conversation, but only through two clearly differentiated voices" (Baxter, 1994, p. 25). Entering into dialogue is risky, for it means assuming responsibility for a shared life. Franklin (1998), however, believes that refusing to undertake these risks is potentially even more dangerous: "In trying to rebuild a world that we can take for granted, we succeed only in constructing a rhetoric or facade of certainty and common sense over the intense activity of change" (p. 3).

A collaborative dialogue with squeegee kids (or other members of marginalized groups) requires moving beyond rigid, authoritarian, blame-connoting politics. A true dialogue would acknowledge alternative views rather than assimilate or ignore them altogether. Falzon (1998) speaks to the conditions of this dialogue:

Openness to the other implies an attitude of respect towards otherness, a willingness to let the other speak and to listen seriously. By the same token, it also means an abandonment of the security, the comfort that comes with an all-embracing view of the world where the other is completely mastered and predictable. It means promoting risk, instability, uncertainty, and the possible transformation of prevailing principles and forms of life. (pp. 60–61)

Franklin (1998) goes on to suggest how these themes of dialogue and risk are coterminous: "The politics of risk society requires a relationship between the public, experts and politicians in which mutual respect and democratic dialogue replace the blind faith and mutual contempt which have characterized the political process" (p. 7). Communication through dialogue implies the existence of some common ground, even as it recognizes that this landscape may be antagonistic and conflict-ridden. Thus, a truly civic discourse over squeegee kids does not mean simple openness, but the capability to move beyond monologue.

CONCLUSION

The January 2000 attempt to purify urban spaces in Ontario generated a heated, if uneven, debate over who has the right to access and use public spaces. The major stakeholders in the dispute (the squeegee kids) were notably absent. Others communicated through monologues or rhetorical attacks. Defensiveness, the statement of anxieties, and contrary visions of public life characterized media coverage of the issue. As the example of the squeegee kids illustrates, battle lines drawn between politicians and advocacy groups, social workers, and outreach agencies caught the public in the middle. A less rigid discourse would not have framed the issues in terms of "us versus them" or supported exclusionary policies of social purification. Imagining a different and more inclusive future would involve focusing politics less on risk aversion and more on inclusion—framing public policies that do not excommunicate the public.

Squeegee kids—and our relations with them—constitute a site of political struggle. We can see the role of communication in this struggle, in the way the discourse is played out in the media, negotiated and contested by individuals, and acted out in the streets. This issue is far more than a mild irritant or a transitory concern on the legislative radar. The broader issue at stake—more important than whether or not squeegee kids pose a real threat to everyday life—is how this discourse is structured and why certain responses are preferred over others. We must, in fact, confront the question of why squeegee kids were defined as a political problem in the first place. Here, the dominant terms of the discourse have been socially constructed around fears. Negotiating these fears is never easy and resolving such issues is never straightforward. In the wake of the recent Ontario provincial legislation, however, there certainly seem to be fewer squeegee practitioners plying their trade in the streets. Their absence may be taken as further evidence that a dominant ideology of social purification is present in practice, as well as in discourse.

REFERENCES

Aho, J. A. (1994). *This thing of darkness: A sociology of the enemy*. Seattle: University of Washington Press.

Bauman, Z. (1987). *Legislators and interpreters*. London: Polity Press.

Bauman, Z. (1997). *Postmodernity and its discontents*. New York: New York University Press.

Bauman, Z. (1999). *In search of politics*. Stanford, CA: Stanford University Press.

Baxter, L. A. (1994). Thinking dialogically about communication in personal relationships. In R. Conville (Ed.), *Uses of structure in communication studies* (pp. 23–37). Westport, CT: Praeger.

Berger, P. L., & Luckman, T. (1966). *The social construction of reality*. Garden City, NY: Doubleday & Co.

Botchford, J. (1998, October 6). Privacy be damned. *Toronto Sun*, p. 4.

Clark, H. H. (1996). *Using language*. Cambridge, MA: Cambridge University Press.

Cofell, D. W. (1998, July 28). Squeegee "kids" aren't really kids. *Toronto Star*, p. A15.

Dawson A. (1999, November 16). Panhandling laws "vicious." *Toronto Sun*, p. 8.

Demian, I. (1998, August 4). The squeegee kid debate. *Toronto Star*, p. C2.

Douglas, M. (1966). *Purity and danger*. London: Routledge & Kegan Paul.

Ebner D., & Spears, T. (1998, August 3). Time to wipe out squeegees, survey says. *Ottawa Citizen*, p. B1.

Edelman, M. (1988). *Constructing the political spectacle*. Chicago: University of Chicago Press.

Falzon, C. (1998). *Foucault and social dialogue*. London: Routledge.

Franklin, J. (1998). Introduction. In J. Franklin (Ed.), *The politics of risk society* (pp. 1–8). Cambridge, MA: Polity Press.

Freeze, C. (1997, July 25). Work fast, be patient, clean up. *Ottawa Citizen*, p. D1.

Frum, D., & Duffy, J. (1999, May 13). Liberals sleeping as society crumbles. *National Post*, p. A6.

Furedi, F. (1997). *Culture of fear*. London: Cassell.

MacIntyre, A. (1970). *Sociological theory and philosophical analysis*. New York: Macmillan.

Maloney, P. (1997, June 17). A squeegee solution. *Toronto Star*, p. A1.

Marshall, B. (1997, July 3). Squeegees turn Spadina into toll road. *Toronto Star*, p. A22.

McCarten, J. (1999, November 3). Ontario Tories move to wipe out squeegee kids. *Calgary Herald*, p. A9.

Mitchell, D. (1995). The end of public space? *Annals of the Association of American Geographers 85* (1), 108–133.

National Anti-Poverty Organization (NAPO). (1999). *Short changed on human rights: A NAPO position paper on anti-panhandling by-laws*. Ottawa. http://www.povnet.org/human_rights/NAPO%20TOC.htm.

Palmer, B. (2000, September). The riot act: Reviving protest in Ontario. *Canadian Dimension 34* (5), 28–32.

Rankin, J. (1998, May 31). Squeegee kids get squeezed. *Toronto Star*, p. A6.

Sibley, D. (1995). *Geographies of exclusion*. London: Routledge.

Young, I. M. (1990). *Justice and the politics of difference*. Princeton, NJ: Princeton University Press.

Chapter 5

Spatial In(queer)ies: Queer Space as Queer Voice in Calgary

Dawn E. B. Johnston

> Though lesbians and gay men, as well as aspects of our culture, have existed for thousands of years in every known society and nation, our existence, history, and transformations are rarely represented in any work in the social sciences fields. Our culture has been trivialized as "lifestyle" and our places, spaces, and geography are unknown and invisible to most people. (Wolfe, 1997, p. 303)

These words echo the experiences of many minority groups within urban spaces. The cases of inaccessible histories, erased cultures, and invisible spaces are innumerable; but with the recent identification of race, class, and gender as crucial points of intersection in academic research and scholarly writing, research has begun to uncover those histories and make those experiences culturally significant. Most recently, sexual orientation has joined race, class, and gender as a recognized site for the constructing of identity, community, and power. A shift in scholarly attention has propelled this recognition of this shift in thinking. Slowly and carefully, individuals within academia are responding to the call for attention to gay, lesbian, bisexual, and transsexual lives, and are taking on the challenge of writing "queer" histories and theorizing about queer cultures.

However, it is no surprise to discover that the majority of this scholarly work focuses on large urban centers with visible and active gay populations. Much has been written, for example, on the gay ghettos of Montreal, the gay neighborhoods of Toronto and Vancouver, and the ever-queer Castro district of San Francisco. But what about the less visible queer communities? If no one is hanging rainbow flags from a neighborhood of houses or dominating the ownership of businesses in a particular area, where is the queer community in Canada? If we cannot see evidence of this community in a city like Calgary, Alberta, does it exist? How concretely is a culture tied to its places, its spaces, and its geography? How does a queer landscape operate as a social and political face or voice? This chapter, which grew out of original research I completed in 1999, explores these questions about queer communities and spaces in Calgary.

Ingram, Bouthillette, and Retter (1997) assert that "queer space enables people with marginalized sexualities and identities to survive and to gradually expand their influence and opportunities to live fully" (p. 3). In speaking of the limitations of movement and self-statement that gays and lesbians have experienced by being "ghettoized," Rich has coined the phrase "politics of location" (cited in Ingram et al., 1997, p. 2). Foucault (cited in Ingram et al., 1997) speaks of a "desanctification of space" in which definitions, descriptions, and boundaries of spaces may become increasingly blurred with gay and lesbian community formation (p. 13). There is no doubt that places and spaces are significant in formation of community and development of culture, but in Calgary, those spaces are not entirely visible. Gay and lesbian bars and dance clubs are scattered throughout the four quadrants of the city. Gay male cruising spots range in location from public washrooms to parks in low-income neighborhoods to the Calgary Zoo parking lot. No one definitive gay housing area exists. Few, if any, of these queer spaces are identifiable by any method other than word of mouth. Considering the conservative social and political environment of Calgary, this deficit is not entirely surprising. Alberta was the last Canadian province to protect sexual orientation under the human rights code—and only under duress from the federal government and the Supreme Court following the Delwin Vriend case.[1] The city's mayor has refused to write or support a declaration of Gay Pride Day.

Yet queer communities and spaces in Calgary do exist, even in the face of such blatant public and political homophobia. This reality raises many questions. How have gays, lesbians, transsexuals, and bisexuals found one another without public identification of gay ghettos? What constitutes queer communities? Most importantly, how do Calgary's queers seek out, identify, and create safe spaces for social and sexual self-statement in a city commonly recognized as socially, politically, and morally conservative and—in many cases—overtly homophobic? Exploring these questions through both interviews and theory has illuminated some interesting observations on construction of space, the materiality of lived relations in space, the sexualizing of space, the politicizing of location and sites of congregation, dialectics of public and private space, differences between legal equality and spatial equality, and notions of civic rights in this city.

Ingram and colleagues (1997) explore many explanations, limitations, and potentialities of queer space that challenge definitions of the terms *queer* and *space*. Not surprisingly, these terms are highly contestable, as they mean different things to almost everyone who identifies as queer and appropriates queer space. For some, the word *queer* is interchangeable with *gay*. For others, the term is much more political, suggesting "different from the norm," "strange," "twisted," or "unpredictable." And for still others, it is an extremely active word, a deliberate de-normalization or de-stabilization of heterosexual norms. For some queers, queer space is anywhere they go. For others, the space has to have a queer history. Some require just queer-friendliness, others demand that their spaces offer queer exclusivity. The language—like the politics of community—is contentious. Perhaps this is why, as Ingram suggests, queer spaces tend to be so ambiguous:

Queer sites are usually characterized by contradictions and ambiguity, allowing for a wide range of erotic and other forms of social contact. Rather than constructing sites explicitly for homoerotic communality and statement, much formation of queer space has concentrated on transcending heteronormative constraints. In times of repression and culturally enforced conformity, the least constraining places are those that are neither totally public or private, containing rich striations within short physical distances. (Ingram et al., 1997, p. 295)

That contradiction of public and private is notably present within queer spaces. Cruising areas, back rooms of bars, bathhouses—these are the spaces that combine private activities with public settings, heightening eroticism and pushing boundaries. The intersection of public and private raises many questions about ownership of space, politicizing of space, and the making of neutral places into meaningful spaces.

Leap (1999) and Foucault (1978) are both fascinated with the intersection of private acts and public places. Leap tries to understand and make sense of public sex through an analysis of place, space, and landscape. He discusses the way in which concepts of ownership and politicization of space are "continually being constructed, negotiated, and contested" (p. 7). Leap offers the appeal of danger as a possible explanation. Foucault, on the other hand, looks purely at the pleasure offered by the public places in which sexual encounters are commonplace:

[In Europe] the bath was sort of a cathedral of pleasure at the heart of the city, where people could go as often as they want, where they walked about, picked each other up, met each other, took their pleasure, ate, drank, discussed. . . . Sexuality was obviously considered a social pleasure for the Greeks and the Romans. What is interesting about male homosexuality today—this has apparently been the case of female homosexuals for some time—is that their sexual relations are immediately translated into social relations and the social relations are understood as sexual relations. For the Greeks and Romans, in a different fashion, sexual relations were located within social relations in the widest sense of the term. The baths were a place of sociality that included sexual relations. (p. 167)

Foucault's words suggest a connection between the sexual and the social and collapsing of boundaries between public and private, in keeping with the philosophies of poststructuralism and postmodernism and, in turn, with attitudes toward the queering of space.

Like de Certeau's (1984) suggestion that space is practiced place, Desert (1997) asserts that space becomes queer through a combination of practice and wishful thinking:

Queer space is in large part the function of wishful thinking or desires that become solidified: a seduction of the reading of space where queerness, at a few brief points and for some fleeting moments, dominates the (heterocentric) norm, the dominant social narrative of the landscape. The observer's complicity is key in allowing a public site to be co-opted in part or completely. So compelling is this seduction that a general consensus or collective belief emerges among queers and non-queers alike. (p. 21)

The logic is circuitous: space is queer because queers go there, and queers go there because the space is queer.

The construction of queer spaces that are *intended* as queer spaces is more simply explained. Gay business owners have the option of choosing a queer market as a target market, and although success is never guaranteed, the use of queer advertising, queer signifiers, and word-of-mouth techniques helps the queer proprietor to create a queer space. As several of my respondents pointed out, there is a tendency in any community to support business owners who treat their clients well and appreciate their business. This is certainly true of queer communities.

However, the most interesting queer spaces are those "natural" or "neutral" places that are appropriated (i.e., consciously queered). According to de Certeau (1984), anyone can make a place his or her own, simply by "practicing it": "The street geometrically defined by urban planning is transformed into a space by walkers" (p. 117). A city park becomes a queer space when gay men choose to use it as a cruising area. Ingram and colleagues (1997) suggest that the process is a response (conscious or unconscious) to mainstream heterosexual norms:

Just as queer identities are constructed within the context of heteronormativity, queer places have been forged within spaces not originally intended for gay use. Identifying a place as queer is a deliberate action parallel to "coming out." Although certain sites have been the focus of gay activities for many years, the nature of these queer places changes, just as identities and modes of contact do. Without a conscious effort to constantly reinvent the queerness of such places, heteronormative forces in society often overwhelm and push out networks of sexual minorities. (p. 295)

By day, the parking lot of the Calgary Zoo shows no signs of queerness, except to the practiced eye or to those who are acquainted with its nighttime activities. In the same way, the Victoria Park Community Center is the site of monthly dances ("outings") for the Alberta Rockies Gay Rodeo Association. (See Ingram et al., 1997 for a discussion of the term *outings*.) This claiming of territory by Calgary's queer communities supports de Certeau's (1984) assertion that, through activity, "place" becomes "space."

So the question becomes, "Who or what constructs that space?" So often we assume that dominant social forces construct spaces and use their power to maintain the margins. Cultural theorist Pile (Pile & Keith, 1997), however, disagrees with the tendency to begin "stories of resistance with stories of so-called power" (p. 3). He maintains that queer spaces, like the spaces of other marginalized groups, are often constructed by those who make places their own rather than by those who seek to contain or control them.

Too often, political activism has been seen as the direct outcome of opposition to the things that the powerful do. Too often, the terrain of political struggle has been thought of as being constituted by practices of the dominant . . . but political identities and political actions take place on grounds other than those defined only through the effects of the powerful. . . . Thinking through geographies of resistance shows precisely that resistance seeks to occupy new spaces, to create new geographies, to make its own place on the map. (p. 1)

Rather than being ghettos or places to hide, queer spaces are developed, practiced, and owned.

De Certeau's (1984) and Pile's (Pile & Keith, 1997) explanations of space-making have their limits, however. If we accept that, theoretically, a street can be owned simply by walking it, we must also accept that Calgary's queers have only to select and use spaces in order to appropriate the space. This suggestion undermines the political and social realities of this city—of any city, for that matter. Inevitably, there are individuals and groups within a particular society who do not want to see expansion of space for queer communities. Those people will challenge the queering of city spaces. Moreover, places are rarely practiced by only one person or even by one *group* of people, and when opposing forces contest the same space, the majority usually wins. For this reason, some members of the queer community keep a low profile. I interviewed one of the co-owners of Calgary's most popular lesbian bar, a space that had no rainbow flag or other gay signifier to designate it as a lesbian establishment. When asked about the lack of signifiers, she indicated that this decision was intentional, as she did not want the residents of the neighborhood to try to close the place or force a change in clientele. (It is interesting to note that this bar changed locations in the winter of 2001. It is now located in the gay-friendlier city center.) The reality of social and political inequality in Calgary places limits on the growth and development of queer communities, and in turn, queer spaces. So, while de Certeau's explanation of "space as practiced place" holds true to a certain extent, it would be inappropriate to extend this logic to suggest that queers have limited space simply because they are not trying hard enough.

Looking at how and why space becomes queer leads naturally to looking at what queer space provides for its clientele. In her study of lesbian bars of the 1950s, Wolfe (1997) provides an explanation of what queer spaces offer—an explanation that, according to the responses from my participants, still holds true. She describes lesbian bars as places of comfort and reprieve for sexual minorities:

In a world where most of us cannot openly exist, lesbian bars provide a momentary safe separate place to meet other lesbians. They can be the place where people thrown out of their families can create a new support network or where lesbians can do things they might get hassled for somewhere else, such as playing pool or dancing with other women. Yet they are not really private in the sense of autonomy, or of controlling the environment, or for many, of choosing them over some other place where we can be "out." (p. 319)

When asked what constituted queer space for them, the participants echoed these same sentiments. Concepts like safety and support and comfort form the basis for choosing a queer social space, I heard again and again. But, as Wolfe (1997) points out, those spaces are not entirely "private" or "owned." In a city the size of Calgary, most queer people do not have a host of options in choosing their space.

Similarly, the concerns of queer business owners, with regard to their responsibilities to their clients, have changed little since the 1950s:

To insure continued patronage and to protect their premises (or if lesbian-owned, their users) from men passing by who might break the windows, or who come in to beat up women or assert their male prerogatives to go anywhere they want, most lesbian bars have no windows, or cover up their windows. The lights are generally very dim to protect their users from recognition should unwanted people enter purposefully or unknowingly. Lesbian bars generally don't have signs or names or other distinguishing outside physical features that might give them away to non-lesbian citizens. Even today, generally the dance floors or even the entire bar are not visually accessible from the front entrance. (Wolfe, 1997, p. 318)

Wolfe's words sound remarkably similar to those of the co-owner of Rook's Bar and Beanery.

Queer space functions on several levels—to create spaces of safety and comfort for queers, but also to create signified spaces of pride. In a city like Calgary, the small rainbow stickers and inverted pink triangles in the windows of many queer establishments are subtle indicators of this pride. But in Toronto's Church/Wellesley village and San Francisco's Castro district, entire neighborhoods are emblazoned with these familiar signs. The signs send an important message to queers and "hets" alike (Desert, 1997). External queer signifiers of this type indicate ownership of space by the entire queer community, not just by the technical proprietors of businesses. Queers *own* these neighborhoods, in the same way that heterosexuals assume ownership of the vast majority of urban space; and such visibility—such ownership—has immeasurable weight in the development of a civic or cultural voice.

This leads us to perhaps the most important aspect of queer space as queer voice in urban centers. The interviews and the literature have pointed to numerous ways in which queer space is constructed, what the space looks like, and what it offers to its patrons. But why is queer space so important? Why is it necessary to bring sexuality out of the home and into the bar or the restaurant or the park? Why do we insist on blurring the lines of private and public, place and space, personal and political? Ingram and colleagues (1997) offer a suggestion:

Most public space offers little representation of queer experience and imagery. Billboards, statues, memorials, and outdoor art depicting aspects of our lives are scant—even in those neighborhoods with large gay communities. Most queer sites, especially those inhabited by racial and cultural minorities, are virtually invisible, and only informed members of those communities know how to find them. This can lead to a sense of cumulative discouragement about claiming outdoor space as queer territory. (p. 92)

Perhaps it is a desire to challenge the political or aesthetic status quo; or maybe it is an interest in forcing people to reconsider the solidity or unity of their own sexual identity. Most likely, it is a combination; but above all, the presence and visibility of queer space challenges popular notions of equality—legal, civic, and spatial.

In Calgary, all of these equalities are at risk. As previously noted, Alberta was the last of the ten Canadian provinces to introduce legislation prohibiting discrimination on the basis of sexual orientation—and only reluctantly. The province does not recognize common-law partnerships between same-sex couples. Civil servants are not entitled to same-sex health or pension benefits. In the eyes of the law and the government, heterosexual unions are the only ones that are recognized. So for Calgary's queers, although there may be legal equality on paper, that equality is not recognized at the most basic level of human rights. Its benefits are not reaped. Because gays, lesbians, and bisexuals have their rights threatened on a daily basis, the fight for civil rights demands a publicity of self that heterosexual citizens are never asked or expected to display.

Patton (1993) says that the quest for civil equality requires a commitment to "coming out":

If agents in possession of gay identities make demands for minority status within the political sphere, this is not because acquisition of gay identity strips away ideology and allows a homosexual body to realize its desire for civil rights that are simply waiting around for the asking. Rather, the demand for civil rights is an intrinsic effect of coming-out rhetoric, altering both the meaning of civil rights and the meaning of homoerotic practices. Coming-out rhetoric, in effect, articulates gay identity to civil rights practices, articulates homoerotic practices to the political concept of minority. The person who takes up a post-Stonewall gay identity feels compelled to act in a way that will constitute her or himself as a subject appropriate to civil rights discourse, and thus, deserving of the status accruing to successful claims to minority status. In the process of queer enunciation, the meaning of civil rights, indeed, the capacity to hold apart the political and social, the public and private, have been radically altered. (p. 173)

The performance of queerness becomes a requirement in the struggle for equality. Queers are forced to prove their status as minorities before they can prove their need for equal rights. We must de-normalize our "lifestyles" in an effort to secure the rights and privileges of a "normal" life. Declaring oneself in such a manner reminds everyone involved of the inequalities associated with a queer identity.

Queers in Calgary are also made constantly aware of their spatial inequalities. The lack of queer spaces in this city is a persistent reminder that there is no equality when it comes to sexual orientation. Queer spaces offer safety for social and sexual statement and interaction, but as we walk out of the doors of these spaces, the freedom and safety disappear. Queer spaces are simultaneously liberating and limiting. They create a two-tiered world in which our sexuality can only be displayed in marked and signified spaces.

Without a doubt, the socially, politically, and morally conservative atmosphere in Alberta has affected the construction and representation of queer space. At the same time, it would be irresponsible to dismiss the future growth or strengthening of queer space simply because the city's or province's politics provide a challenge. As well, Ingram et al. (1997) have suggested that queer community and queer space are changing as we enter a new century:

In the 1990s, the ghettobusting of queer nationalism and the rapid globalization of real estate markets have transformed queer space, pushing it beyond the bounds of the ghetto and inspiring new linkages within and among communities. . . . In the fragments of queer-friendly public spaces available today, a basis for survival, contact, communality, and sometimes even community has begun. (p. 3)

These words gave me a new lens through which to view Calgary's queer spaces. I became aware that, in some senses, Calgary is an anomaly. Our queer spaces are not centrally located in one distinct neighborhood. There is no gay ghetto. I had considered Calgary to be backward or behind the times in this sense—but perhaps not. If, as Ingram suggests, the "new" queer nationalism is about "ghetto-busting," perhaps Calgary is ahead of its time. Calgary's queer community, particularly with regard to its spaces, can certainly be described as "fragmented." Perhaps such fragmentation will define the queer landscapes of the twenty-first century.

Moreover, the theorists are not the only ones who hold such views. An interview with Glen Murray (1999), the mayor of Winnipeg, appeared in a recent issue of *Outlooks*, a newspaper that serves Alberta's queer community. When asked about the state of gay communities on the Prairies, the openly gay Murray provided a thoughtful—and thought-provoking—response.

I think that places like Winnipeg and Calgary are probably the first two post-urban ghetto centers for gay and lesbian cultures. We don't live in isolation like people can in gay "meccas" like Toronto or Vancouver, we're part of the larger community and we're more integrated. More and more young people are staying in places like Winnipeg and Calgary because of this. We are not "ghettoized"—our bars and businesses are interspersed here throughout the city. I think a lot of gay and lesbian people early on ran to the ghettos of Montreal, Toronto, and Vancouver, because they didn't think the world was ever going to catch up, that they wouldn't ever actually be accepted. But this is starting to change. People in places like Edmonton, Calgary, Winnipeg, Regina, et cetera, have *had* to build stronger communities outside of the ghettos. I think there is a greater sense of inclusion within smaller gay communities because we can't segregate ourselves, we have to be strong in a fragmented way. And I also think that there is a great sense of humanity about people on the prairies—we have had to work together in isolation from large centers. (p. 7)

The limited visibility of Calgary's queer communities and spaces has long been criticized and lamented, but Murray's words put a new spin on the construction of queer space on the prairies. This heralding of fragmentation, in conjunction with theories of " '90s ghetto-busting," provides a new perspective on Calgary's queer spaces.

A commitment to the development and nurturing of exclusively queer spaces may appear counterproductive in terms of integration and normalization, but queers need the comfort and solidity of owned spaces in order to expand their influence and to challenge homophobia, heterocentricism, and heteronormativity. The practicing of place and the ownership of space facilitate this battle. Rich (1993) says that "a place on the map is also a place in history" (p. 212). To queer the history of Calgary and Alberta— that is, to challenge the popular perception of Western cities as conservative, corporate, and "cowboy"—we need a place on the map.

NOTE

1. Delwin Vriend is an Alberta teacher who was fired in 1991 when he revealed that he was gay. The Court of Queen's Bench determined that his dismissal was wrongful, but the Alberta Court of Appeal overturned the ruling, stating that the courts could not rule on provincial jurisdiction. In April 1998, the Supreme Court of Canada ruled in Vriend's favor, and the Alberta Provincial Government decided not to constitutionally override the decision.

REFERENCES

De Certeau, M. (1984). *The practice of everyday life*. Los Angeles: University of California Press.

Desert, J. (1997). Queer space. In G. Ingram, A. Bouthillette, & Y. Retter (Eds.), *Queers in space: Communities/public places/sites of resistance* (pp. 17–26). Seattle, WA: Bay Press.

Foucault, M. (1978). *The history of sexuality: An introduction*. New York: Random House.

Ingram, G., Bouthillette, A., & Retter, Y. (Eds.). (1997). *Queers in space: Communities/public places/sites of resistance*. Seattle, WA: Bay Press.

Leap, W. (1999). *Public sex/gay space*. New York: Columbia University Press.

Murray, Glen. (1999, April). Interview. *Outlooks*, 6.

Patton, C. (1993). Tremble, hetero swine! In M. Warner (Ed.), *Fear of a queer planet: Queer politics and social theory* (pp. 143–177). Minneapolis: University of Minnesota Press.

Pile, S., & Keith, M. (1997). *Geographies of resistance*. London: Routledge.

Rich, A. (1993a). Blood, bread and poetry: The location of the poet. In A. Rich (Ed.), *Prose and poetry* (pp. 239–254). New York: W.W. Norton and Company.

Rich, A. (1993b). Compulsory heterosexuality and lesbian existence. In A. Rich (Ed.), *Prose and poetry* (pp. 203–224). New York: W.W. Norton and Company.

Wolfe, M. (1997). Invisible women in invisible places: The production of social space in lesbian bars. In G. Ingram, A. Bouthillette, & Y. Retter (Eds.), *Queers in space: Communities/public places/sites of resistance*. Seattle, WA: Bay Press.

Chapter 6

The Discourse of the Leading Actors in the Fight against Poverty: An Analysis of the Québec Print Press

Marie-Nicole Cossette

Canadian society adheres, in principle, to equal opportunity for all citizens. Yet poverty is a significant inequality, a condition that calls for remedy; and its existence contradicts the ideals of a just society. For these reasons, the fight against poverty is an important topic of social discourse, both within government and civil society as a whole. Those most committed to eliminating poverty often disagree, however, on the goals of the fight, definitions of what constitutes poverty, and solutions to poverty. The polysemic nature of poverty explains our inability to achieve a definition that is universally and internationally accepted. In popular usage, the word refers to many different realities. Not all agree, for example, that poverty denotes lack of resources.

At an international level, the United Nations Development Program (UNDP, 1998) sees freedom from poverty as a human right. If people who live in poverty are unable to attain the living standards of the rest of society, then the term also suggests an absence from participation in the social order. For the UNDP, poverty is a process and not a condition. Rather than viewing the poor as passive victims, the UNDP sees the most disadvantaged members of society as leading figures in the fight against impoverishment. Instead of focusing on the weaknesses of the poor, they say that we should expand our concept of poverty to encompass the potential of the poor and the resources they need to rise above the poverty line.

Statistics Canada concurs that low income is not necessarily a sign of poverty (Fellegi, 1997). However, civil society groups accuse the Canadian government of wanting to adopt a criterion other than the basket of goods in order to artificially reduce the poverty statistics. In short, the choice of facts and their interpretation largely depend on fundamental values. Friedman (1996) divides discourse on poverty into five categories: administrative, moralizing, scientific, the voice of the poor, and empowerment.

The goal of this study was to learn more about how the Québec press defines and covers the concept of poverty and to uncover the views of the various actors in the fight against poverty. The metaphor of fighting is widely used when talking about poverty. As in all fights, people play different roles. Sometimes the actors are adversaries, and the roles are oppositional. At other times, the actors are allies, working together and agreeing on goals. How does the press depict the "fight" against poverty? Who are the actors? Finally, do the actions of the leading actors in this fight conflict with what they say about poverty? What meaning do the actors give to poverty? If the previous discussion is correct, we can expect to find a wide variety of opinions and definitions appearing in press coverage of poverty.

To accomplish the purposes of this study, I analyzed 306 articles from four major French-language daily newspapers. The articles appeared in the Québec press between October of 1998 and September of 1999. The ATD Fourth World Movement in Montréal (Atd Quart Monde, 1998–1999) had identified these articles as relevant to the topic of poverty. The distribution of the articles, by newspaper, was as follows: *Le Devoir*, 100; *La Presse*, 110; *Le Journal de Montréal*, 66; and *Le Soleil*, 30. The decision to analyze newspaper coverage grew out the fact that this traditional print medium reflects, as well as molds, societal views.

RESEARCH METHOD

To better define the specific dynamic of the fight against poverty and the roles of the main actors, I conducted a systematic study of each of the 306 articles in the research corpus. I identified nine questions that could frame the content analysis. Landry (1997) argues that responding to questions in a content analysis generates data that are similar to the results of survey research. In framing the nine questions (i.e., in arriving at these questions), I referred to a study by Ilouz (1994), who had identified four distinct themes in news coverage of poverty: characteristics of the poor, causes of poverty, solutions, and the people in charge of solving the problem of poverty. These findings led to questions that became part of my research design. I also referred to the broader literature on the discourse of poverty to generate the questions.

In brief, my content analysis responded to the following questions: (1) Who talks about poverty or participates in the fight against it? (2) What meaning do the actors give to the concept of poverty? (3) What are the demands of different individuals and groups? (4) Which of these actors appear to be held responsible for eliminating poverty? (5) What solutions are proposed? (6) What roles do the poor play in this fight: actor or beneficiary? (7) What is the tone of the articles? Are they positive (offering a defense of the poor) or negative (accusing the poor)? (8) Does the press convey the idea that inequalities exist between women and men, rich and poor? (9) What do the articles identify as the causes of poverty? I also tried to identify actors who agreed and disagreed on the answers to these research questions.

In responding to the questions, I designated the theme as the unit of analysis (rather than the article). For that reason, the totals in my tables do not match the total number of articles in the study. (Sometimes the totals are larger; sometimes they are smaller.) Not every theme appeared in every article. That is, I was not able to find the answers to every question in each article. Some articles responded to some questions, other articles responded to others.

RESULTS OF THE ANALYSIS

In discussing the results of the analysis, I have added quotations from the articles to the quantitative data, in the hope of going beyond a simple description of the content. Simplistic interpretations prevent us from grasping the complexity of the problems involved in the fight against poverty. The following discussion highlights some of the most interesting findings of the research but does not attempt to be comprehensive. The tables, however, provide additional information.

Images of Fighting against Poverty

The metaphor of fighting appears often in news coverage of poverty issues. The fight is couched in the language of war: "The poor are climbing the barricades: Ottawa called upon to condemn discrimination against the poor" (*Le Devoir*, April 12, 1999). There is an "anti-poverty crusade led by Christiane Gagnon" (*Le Soleil*, March 26, 1999). "Yesterday, two generals in the social justice movement delivered a symbolic demand to the Montréal office of Prime Minister Lucien Bouchard" (*Le Devoir*, December 10, 1998).

Two opposing conclusions to the fight (the worsening of poverty and the reduction/elimination of poverty) characterize the newspaper coverage of the "fighting poverty" theme. The following examples illustrate the position that the poverty situation is worsening: "Poverty on the rise in Montréal" (*Le Devoir*, May 13, 1999); "Poverty is gaining ground on the Island of Montreal and is spreading its tentacles further and further" (*La Presse*, April 23, 1999). Writers suggest that the fight is clearly being lost: "The situation of homeless people is reaching critical proportions" (*Le Devoir*, July 13, 1999). This deteriorating situation calls for emergency measures: "Emergency measures for street youth" (*Le Devoir*, December 18, 1998). Less frequently, the press reports successful efforts to reduce or eliminate

Table 6.1
Who Speaks on the Subject of Poverty or Takes Action against It?

	Le Devoir	La Presse	Le Soleil	Le J. de M.	
Politicians	13	13	3	5	34
Journalists	5	6	0	4	15
NGO	35	50	18	34	137
Individuals	2	4	1	6	13
Government	22	26	8	13	69
Poor	9	16	5	7	37
Experts	27	9	2	2	40
	113	124	37	71	345

poverty: "Anti-poverty fund created, employers to participate" (*La Presse*, February 15, 1999).

The Leading Actors in the Fight against Poverty

Assuming that the fight against poverty involves a conflict between op-posing forces, who are the social actors in this fight? The processing of information by the media means that not every voice appears in the press. In its editorial function, the press selects certain themes to highlight, as well as certain actors to present. In the case of poverty, I was interested to know whose voices appeared in the press and, alternatively, whose voices were absent (see Table 6.1).

Non-governmental organizations (NGOs) indisputably play a leading role in the fight against poverty. NGOs include unions, churches, women's groups, rights groups for welfare recipients, artists, community organiza-tions, the United Way, and the Social Justice Centre. This role received much recognition in the press. My analysis found that NGOs appeared in 39.7 percent of the 345 references to actors in the fight against poverty. Twenty percent of the 345 mentions referred to government actors. In-cluded in this category were ministers and bureaucrats, municipal repre-sentatives, school boards, and health boards. Experts (including statisticians, sociologists, and economists) came third in total number of mentions, at 11 percent. Only 10.7 percent of the references to social actors mentioned the poor as active participants in the fight against poverty. Pol-iticians (i.e., the members of the opposition) received 9.9 percent of the mentions, journalists (editorialists and columnists) 4.3 percent, and indi-viduals 3.8 percent. The imbalance was evident from the start. The news-papers framed most of their reports on poverty around two actors (NGOs and government representatives). All of the other actors played secondary roles in the press coverage. However, *Le Devoir* presented a very different picture. Approximately 23.9 percent of its references to actors in the fight against poverty included experts.

Poverty as Seen by the Leading Actors

The concept of poverty has different meanings to different people (see Table 6.2). The second question asked the following: Which of the many interpretations of poverty appear in the Québec press? Which appear to be favored in press coverage? How does the press present the opinions of each social actor?

Thirty-six percent of the 362 poverty-related themes defined poverty in terms of lack of basic necessities: food, adequate housing, electricity, medicine, and transportation. Headlines that exemplified this approach were the following: "Students going hungry" (*Le Devoir*, January 22, 1999). Housing is also among these necessities: "People should not have to choose between paying rent and eating" (*Le Journal de Montréal*, March 4, 1999). Lack of money was linked to poverty in 16 percent of the thematic discussions. Examples of references to money include the following: "There are more people without an income than ever" (*Le Soleil*, April 29, 1999); "For the poorest people, the fight against the deficit means less money for meeting basic needs" (*La Presse*, March 4, 1999). The majority of the actors held the same opinion in this regard: poverty means a lack of basic necessities or a lack of money. Adding the category of money (16%) to the category of basic necessities (36%) gives a total of 52 percent.

Seventeen percent of the 362 references to poverty made a bridge to lack of education (or resources necessary to acquire an education): "One student out of four in Montréal comes from a poor family" (*La Presse*, October 24, 1998) and "4000 children need $100 of school supplies" (*Le Devoir*, August 19, 1999). Twelve percent of the 362 thematic units regarded poverty as a lack of rights: "It really is a violation of human rights—probably the most common violation" (*Le Devoir*, November 30, 1998). Those most likely to link poverty to rights were NGOs and government representatives.

The theme of employment (or unemployment) appeared in 11 percent of the 362 thematic units: "Poverty is when access to jobs and services is lost" (*Le Journal de Montréal*, November 21, 1998); "This increase in self-employment translates into an increase in poverty among women" (*Le Devoir*, March 6, 1999). Experts often blamed poverty on job shortages and poor working conditions. Journalists and NGOs also made this same argument, but not as often as experts. Other actors blamed factors other than employment for the existence of poverty in Canada.

Seven percent of the 362 thematic units associated poverty with distress and exclusion from the social order: "Poverty has adverse effects that trans-

Table 6.2
What Meanings Do the Different Actors Give to the Concept of Poverty?

	Poor	NGO	Governments	Politicians	Experts	Journalists	Individuals	
Education	5	25	19	5	8	1	0	63
Employment	1	19	6	2	11	2	0	41
Basic necessities	12	61	27	6	14	6	5	131
Money	7	19	11	10	8	1	3	59
Distress, exclusion	1	13	8	0	1	1	0	24
Rights	4	18	4	5	6	4	1	42
Dignity	0	2	0	0	0	0	0	2
	30	157	75	28	48	15	9	362

late into psychological distress, parents' worries about their children, their inability to cope, the loss of self-esteem, and the search for anonymity" (*Le Journal de Montréal*, November 21, 1998); "Poverty is when we become Mr. or Ms. Nobody" (*Le Journal de Montréal*, November 21, 1998); and "Along with poverty comes deep-seated distress" (*Le Devoir*, January 9, 1999). *Le Journal de Montréal* (November 12, 1998) noted: "Poverty imposes social and psychic slavery. This situation is intolerable and does not respect human dignity." The only social actors who discussed these themes were government organizations, NGOs, and journalists. Other social actors did not make these links. Finally, only 1 percent of the 362 references (NGOs) equated poverty with loss of dignity.

Thus, in descending order of importance, the following meanings for poverty appeared in the Québec press: lack of basic necessities and money, lack of education, lack of rights, lack of employment, psychological distress, exclusion from participation in the social order, and lack of dignity.

The Major Demands in This Fight

The next part of the analysis responded to the following question: What are the demands of the poor and their spokespersons? (see Table 6.3).

My analysis found that the poor want "rights" rather than "charity." Thirty-eight percent of the 210 demands reported in the press included references to rights, laws, and justice. One newspaper headline expressed this change eloquently: "From charity to rights" (*Le Soleil*, September 16, 1999). Other statements that supported this emphasis were the following: "Two demands made by the poor in their fight against poverty: over the short term, incorporate the principle of minimum levels of assistance in social assistance legislation and, over the medium and long term, pass comprehensive legislation to eliminate poverty" (*Le Devoir*, November 19, 1998); and "Three MPs wish to include social conditions among prohibited grounds for discrimination" (*La Presse*, March 23, 1999).

Seventeen percent of the 210 demands that appeared in the press were for money; another 16 percent were for basic necessities. In other words, 33 percent of the thematic units included demands for money or essentials to live: "They demand an end to lower benefits in cases of shared housing, an end to the seizure of social assistance cheques for unpaid rent, and free medication for all people living below the poverty line" (*La Presse*, March 16, 1999). NGOs and government organizations agreed on the appropriateness of these demands.

Thirteen percent of the 210 demands called for more attention to issues of dignity: "In the fight against poverty, people must be given the means to be proud of themselves" (*Le Journal de Montréal*, November 21, 1998); and "He [Bertrand Tavernier] focuses on a nursery school director's constant struggle to offer a semblance of dignity" (*La Presse*, September 11,

Table 6.3
What Demands Are Made by Individuals and Groups?

	Poor	NGO	Governments	Politicians	Experts	Journalists	Individuals	
Basic necessities	7	18	3	1	3	0	1	33
Education	3	3	8	1	4	0	0	19
Money	6	16	6	5	1	1	0	35
Employment	2	7	0	1	2	0	0	12
Support network	0	1	2	1	0	0	0	4
Rights	11	34	8	13	7	3	4	80
Dignity	5	15	3	1	1	2	0	27
	34	94	30	23	18	6	5	210

1999). Those who demanded dignity for the poor included the poor them-selves, journalists, and NGOs.

Nine percent of the 210 thematic units included a demand for more emphasis on education in fighting poverty. "If we want to avoid social disengagement and economic insecurity over the long term, we must help young people by preparing and equipping them, from adolescence and even childhood, to become active citizens and to be successfully integrated into society, both socially and economically" (*Le Devoir*, August 27, 1999). Except for the experts, leading actors in the fight against poverty assigned little importance to employment. This last variable received attention in only 11 percent of the thematic units. Another 2 percent of the thematic units included demands for better support networks for the poor.

In short, the demands, in descending order of importance, were rights, basic necessities, and money, followed by dignity, education, employment, and better support networks. NGOs and the poor agreed on this ordering. The other actors had a variety of positions. This ordering deviates signifi-cantly from the most common meanings attributed to poverty, where rights and dignity receive much less attention.

Who Is Responsible for Eliminating Poverty?

My analysis revealed that 69 percent of the 168 thematic units conveyed the viewpoint that governments are responsible for solving the issue of poverty in Canada (see Table 6.4). All the actors shared this opinion except the members of the governments themselves, who are often branded as the enemy of the poor and adversaries in the fight against poverty. The experts expressed the strongest condemnation of government (81% of the thematic units included their criticisms): "Ottawa blamed for its feeble support of the fight against poverty" (*La Presse*, February 25, 1999); and "I think they have reneged on their commitment to fight poverty" (*Le Devoir*, Feb-ruary 17, 1999). Sometimes journalists were also very critical of govern-ments' actions: "Landry gives welfare recipients a slap in the face" (*La Presse*, April 24, 1999). However, some articles did portray governments in a more favorable light: "Montreal and Québec City are aiming for a comprehensive approach toward eliminating poverty" (*Le Journal de Mon-tréal*, July 17, 1999).

There were also many calls for society in general to make solidarity and justice a reality. In all, 22 percent of the thematic units included references to the need for society to be held accountable for eliminating poverty. The poor themselves and journalists most often expressed this point of view. Five percent of the 162 thematic units expressed the belief that the business world (specifically companies) could offer solutions. Four percent of the thematic units held the poor responsible for devising solutions to their problems.

Table 6.4
Which Actors Are Presented as Being Responsible for Eliminating Poverty?

	Poor	NGO	Governments	Politicians	Experts	Journalists	Individuals	
Governments	10	47	23	16	13	5	2	116
Poor	2	2	1	1	0	1	0	7
Society	5	13	7	5	2	2	3	37
Business world	2	4	0	1	1	0	0	8
	19	66	31	23	16	8	5	168

In short, the Québec press appears to hold governments, in particular, responsible for solving the issue of poverty. Other groups may be involved, but they are secondary in importance.

What Solutions Are Proposed?

The press included references to a number of solutions and services offered by the major actors in the fight against poverty (see Table 6.5). In spite of the wide variety of solutions advocated, 29 percent of the 89 thematic units focused attention on basic necessities. Another 11 percent focused on money as a solution to poverty (40 percent of the thematic units included a reference to one or both of these solutions). Exemplifying this approach was the following headline: "Moisson Beauce to distribute 1,300 Christmas baskets" (*Le Soleil*, December 12, 1998). The four groups who gave priority to solutions involving meeting the basic necessities of the poor and giving money were NGOs, politicians, government organizations, and the poor.

Education as a means of alleviating poverty was a topic in 16 percent of the thematic units, employment in 10 percent, and support networks in 9 percent. The focus in these discussions was on providing the tools necessary to reintegrate the poor into society, in order to break their solitude. "Resto Plateau is a tool for re-entry into society" (*La Presse*, March 3, 1999). Only two major actors contributed to these discussions: NGOs and government organizations.

Solutions geared toward addressing issues of dignity were mentioned in only 7 percent of the thematic units. "Attentive readers will have already noted that it's not just the small victories that count in the life of people with literacy problems trying to function in society; it's a matter of pride" (*Le Devoir*, September 4, 1999). "Street kids speak their mind" (*Le Journal de Montréal*, August 19, 1999). Only NGOs, government organizations, and journalists offered solutions and resources related to the restoration of dignity. Fewer still proposed solutions to rights-related issues. In short, contributors tended to focus on material goods and money, education, and employment as the solutions to the problem of poverty. They did not focus on restoring dignity or rights to the poor.

What Role Do the Poor Play in This Fight, Actor or Beneficiary?

In the articles analyzed, all of the actors agreed, except for the poor people themselves, that they are seen as passive (see Table 6.6). Eighty-five percent of the thematic units referred to the poor as beneficiaries and not actors. The poor seem to have accepted this stereotype. They have become "victims of injustice" (*Le Devoir*, September 13, 1999). "The poor have

Table 6.5
What Solutions Have Been Proposed?

	Poor	NGO	Governments	Politicians	Experts	Journalists	Individuals	
Basic necessities	1	19	7	2	0	0	0	29
Education	0	9	5	0	0	2	0	16
Money	0	1	7	2	0	0	1	11
Employment	0	7	1	1	0	1	0	10
Support network	0	7	2	0	0	0	0	9
Rights	0	1	4	0	0	1	0	6
Dignity	0	4	3	0	0	1	0	8
	1	48	29	5	0	5	1	89

Table 6.6
What Role Do the Poor Play in This Fight, Actor or Beneficiary?

	Poor	NGO	Governments	Politicians	Experts	Journalists	Individuals	
Beneficiary	16	115	54	27	27	10	9	258
Actor	12	17	5	5	2	3	3	47
	28	132	59	32	29	13	12	305

paid a heavy price in the war against the deficit" (*La Presse*, March 4, 1999).

A number of the articles discussed how to transform this dependence into independence. "The system will drop the social assistance philosophy and will become a tool for integration and achievement" (*Le Journal de Montréal*, March 8, 1999), said the Minister of Social Solidarity. "The Resto Plateau Program is helping to break the vicious cycle of dependence" (*La Presse*, March 3, 1999). The concept of the poor doing something to change their own situation was not a major theme in the press coverage; rather, the organizations, working to develop strategies and tools to foster independence, were seen as the active players in the fight against poverty.

The poor viewed themselves in a very different light. Twenty-eight of the thematic units included the views of the poor. Out of these 28 thematic units, the poor saw themselves as actors in the fight against poverty in almost half of the references. "The homeless are taking their future into their own hands"(*Le Soleil*, May 31, 1999); "They are going back to school for their children" (*Le Devoir*, May 18, 1999); "Renters suggest that Minister opt for joint management of low-income housing" (*La Presse*, July 21, 1999).

Tone of the Article: Positive or Negative

Fear of the poor seems to be abating: "People on social assistance are no longer treated as dangerous" (*La Presse*, April 29, 1999); "The vast majority of people on social assistance pay their bills," says the former president of the Régie du logement, Rodrigue Dubé (*Le Journal de Montréal*, January 30, 1999). And even if the press depicted the poor as passive, they did not condemn them (see Table 6.7). Eighty-three percent of the 305 thematic units referred to the fact that the poor defend themselves. The same percentage viewed the poor as worthy of help. They are destitute (*Le Journal de Montréal*, November 14, 1998) and living "below the poverty line" (*Le Journal de Montréal*, May 27, 1999). In short, all of the major actors agreed: society must defend, not condemn, the poor. If one regards expressions of empathy for the poor as positive press coverage, then the poor have a positive image in the Québec press.

Inequalities between Rich and Poor, between Women and Men

In regard to the study of perceived inequalities, the results are quite surprising (see Table 6.8). Even though the major demands of the social actors involved in the fight against poverty focus on rights, few of the articles discussed the issue of inequality between rich and poor. In fact, only 24 out of 306 thematic units, or 7.4 percent, included such a discussion. "Economic growth only benefits executives" (*La Presse*, October 23, 1998);

Table 6.7
What Is the Tone of the Article?

	Poor	NGO	Governments	Politicians	Experts	Journalists	Individuals	
Positive	23	98	37	20	21	7	11	217
Neutral	0	3	6	1	0	3	2	15
Negative	1	12	11	2	1	2	0	29
	24	113	54	23	22	12	13	261

Table 6.8
Are There Inequalities between Rich and Poor? Women and Men?

	Poor	NGO	Governments	Politicians	Experts	Journalists	Individuals	
Women and men	0	6	3	3	4	0	0	16
Rich and poor	2	10	3	0	8	1	0	24
	2	16	6	3	12	1	0	40

Table 6.9
An Examination of Which Causes of Poverty Are Identified in the Articles

	Le Devoir	La Presse	Le Soleil	Le J. de M.	
Social injustice	1	0	0	0	1
Human weakness	0	0	1	0	1
Fate	0	0	0	0	0
Lack of resources	0	1	0	0	1
Government action	4	0	0	0	4
Economic situation	2	2	0	0	4
	7	3	1	0	11

"The system takes from the poor and gives to the rich" (*Le Devoir*, July 14, 1999). Only 16 out of 306 thematic units, or 5 percent, raised the issue of male-female inequalities. "The Canadian tax benefit discriminates against women" (*Le Devoir*, December 8, 1998). In fact, the Québec press did not make linkages between poverty and social or gender inequalities, nor did the articles discuss the causes of poverty, as we will see below.

What Are the Causes of Poverty?

The articles provided little help in answering this question. Only 11 articles published in the four newspapers identified causes (see Table 6.9). The causes identified were government action (or inaction) and the general economic situation. "The employment insurance plan continues to impose the poverty upon the regions" (*La Presse*, February 3, 1999). Nevertheless, the articles did not pin the blame for poverty on such a general culprit as fate (destiny) or on human weakness (illness, laziness).

INTERPRETATION OF THE RESULTS

The study showed a consensus among many of the major actors on certain issues. Even though some players define the fight against poverty as a matter of human rights, the press still associates poverty primarily with a lack of basic necessities and money. Education ranked second as part of the definition of poverty and second as a solution to this condition. Few of the actors demanded jobs for the poor. Only the experts placed importance on the issue of employment. The overall impression was that the poor are aid recipients, not potential workers.

The perceived role of the actors varies considerably. In the fight against poverty, the NGOs act as the main spokespersons for the poor. They also provide them with many services. NGOs appear to be the primary definers of poverty, as the press depicts the issue. They appear as the allies of the poor, those who act on their behalf.

The perceived role of government organizations is a paradoxical one. The press presents governments as adversaries, responsible in some cases for the worsening poverty situation. However, they also depict them as prime actors, who hold the key to numerous solutions to poverty. These perceptions, contradictory though they may be, confirm that governments occupy an important role in Québec society. Those who write about poverty see that the solution lies in concerted collectivity, not just individual action.

The press depicts the poor as secondary characters in the fight against poverty, rarely speaking or acting in their own defense. Less than 10 percent of the thematic units gave voice to their opinions. Actors such as NGOs make demands for them. These major social actors (the NGOs) have claimed the lofty role of provider of education, material goods, money, and rights for the poor. In this view, the poor become mere receptors of whatever is given to them, but they do not know how to give back. The exchange process is in a state of imbalance. The press presents the poor simply as beneficiaries, not as actors who are fighting to improve their situation in life.

Articles devote little space to the causes of poverty. No one talks about the relationship among poverty, neoliberal government policies, globalization, and new forms of work. There is no search for the cause, and there is no attempt to address the origins of the problem. Social and political analysis is of secondary importance. The only groups to express their anger and indignation openly are artists (Le Devoir, September 9, 1999) and people in the theater business (Le Journal de Montréal, June 12, 1999). Moreover, the emphasis on individual human rights seems to have obscured any reference to class and gender inequalities.

In the final analysis, the discourse presents poverty from the perspective of external agents. That is, the poor are defined by what others think of them and not as thinking, acting beings. Their daily struggle against poverty, their concerns, and their points of view are almost ignored. Their experience and knowledge of life below the poverty line is cut out, as often happens in administrative and academic writing. Ironically, it was a representative of a large corporation, Paul Desmarais (president of Power Corporation), who reminded everyone of the knowledge base of the poor. "He realized how much the rich and poor can learn from each other and how knowledge dispels fear and prejudice" (La Presse, December 18, 1998).

CONCLUSION

This study demonstrated that the discourse on the fight against poverty in the print media unfolds in an environment of cooperation and antagonism between two major actors: government organizations and NGOs. The poor themselves are excluded from the discourse, and actors other than these two groups take on a secondary role in the discourse. Three levels of action become apparent in the struggle against poverty: ad hoc strategies to provide basic necessities, long-term educational strategies, and demands for human rights. The study also showed the importance of a very active civil society working alongside government organizations, which have traditional and more ambiguous roles.

We can also see how little interest the media have shown in the causes of poverty: the job shortage, globalization, and the process of disaffiliation and disengagement. In addition, those who speak out in the print media offer little hope to the poor. As governments withdraw from social programs, the concept of equality of opportunity enshrined in international conventions loses its credibility.

At the dawn of the new millennium, the interrelationships of politics, the economy, and society are undergoing profound transformations. Perhaps a new balance of power will be created at the interface of these three sectors, and effective strategies to eradicate poverty will develop. It is up to all of us, from ordinary citizens to experts and journalists, to become more involved and to invent new forms of social dialogue. Above all, we must find new paradigms that allow the full range of society (rich and poor) to become full-fledged actors in their own lives and co-authors of the discourses that concern them.

REFERENCES

Atd Quart Monde, Revue de Presse. (1998, October–1999, September). *Atd Quart Monde of Montreal.*

Fellegi, I. P. (1997). On poverty and low income. Statistics Canada. http:// www. statcan.ca/english/concepts/poverty/pauv.htm.

Friedmann, J. (1996, June). Rethinking poverty-empowerment and citizen rights. *International Social Science Journal 148:* 61–172.

Ilouz, E. (1994, Winter). Defense or prosecution: The ideology of poverty in elite and popular press. *Journal of Communication Inquiry 18,* 45–62.

Landry, R. (1997). L'analyse de contenu. In B. Gauthier, *Recherche sociale, de la problématique à la collecte de données* (pp. 329–356). Ste-Foy: Presses de l'Université du Québec.

La Presse (1998, October–1999, September).

Le Devoir (1998, October–1999, September).

Le Journal de Montréal (1998, October–1999, September).

Le Soleil (1998, October–1999, September).

United Nations Development Program (UNDP). (1998). *UNDP Poverty Report. Overcoming human poverty.* New York: UNDP.

Chapter 7

Protecting the Kids? Debates over Internet Content

Leslie Regan Shade

This chapter will examine debates in Canada about how to protect children from offensive and illegal content on the Internet. The stakeholders in this debate include government, industry, parents, educators, librarians, and public interest groups. After looking at the type of content that has been targeted, I will relate the discussion to earlier and ongoing concerns about "moral panics" surrounding children and media content. I will then look at how diverse stakeholders have addressed the issue of offensive and illegal content, particularly pornography. Tensions highlighted include the need to achieve a balance between freedom of speech and censorship, self-regulation and governmental regulation, and technological solutions and education and awareness.

TARGETED CONTENT ISSUES

Studies indicate that children and teens access the Internet at school and home. The *YTV Tween Report 2000* reported that two-thirds of "tweens" (kids aged 7–14) with computers at home have access to the Internet, and they spend an average of 3.8 hours a week surfing it (Media Awareness Network, 2000b). Statistics Canada *General Social Survey: Internet Use 2000* reported that teens are one of the largest groups of Internet users, with "nine out of every 10 teenagers aged 15 to 19 report[ing] using the Internet at some time in the 12 months prior to the survey" (Statistics Canada, 2001). Educators and governments have promoted the use of the Internet as a necessary educational tool for the knowledge-based economy, often, critics say, to the detriment of art and music training (Moll, 2001). But, alongside the widespread celebration of the Internet as a vital educational and learning tool for children and teens are cautions and grave concerns about Internet content deemed inappropriate for children.

Inappropriate content includes illegal and potentially offensive web sites, such as those containing gambling, pornography, hate, violence, alcohol, tobacco, and gender stereotypes. The issue of problematic content has received much attention from a variety of sectors, including federal and international governing bodies, public interest groups, research foundations, public libraries, and the Internet industry. Not surprisingly, the majority of stakeholders have targeted pornography as one of the primary content issues to address.

Canada's hate speech laws, as they appear in both the *Criminal Code* and the *Human Rights Act*, can be applied to the regulation of online hate. However, laws are fuzzier with regard to pornography. Hecht and Neufeld (2000) say that it is necessary, in considering what is harmful to children, to differentiate between legal and illegal content. Certain forms of pornography are legal, whereas child pornography (especially where children are implicated in its production) is illegal. Bill C-15, an act to amend the *Criminal Code*, announced in March 2001, established the government position with respect to child pornography on the Internet. The *Criminal Law Amendment Act, 2001* proposes specific penalties for distributing, possessing, and accessing child pornography on the Internet. The bill also stipulates that it is a crime for anyone to use a computer to communicate with "a person who is, or who the accused believes is, under the age of 18 years" for the purpose of "facilitating the commission" of illegal acts with a minor (Government of Canada, 2001).

Canada still grapples with the issue of whether existing laws meet the challenges posed by pornography on the Internet. Does Section 163 (1) of the Canadian *Criminal Code* apply? Does, or should, the standard of "knowingly" publishing, distributing, or circulating pornography be applied to the Internet? Can the concept of "community standards" be applied to Internet content?

A NEW MORAL PANIC?

> Moral panics have become the way in which daily events are brought to the attention of the public. They are a standard response, a familiar, sometimes weary, even ridiculous rhetoric rather than an exceptional emergency intervention. Used by politicians to orchestrate consent, by business to promote sales in certain niche markets, and by media to make home and social affairs newsworthy, moral panics are constructed on a daily basis. (McRobbie & Thornton, 1995, p. 560)

Cultural debates on children and the media are polarized "between children's advocates and researchers, on the one side, calling for more responsible programming and policies from media producers, broadcasters, advertisers, and government agencies on the other" (Kinder, 1999, p. 1). Children's advocates and researchers, Kinder says, are split between those who see children as passive victims of an increasingly commercialized and sensationalistic culture and those who perceive children as active participants and negotiators of media. Decrying the "loss of childhood" (Buckingham, 2000, p. 21), members of the former camp deploy this rationalization in their crusade against what they perceive to be a moral decline in society. These advocates further believe that the media's increasing emphasis on "tabloidization" and titillation, as well as "sexualization," and sensationalism, reinforces this moral decline.

New communication technologies have always provoked debate over the acceptability of content designed for children (Hein, 2001). In the 1950s, Wertham (1954) led a crusade against violence in comic books. His book *Seduction of the Innocent* galvanized parents, educators, and the media to protest the violence. At his urging, comic book publishers formed the Comics Magazine Association of America. When the U.S. Senate hearings identified a possible connection between comic book content and juvenile delinquency, the Comics Magazine Association instituted the comics code seal that regulated comic book content. In the 1990s, debates over violence and sexually provocative content on television led to the V-Chip. After "reading" information encoded in the rated television program, the V-Chip blocks programs on the basis of the rating selected by the parent. The V-Chip is now required in all new televisions produced in the United States (V-Chip Education Project, n.d.). The Entertainment Software Rating Board created a similar rating system for video games.

MEDIA RESPONSES: SENSATIONALISM SELLS

> A dark, violent and persuasive netherworld wants to lure your child's imagination, especially if you're a parent who's not paying attention. . . . The nightmarish side of the Net includes more than 20,000 e-mail addresses of known pedophiles and Web sites of child pornography. The briefest of searches quickly churns out a site called Nazi Pedophiles. A few mouse clicks away are web pages filled with racist diatribes, chat rooms stalked by child molesters, newsgroups poisoned by vitriolic rants. (Lowey, 1999, p. A3)

An attempt by the United States to legislate illegal and offensive content through the *Communications Decency Act* precipitated widespread media interest.[1] This legislation stimulated many international debates and polarized sentiments between free speech advocates and politicians, parents, and children's rights organizations. Free speech advocates argue that any effort to legislate content (even offensive content) constitutes censorship. Politicians and rights organizations disagreed. Various other countries made similar efforts to regulate content (Akdenizof, 2000).

The 1999 Columbine incident generated a further wave of newspaper articles and commentary calling for more vigilant oversight on Internet content. Two male high school students went on a killing rampage at Columbine, an act that many believed to have been strongly influenced by an increasingly violent media culture. Reports that the two young perpetrators had posted a hate web site, which targeted some of their classmates, triggered the debate. When the public learned that information about explosives had also been posted online, the debate intensified (Gibbs, 1999). Canada was certainly not removed from these discussions. Extensive newspaper and television coverage of the events brought the issues to Canada, and a copycat episode in western Canada followed on the heels of Columbine.

A content analysis, which examined 1999 newspaper coverage of the effects of the Internet on children and families, revealed the following conclusions. Overall, the press presented the Internet as a place where more problems (almost 60 percent) than benefits (almost 40 percent) exist. The majority of articles focused on problems such as child pornography (31 percent), online crime (13 percent), and pornography in general (13 percent). The benefits of the Internet described in the articles included educational value (43 percent), social uses (29 percent), and e-commerce benefits (17 percent). Only 8 percent of articles talked about the Internet in terms of recreational use or entertainment. Privacy issues (11 percent), marketing to children (9 percent), and hate sites (8 percent) were other problems mentioned in the articles.

Despite these reservations, only 6 percent of the articles questioned the value of the Internet or its use by children and in schools. Only 5 percent of the articles looked critically at Internet use and participation by children and young people in relation to digital divide issues (Shade, 2000).[2] Without a doubt, media coverage of Internet issues related to families and children tended to concentrate on problem areas (particularly child pornography, pornographic content in general, and criminal content). Is the media, then, whipping up a moral panic about children and exposure to Internet pornography?

Suggestions for improving coverage of the Internet as it relates to children and families include the following. Coverage should be extended to include more critical analysis of the role of Internet technology in the everyday lives of children and young people. Newspapers should more critically assess the commercialization of web content that is directed toward children. Privacy issues should be examined more critically, especially online marketing practices that secure personal information on children. More youth, educators, and public interest groups should be consulted on stories about the Internet and children.

More nuanced debates on the digital divide in Canada should take place. Although the media rarely consider access issues, they depict the young "entrepreneurs" who use the Internet for e-commerce applications in heroic terms. The media fail to adequately explore the overall media culture of children. Apart from the many articles ruminating over the Columbine tragedy, the media tend to present unsavory Internet content as divorced from the overall media culture, when in fact, the "sexualization" and "tabloidization" of popular culture has become commonplace (Shade, 2000).

PUBLIC INTEREST RESPONSES: MEDIA AWARENESS NETWORK

The Media Awareness Network (Mnet) is a non-profit media literacy organization which focuses on developing web awareness modules for schools and libraries. In 2000, Mnet and Environics Research Group surveyed parents to learn more about their children's Internet use.[3] The survey was particularly concerned with assessing the effectiveness of measures used to address Internet safety issues and to deal with inappropriate online content. The report, *Canada's Children in a Wired World* (Media Awareness Network, 2000a), revealed that most Canadian parents are optimistic about the Internet, believing that the benefits outweigh the risks. Sixty percent of parents reported that education is the biggest benefit of their children being on the Internet, while 51 percent say their biggest concern is inappropriate content. When asked if their children had come across sexually explicit material—that they were aware of—21 percent reported that they had. Six percent of the parents revealed that their children had been sent unsolicited sexual material. (More may have been unaware of their children receiving unsolicited material with sexual content.) Parents cited "educating children" (94 percent) and "educating parents" (97 percent) as effective strategies for ensuring wise use of the Internet at home.

LIBRARIES: TO FILTER OR NOT TO FILTER?

Concerns about open access to the Internet in public libraries, particularly in Toronto and Calgary, led to vociferous debates. In Toronto and Calgary, public library officials and the community argued whether or not libraries should install filtering software on Internet-accessible computers. A major controversy surrounded the conflict between issues of Internet censorship and preventing children from being exposed to inappropriate content while on the web. Calgary Alderman Patti Grier was adamant in saying that children should not be exposed to "accidental or intended peep shows," particularly when public libraries are "funded with public dollars" (Dolik, 1999, p. B8).

The Canadian Library Association (CLA) has closely monitored the situation in the United States. The American Library Association (ALA) (a national association) "strongly encourages local libraries to adopt and implement Internet policies that protect access to information and promote a positive online experience while respecting parents' rights" (Kranich, 2000, p. 45). However, the association has protested attempts to mandate the use of filtering software on publicly accessible Internet terminals, arguing that "only about 1.5% of Internet sites are considered pornographic, and the best filters block about 75% of those" (Kranich, p. 43). The CLA has responded in kind, producing a web-based toolkit, *Net Safe; Net Smart: Managing and Communicating about the Internet in the Library* (n.d.). The toolkit contains practical resources for use in staff and board training and public education programming.

INDUSTRY RESPONSE: SELF-REGULATION

Industry is concerned about being held legally responsible for the content of their users. So Internet service providers have championed self-regulation and user codes of conduct. For instance, the Canadian Association for Internet Providers (CAIP) includes provisions in its *Code of Conduct* stating that "CAIP members are committed to public education about Internet issues and technology" and that "CAIP members will not knowingly host illegal content [and] CAIP members will share information about illegal content for this purpose" (CAIP, 1997).

In February 2001, the CAIP launched its "protection portal" as part of the government's "cyberwise" strategy. This portal provides information on several organizations that "combat" illegal and offensive content on the Internet. Those organizations include the Simon Wiesenthal Center, which documents the rising incidence of hate online; the Media Awareness Network's Web Awareness project; the creators of "Missing," a videogame and web site that warns children about online predators; and Industry Canada Minister Brian Tobin and the cyberwise strategy (discussed below).

Industry has touted technological solutions as a means to protect children from offensive and illegal content. A plethora of software filters are available on the market (Cranor, Resnick, & Gallo, 1998). Many such as Net Nanny, Cybersitter, Cyber Patrol, Net Shepherd, and Safe Surf specifically target parents; but the efficacy of filtering software has been a huge issue, with many groups claiming that filters censor more than they control content. In one study, the Electronic Privacy Information Center (1997) claimed that filtering software prevents "children from obtaining a great deal of useful and appropriate information that is currently available on the Internet." Powell (2000) described filtering software as a "vaccination" of children against offensive content, rather than "isolation" of children from portions of the Internet (p. 40).

Others have promoted self-regulation as a means to protect children and to deal with the problem of illegal and harmful content on the Internet. The Bertelsmann Internet Content Summit recommended a coordinated effort, including self-regulation of the Internet industry, self-rating and filtering by individuals and families, the use of hotlines as a feedback mechanism for users, and reliance on law enforcement and the role of legal provisions in supporting self-regulation (Bertelsmann Foundation, 1999).

GOVERNMENT RESPONSE: NO REGULATION

In May 1999, the Canadian Radio-Television and Telecommunications Commission (CRTC) released its report on new media hearings, which looked broadly at issues of Internet content and regulation. The CRTC, the report said, would not regulate new media activities on the Internet under the *Broadcasting Act*. With regard to illegal and offensive content, the Commission recommended industry self-regulation and the development of codes of conduct to help combat the distribution of offensive material. It also recommended acceleration in the process of establishing complaint lines, appointing industry ombudsmen, and developing cooperative links with law enforcement agencies, in Canada and abroad. In addition, the report suggested that content-filtering software should "assist those who wish to control access to material that they feel is inappropriate." The regulation of offensive content—and particularly hate propaganda—was deemed to be beyond the regulatory jurisdiction of the *Broadcasting Act*, according to the CRTC, because it consists predominantly of alphanumeric text. That is, the CRTC perceived the Internet as being mostly text-based, rather than carrying broadcast material.

Certainly, the Canadian government has had to consider the proposals of other governments with respect to regulation of offensive Internet content. The United States has approved several pieces of legislation. Congress passed the *Child Online Protection Act of 1998* (Pub. L. No. 105–277, 112 Stat. 2681–736) to restrict the commercial distribution of material that could be considered harmful to minors on the Internet. The act also established a commission to examine the extent to which current technological tools effectively help to protect children from inappropriate online content. The *Child Online Protection Act* attempts to protect children by prohibiting commercial web site operators from making sexually explicit material that could be deemed "harmful to minors" available to those under the age of 17. Web site operators found in violation of the law may be sentenced to six months in jail and fined up to $150,000 for each day that the offensive web site is up (see *Children's Online Protection Act*; also Powell, 2000). The *Children's Internet Protection Act* was passed by Congress and signed into law by former President Bill Clinton in December 2000. This law requires public libraries and schools to install pornography-blocking software on computers or risk losing federal funds and assistance (ALA, 2001).

Australia recently passed legislation aimed at protecting children from exposure to inappropriate Internet content. The *Broadcasting Services Amendment Act* (1999) establishes a complaints-based legal regime, which uses existing systems and methods of classifying content. The Australian Broadcasting Authority is mandated to regulate carriage of content over the Internet. However, the act also encourages the development of industry codes of practice. Since primary responsibility for material lies with its creators, Internet service providers are not liable for material carried on their service. The act also defines prohibited categories of Internet content (hosted in Australia). Any content classified as *RC, X* or *R* requires adult verification. Prohibited categories for overseas-hosted content are *RC* and *X* (Australia, *Broadcasting Services Amendment Act*, 1999). In both the United States and Australia, various public interest groups have protested this kind of government legislation. For example, the American Civil Liberties Union (ACLU) and the ALA have argued that such legislation violates the First Amendment tenets of free speech.

In February 2001, the Government of Canada unveiled its strategy for dealing with illegal and offensive content on the Internet. Borrowing extensively from the research and educational strategies of the Mnet, the government advocates "safe, wise, and responsible" Internet use. Its "cyberwise" strategy focuses on educating and "empowering" users (not through new regulation, but through strengthening the enforcement of existing laws on the Internet), promoting industry self-regulation, implementing hotlines and complaint-reporting systems, and supporting consultation, nationally and internationally (Industry Canada, 2001).

CONCLUSION: THE DARK SIDE OF THE NET?

> The various approaches to addressing Internet content must therefore take into account the guarantee of freedom of expression enjoyed by Canadians; any efforts to regulate Internet content must be "demonstrably justified in a free and democratic society"—a standard that is very high indeed. (Pierlot, 2000)

Regulating content on the Internet is a messy affair. Even mentioning regulation sends many into a tailspin—and not just techno-libertarians and free speech advocates. The more palpable fear seems to be that regulation implies governmental control, and in North American societies, such a suggestion raises the specter of totalitarian regimes. The easy line to tow is that of self-regulation (industry), enforcement of existing laws and legislation (government), and education and awareness programs (libraries and public interest groups).

Does the focus on pornography distract from more important content issues, such as hate and commercialization? Hate content (whether anti-Semitic, racist, sexist, or homophobic) is insidious (Mock, 2000). Sunstein (2001) argues that hate groups "expressly attempt to encourage both recruitment and discussion among like-minded people" (p. 63) and also provide links to other like-minded extremist groups. In particular, hate groups target young kids through a variety of techniques: "kiddy" and glitzy graphics, games and activities, and special kids' sections. One example is the neo-Nazi "World Church of the Creator" site; its "Creativity for Kids" section features crossword puzzles with racist content (Media Awareness Network, n.d.).

Targeting children as a viable and lucrative market has been the goal of many commercial web sites. Often the commercial aspects of the web sites are thinly veiled; at other times, the commercial content is blatant. Interactive quizzes and games, the creation of virtual meeting places such as chat and web forums, and contests and cross-licensing promotions are just a few of the strategies employed. Privacy is one of the key areas under threat (Montgomery, 2000).

Why, then, has pornography received the bulk of attention as the content area that most threatens children and young people? Could its obvious visible nature (rather than the medium that carries it) explain why debates rage amongst and between free speech advocates, feminists, and the Christian right? Lessig (1999) points out that in real space (contrasted to cyberspace), pornography is extensively regulated—through legislation, law, and social norms. Social norms, for example, include age restrictions related to the purchase of magazines and videos, and venders must position pornographic magazines so that children and youth cannot easily access them. In other words, as Lessig argues, an architecture regulates access to pornography.

The Internet is different, however, as its technical architecture allows for anonymity (users can create multiple identities), deception (users can lie about their ages, race, ethnicity, and gender), and bypassing (information can be sent through multiple channels, in multiple formats, and via different routes). An architecture that zones speech (in this case, pornography) could demand a "Kids-ID" or an "Adults-ID." Browser profiles or the establishment of digital certification are other zoning solutions (Lessig, 1999), but in both instances, the adult bears the burden to prove that he or she is validated to receive "adult speech" (pp. 176–177).

Not heard in the policy debates over Internet content are the voices of children and teens. In an analysis of policy documentation, press articles, and interviews with those involved in policy design and implementation in the United Kingdom, Oswell (1999) looked at governmental, industry, and parental responses to Internet content regulation and child protection. Internet content regulation and child protection, he remarked, "make[s] visible how governance is a socio-technical process" (p. 57) and how regulatory practices deny agency, rights, and citizenship to children when they fail to involve them in policy formation.

Should children and youth be consulted on these issues? Ostensibly, adults (parents, educators, and government officials) represent and protect children and youth. In the debates over Internet content and children, the delicate balancing act has been how best to balance the right to freedom of expression (for adults) with the protection of children. So far, the onus has been on adults to self-regulate, provide technological solutions, and promote education and awareness programs. Unfortunately, in Canada, most of the debates have centered on pornographic content, not hate speech or overtly commercialized sites that target kids. This more insidious content may be more threatening to children than pornography. The debates need to shift to reflect these concerns. Perhaps what is also needed is more creativity in the design of Internet architecture, so that "offensive" content can be zoned.

NOTES

1. The CDA made it a crime to post sexually explicit material on the Internet. In 1997, the U.S. Supreme Court struck down the CDA. See Lessig (pp. 174–176) for more discussion.

2. The content analysis focused on articles found in eight major daily Canadian newspapers, chosen for their geographic representation. The complete analysis can be found in Shade, May 2000. http://www.media-awareness.ca/eng/webaware/netsurvey2000/medconanalysis.htm.

3. The *Canada's Children in a Wired World* questionnaire was divided into three sections: (1) family use of the Internet; (2) general knowledge and perceptions about issues related to children and the Internet, including online activities and practices in the home; and (3) responses and proposed solutions in regard to issues involving children and the Internet. Environics polled 1,080 randomly selected Canadian families who owned a home computer and had children between ages 6 and 16. Over 70 percent of parents surveyed indicated that they had Internet access at home, and 86 percent of these parents said their children used the Internet. More information can be found at http://www.media-awareness.ca/eng/webaware/netsurvey2000/index.htm.

REFERENCES

Akdenizof, Y. (2000). *Regulation of child pornography on the Internet: Cases and materials related to child pornography on the Internet.* London: Cyber-Rights and Cyber-Liberties Group. http://www.cyber-rights.org/reports/child.htm.

American Library Association (ALA). (2001). CIPA web site. http://www.ala.org/cipa/legislation.html.

Australia. *Broadcasting Services Amendment Act* (Online Services) 1999, No. 90. (1999). http://www.noie.gov.au/legreg/content/index.htm.

Bertelsmann Foundation. (1999, September). *Memorandum on self-regulation*, from the Bertelsmann Internet Content Summit. http://www.stiftung.bertelsmann. de/Internetcontent/english/download/Memorandum.pdf.

Buckingham, David. (2000). *After the death of childhood: Growing up in the age of electronic media*. Cambridge, MA: Polity Press.

Canadian Association of Internet Providers (CAIP). (1997). *Code of conduct*. http: //www.caip.ca/caipcode.htm.

Canadian Association of Internet Providers Protection Portal. (2001). http://www. caip.ca/portal/index.html.

Canadian Library Association (CLA). (n.d.) *Net safe; net smart: Managing and communicating about the Internet in the library*. http://www.cla.ca/netsafe/ netsafe.htm.

Child Online Protection Act. http://www.epic.org/free_speech/censorship/final_ hr3783.html.

Canadian Radio Television and Telecommunications Commission (CRTC). (1999, May 17). New media, broadcasting public notice. CRTC 1999–84-Telecom Public Notice CRTC 99–14. http://www.crtc.gc.ca/eng/BCASTING/ NOTICE/1999/P9984_0.txt.

Cranor, L. F., Resnick, P., & Gallo, D. (1998, December). *Technology inventory: A catalog of tools that support parents' ability to choose online content appropriate for their children*. Prepared for the Internet Online Summit: Focus on children. Revised for America Links Up, September 1998. http:// www.research.att.com/projects/tech4kids/.

Dolick, H. (1999, October 28). Library staff to study Internet filter issue. *Calgary Herald*, p. B8.

Electronic Privacy Information Center. (1997, December). *Faulty filters: How content filters block access to kid-friendly information on the Internet*. http:// www2.epic.org/reports/filter-report.html.

Gibbs, N. (1999, May 3). The monsters next door. *Time Magazine* (Canadian edition), 25–34.

Government of Canada. (2001). The *Criminal Law Amendment Act, 2001*. http: //www.parl.gc.ca/37/1/parlbus/chambus/house/bills/government/C-15/C-15 _1/90148bE.html.

Hecht, M. E., & Neufeld, R. (2000). The Internet and international children's rights. In S. Hick, E. F. Halpin, & E. Hoskins (Eds.), *Human rights and the Internet* (pp. 153–165). New York: St. Martin's Press.

Hein, M. (2001). *Not in front of the children: Indecency, censorship and the innocence of youth*. New York: Hill & Wang.

Industry Canada. (2001). *Illegal and offensive content on the Internet: The Canadian strategy to promote safe, wise, and responsible Internet use*. http:// connect.gc.ca/cyberwise/.

Kinder, M. (1999). Kids' media culture: An introduction. In Marsha Kinder (Ed.), *Kids' media culture* (pp. 1–28). Durham, NC: Duke University Press.

Kranich, N. (2000). Assessing Internet access. *Media Studies Journal* 14 (3), 42–45.

Lessig, L. (1999). *Code: And other laws of cyberspace*. New York: Basic Books.

Lowey, M. (1999, May 2). Internet provides troubling forum. *Calgary Herald*, p. A3.

McRobbie, A., & Thornton, S. L. (1995). Rethinking "moral panic" for multi-mediated social worlds. *British Journal of Sociology 46* (4), 559–574.

Media Awareness Network (Mnet). (2000a). *Canada's children in a wired world: The parent's view*. Ottawa: Media Awareness Network. http://www.media-awareness.ca/eng/webaware/netsurvey2000/index.htm.

Media Awareness Network (Mnet). (2000b). *YTV tween report 2000*. http://www.media-awareness.ca/eng/issues/stats/usenet2000.htm#tweens.

Media Awareness Network (Mnet). (n.d.). Recruitment on the net. http://www.media-awareness.ca/eng/issues/internet/safety/hate/recruit.htm.

Mock, K. (2000). Hate on the Internet. In S. Hick, E. F. Halpin, & E. Hoskins (Eds.), *Human rights and the Internet* (pp. 141–152). New York: St. Martin's Press.

Moll, M. (2001). Pianos vs. politics: Sustaining public education in the age of globalization. In M. Moll & L. R. Shade (Eds.), *E-Commerce vs. E-Commons: Communications in the public interest* (pp. 109–127). Ottawa: Canadian Center for Policy Alternatives.

Montgomery, K. (2000, August). Youth and digital media: A policy research agenda. *Journal of Adolescent Health 27*, 61–68.

Oswell, D. (1999). The dark side of cyberspace: Internet content regulation and child protection. *Convergence: The Journal of Research into New Media Technologies 5* (4), 42–62.

Pierlot, P. A. (2000). Self-regulation of Internet content: A Canadian perspective. *Proceedings of INET 2000*. http://www.isoc.org/inet2000/cdproceedings/8k/8k_2.htm#s26.

Powell, A. C. III. (2000, Fall). Children, the Internet, and Free Speech. *Media Studies Journal 14* (3), 36–41.

Shade, L. R. (1999). *Content analysis of media coverage of Internet content issues related to children and families in Canada*. Prepared for Media Awareness Network, May 2000. http://www.media-awareness.ca/eng/webaware/netsurvey2000/medconanalysis.htm.

Statistics Canada. (2001, March 26). General Social Survey: Internet Use 2000. *The Daily*. www.statcan.ca.

Sunstein, C. (2001). *Republic.com*. Princeton, NJ: Princeton University Press.

V-Chip Education Project. Center for Media Education and Henry J. Kaiser Foundation. (n.d.) http://www.vchipeducation.org/.

Wertham, F. (1954). *Seduction of the innocent*. New York: Rinehart.

Part III

Strident Voices, Organized
Protest, and Virtual Communities

Chapter 8

Anarchy Makes a Comeback

Evan Potter

A veritable Noah's Ark of opposition from around the world, including Flat Earth advocates, feminists, gays, members of the John Birch Society, and trade unionists—clad in everything from designer black to turtle costumes—converges on Main Street. Environmentalists trade barbs in equal measure with anarchists and heavily armed, jack-booted riot squads; dazed politicians and tear-gas choked officials run a gauntlet of police and rioters. Calls to the barricades are flashed on listservs and web sites of "progressive" organizations around the world. Alternative media organizations vie with broadcast networks and the elite press to get their stories out to their supporters. Tens of thousands of protestors take to the streets to demonstrate against the World Trade Organization (WTO), and television cameras record the tumultuous events for a global audience.

As we have seen from the intense preparation for the Summit of the Americas in Québec City (2001), the specter of Seattle in December 1999 (itself a stunning follow-up to organized resistance against the Multilateral Agreement on Investment [MAI] negotiations of 1998) continues to haunt governments intent on promoting the benefits of liberalized trade to their citizens. Anti-globalization protests have become serial events that dog international meetings around the world. Some dismiss the anti-globalization movement as nothing more than a collection of fringe groups (whether of the non-violent, naive "do-gooder" or window-smashing anarchist varieties). Others see in these protests an important shift in the political culture. For trade negotiators—long accustomed to making important binding, national decisions following selective consultations and far from the public's prying eyes—the highly visible protests of recent years have raised important questions about the impact of global citizens' movements on the process of economic diplomacy (interstate negotiations over market access).

Although McLuhan's global village has not replaced the nation-state, today's villages are so thoroughly interconnected that we can scarcely recognize the "Westphalian world in which modern diplomacy was born" (Fulton, 1998, p. 13). Global mass communications and advances in information technologies (ITs) pose a fundamental challenge to the traditional conduct of economic diplomacy by dispersing authority to multiple levels, increasing the activism of a global civil society, and driving the expansion of global finance and trade. As Canadian scholar Harold Innis (1951) observed a half century ago, if "sudden extensions of communication are reflected in cultural disturbances" (p. 31), then we are experiencing a cultural disturbance of global proportions, one that may rival the move from the oral tradition to printing.

We stand on the threshold of an information revolution in which electronic forms of communication, largely immune to regulation, will be the primary means of communication. As noted in a 1998 report by the Washington-based Center for Strategic and International Security (CSIS), "hierarchy is giving way to networking," "openness is crowding out secrecy," and "ideas and capital move swiftly and unimpeded across a global network of governments, corporations, and non-governmental organizations" (Fulton, 1998, p. 8). The notion of a cultural disturbance is apt since nations once connected primarily through foreign ministries and traders are now linked "through millions of individuals by fiber optics, satellite, wireless, and cable in a complex network without central control" (p. 8).

These trends have resulted in considerable speculation about the future shape of the multilateral trade system itself, as well as how governments conduct their international trade negotiations. Some practitioners and scholars have suggested that the media's infatuation with de-contextualized, emotion-evoking images (e.g., small Greenpeace boats confronting gargantuan oil tankers, or tree sit-ins) turns public opinion against globalization. They have also suggested that interest groups drive government trade agendas and that trade ministries are increasingly irrelevant. Meanwhile, ordinary members of the public, using available communications technologies, are developing new competencies that will facilitate global engagement and mobilization on a cross-section of economic and security issues. Certainly, the negotiation of international trade agreements has become more complex, as global audiences have acquired the ability to access greater quantities of information in real time. The increased availability of the information and the speed with which it is delivered have made the public dimension a central element of economic diplomacy.

The organized protests against globalization that followed the collapse of the MAI in 1998—the "Battle in Seattle," smaller scenes in Washington, DC and Prague, and the most recent eruption in Québec City—pose a number of questions to which this chapter will respond. What role did new communications technologies such as the Internet play in activism surrounding the MAI and WTO ministerials?[1] How did civil society networks use the Internet to achieve their purposes? Can we conclude that the worldwide campaigns were the product of the communications technology, or would it be more accurate to conclude that these technologies amplified activism already in place? If the evidence shows strong correlations between Internet use and the capacity to mobilize campaigns against the liberalization of international trade, will increased usage lead to more and more citizen-led anti-globalization campaigns? An affirmative response to this last question leads to two additional questions. Does a more active movement necessarily mean a more effective movement? That is, do increases in levels of activity imply greater impact on the management of economic diplomacy? And will this hypercommunications environment require a more aggressive communications strategy by governments?

The chapter proceeds as follows. In the first section I describe the nature and impact of the new communications technologies. In the second section I explore the fit between the new communications networks, made possible through advances in technology and global social movements. The third section compares the MAI and Seattle experiences and establishes a theoretical framework for assessing the effectiveness of the Internet as a tool for mobilizing opposition groups. This discussion relies on the work of Deibert (1999) and Smith and Smythe (2000) but also draws on my own experience as a communications officer at the Canadian Department of Foreign Affairs and International Trade (DFAIT) during the Seattle demonstrations. In the fourth section, I evaluate the economy, efficiency, and effectiveness with which the Internet functions in mobilizing civil society groups. Finally, I respond to the question of whether the anti-globalization protests affect the views of the mass public. I conclude with some observations on how the Internet has established a new set of rules of engagement for trade policy makers and civil society organizations.

THE EFFECTS OF COMMUNICATION TECHNOLOGY

If we were to summarize the effects of the new information and communication technology, we would talk about *interconnectivity, decentralization, acceleration, amplification* (Rothkopf, 1998) and *hypertextuality* (de Kerckhove, 1997). Higher connectivity among individuals, institutions, and communities results from the exponential increases in contacts made possible by public and private telecommunications infrastructures. This connectivity in turn leads to decentralization and the possibility of bypassing traditional authorities, whether in the public or private domains.

The digitalization of information allows any content (video, text, still pictures) to be stored in a variety of media formats (tape, computer, disk,

CD) or transmitted through any medium (wire, ether, infrared, fiber optic). This capacity to store and transmit information, combined with more powerful digital processors, increases the pressure on decision makers to respond in real time. With increasing processing power and bandwidth amplification, users can access unprecedented volumes of information from anywhere at any time (e.g., the World Wide Web) at lower and lower cost, leading to a state of "hypertextuality." Interactivity, in turn, results from the combination of all these factors—lowered costs, vast content storage capabilities, and acceleration of user demands. Seemingly isolated and often unpredictable actions create greater global volatility.

The less obvious effects of this digital revolution are *dislocation* and diminishing *asymmetry*. Dislocation refers to the disconnecting of transactions from physical location. For example, interest groups can move readily from one location to another, without having a national "home"; and asymmetry refers to the traditional advantage in information control enjoyed by states and corporations. A by-product of advances in communications technology is that much smaller organizations—sometimes even individuals—are able to compete in a way not possible in the past. Many of the newly formed communication networks bypass the traditional gatekeepers of information, both state and private.

The degree of global transparency will increase by several orders of magnitude in the next decade as a result of the reduced cost, lighter weight, and miniaturization of technology (e.g., satellite up-link equipment, satellite telephones); the introduction of commercial high-resolution remote sensing abilities; and the exponential growth of the Internet. As we will see in the next section, the cumulative effect of these innovations on global social movements has been profound.

IDEAL FIT: COMMUNICATIONS NETWORKS AND GLOBAL SOCIAL MOVEMENTS

More than 15,000 non-governmental organizations (NGOs) around the world are actively involved in international affairs (*Yearbook of International Organizations*, 1997). The NGOs range from major, well-known ones such as Amnesty International and Greenpeace to smaller national groups such as Canada's Council of Canadians and the East Timor Alert Network. Although long recognized as international players, these civil society organizations only began to challenge the dominance of governments and transnational corporations in international relations in the early 1990s. Early examples were the Rio Conference and the 1995 United Nations Fourth World Conference on Women. One explanation is that the new communications networks and technologies appear tailor-made for global social movements.

By becoming increasingly skilled at using traditional media (e.g., short-wave) and the lower cost new media (particularly the Internet), NGOs have become a more visible presence and audible voice in the international marketplace of ideas. They can now build international coalitions that compete effectively for the public's attention at the same time that the neoliberal, welfare governments of the industrialized world retreat in the face of globalization. Case studies of environmental, women's, and human rights movements show that they have become more assertive and prominent as social actors in their own rights, through their enhanced ability to use the new communication technologies to reach out quickly to widely dispersed supporters. Pal (2002), for instance, describes the human rights sector as a distributed network with "a jumble of thousands of sites, but with a handful of slightly prominent core nodes that provide access, authenticity, and reliability." In common with the environmental and women's movements, the human rights movement places a premium on networking and amplifying the capacities of many different grassroots organizations. As a network, the human rights sector has weak ties, which (at first glance) make it appear too disorganized to accomplish anything. Pal notes that, paradoxically, its very weakness is its strength. If the goal of a human rights network is to circulate information as widely as possible, then the human rights network on the Internet is ideally designed to get information out rapidly.

What then can be said of the impact of these technologies on the broader tent of the anti-globalization movement? Trade and economic policy, for much of the last half century, was the preserve of the business community and policy makers. Businesses identified their objectives (usually in terms of desired tariffs and border measures), and governments negotiated on their behalf. Citizens generally watched from the sidelines. Economic diplomacy, conducted away from the public eye, began to change during the 1988 and 1993 trade negotiations (Canada–U.S. Free Trade and North American Free Trade). These negotiations took place under close public scrutiny, with the focus moving from traditional trade policy objectives such as tariffs to the intersection between trade policy and social and political concerns: culture, health, water, the environment, and education.

This shift was not surprising. The confluence of growing global economic interdependence, coupled with the end of the cold war, meant that by the early 1990s focus had shifted from geopolitics to geoeconomics. Governments had to engage increasingly often in public diplomacy, as they turned to global markets in an effort to maintain domestic growth. This state of affairs led, in turn, to a clash between their desire to promote trade liberalization on the one hand and their need to preserve control over domestic social policy on the other hand. At the same time, citizens have grown ever more cynical about the ability of national governments to represent their concerns. With the advent of the new communications technologies, citizens' groups have had the incentive and opportunity to press for greater transparency in international negotiations and to internationalize their opposition to global trade liberalization. This opposition has presented itself in the growing numbers and varieties of citizens' protest groups.

PROTESTING GLOBALIZATION: THE MAI AND THE "BATTLE IN SEATTLE"

The anti-globalization protests against the MAI and the multilateral trade ministerial at Seattle provide unique case studies for exploring the impact of new communications technologies on trade negotiations. However, before examining this impact, it is useful to review some of the similarities and differences in these two episodes.

The supporters of the MAI—which ultimately failed—argued for a clear set of multilateral rules on investment (applied uniformly among signatories) and an effective dispute settlement mechanism. Achieving these two objectives would further liberalize international trade and investment. Deibert (1999) estimated that the anti-MAI forces total as many as 600 non-governmental organizations from at least 70 countries, "in areas such as environment, labour, culture, each with its own set of sectoral criticisms" (p. 13). Protesters were against growing corporate power and rights at the expense of state sovereignty. Under the proposed MAI, so the argument went, corporations would have the right to sue states if they believed that local or national laws discriminated against them. The rights of corporations, critics believed, would supercede the rights of individuals. At some point, it became clear to the negotiating governments that the political costs of an agreement were not worth the economic gains, and a number of key players such as the United States lost their enthusiasm. France eventually withdrew from negotiations, and any real hope of an agreement disappeared.

Although the protests against both agendas (the MAI and the WTO) aimed to check or completely halt the process of globalization, four important differences also existed. These differences became evident in an in-depth study of Canada's preparations for the 1999 trade ministerial meetings in Seattle. Stairs (2000) concluded that the failure of the MAI "triggered the new and much more expansive approach to consultation" on a full range of issues relating to the agenda of the WTO (p. 16). The desire not to repeat the MAI experience resulted in a Canadian Parliamentary committee receiving oral testimony from 450 witnesses and engaging in ongoing consultations with experts, industry, and NGO representatives. DFAIT's launch of a "Trade Negotiations and Agreements" web site also reflected this more consultative approach.[2]

Second, the Seattle exercise, by definition, was much broader in scope than the MAI negotiations, designed as it was to launch a new round of international trade negotiations and to build on the "successes" of previous multilateral trade rounds. The WTO response to civil society organizations was also different. Whereas the WTO had made few formal links with civil society representatives in the period preceding the MAI negotiations, it consulted extensively with the NGO community before the Seattle meeting, and national delegations such as Canada's actually included representatives from industry associations and civil society. In addition, there was an opportunity for non-governmental interest groups (business and civil society) to register independently at the Seattle conference. Sixty-five private Canadian organizations ranging from the Chicken Farmers of Canada to Oxfam Canada and the Sierra Youth Coalition took the opportunity to do so (Stairs, 2000).

Third, in Stairs' (2000) view, unlike the case of the MAI, Seattle "acted as a magnet for an extraordinarily vigorous and diverse display of often-incompatible preferences and positions. . . . The spectacle of American stevedores and airline pilots campaigning . . . against further elaboration of a rule-ordered multilateral trade regime could easily leave the more innocent of onlookers completely baffled" (p. 28). Fourth, having set the public policy agenda for the MAI and put governments on the defensive, the global citizens' movements (led, it seemed to Canadian officials and ministers, by Maude Barlow and the Council of Canadians) were primed and resourced to gain as much mainstream media coverage as possible at Seattle. They hoped to raise their concerns in the public consciousness by both peaceful and violent means.[3]

Deibert (1999) and Smith and Smythe (2000) were, however, careful to point out that no opposition groups (even those armed with Internet technology) can take full credit for the failure of the MAI—nor, by extension, Seattle. The failures in both cases arose from a multiplicity of reasons. Had the French and Americans persevered, an agreement on investment might have resulted. The negotiations at Seattle failed for many more reasons than those associated with tens of thousands of vocal protesters. The meeting failed because of poor preparation on the part of a new and naive WTO secretariat and poor preparation on the part of the Clinton administration, which used the event for blatant domestic politicking. Perhaps, most importantly, Seattle failed because of the irreconcilable differences among the main players (particularly Europe and the United States) over the scope and context of the negotiations. Certainly, what happened inside the Seattle convention center was overshadowed in the public eye by what happened in the streets. This reality does not mean, however, that the protests were enough in themselves to explain Seattle's failure. It would be more accurate to state, in the words of Smith and Smythe (2000), "Political delays and disagreements created an opportunity which these groups were able to exploit effectively to mobilize domestic opposition in a number of countries" (p. 18). In other words, rather than taking a highly deterministic approach to the impact of the new technology, we have to view its impact relative to other causal factors.

Deibert (1999) describes three main ways in which the Internet, as one causal variable, played a part in the anti-MAI activism. His observations are applicable equally to Seattle. First, web sites, listservs, and e-mail were crucial for gathering, sharing, and mobilizing supporters; and access to a "large stock of detailed information buttressed the strength and intellectual capacity of the campaign" (p. 21). The Internet was key in communicating information swiftly among members of the anti-MAI and anti-Seattle lobbies—lobbies dispersed across several state jurisdictions in both developed and developing countries. Those who had opposed the earlier free trade agreements (FTA and NAFTA) would have scarcely recognized the speed with which local activists gained access to policy papers and material (e.g., draft negotiating texts) and forwarded them to other people on their listservs and e-mail lists. Smith and Smythe (2000) report that, during the MAI campaign, some e-mailed lists included 1,000 to several thousand names. As Deibert says, "In this way members of the anti-MAI lobby were kept apprised of negotiations, meetings, protests, letter campaigns, editorials, news items, websites of interest, and general information. . . . By providing a form of distributed intelligence, the listservs helped augment the knowledge, capacity, and responsiveness of the anti-MAI network in a way telephones and faxes could not" (p. 18). The use of electronic mail allowed anti-globalization strategists to quickly share strategy as events unfolded. As Smith and Smythe note, the combination of speed, ease, and low cost of communications technology provided people with resources that they would not have otherwise had. This use of e-mail communications was even more evident in the case of Seattle, since the technology had spread to more users by that time.

The Internet was also important in publicizing information about the MAI and Seattle ministerials and in providing activists' interpretations of these meetings and their agendas. Anti-MAI listservs (e.g., MAI Not and Stop MAI—Australia) and the web sites of organizations such as the Council of Canadians were central "nodes" of information distribution. These nodes offered updates on the "progress of negotiations, secondary interpretations and essays on the MAI and globalization, tips on how to become an anti-globalization activist, and notification of speeches and demonstrations" (Deibert, 1999, p. 19). The advantage of the Internet over more traditional forms of media was that persons with "little technical expertise could post images, text, graphics, audio and video to a global audience" (Deibert, p. 19); and organizations with few resources now had a global reach. The cross-referencing of web sites meant that each author had a public exposure that would have been unthinkable without the Internet. In addition, at Seattle, an alternative media broadcasting center allowed 24-hour broadcasting.

The capacity to collect data, distribute interpretations, and broadcast internationally at low cost meant that the Internet helped "to break the information monopoly enjoyed by business, government leaders, and [in the case of the MAI] OECD officials" (Smith & Smythe, 2000, p. 31). The Canadian decision to engage in a comprehensive and expensive consultation exercise, leading up to the Seattle ministerial, may have resulted from the belief by MAI negotiators that groups had arrived "armed" with outdated or misleading information gleaned from the Internet (Smith & Smythe, p. 31). In the case of the Seattle ministerial, some Canadian government officials felt consternation that Canadian NGOs, who had received unparalleled access and briefings, seemed intent on making the negotiations fail. The government had believed that increased transparency and the sharing of "insider knowledge" would lead to NGO positions that hewed closer to the official lines.

NGOs also used the Internet to put direct pressure on politicians and policy makers in member states. Deibert (1999) reports that many anti-MAI sites provided the e-mail addresses of Members of Parliament (MPs) and state representatives, and many anti-Seattle sites employed the same tactic (e.g., form letters to voice concern). In the case of Seattle, DFAIT monitored all web sites regularly and reported to ministers' offices. Analysis showed that most correspondence from constituents criticized the government's position. Ironically but not surprisingly, policy makers were more sensitized to the secondary coverage of anti-globalization views (as reflected in newspaper accounts) than to the primary sources (web site messages posted by civil society organizations). Government representatives assume that far larger audiences will see the views expressed in mainstream media.

ITs: A QUESTION OF ECONOMY, EFFICIENCY, AND EFFECTIVENESS

In the end, how important was the Internet to the anti-globalization campaigns? Did the Internet generate new activism, or did it function more as a facilitator for existing activism? To what extent did the Internet activism influence the Canadian government's policy positions, and how did the trade negotiators react? What was the impact on broader public opinion? The first question (How important was the Internet to the anti-globalization campaign?) can also be reframed in more specific terms. In the case of the MAI and Seattle ministerials, did the Internet operate with (1) economy (its ability to reduce costs), (2) efficiency (impact relative to costs), and (3) effectiveness (the ability to prompt changes in policy objectives and, over the longer term, to have an impact on public policy outcomes)?

Deibert (1999) and Smith and Smythe (2000) conclude that the anti-MAI campaign would not have been as efficient without the Internet. However, more efficient communication among the committed protesters does not mean that the Internet created the protests; nor does it imply growth in the total number of individuals committed to anti-MAI protests. Protesters were unable to stop the Seattle ministerial meeting. As Deibert states, if the Internet had spontaneously generated the anti-MAI network, one would have expected a more evenly distributed set of participants from across the Internet, "corresponding roughly to Internet participant demographics on a country by country basis" (p. 23). But, as Smith and Smythe discovered, the United States and Canada displayed a disproportionate amount of interest, with these countries hosting almost 50 percent (31.9% in the United States and 17.6% in Canada) of all web sites devoted to the MAI. The Canadian and American sites also contained the most original information. This finding indicates that other reasons, besides the Internet, account for the high level of protest activity in North America.

It is certain that some form of citizen activism would have emerged to lobby against the MAI and the WTO in Seattle—with or without the Internet. The contribution of the technology was to "add a dense layer of daily interaction to these links, intensifying the bonds between disparate members and fomenting a sense of international commonality" (Deibert, 1999, pp. 18–19). Older forms of communications technology (telephone-based networks and even fax campaigns) lacked the interactivity, responsiveness, and flexibility of computer networks. And, as Deibert points out, listservs allow information to be "posted and redistributed, often with comments by participants, such that the same core message may circulate dozens of times through the network modifying and changing as it goes from listserv to listserv" (p. 24). Significantly, unlike telephones, faxes, hand-delivered flyers, and pamphlets, the World Wide Web has a permanent presence and international reach. Thus, while the Internet may not create an international community, it does facilitate communications among existing communities.

One could conclude from the MAI and Seattle experiences that the Internet was certainly a very economical way for citizens to communicate and mobilize, given its low cost, and that it was efficient, given its ability to distribute large amounts of information quickly. Assessing the Internet's effectiveness, however, leads to a more qualified conclusion. The likely impact of non-technological factors (such as intergovernmental impasses) on these negotiations raises questions about the influence of citizens' movements on policy positions. Any recognition of multiple causal factors diminishes the importance of the Internet's role and qualifies its effectiveness.

One way to test this proposition is to examine the reaction of the Canadian trade negotiators and DFAIT to the failure of the MAI. Stairs (2000) suggests that Canadian policy makers and politicians reacted seriously to the force of civil society activism. Trade Minister Sergio Marchi, who had felt "blind-sided" by the MAI experience (and by extension the Council of Canadians), was determined that Canadian delegates would not be "similarly confounded" at the Seattle meeting (p. 17). He therefore instructed

DFAIT to initiate "a wide-open public consultation process" (p. 17) as part of the general preparations for Seattle. As Stairs describes, the elaborate consultative activities did not end with the departure of the Canadian delegation to Seattle. Canadian ministers and officials continued these consultations on-site, where they found themselves in constant briefing mode: "A very elaborate apparatus for communication between diplomats engaged in front-line action on the one hand and their interested constituents [NGOs and business representatives] on the other" developed (p. 28). Judged by the traditional standards of statecraft, such interactions with the public were unusual, to say the least, but they very much reflected the shift toward greater public diplomacy. So intense was the activity that DFAIT's "Trade Negotiations and Agreements" web site was revised on a daily basis, so that citizens who were not actually in Seattle could compare DFAIT's information with information gleaned from other sources.

If effectiveness implies the ability to have a *much greater* direct influence on government policy direction, then any assessment of the Internet's impact in the case of Seattle must be a qualified "not yet." The Canadian government did initiate an unprecedented outreach effort, but this high level of consultation did not lead directly to the fundamental policy changes demanded by the NGOs (e.g., reversing the process of trade liberalization and establishing new labor codes). Information, communication, and mobilization can all increase without necessarily leading to policy change. Other factors were at play in the failures of both the MAI and Seattle negotiations; and, as the example of the negotiations leading up to NAFTA shows, even democratic regimes are sometimes immune to public pressure. In 1993, when Canada sought to be included in the U.S.–Mexico free trade negotiations, Decima Research and Goldfarb Consultants found that only 37 percent of Canadians supported the practice of trilateral free trade. Despite this public sentiment, the Liberal government ratified NAFTA when it formed the government in 1994—a reversal of its earlier position as official opposition. Thus, we can assume that, with or without the Internet, some government policy positions will be immune to the types of public pressures adopted by citizens' movements.

The power of citizen mobilization should, therefore, not be overstated. Certainly, the state is losing its monopoly of information, and the phenomenon of diminishing asymmetry is very real. The state nonetheless retains privileged access to information and maintains the capacity, given sufficient political will and investment, to project its image and voice into the emerging hypermedia. Canada's foreign and international trade ministry employs over 7,000 individuals, who are stationed at headquarters in Ottawa and in 160 embassies, consulates, and trade offices abroad. Despite the emergence of a global civil society fuelled by communications technologies, an industrialized country such as Canada still has considerable infrastructure with which to project its views and engage in public diplomacy. This conclusion leads, in turn, to the observation that, in the face of information overload, credibility is the new "edge" in international relations and a key element of effective policy making (Nye & Owens, 1996). The paradox of the information age is the inverse relationship between information flow and information reliability. The risk associated with overabundance of information is the potential to drown out knowledge, a phenomenon that would increase rather than lessen the import and profile of official communications from governments.

Indeed, it has been tempting to jump to the conclusion that, in an age of civilian satellites, citizens' movements will be competing with and defeating states in information wars. In an information era when credibility is crucial, inaccurate interpretation by well-intentioned amateurs is a real risk. Erroneous interpretations of information could do incalculable damage to organizations that depend almost exclusively on public donations for their survival. Some NGOs have already learned the hard way that they pay a high price when they dabble in exaggeration in a real-time news environment. As Gowing (1998) points out in his study of NGO responses to the Great Lakes crisis of 1996–1997, the medium- to long-term cost in credibility, integrity, and image to NGOs may be far higher than any short-term tactical advantage.

Related to questions of effectiveness and credibility is the anti-globalization movement's impact on the body politic. As could be expected, the leaders of the protest movements at Seattle argued that, following the MAI experience, Seattle was not a fluke; it represented, as Nevitte (1996) concluded, a shift in underlying public attitudes that had been apparent for at least two decades in industrialized countries.[4] Van Rooy (cited in Mendelsohn & Wolfe, 2000), for example, argued: "Canadians, and others, are uneasy about globalization. Not all identify it entirely with corporate greed to be sure, but most are deeply wary about the impact of this perceived roller coaster on their lives" (pp. 9–10). Two national surveys (2000 and 2001) confirmed that Canadians see the benefits of trade liberalization accruing more to governments and corporations than to themselves and their families (Ekos Research Associates, 2000, 2001). These attitudes do not mean that Canadians are against globalization. In fact, by a two-to-one margin (46% compared to 24%), Canadians tend to have a more optimistic than pessimistic attitude toward globalization (Ekos, 2000) and almost three-quarters now support NAFTA.

The "myth" of the MAI and Seattle experiences appears to be that media images of protesters fighting "unaccountable institutions" has further reinforced the public's angst and antipathy toward trade liberalization. This conclusion is not entirely accurate. Public opinion research, commissioned by DFAIT in the immediate aftermath of Seattle (December 1999 and March 2000), indicates that the protests at Seattle had little immediate effect on the public mood. That is, they were not effective at changing public opinion in the short term. According to Angus Reid (1999), the majority of Canadians (63%) surveyed said the protests made them feel neither more positive nor negative about Canada's participation in the talks. About the same proportion of Canadians believed that the protests had made them "more positive" toward trade talks as believed the protests had made them "more negative" toward the trade talks.[5] Overall, according to Angus Reid, 84 percent of Canadians support Canada's role in trade negotiations, and an even higher proportion (93%) believe it is important for Canada to take a lead role in setting global trade rules. In Québec, two weeks after Seattle, almost two-thirds of the populace said they had not even heard of the "battle in Seattle."

Nonetheless, can protesters at these events be considered irrelevant gadflies? Mendelsohn and Wolfe's (2000) examination of two decades (1980–2000) of Canadian trade surveys indicates that the public's broad support for trade liberalization, while real, is also shallow and not very crystallized. Attitudes shift, depending on the wording of survey questions and the state of the domestic economy. As a result, the researchers conclude "there is no compelling evidence that the public does not believe at least the milder versions of the anti-global governance protests" (p. 27). Furthermore, recent data by Environics Research (September 2000) indicates that, although the majority of Canadians articulate "moderate" support for the WTO, few indicate "high" support. The soft support for trade liberalization translates into a window of opportunity for the anti-globalization citizens' movements. An April 2001 survey by Ekos Research Associates (commissioned by DFAIT and undertaken before the Summit of the Americas) supports this trend in public opinion. The 2001 survey found that a majority of Canadians (53%) now believe the anti-globalization protests are about "valid issues which a great many of Canadians care about." This belief is strong across all age groups but especially among younger Canadians, 73 percent of whom feel this way.

Paradoxically, when asked if the coverage of anti-globalization protesters (i.e., the newspaper commentaries and televised scenes of the "mobilized citizens" in the streets) had any impact on their attitudes, 6 in 10 Canadians believe that this coverage had no impact on their views toward trade liberalization. We are left with the sense that Canadians have become more sensitized to the issues promoted by the anti-globalization movement (especially messages about the impact of trade on the environment and human rights). They are also less inclined to view mobilized citizens as members of "fringe groups." Even so, they are not yet ready to credit their increased awareness to the successful use of new communication technologies by citizens' groups. They do not acknowledge the contribution of these citizens' groups in putting these trade issues on the media, and, therefore, public policy agenda. Academic observers, however, are more quick to recognize the role of civil society:

Citizens and groups that were well-coordinated (through the use of the Internet) and armed with detailed information and analysis were much harder for negotiators . . . to dismiss as uninformed, nationalist or fringe elements. In a number of cases NGOs felt the presence of anti-MAI information on the Internet had shaped domestic media coverage and citizen opposition. (Smith & Smythe, 2000, p. 35)

CONCLUSION

This chapter has shown that the Internet played an important role in the anti-MAI activism, contributed to the high media profile of protesters at Seattle, and helps to explain the rapid mobilization of opposition to every major subsequent international economic conference. Research strongly suggests that the new Internet technology generated more activism than would have been the case without the technology; and while the Noah's Ark of opposition hardly qualifies as a community, it was more than a collection of isolated groups. United by a sense of destiny gained from the MAI protest, the disparate groups that gathered in Seattle sought to deliver yet another blow to what they saw as weak-kneed governments capitulating to a global corporate agenda, set by a secretive global bureaucracy, housed in international organizations such as the WTO.

The cases of the MAI and Seattle demonstrated that the emergence of new communications technologies facilitated activism already in place, increased the public profiles and roles of civil society actors (including allowing them to formally join Canada's official delegation in Seattle), and thus broke the "information monopoly" that had long been enjoyed by business and government in international trade negotiations. The less the state is able to monopolize knowledge about the substance of specific trade negotiations (with negotiating texts available either broadly online or distributed for comment to a select number of representative citizens' groups), the more citizens can enter the policy arena with their special issues and points of view. While we cannot draw a causal connection between the increasing availability of communications technology and substantive changes in the composition of trade policies, we can say that the increased level of global transparency brought about by these technologies has fundamentally changed the nature of citizens' relations with their governments.

We cannot say for sure whether a mobilized citizenry led the framers of the *Declaration of Québec City*[6] (Summit of the Americas, April 2001) to insert terms such as *democratic development, fundamental freedoms,* and *connectivity* into their draft documents; nor can we unquestioningly attribute the commitment of participating governments to an *Inter-American Democratic Charter*[7] to the actions of these opposition groups. But there can be no doubt that political perceptions of the "saleability" of free trade in the Americas led to the insertion of the numerous democratic "clauses" in the Summit's final declaration. With regard to public opinion, it is true that the public is aware of resistance to globalization. Yet the sound and fury of Seattle has not dented Canadians' confidence in their ability to manage globalization.

The new communications technologies help to rebalance a fundamentally asymmetrical power relationship among states, corporations, and citizens. A sophisticated citizenry with access to multiple sources of information will no longer tolerate the traditional levels of secrecy and hierarchical control of information in international trade negotiations. However, with regard to the effectiveness of the communications technology used by the protest movement, more empirical study is required to test the degree to which the new communication technology has been effective (i.e., enabled social movements to effect change in public policy positions). Most observers agree, for example, that many causal factors (other than the citizen movements) contributed to the failures of the MAI and Seattle. They also conclude that few policy changes followed the protests. It would be wrong to suggest that social movements will gain the upper hand any time soon.

Governments' abilities to pursue policy objectives have not yet been deeply compromised by the hypermedia environment. The same technologies, employed by members of the anti-globalization movement, can be used by the state for purposes of advocacy and surveillance; and while the protest movements have scored some easy public victories in recent years by embarrassing a large bureaucracy that is far less nimble, this situation may change in the near future. Government officials in Westminster parliamentary systems have traditionally taken a low-keyed, anonymous approach, taking care not to overshadow their ministers. However, with so much information (much of it inaccurate) spilling out into the public domain, government will have to make more use of its "brand" (qualities of credibility, integrity, knowledge, and honest policy advice). Public servants will need to assume a more public role in explaining public policies and countering myths. The government will need to devote more attention to creating intergovernmental communication systems for enhanced dialogue between national and provincial officials, as well as with foreign governments. These strategies may challenge the earlier successes of opponents of the MAI and Seattle. In short, this new hypercommunications environment requires an aggressive and visible government communication strategy.

As the two case studies show, traditionally hidebound institutions such as foreign and trade ministries will no longer be given the latitude to make major decisions behind closed doors. Extensive consultations before, during, and after trade negotiations will become routine. The organizers of all future international trade conferences will have to take as a given that there will be organized demonstrations and that a dialogue will have to be initiated with the public. As the DFAIT's actions during the Seattle ministerials demonstrate, more collaborative relationships with the public will be a necessity, not a choice. In a networked world, governments will not only consult regularly with their own citizens, but they will also simultaneously consult with citizens of key target countries. They will no longer be able to speak differently to different audiences; they will have to adopt the language of what Pal (2002) calls "emotional persuasion" rather than the technical discourse of traditional diplomacy. This transition will not be easy, nor will it be rapid. Decentralized networks coexist and interact uneasily with the hierarchical nature of traditional bureaucratic organizations, which tend to control and compartmentalize information.

What we are hearing is not the death knell of traditional economic diplomacy; what we see as passé is the pursuit of a diplomacy that self-consciously diminishes and underfunds its public face—its public diplomacy. Indeed, what stands out is not the decline of economic diplomacy but its ability to adapt—albeit slowly—to the promises and challenges of the networked age. The public's sober reaction to the protest movement and the state's capacity to adapt to the new environment will ensure that, although anarchy may reign in the virtual world, it has not yet gained a foothold in the real one.

NOTES

1. At the time of writing, the Summit of the Americas was just ending. For this reason, the chapter concentrates on the experiences of the MAI and Seattle ministerials, two events for which there is insufficient data to draw definitive conclusions on the impact of communications technology on citizen mobilization.

2. As Stairs (2000) describes, the Canadian government had a well-established consultative mechanism in place with the business community, known as the Sector Advisory Groups on International Trade (SAGITs), that dated from the free trade negotiations. What the MAI experience accomplished, in effect, was to force DFAIT to reach beyond the business community to civil society organizations.

3. Given the diversity of views of the protesters, it is difficult to isolate a common theme other than the most general antipathy toward globalization. With tongue in cheek, one could characterize the uniting factor as a belief that the corporate agenda was dedicated "to cutting down all the trees of rainforests; polluting rivers and skies; undermining health, environmental and labor standards; and forcing the citizens of the developing world to work for a pittance and thus cause greater unemployment in the industrialized countries." I am indebted to my colleague, Colin Robertson, for this pithy attempt to summarize the collective anti-globalization view.

4. Nevitte (1996), using data from the World Values Survey, discusses the rise of a postmaterialist citizenry in Canada, who are less deferential and more willing to engage in protest behavior. In fact, he points out that Canadians are the most protest-oriented of all the national samples.

5. DFAIT commissioned a short survey by Angus Reid on Canadian attitudes toward international trade and the protests. The survey, which took place in the weeks following the conference, revealed that only 2 in 10 views were negatively affected by the protests. This lack of impact was corroborated by a larger survey

on Canadian attitudes toward international trade, conducted by Ekos Research Associates in March 2000 for DFAIT.

6. The Declaration of Québec City can be found at http://www. americascanada.org/eventsummit/declarations/declare-e.asp.

7. The Inter-American Democratic Charter can be found at www.oas.org/charter/docs/resolution1_en_p4.htm.

REFERENCES

Deibert, R. J. (1999, August). Civil society activism and the world-wide web: The case of the anti-MAI lobby. Paper presented to the Global Trends Project, Ottawa.

de Kerckhove, D. (1997). *Connected intelligence: The arrival of web society.* Toronto: Somerville House Publishing.

Ekos Research Associates. (2000, 2001). Canadian attitudes towards international trade. Two annual surveys commissioned for the Canadian Department of Foreign Affairs and International Trade.

Environics Research Group. (2000, September). Focus Canada. Annual syndicated survey.

Fulton, B. (1998, October). Reinventing diplomacy in the information age: Final draft. Washington, DC: Center for Strategic and International Studies. www.csis.org/ics/dia.

Gowing, N. (1998). New challenges and problems for information management in complex emergencies. Ominous lessons from the Great Lakes and Eastern Zaire in late 1996 and early 1997. Conference paper delivered at "Dispatches from Disaster Zones: Reporting of Humanitarian Emergencies," London, May 27-28.

Innis, H. A. (1951). *The bias of communication.* Toronto: University of Toronto Press.

Mendelsohn, M., & Wolfe, R. (2000). Probing the aftermyth of Seattle: Analysis of available Canadian public opinion data on international trade. A research report prepared for the Canadian Department of Foreign Affairs and International Trade, Ottawa.

Nevitte, N. (1996). *The decline of deference.* Peterborough, ON: Broadview Press.

Nye, J. S., Jr., & Owens, W. A. (1996, March–April). America's information edge. *Foreign Affairs,* 20–36.

Pal, L. A. (2002). Bits of justice: Human rights on the Internet. In E. H. Potter (Ed.), *Cyber-diplomacy: Managing foreign policy in the 21st century.* Unpublished manuscript provided to the author.

Reid, Angus. (1999, December). Attitudes towards international trade. Public opinion survey commissioned by the Canadian Department of Foreign Affairs and International Trade.

Rothkopf, D. J. (1998). Cyberpolitik: The changing nature of power in the information age. *Journal of International Affairs 51* (2), 334–336.

Smith J. P., & Smythe, E. (2000, March). Globalization, citizenship and technology: The MAI meets the Internet. Paper presented at the International Studies Association annual conference, Chicago.

Stairs, D. (2000, December). Foreign policy consultations in a globalizing world. *Policy Matters 1* (8). Montreal: Institute for Research on Public Policy.

Yearbook of international organizations (34th ed.). (1997). Munich: K. G. Saur Verlag. www.uia.org.

Chapter 9

Standoff at Oka: Take Me to Your Leader

Sherry Devereaux Ferguson

A 1990 dispute over ownership of a municipal golf course at Oka, Québec, escalated into a face-off between Mohawks, the police, and ultimately the Canadian army. The crisis was a significant one, estimated to have cost Canadian governments over $200 million (Editorial, *Edmonton Journal*, May 6, 1991) and a tremendous loss of credibility in the international community. The European Parliament, which passed a resolution condemning Canada for its treatment of Natives, sent a fact-finding delegation to Canada. In the same period, the Mohawk flag was raised at the Hague (MacLeod, 1993). One film historian wrote, "While the government was on holiday, the country was on the brink of civil war" (MacLeod, 1993). The final cost of the crisis, one observer noted, may never be known.

This chapter examines the dynamics of the crisis at Oka, a situation in which many voices clamored for an audience and many groups argued for their right to be accepted as spokespersons. Governments, for their part, played a game of "hot potato" with the public, passing responsibility for management of the crisis from one level of government to another and from one department to another. The dominant characteristic of the crisis at Oka was confusion over leadership and authority questions. Whose crisis was it? And who was responsible for managing it? To better understand the events of 1990, I will construct a theoretical framework against which to view the particulars of Oka. First, however, I will detail the history of events leading to Oka.

THE MAKING OF A CRISIS

While many definitions of crisis exist, most incorporate the elements of surprise and perceived threat, real or imagined, to the survival and well-being of the organization (e.g., Privy Council Office, 1987). Still, some crises are more anticipated than others. In the case of Oka, the element of surprise should not have been present, as this particular conflict was 270 years in the making. The catalytic event was a decision by the municipality of Oka, Québec, to expand a 9-hole golf course into an 18-hole golf course. This expansion necessitated the appropriation of sacred land, traditional burial grounds for Mohawks, who inhabited the "patchwork quilt of territory" known as Kanehsatake (Roth, 1993, p. 319). Outraged, the Mohawks demanded that the town council reconsider its decision to proceed. When the mayor of Oka refused, the Mohawks responded on March 11, 1990, by erecting a barricade on a recreational dirt road leading into the contested area. This barricade was largely symbolic, as the road did not constitute a main travel route (Obomsawin, 1993). Subsequent negotiations in which federal Indian and Northern Affairs Minister Tom Siddon met independently with representatives of the town of Oka, the Kanehsatake Band Council, and John Ciaccia (the Minister of Native Affairs) failed to settle the dispute.

The crisis escalated on July 11, 1990, when the Sureté du Québec (S.Q.) sent 250 members of a SWAT team to Oka. The provincial police officers used tear gas and concussion grenades in an attempt to disperse armed Mohawk Warriors, who were defending the barricades. The direction of the wind changed, however, and the tear gas became a weapon against the S.Q. In the ensuing confusion, a police officer died in "friendly" cross-fire (MacLeod, 1993; Obomsawin, 1993). In the aftermath of these events, Mohawks extended their blockade onto a main highway, and Natives from a nearby reserve (Kahnawake) erected a sympathy barricade on the Mercier Bridge leading into Montreal. This second blockade, which added two hours to the commuting time of Chateauguay residents employed in Montreal, fueled the emotions of non-Native townspeople. When several hundred members of the Royal Canadian Mounted Police (RCMP) arrived to assist local police, they confronted 4,000 non-Native rioters, who were throwing Molotov cocktails and burning Mohawk Warriors in effigy (Green & Stier, 1991; Obomsawin, 1993). Natives accused S.Q. officers of dressing in plain clothes and inciting the civil unrest (MacLeod, 1993). Premier Robert Bourassa appealed to the federal government for military intervention.

In an attempt to resolve the crisis without further escalation, federal ministers announced that the Government of Canada was prepared to purchase the land from the municipality of Oka. However, Indian Affairs Minister Siddon said that the provincial government must, first, expropriate the contested area from the municipality, and second, resolve the matter of the armed standoff (Green & Stier, 1991). Minister Ciaccia pledged that his government would meet these federal demands. Mohawk negotiator Joe Deom balked, stating, "This land is ours; it has always been ours; so I don't understand this talk about buying land" (Begin, Moss, & Niemczak, 1990, p. 4).

The blockades and rioting continued into early August, when the province made a second request for federal intervention (Cogden, 1990, p. 116). On August 8, 1990, Prime Minister Brian Mulroney appointed Alan Gold, Chief Justice of the Superior Court, to mediate an agreement on the preconditions to full negotiation of the conflict. Finally, on August 12, the governments of Québec and Canada reached an agreement with the Mohawks on preconditions. On that same day, the prime minister placed approximately 4,000 Canadian troops at the disposal of Premier Robert Bourassa; and within two days, 2,500 soldiers moved into four locations near Oka and Chateauguay. Under these tense conditions, formal negotiations began (Begin, Moss, & Niemczak, 1990).

Negotiations stalled, resumed, then stalled again. Mohawks argued among themselves over matters of representation. The federal government rejected Native demands as "bizarre" (MacLeod, 1993). Within the week, federal negotiator Bernard Roy announced that the talks had reached "a serious impasse over some of the most fundamental issues"—the dismantling of the barricades, surrendering guns, and Mohawk demands for immunity from prosecution (Begin, Moss, & Niemczak, 1990, p. 5). By August 21, a military solution looked inevitable, and army troops replaced the S.Q. at the barricades (Cogden, 1990). Prime Minister Mulroney threatened to remove the barricades by force, if necessary; and on August 30, Premier Bourassa gave the order.

By September 2, Canadian armed forces had forced the Mohawks to retreat from the barricades to an alcohol treatment center on the Kanehsatake reserve. After 62 days of Native occupation, the army reopened the Mercier Bridge at Chateauguay. A few days later, the army raided the Warrior Society Longhouse at Kahnawake; when Native women resisted, one was injured. The army claimed to have confiscated weapons, but Natives countered that they found only cigarettes and beer (Obomsawin, 1993).

By September 9, the federal position had hardened. Minister of Justice Kim Campbell stated: "The Warriors do not represent legitimate native grievances legitimately advanced. They carry guns, they are resisting enforcement of the law and we will not negotiate with them. We will only discuss the terms of the surrender of their firearms" (Begin, Moss, & Niemczak, 1990, p. 5). On September 18, the military escorted S.Q. forces onto Tekakwitha Island, near Kahnawake, in search of weapons. The raids ended in violence and scuffles, the firing of warning shots and tear gas, and an injured soldier (Cogden, 1990). The military gave a televised press conference in which they displayed some of the weaponry they had allegedly seized (MacLeod, 1993).

The standoff at Oka ended on September 26, 1990, a day earlier than had been negotiated with the armed forces (Anonymous participant in Post-

Oka Communications Symposium, 1990). Refusing to acknowledge surrender, approximately 30 Warriors and 20 women and children left the
treatment center. Cameras captured the resulting chaos of men, women,
and children being wrestled to the ground by surprised army troops
(Obomsawin, 1993). Cynical observers accused the Natives of surrendering
at 6:00 P.M., which is prime time on television (Anonymous participant,
1990). The army took the adults into custody, and Indian Affairs Minister
Tom Siddon announced that he would meet with Mohawk representatives
to discuss a plan of action for negotiation of the disputed land. The judicial
process later found 32 Mohawks guilty of crimes committed during the
confrontation, but follow-up appeals resulted in acquittals. The Canadian
government purchased land from the municipality, but Natives claim that
they bought the wrong land and that the township is still claiming the
property where bloodshed occurred in 1990 (MacLeod, 1993).

Tensions rose again in 1994 when the Mohawks announced their claim
to 260 square miles around Kanehsatake—an area that included a major
international airport and a number of Montreal suburbs. Such actions led
one observer to note that chances for a final resolution are bleak, as "the
conflict is much more than a fight for a small parcel of land in and around
the cemetery" (Emond, 1994, n.p.).

DEVELOPING AN ANALYTICAL FRAMEWORK FOR
UNDERSTANDING THE EVENTS AT OKA

The answers to the following three questions can help the analyst to
understand not only what happened at Oka, but what happens in many
crisis situations: (1) Who owns the issue? (2) Who are the stakeholders?
(3) What is their power capability? (Ferguson, 1994, 1999).

Deciding Questions of Ownership

In any crisis situation, the first question that must be answered is the
following: Does the issue fall within the mandate and mission of the organization? Does the organization have the jurisdiction to act in the crisis?
Most issue management specialists agree that few issues will disappear as
a consequence of being ignored by the organization. Nonetheless, responding to issues that reside outside the organization's mandate and mission
implies risks.

In the case of the Mohawk standoff at Oka and Chateauguay, confusion
over ownership of issues made management of the crisis extremely difficult.
This confusion existed at all levels of the Canadian government (federal,
provincial, and municipal) and between the two main governing councils
at Kanehsatake, factions within those councils, Mohawks on other reserves
and those who lived in Oka, and the First Nations Assembly (which rep-

resented the Indian community across Canada). In the void, Mohawks asserted their right to speak for the Indians at Kanehsatake and Kahnawake. However, disputes over these claims to leadership made it difficult for the federal or provincial governments to identify appropriate negotiators to represent the Native position (Roth, 1990). In actual fact, no one Native position existed, and ownership of the various dimensions of the issue was subject to much ongoing debate. This situation is not uncommon in crises that evolve out of a larger historical context, in which the issues are complex and intertwined.

As the situation worsened, the Canadian public expected the federal government (in particular, the Department of Indian and Northern Affairs) to intervene and reach a settlement with the Natives. Opposition political groups and Québecers accused the prime minister and the Minister of Indian and Northern Affairs of failing to act in a rapidly deteriorating environment. In defense, Indian Affairs Minister Tom Siddon said that the federal government lacked jurisdiction over the public and administrative issues involved in the crisis. He said the hands of the federal government were "partly tied" (Green & Stier, 1991, p. 25), as the provincial government had not expropriated the land from the municipality. Like the federal government, the provincial government claimed that it had no mandate to solve the crisis (MacLeod, 1993).

The refusal of the politicians to accept ownership of the land claim issues persisted throughout the crisis and guaranteed the failure of negotiations. The federal government did agree to assume ownership of the "law and order" issue—but only when the province requested the intervention. Commodore David Cogden (1990), director general of public affairs, Canadian National Defence Headquarters, explained how the transfer of ownership on the "law and order" issue took place in two stages: "Initially, the military involvement was purely in support of the Sureté; a limited response" (p. 117). According to the communication plan followed by the Department of National Defence ("Operation Salon"), this limited response included the provision of equipment and non-lethal support to police. However, in mid-August, the army responded to a provincial request for intervention by stationing several thousand troops near Montreal. A week later, the army replaced the S.Q. at the barricades.

The army maintained ownership of the "law and order" dimension of the crisis until October 31, 1990, when the last troops returned to their home base at Valcartier. Cogden (1990) described the gradual return of authority to the provincial police force: "By 5 October, all individuals had been released on bail or had voluntarily transferred to a Sureté detention facility. Once the barricades had been removed and all involved Warriors had surrendered, the military presence was reduced to a backup status, allowing the gradual re-introduction of the law enforcement agencies" (pp. 125–126).

The army had the clearest mandate of any stakeholder in the crisis. Cogden (1990) emphasized the importance of this point to their operations:

People must realize that the military are not policymakers. We had nothing to do with the policy that was going on. . . . I think people in Canada still don't know what the issue. . . . I mean, was it a law and order issue? Was it a native issue? I don't think people really know. . . . But we knew—for us, it was a very clear issue. It was a legal issue—we were tasked legally through the Province of Québec. . . . It was a simple law and order issue. It was not a native issue; it was not a federal-provincial issue. (pp. 127, 134)

Another member of the Canadian armed forces reiterated this position: "From our perspective, we were not dealing with the other issues. . . . We had our mandate and we stuck to our mandate and did our mandate, and our mandate was legal" (Anonymous participant, 1990, pp. 140–141).

Second Lieutenant Dave Scanlon (1990) said that there were "finite limits" (p. 83) to the communications mandate of the armed forces. Nonetheless, in the absence of comment from the political arm of the government, senior army officials often had to explain federal policies or policy reversals. Lieutenant Scanlon said that army spokespersons sometimes complained, off the record, that "they were left holding the bag" (p. 84), forced to assume ownership of issues that they lacked the jurisdiction to resolve.

Ownership questions also arose concerning who was responsible for the death of S.Q. officer Lemay. Many blamed the mayor of Oka for creating the conditions that gave rise to the attack. The mayor, for his part, claimed that he had transferred decision-making powers to the provincial government, who then decided to launch the offensive against the Natives. The mayor formally passed this responsibility to the province in a televised interview: "We're giving you the case to have someone to respect the law. The way they do it, it's not my concern. It's not my job" (MacLeod, 1993). He refused, in subsequent interviews, to acknowledge any responsibility for the violence that ensued.

Some alleged that the S.Q.—not the provincial government—issued the order to attack on July 11 (Green & Stier, 1991). However, the point is a rhetorical one, as the S.Q. answers to the province. In essence, no one accepted ownership of the events that resulted in an escalation of the crisis and the death of a police officer. Ray (1990), employed on the radio side of the Canadian Press, noted the absence of an S.Q. presence after early July:

I went up there on July 11th. I saw an S.Q. public relations guy there, parked in his car just down below the barricades just half an hour before a shoot-out. I went back there in one hour, and he got in his car and took off. From that point until the news conference by the head of the S.Q., halfway through the summer, there was not a word to be heard from them. And I'm also a member of the Association of Journalists, and we also tried to get a member of the S.Q. to attend our panel, to explain their involvement and they also refused. (pp. 89–90)

Within the Native community, a long-term dispute over questions of leadership had its impact on the ability of governments and Mohawk leaders to manage the crisis. The Kanehsatake Band Council (elected by democratic vote, in accordance with procedures set out in the *Indian Act*) and the Longhouse government (chosen by the clan mothers, in compliance with Indian traditions) vied for decision-making powers. This conflict also had historical roots, dating back to the institution of the *Indian Act* in 1889. While some Mohawks had accepted the government policies that forced the Indians to conform to a European electoral model, the majority had rejected the model. Green and Stier (1991) described the outcome of this historical disagreement:

In order to deal with the unpopular decision the Mohawks returned to the Six Nation Confederacy, with the building of a Longhouse and the opening of a Grand Council in 1927. . . . The different events led to a parallel organization where the Mohawk Council was dealing with national affairs between settlements and countries and the Band Council handled business with the Department of Indian Affairs. After the review of the *Indian Act* the Band Council and the Longhouse became more and more distant from each other, both in the way they acted and the way their policies were defined. (p. 78)

Even within the traditional government, factional disputes arose among members of the Longhouse government of Kanehsatake and the Warriors, an independent and more radical group of Mohawks whose membership was not restricted to the Kanehsatake Natives. The Warriors claim that their mandate comes from the Great Law of Peace, the Constitution of the Iroquois Confederacy, which charges all Mohawk men with the task of defending the Mohawk nation. However, not all accepted the legitimacy of this mandate. On August 13, 1990, the day after the Pines negotiating committee (representing the Mohawks) signed the prenegotiation agreement with the governments of Canada and Québec, Kanehsatake leader and former Chief Clarence Simon denounced the agreement "as void and nonexistent, objecting to the lack of representatives from Kanehsatake on the committee" (Green & Stier, 1991, p. 28). Mohawks from other reserves also entered the fray. The Six Nations Traditional Hereditary Chiefs of the Brantford reserve claimed that some bands had not been represented on the Pines negotiating committee and that "a select negotiating committee," controlled by minority external interests, had commandeered the process. They said that outsiders had been "implanted" in the community (p. 27) and decried the fact that Québec and Canada "have chosen to sign an agreement with the Warriors Society, which is a terrorist organization, rather than with the Kanehsatake Band Council" (p. 28).

The Delta Tribal Council in the Northwest Territories also called the Mohawk Warriors "thugs" and "criminals" and condemned the fact that the Warriors had resorted to weapons to settle their land claims disputes (Green & Stier, 1991, p. 31). Six Nations Confederacy Chief Orion Lyons said: "During the past two weeks, many letters, communications and press releases have been put out by a group of people claiming to speak on behalf of the Confederacy, and by the Mohawk Nation office at Kanewake. Those people are not authorized to act, or speak on the behalf of the Confederacy and have no sanction from the Grand Council to do so" (p. 31).

Nonetheless, moderates within the Mohawk community argued that the Warriors were standing up for Indian rights in a long-standing territorial issue (Monpetit, 1990), and Oneida Chief Terry Doxtater (who also spoke for the Six Nations Confederacy) said that "this statement is the first of our warnings to the Government of Canada and Québec that our patience runs short, that we are now setting in motion plans for the liberation of our defenders of the Nation of Kanehsatake" (Green & Stier, 1991, p. 31). Assembly of First Nations Chief George Erasmus issued an equally strong statement, saying that his organization was looking for ways to bring Canada "to its knees" (p. 31). Internal strife was further evident when the well-respected Chief Elijah Harper of Western Canada submitted a peace proposal, presumably on behalf of the Six Nations Confederacy, which was later disclaimed by the Confederacy.

Harry Swain, the Deputy Minister of Indian and Northern Affairs Canada, was quick to note the conflict among groups competing for the right to represent the Native voice. In a briefing to the media on July 23, 1990, Swain said that the Warriors had "hijacked the process dealing with this land claim and that the people at Oka are not calling the shots now and . . . the Warriors . . . are not blessed by the community, by the Longhouse, by the traditional government or by the Iroquois confederacy" (Begin, Moss, & Niemczak, 1990, p. 3). Although reticent to bless Swain's statement, Indian and Northern Affairs Minister Tom Siddon confirmed that some of the hereditary chiefs (at Kanehsatake and Native reserve areas) had expressed concerns that the Mohawk Warrior Society did not represent the views of the larger Native community. In a television interview with Native political leader Phil Fontaine, television commentator Pamela Wallin (1997) pointed to the negative impact of such confusion on former chief Ovide Mercredi's efforts to stimulate public support and political action. (Mercredi was Fontaine's predecessor as Assembly of First Nations chief.)

Ambiguities arose in part because the legal status of Indians in Canada is unclear. Green and Stier (1991) noted that Mohawks live at the "border of the legal system" (p. 87). For example, 15 of the Warriors who manned the barricades at Oka came from the Ganienkeh reserve in New York state; six came from the Akwesasne reserve, which spans Québec, Ontario, and New York. The Warrior who received the most media attention was Ronald Cross (alias "Lasagna"), a "Canadian" Indian who had lived and worked in Brooklyn, New York. (Cross has since died.) Political analysts noted that Cross' case is not uncommon, as many Canadian Indians seek employment in the United States (Monpetit, 1990; Roth, 1990). The Natives do not recognize the American/Canadian border as relevant to their status as North American Indians. This ambiguity in the status of the Natives had an impact on negotiations in the Oka crisis, as some of the negotiators in the territorial disputes lived on the American side of Akwesasne but carried Mohawk passports stamped in Canada.

Further ambiguities concerning leadership related to the matriarchal nature of Mohawk society. Soon after army troops had reopened the Mercier Bridge at Chateauguay, the women of Kahnawake staged the largest demonstration of the summer. In a show of support for the last holdouts at the Oka pines, they blocked a single-lane highway leading to the bridge. A spokesperson for the women made a statement: "Women in Kahnawake are serious about supporting men, women, and children in Kanehsatake. We feel this is our time to point out to the country, the world, that women in Kahnawake are serious. . . . It has not come across enough that we brought up those men to do what they are doing" (MacLeod, 1993). Two weeks later, other women led a march to the Kahnawake Longhouse to issue an eviction notice to the army and the police. As one commentator observed, "The army had only negotiated with the men. Now they are made to realize that the women are a real political force in the community" (MacLeod, 1993). Throughout the crisis, a number of women acted as spokespersons for the Native community. Kroker (1992) observed that "what makes the Mohawks really dangerous for the Quebec and Canadian states is their creation of a democratic politics model based on matriarchal principles of rule." Ellen Gabriel, a major spokesperson during the 1990 crisis, argued that the women of the Mohawk nation are the "only rightful title holders because they are the caretakers of the land by traditional law, and they have never sold or ceded the land" (Horovitch, 1994, n.p.).

In summary, responding to the crisis situation was made more difficult by the confusion over ownership—among the different levels of government (municipal, provincial, and federal), among different departments within each level of government (e.g., Indian and Northern Affairs; National Defence, and the Solicitor General [responsible for the RCMP]), and within the Indian nation itself (comprised of many councils and bands, vying for leadership, and with an ongoing tension between the traditional selection of leaders by the clan mothers and the electoral process imposed by the Europeans). Lack of agreement on who should be conducting the negotiations made resolution of the crisis almost impossible. When spin-off crises occur within the framework of a larger crisis situation, sorting out ownership questions on the mini-crises can create additional complications. As Robinson (1990) observed, "Communicational situations are by definition messy situations . . . with the gray areas that are brought out in trying to unravel who's in charge of what; who is to be made accountable for what" (p. 173).

Where debates over ownership take place within the boundaries of the organization (e.g., within different branches of government), management of the crisis becomes still more difficult. For instance, the Canadian Department of the Solicitor General has a Correctional Services Branch and a Parole Branch. When murders occur at halfway houses, debates often erupt over which branch of government has failed to protect the public—the Parole Board (which decides when to release an offender) or Correctional Services (which oversees the conduct of the offender while on parole). This same kind of situation developed at Oka with the army and the S.Q., who were supposed to be working together to resolve the "law and order" issues. Yet when a controversy arose over the disarming of Native peacekeepers (the Mohawk equivalent of the local police), neither the army nor the S.Q. would claim responsibility for the decision. Faced with criticism, both peacekeeping contingents became involved in "bouncing the ball back and forth" between each other (MacLeod, 1993). When the media picks up and carries these debates over ownership, those in positions of leadership face a no-win situation.

Identifying Stakeholders

The term *stakeholder* refers to "any individual or group who can affect or is affected by the actions, decisions, policies, practices, or goals of the organization" (Freeman, 1984, p. 25) or "groups of individuals whose interests coincide in one or more ways with the organization" Brody, 1988, p. 81). Stakeholders in an issue may be defined by a region (e.g., community, city, state, nation), an ethnic or racial grouping, political orientation, or other demographic or psychographic factors. Within government, it is not uncommon for several departments to have a stake in the same issue. In the case of Oka, the Department of Indian and Northern Affairs was ultimately concerned with broader land claims issues. When the federal government sent the RCMP into Oka and Chateauguay, the Department of the Solicitor General became a stakeholder. The subsequent involvement of the military made the Department of National Defence a stakeholder.

To identify stakeholders in a political crisis, it is useful to look at the dimensions of the issue. Most crisis issues can be examined against the following dimensions: *political, social/cultural, legal/criminal, human rights, economic, technological, ecological, regulatory, public health,* and *public safety* (Ferguson, 1999). Because these categories relate to areas of social concern, they also describe the social institutions that have evolved to meet these concerns. Governments institutionalize these areas of concern in the form of departments or agencies. Examples include the following: the Environmental Protection Agency (*ecological concerns*), the Department of Health Services (*public health concerns*), and the Department of the Interior (*cultural concerns*).

A Washington executive described how the issues of concern to his organization tended to cluster into groups that relate to specific House and Senate committees:

Members of my staff follow their issues into the House, the Senate, executive branch agencies—wherever they lead. And their bundles of issues change very little because they relate to congressional committees. Tax and trade issues, for example, center in the House Ways and Means Committee and the Senate Finance Committee, falling into one natural bundle. The same with the Public Works Committee and the Environmental Committees. The Committee structure on the Hill dictates the issues assignments. (Lusterman, 1988, p. 3)

In general terms, it can be said that the greater the number of dimensions to an issue, the greater the number of stakeholders; and the greater the number of stakeholders in an issue, the more complex and difficult the issue will be to manage (Ferguson, 1999). In the case of Oka, the Canadian federal government's decision to accept partial ownership of the issues implied the need to involve the multiple stakeholders: *legal/criminal* dimension (Justice Canada and the Department of the Solicitor General, which includes the RCMP), *social/cultural* dimension (the Department of Indian and Northern Affairs), *political* dimension (the Prime Minister's Office), *public safety* dimension (the Department of National Defence), and *ecological* dimension (the Department of the Environment). As the crisis progressed, other dimensions became important. Health Canada and the Human Rights Commission became stakeholders when the S.Q. stopped the movement of food and medical supplies into Kanehsatake and Kahnawake. Health Canada is responsible for public health on Native reserves, and the Human Rights Commission monitors *human rights* concerns.

Using the same diagnostic tool, it is possible to identify stakeholders from other jurisdictions: *legal/criminal* dimension (Justice Department of Québec); *social/cultural* dimension (the Native Affairs Ministry, other Native societies, and some multicultural groups); *political* dimension (the premier of Québec, his cabinet, the Iroquois Confederacy, the First Nations Assembly of Canada, the Band Councils across Canada, the Longhouse governments, governing bodies on other Mohawk reserves who are currently negotiating land claims disputes, and the international community); *public safety* dimension (Sureté du Québec, the Oka police force, and Native peacekeepers); *ecological* dimension (Native groups across Canada who demonstrate against clear-cut forestry practices, building of dams, and other environmental issues); *public health* (the Ministry of Health); *human rights* (the Human Rights Commission and the United Nations Human Rights Commission).

The communication plan generated by the Canadian armed forces reduced these stakeholders to four major groupings: (1) the media, (2) the local populations, (3) national and international publics, and (4) the Native communities. Army strategists believed that national and international publics would sympathize with the Warriors and oppose the intervention of the military (Cogden, 1990). As a consequence, the communication strategists decided to stress "the legal aspect of the Canadian Forces presence" with this audience (p. 119). The decision to involve General Foster, the Commander of the Army, as spokesperson told Native audiences that the Canadian government was taking the issues seriously. The engagement of high-level officials was also appropriate in meeting the needs of the general public, who expect organizations to take "high outrage" risks more seriously than "low outrage" risks (Sandman, 1993). They expect that top leaders will speak for the organization on the most serious issues.

Evaluating the Power Capability of Stakeholders

The term *power capability* refers to the property of an individual or group that enables the party to be politically influential (Adams, 1967; Anderson, 1967). The power for managing a political crisis can reside within the organization (e.g., in its human and financial resources or its credibility) or outside the organization (e.g., in public or celebrity support).

Financial resources give obvious advantages to an organization:

Resource-rich sources enjoy certain advantages that place them in a much stronger position to bargain with reporters and to manage the news than resource-poor groups. These advantages stem from conventional criteria of newsworthiness applied in newspapers, from the structure of the beat and specialist systems, and from the capabilities of rich sources to ease the reporter's job in collecting the news. (Goldenberg, 1975, p. 145)

Technical skills can also enhance the power capability of a group (Meng, 1992). General public support can constitute a power capability—whether in Argentina under Peron or Canada in the aftermath of a political accord that failed, in large measure, because of its disregard for Native and Western politics. Celebrity spokespersons like Meryl Streep, Elizabeth Taylor, or Jane Fonda can keep an issue on the media agenda for weeks, thus qualifying as a notable power capability for the stakeholders that they represent. (See Rose, 1991, for a discussion of Streep's influence on the Alar environmental issue.)

Another power capability relates to credibility. Like individuals, organizations project an image. A good image, based on laudable past actions, enhances the possibility that the organization can weather the difficulties posed by political or other crises. A bad image makes management of crises extremely difficult. In the same way, opposition stakeholders with high credibility can mount a stronger threat than those with low credibility: "Ralph Nader and other public interest lawyers have become respected celebrities . . . embodying solid expertise and mainstream reliability. They have learned how to make the journalistic code book work for them" (Gitlin, 1980, p. 284).

In the case of Oka, the Canadian federal government had an image problem in the person of Indian and Northern Affairs Minister Siddon. Trouble seemed to follow Siddon wherever he went. During Siddon's earlier tenure as Minister of Fisheries and Oceans, another crisis had occurred, a crisis that some dubbed "Tunagate." Under pressure from the StarKist Company of St. Andrews, New Brunswick; its American parent company, H. J. Heinz; and the government of New Brunswick, Siddon had approved the sale of more than one million tins of tainted tuna—tuna declared "unfit for human consumption" by federal fish inspectors. Heinz had threatened to close the New Brunswick plant if Siddon refused to release the disputed tuna for public sale. The plant closure would have cost 400 existing jobs and another 100 anticipated positions. Despite the fact that Siddon was able to demonstrate that the tainted tuna did not pose a serious health threat, an outraged Canadian public demanded the minister's resignation. This crisis took place in April 1985, some five years before Oka, but most Canadians remembered the scandal. The situation was not improved by the low popularity ratings of Prime Minister Brian Mulroney.

Québec Premier Robert Bourassa also had ongoing image problems. His liberal government had been under assault for its staunch anti-separatist position, and Native issues only complicated the crisis of leadership. The Natives wanted no part of sovereignty. They had threatened to separate from Québec if Québec separated from Canada. Some believed that political exigencies were at the foundation of Bourassa's unyielding position on the Native protest (MacLeod, 1993), and many recalled an earlier period in Québec history when Bourassa had called upon Prime Minister Pierre Trudeau to establish military rule in Montreal. In the case of the "October Crisis," both Bourassa and Trudeau had been severely criticized for their recourse to a military solution to a political crisis.

Other stakeholders in the crisis at Oka also had image problems. Some political observers said that the need to resort to military rule reflected badly, not only on the credibility of Bourassa, but also on the provincial police force (T. J. Scanlon, 1990). The S.Q. entered the crisis with a sullied image. This organization did not have a reputation for treating Natives in a fair and equitable manner. Mohawks claimed that the S.Q. had harassed them in the period from 1975 to 1976, often arresting and taking Mohawks into custody for no legitimate reason. Questions also lingered over police responsibility for the death of Mohawk David Cross in 1979. The S.Q. claimed that it had killed in self-defense; however, Mohawks retorted that you do not shoot a person five times in self-defense. The 1979 killing had received much media coverage. Another source of conflict had occurred in 1985, when the Québec government gave the S.Q. the right to arrest intoxicated persons on the Kahnawake reserve (Green & Stier, 1991).

Some S.Q. actions during the crisis were also seen as unacceptably racist (Monpetit, 1990). Observers were particularly offended by one incident, in which the police stood silent as protesters stoned Mohawks who were evacuating Kahnawake. The people leaving the reserve were older adults, children, and women. In the ensuing violence, one older man died from a heart attack. Mohawks believed that the provincial police were persecuting them for their part in defeating the Meech Lake Accord (an attempt to bring Québec into the Constitution). A veteran of World War II, Joe Deer, expressed the sentiments of many Mohawks when he said: "When they lost the Meech Lake Accord, that's when they really started kicking us around" (MacLeod, 1993).

Two groups of stakeholders enjoyed an initially higher level of credibility than the others. The Meech Lake talks had given Native leaders such as Elijah Harper and Ovide Mercredi enhanced profiles, and many more Canadians sympathized with the Native cause after the constitutional debates. However, as previously noted, Québecers as a whole did not share the sentiments of the larger population. They felt threatened by the Natives' talk of sovereignty, at a period in history when they were negotiating their own sovereignty (Monpetit, 1990; Robinson, 1990; Roth, 1990). Some Canadians believed that the Native cause gained further impetus as a consequence of the coverage at Oka. Bain (1990), Ottawa columnist and retired Dean of Journalism at King's College, commented: "The natives were reported upon more and in a more favorable light than those on the other side of the issue, which is to say, two governments, the police, and the Army. The natives were presented as the victims, romantic, colorful victims" (p. 47). Bain claimed that the story was written as a Native story, a story of protest, from the point of view of the Warriors.

The army, known predominantly for its peacekeeping missions around the world, entered the crisis with a better image than other federal stakeholders. At that point in time, it had not yet experienced its most serious crisis: widespread media coverage of misconduct by Canadian peacekeepers and allegations of complicity in the murder of Somalian civilians. Robinson (1990) concluded that the army maintained this positive image during the Oka crisis: "I think there was general agreement on this, that the Canadian Armed Forces won the minds of Canadians" (p. 175). Allen (cited by Robinson) proposed that the Canadian Forces accomplished this task by using psychological tactics, restraining the movements and activities of journalists, using various communication media to inform relevant publics, and creating a credible down-to-earth style of communicating.

Roth (1990) compared the strategies of the army to that of the S.Q.:

The S.Q. did not seem to have a very sophisticated public relations strategy in comparison with the Canadian Armed Forces. For example, the S.Q. refused to talk directly with journalists, whereas the military held regularly scheduled press conferences twice a day. They also gave press tours on a regular basis to the razor wire barricade closest to the treatment centre. . . . Their appearance as a "peacekeeping" force was in direct contrast to the policies and practices of the S.Q., which was the "law and order" arm of the Québec government. (p. 13)

Cushing (cited by Allen, 1990) agreed that the army's success was due, in large part, to its "brilliant public relations campaign." Julian Sher, president of the Canadian Association of Journalists, said, "If you have to make a scorecard of the whole affair, I think you'd have to say the Army 1– Media 0" (p. 77). In an attempt to identify the basis of their success, Allen (1990) noted that army strategists prepared or organized 45 press releases, 25 question-and-answer briefs for spokespersons, and 10 press conferences during the 77-day period of the crisis. At some press conferences, they distributed videos, some of which detailed weapons allegedly owned by the Warriors (p. 63). Army spokespersons confirmed that, in the post-Oka period, the Canadian forces experienced a 30 percent increase in the number of young people wishing to enlist (Jean Claude Cloutier, quoted by Allen, 1990). Informal discussions with communication officers from National Defence Headquarters suggested that they were well satisfied with their efforts at managing the crisis.

Not all agreed, however, that the army left Oka with a spotless image: "The armed forces provided strong-arm back-up for a Police Force raid on the Kahnawake longhouse. That began a string of events in which the Army lost much of its image as peacekeeper, and took on the trappings of the S.Q.'s bully-boy" (Bury, 1990, p. 2). Bury spoke of the "enforcer image" that the army acquired during the last days of the Mohawk dispute, and York (1990) accused the army of coming close to provoking a "blood bath" (p. 100). Mohawks also shared this sentiment; they called the army a "puppet of the S.Q." (MacLeod, 1993). They said that the army was acting as an "escort" for the provincial police to "do whatever they want" (MacLeod, 1993). On September 8, 1990, a squad of soldiers badly beat a Warrior whom they found sleeping in a trench. Journalists and Mohawks alike complained about the psychological warfare that the army conducted against media personnel and Warriors who took refuge at the treatment center. Bury said that the journalists felt like "animals in a zoo" (pp. 2–3).

A content analysis of 11 Canadian newspapers in the period from July

11 to September 29, 1990 reached the following conclusions regarding the terminal credibility of stakeholders in the crisis:

An overall image apparently skewed negatively against the Warriors and their cause emerges. But by the same token, both the federal and Québec governments also are presented in a negative light of comparable starkness. Moreover, if less dramatically, the statistical portraits painted of both the Sureté du Québec and the involved non-Indian community also are generally negative. In fact, only the non-Warrior Mohawks of the crisis area and the Army emerge to be seen positively. (Osler & MacFarlane, 1991, p. 7)

It is possible to gain additional insights by examining what happened to the careers of government leaders most directly involved with managing the Oka crisis. After the crisis at Oka had ended, Québec Native Affairs Minister John Ciaccia and Minister Sam Elkis, in charge of the S.Q., were demoted (MacLeod, 1993). The individual responsible for communications at the Privy Council Office (the central agency responsible for managing the crisis for the Canadian government), however, received a promotion soon after the crisis ended (D. Scanlon, 1990).

CONCLUSION

Lines of ownership were blurred in the crisis that erupted at Oka in early 1990. The disputed land was claimed by the federal government, the province, the municipality, and the Indians, who based their claim on 4,000 years of occupancy. This lack of clarity translated into a similar level of ambiguity in regard to ownership of issues that emerged from the dispute. Who should deal with the Native protest at Oka? The federal government, who had ultimate responsibility for the negotiation of land claims? The province, which had been granted entitlement by colonial governments? The municipality, which based its claim on a history of gradual expropriation of the land for community development purposes? Who had the authority to represent the Native position? The Longhouse government, elected by the clan mothers? The Band Councils? The moderates in the community? The First Nations Assembly? Canadian or American Natives? (Can you make the distinction?) The need to restore law and order raised further ownership questions. Who had the mandate and jurisdiction to restore civil order on Native land? (Was it Native land?) The Native peacekeepers? The S.Q.? The RCMP? The military? Who owned the issues that grew out of the death of the Québec police officer? The S.Q.? The Warriors? The mayor who had requested provincial intervention?

Some stakeholders regarded intervention by the federal government as inappropriate and illegitimate. However, in general, the Canadian public—especially Québecers who had experienced firsthand the threat of civil violence and the inconvenience of closed bridges and highways—did not share this view. Oka was a crisis for the federal government, despite the fact that the government inherited many of the subsidiary issues from other levels of government.

The engagement of large numbers of stakeholders in the crisis at Oka created still greater problems for those seeking to manage the issues. The residents of nearby Chateauguay, forced to spend an extra two hours commuting each day to work, certainly believed they had a stake in the dispute. Separatists in Québec felt threatened by the sovereignty issues raised by the Natives. Environmental groups across Canada were activated by the Native cause. Using a "stakeholder identification" tool, it is possible to identify a number of stakeholders with legitimate claims to involvement in the crisis at Oka.

Some stakeholders coped more successfully than others at Oka. The most successful (the army and Native leaders such as Elijah Harper and Ovide Mercredi) had clearly defined areas of ownership, prior credibility, high levels of public support, and the resources to accomplish their task. In the less successful instances (e.g., Indian and Northern Affairs, the Québec government, the S.Q., and the Warriors), questions related to ownership were confused; the parties were under attack by the public; and both initial and terminal credibility were low. The media and the public accused the S.Q. and the provincial government of being driven by political motives. The minister responsible for Indian and Northern Affairs was seen as being ineffectual and weak. The prime minister was experiencing record lows in popularity. The media and others (including Natives) labeled the Warriors as "criminals" and "thugs." They accused the Warriors of being driven by greed (a reference to their alleged involvement with bingo halls and cigarette smuggling). The Indian people, as a whole, however (along with leaders such as Harper and Mercredi), entered and left the crisis with a reasonably high level of credibility. Their cause would have been still further enhanced had their leaders been more able to project a united image, with lines of responsibility clarified. This confusion over leadership continues to impact negatively on the advocacy efforts of Native groups who seek to make their voices heard and their issues visible.

REFERENCES

Adams, R. (1967). Political power and social structures. In C. Veliz (Ed.), *The politics of conformity* (pp. 15–42). Oxford: Oxford University Press.

Allen, S. (1990, November). Transcript of presentation to the Post-Oka Communications Symposium, hosted by the Department of National Defence, National Defence Headquarters, Ottawa.

Anderson, C. W. (1967). *Politics and economic change in Latin America: The governing of restless nations.* New York: Van Nostrand and Reinhold.

Anonymous participant. (1990). Transcript of presentation to the Post-Oka Communications Symposium, hosted by the Department of National Defence, National Defence Headquarters, Ottawa.

Bain, C. (1990). Transcript of presentation to the Post-Oka Communications Symposium, hosted by the Department of National Defence, National Defence Headquarters, Ottawa.

Begin, P., Moss, W., & Niemczak, P. (1990). *The land claim dispute at Oka*. Ottawa: Research Branch, Library of Parliament.

Brody, E. W. (1988). *Public relations programming and production*. New York: Praeger.

Bury, C. (1990, November). Oka 1990: Covering the crisis wasn't easy. Paper presented to the Post-Oka Communications Symposium, hosted by the Department of National Defence, National Defence Headquarters, Ottawa.

Cogden, D. (1990, November). Transcript of presentation to the Post-Oka Communications Symposium, hosted by the Department of National Defence, National Defence Headquarters, Ottawa.

Editorial. (1991, May 6). *Edmonton Journal*.

Emond, A. (1994, May 30). Oka-Kanesatake: An old conflict resurface[s] in Canada. Contribution to Internet news group on native issues. http://nativenet.uthscsa.edu/archive/nl/9406/0011.html.

Ferguson, S. D. (1994). *Mastering the public opinion challenge*. New York: Richard Irwin Publishing.

Ferguson, S. D. (1999). *Communication planning*. Thousand Oaks, CA: Sage.

Freeman, R. E. (1984). *Strategic management: A stakeholder approach*. Boston: Pitman.

Gitlin, T. (1980). *The whole world is watching*. Berkeley: University of California Press.

Goldenberg, E. N. (1975). *Making the papers*. Lexington, MA: D. C. Heath.

Green, M., & Stier, J. (1991). *A minority conflict in Canada: A case study of the Mohawks and the Oka conflict*. Lund, Sweden: Vaxjo University.

Horovitch, A. (1994, May 27). Contribution to Internet news group on native issues.

Kharbanda, O. P., & Stallworthy, E. A. (1986). *Management disasters and how to prevent them*. Brookfield, VT: Gower.

Kroker, A. (1992). *The possessed individual*. New York: St. Martin's Press.

Lusterman, S. (1988). *Managing federal government relations*. New York: Conference Board.

MacLeod, A. G. (Director). (1993). *Acts of defiance* (film). Montreal: National Film Board.

Meng, M. (1992, March). Early identification aids issues management. *Public Relations Journal*, 22–24.

Monpetit, C. (1990, November). Transcript of presentation to the Post-Oka Communications Symposium, hosted by the Department of National Defence, National Defence Headquarters, Ottawa.

Obomsawin, A. (Director). (1993). *Kanehsatake: 270 years of resistance* (film). Montreal: National Film Board.

Osler, A., & MacFarlane, A. (1991, May). How eleven Canadian newspapers reported Oka. Paper presented at the annual meeting of the Canadian Communication Association, Kingston, Ontario.

Privy Council Office. (1987). Proceedings of the Meech Lake meeting of communications managers, Government of Canada, October 8–9, Meech Lake, Ontario.

Ray, P. (1990, November). Transcript of presentation to the Post-Oka Communications Symposium, hosted by the Department of National Defence, National Defence Headquarters, Ottawa.

Robinson, G. (1990, November). Transcript of presentation to the Post-Oka Communications Symposium, hosted by the Department of National Defence, National Defence Headquarters, Ottawa.

Rose, M. (1991, Fall). Activism in the 90's: Changing roles for public relations. *Public Relations Quarterly*, 28–32.

Roth, L. (1990, November). The "Mohawk Crisis": Reflections on French, English, and Mohawk media coverage. Paper presented to the Post-Oka Communications Symposium, hosted by the Department of National Defence, National Defence Headquarters, Ottawa.

Roth, L. (1993). Mohawk airwaves and cultural challenges: Some reflections on the politics of recognition and cultural appropriation after the summer of 1990. *Canadian Journal of Communication 18* (3), 315–331.

Sandman, P. M. (1993). Regulating risk: The science and politics of risk. Summary of a conference presentation, distributed by Health Canada, Government of Canada, Ottawa.

Scanlon, D. (1990, November). Transcript of presentation to the Post-Oka Communications Symposium, hosted by the Department of National Defence, National Defence Headquarters, Ottawa.

Scanlon, T. J. (1990, November). Transcript of presentation to the Post-Oka Communications Symposium, hosted by the Department of National Defence, National Defence Headquarters, Ottawa.

York, J. (1990, November). Transcript of presentation to the Post-Oka Communications Symposium, hosted by the Department of National Defence, National Defence Headquarters, Ottawa.

Chapter 10

Too Far, Too Fast: The Mobilization of Parents against Neoliberal Restructuring in Ontario

Kirsten Kozolanka

Civic unrest has shadowed the Conservative government of Mike Harris in Ontario since it came to power in 1990 on a neoliberal platform of reducing spending and taxes. The government's 1997 plan to restructure and downsize the education system was a typical example of neoliberal policy in both its inception and implementation. The 10-week journey of the *Education Quality Improvement Act* (Bill 160) from introduction to passage into law should have been uneventful, given the majority government's two-year history of similar legislation and policy initiatives. Instead, this legislation galvanized the public in a way that previous initiatives had not. Despite the considerable efforts of the government to close down the legislative process and exclude the public, parents of school-age children organized themselves into lobby groups and mounted grassroots resistance against the bill and in support of public education. Members of the public at large soon joined the protest movement.

This chapter examines how the Bill 160 campaign[1] came to be a testing ground for the government. To accomplish this central purpose, I look at the political and social environment within which the campaign took place; offer a theoretical framework that is capable of explaining the successes and failures of various stakeholders; and finally, evaluate the communication strategies of parents, teachers, and government against this framework. I explore how the creation of entry points in the emerging neoliberal discourse allowed education stakeholders—both official sources (teachers' unions) and unofficial sources (parents' groups)—to influence media coverage and government actions.

POLITICAL AND ECONOMIC ENVIRONMENT

The Conservative government came to power carrying the neoliberal standard of deficit reduction and institutional restructuring, an ideological mission tied to the changing political economy in Great Britain, New Zealand, and the province of Alberta. The party mapped out its electoral policy platform in a document titled the *Common Sense Revolution*. This neoliberal project comprised three main threads: authoritarianism in law and order, union, and monetary areas; classical liberalism in areas of state intervention; and populism in its appeal (Hall, 1988). Its major tenets were downsizing government in the belief that government cannot do everything, reducing spending across all sectors in the belief that taxes are too high, and reducing the deficit and balancing budgets as a means to securing the future (Scott, 1997). Thus, the policy document linked the political environment directly to the economic environment.

Critical to the legislative success of such projects is the "ideological coherence" of the government agenda, established through legislative patterns (Scott, 1997). The government must adhere to simple, narrowly defined messages delivered by single spokespersons. The messages do not deviate from the policy agenda. Margaret Thatcher of Great Britain pioneered the development of the neoliberal discursive terrain with key words such as *choice, quality,* and *value for money* and formulaic phrases such as *parent choice* and *freedom of choice* (Phillips, 1996).

Soon after the 1995 election, the new minister of education and training said that the government would precipitate an artificial crisis in public education by undermining confidence in the education system (Brennan, 1995; Ibbitson, 1997). This statement to government bureaucrats was captured on videotape. A *Toronto Star* editorial (1995) quoted Ontario Minister John Snobelen as saying on the video: "Creating a useful crisis is part of what this will be about. So the first bunch of communications that the public might hear might be more negative than I would be inclined to talk about (otherwise). . . . Yeah, we need to invent a crisis, and that's not an act of courage, there's some skill involved" ("Minister Plotted," p. A3). The strategy was to provoke a moral panic of the nature described by Hall (1978). The success of this strategy was apparent in the results of a 1998 survey, conducted by the Ontario Institute for Studies in Education (OISE) at the University of Toronto. The survey (conducted after the Bill 160 campaign) showed drops in satisfaction with the quality of public education, whereas earlier OISE surveys (through 1996) had demonstrated that Ontarians were increasingly satisfied with the quality of public education.

THE SOCIAL PRODUCTION OF NEWS

Governments depend on—and dominate—the social production of news in order to reproduce the values and messages of their policy initiatives (Golding, 1990). In recent years, government's ability to dominate media agendas has grown largely out of the spectacular growth in resources and people dedicated to public relations (Ryan, 1991; Tiffen, 1989). As Tiffen writes, "Politics is the only sphere where publicity is the *sine qua non* of successful role performance" (p. 3). This exigency intensifies the interdependence of media and state: journalists depend on official news sources for their political messages, and politicians construct the messages that appeal to journalists (Bennett, 1988; Blumler, 1990). Against the routine backdrop of institutionalized access, governments make it easy for the media by providing them with "institutional accommodation" (Tiffen, p. 33).

The concept of issue framing is directly related to the concept of institutional access. In constructing the news, reporters and editors apply "interpretative frameworks or frames to order information into coherent stories" (Ryan, 1991, p. 75). This standard—yet highly subjective and value-laden process—results in a situation where realities, once set, are seldom changed or successfully challenged. Political interests have an institutional advantage in creating a frame that can effectively exclude other possible frames. Which or whose reality is presented depends on a variety of factors, some of which are surmountable (e.g., resources or knowledge of media imperatives), some of which pose systemic difficulties.

Hall and colleagues (1978) say that powerful or privileged institutional positions ("accredited sources") have become the primary definers of social events. The media, which stand in "structured subordination" to the primary definers, play a secondary role, reflecting and reproducing the interests of the powerful. Dominant forces have no need to dictate directly to the media, because the power relationship is built into the news process.

Unofficial sources find it more difficult to gain credibility through news coverage (Molotch & Lester, 1974). Less frequent access means less familiarity, and less familiarity means less credibility. In addition, claims by unofficial sources require more verification by news gatherers (Ryan, 1991). The lack of visibility of sources in news coverage may reflect news values, lack of resources and finances, lowered credibility, or the changing strategies and capabilities of the sources, among other factors (Ryan, 1991). Yet their alternative visions are crucial to the survival of a public sphere (Schlesinger, 1990). Ryan (1991) says that the task of the unofficial source— whom she calls "challengers"—is to "make visible the dominant frame, and then, prove that there is another equally 'natural' way to perceive reality" (p. 70). In addition, diverse sources create greater accountability for all and better news quality.

When pressure groups or unofficial sources do not have institutionalized access, democratic debate and accountability are jeopardized. Lack of access deprives the public of information required for their participation in the social order (Golding, 1990). Schlesinger's (1990) ideas are relevant in understanding what happened in the Bill 160 campaign, a situation in which sources beyond the usual official and dominant ones entered unexpectedly into the field of discourse and experienced considerable success. In the case of Bill 160, the Ontario government followed the neoliberal campaign strategies in an attempt to bypass the public and ensure easy passage. Interested segments of the public, however, were able to interrupt the neoliberal policy path and prevent the government from undemocratically excluding the public from the debate. Against this theoretical framework, the following discussion will consider the campaign against Bill 160, in terms of political actors, media coverage, and public opinion.

POLITICAL ACTORS IN THE BILL 160 CAMPAIGN

On September 22, 1997, Minister of Education and Training John Snobelen announced the first reading of Bill 160, the *Education Quality Improvement Act*. The bill centralized all aspects of power over education in the hands of the provincial government. The legislative proposal simultaneously undermined the role of school board trustees and imposed new working conditions on teachers without allowing for the usual collective bargaining to take place. The bill contained many clauses that gave the government the right to make decisions concerning education through regulation rather than through legislative processes. Mimicking Thatcherist discourse (Phillips, 1996), the government media release justified these actions by claiming that the education ministry would be providing students with "the highest quality education in Canada in the most cost-effective manner" (MEdT, 1997c).[2]

Given the length and breadth of the bill, it would have been normal for the government to hold extensive public consultations. Instead, the government announced only six days of hearings for the entire province. In addition, the ministry submitted a list of groups to the standing committee clerk, with the instruction that these groups should be approached first to make submissions. Usually, the politically neutral standing committee makes these determinations without provincial intervention. In taking these actions, the government revealed that its communications strategy was to control opposition comment. A similar government communications strategy was critical to the success of New Zealand's *Employment Contracts Act* campaign, an initiative in which policy promotion was "minimized" and "the fine details were not publicly released until the draft legislation was introduced to parliament"(Scott, 1997, p. 189). No time was allowed for opposition to build against the bill. (In Great Britain, the unsuccessful legislative process of the poll tax initiative took 29 months; in New Zealand, the successful passage of the ECA took only five months; Bill 160 took 10 weeks.)

The provincial government strategy signaled its ideological coherence through its repeated message: "Government is flexible about reaching its objectives, but will not compromise its goals" (MEdT, 1997b). Formal partisan opposition to the bill by the Liberals and New Democrats was slow to gather strength and lacked credibility. Moreover, the issue of educational reform had obtained little media coverage in the year leading to Bill 160. Deacon and Golding (1994) state, "If an issue is marginalized by the main political parties, it is highly unlikely to attract consistent attention in the media." Opposition from lobby groups, on the other hand, heated up quickly once the bill was tabled. The first to become involved were the five organizations representing Ontario teachers.[3] Leaders of the Ontario Teachers' Federation (OTF) had been formulating a strategy since January 1996. The OTF strategy entailed getting the support of the membership, a group of 126,000 teachers not used to thinking of themselves as part of organized labor. Key messages in the teachers' plan challenged the usual self-interested frame used in industrial conflicts (see Hartmann, 1975–1976; Knight, 1982): "This is about students in the classroom" (OTF, 1998, p. 9). Their print advertising campaign highlighted the "crisis in the classroom" and their belief that the government was "moving too far, too fast" (OTF, 1998, p. 13). The plan further targeted Minister Snobelen. Television advertising featured an out-of-control car and the personalized message: "Where are you taking us, Mr. Snobelen?" The strategy noted: "We had information that the government had focus tested this tv ad and found the messages were all recognized and had resonance—they were surprised by their effectiveness" (OTF, 1998, p. 18).

According to Schlesinger (1990), sources become "political entrepreneurs" when they attempt to interpret political agendas and shape the interpretation of current issues (p. 79). Deacon and Golding (1994) emphasize that some sources hold considerable economic, political and cultural power, whereas other sources may have to lobby loud and hard to be heard. Sources/actors in the Bill 160 campaign can be grouped into Williams' (1973) three categories: dominant, alternative, and oppositional modes. Williams says that the dominant system can accommodate and tolerate the actors who fall into the *alternative* category. Their ideas do not threaten the dominant system. However, *oppositional* groups want to change society; so the dominant system is not able to accommodate or tolerate these sources or actors.

The Ontario Parent Council (OPC) is a *dominant* group that clearly reflected the government's point of view—not surprising since it is made up of 50 percent government appointees. In that sense, OPC could be called an institutionalized parent voice. The OPC's mandate is to advise the minister on educational issues and suggest ways to involve parents in their children's education (OPC, 1994). The OPC's submission to the Bill 160 consultation repeated the government's main message that "the classroom should be the primary focus of education" (OPC, 1997).

A second *dominant* group is the Education Improvement Commission (EIC), set up by the government in January 1997, with a four-year mandate to study and make recommendations on various aspects of education reform. Its first formal report, *The Road Ahead: A Report on Learning Time, Class Size and Staffing*, was released September 11, 1997, 11 days before the introduction of Bill 160. "We will be looking closely at the recommendations. . . . I look forward to hearing more about the many good ideas that are in this report," said Minister Snobelen in a press release (MEdT, 1997d). Many of the EIC's recommendations were included in the bill. In fact, the government's communications strategy for Bill 160 formulated tactics based on "proposed recommendations expected from the EIC report" (MEdT, 1997b). People for Education (P4E) is a Toronto-based parents' group formed in late 1996 to oppose cuts to education funding. An *alternative* group, P4E works within the system to achieve change or reform. The group has had considerable success in garnering media coverage in the tight Toronto media market, mostly because of creative ideas and the receptiveness of the media to its acknowledged leader, Annie Kidder. P4E started the green ribbon campaign, for example, which saw parents across the province wearing ribbons to draw attention to the importance of public education. P4E is still active in public education in Ontario, often sitting on panels to provide the parent voice.

The Ontario Education Alliance (OEA) is clearly an *oppositional* movement. The ultimate aim of this province-wide coalition of groups and individuals is to create a new vision for education that could lead to a new polity in Ontario (Martell, 1998). Its long-term goals include productive and progressive educational reform, an electoral strategy to defeat the government, and the repeal of Bill 160. The OEA is adept at entering the media frame by showing up at government-sponsored public events and demanding to be heard (Latter, 1998). Because of the grassroots nature of its work, the alliance has also been successful at coordinating press releases with other groups outside Toronto. Even after the Bill 160 campaign, the organization continued to develop policy that presupposes major restructuring of the education system.

An Ottawa-based group of parents, the Coalition for Public Education (CPE), organized a rally to oppose the first cuts to education in late 1996. This action responded to a call from P4E. By 1997, the coalition was well positioned to respond to the first piece of educational reform legislation. CPE worked with the *alternative* group P4E, as well as the *oppositional* group OEA, with whom it was affiliated. CPE acquired an excellent success record in gaining access to the media. Several members of its core working group had extensive communications experience and several were politically active. The group typically responded quickly to issues, created its own media events, developed an e-mail network of 200 and a mailing list of 800, participated in government hearings on various policy initiatives, and spoke on panels and at educational forums. By late 1998, members of the initial working group had formed a new group, Our Schools Our Communities. This new organization was formed to respond to school closings, a then-emerging issue. In effect, CPE ceded its oppositional status to a newly sensitized group of parents pursuing an alternative agenda.

Other *alternative* parent-based groups sprang up across Ontario in response to Bill 160: Simcoe Parents Information Group, Wind-Ex in Windsor, Metro Parents Network in Toronto, Public Education Rights Coalition (PERC) in London, Mothers and Fathers for Education in Thunder Bay, People against Cuts to Education (PACE) in Kitchener-Waterloo, and even Grandparents Opposed to Bill 160 in Guelph. These groups experienced various levels of success in their media strategies. The Kitchener-Waterloo organization PACE, for example, achieved little media attention, although the members followed routine communications strategies to obtain news access (Hofstettner, 1998). The parent groups experienced some success, however, in joint activities undertaken with umbrella groups such as OEA.

Two unofficial sources (i.e., outside the government or dominant sphere), including P4E and OEA, have to contend with the constraints in newsmaking imposed by the social production of news. Articles tend to feature the Ontario government and to exclude the alternative/oppositional messages of their organizations. Also, the groups have to fit into an already-established media frame. Often they must rely on disrupted access to gain entry to the 20 percent of coverage in which ordinary people or "low-power constituencies" appear (Ryan, 1991). Another barrier to inclusion is the oral or informal nature of their resistance, which is not simple to reconstruct (Bergvall & Remlinger, 1996).

Golding and Elliott (1979) say that the media typically demand that unofficial sources present their news as "interesting" rather than "important" (p. 117). Thus the public saw countless images of Annie Kidder at her kitchen sink with her children or wrapping schools with green ribbons. Similarly, the media often used voice-overs of school-based members, politicians, and Ministry of Education officials when broadcasting coverage of events sponsored by Ottawa's CPE. The coalition events became the wallpaper for delivering establishment messages.

Despite the trivialization of some of their efforts, the parents' groups helped to make visible the dominant frame and to create a fledgling, albeit uneven, civil society—the very public presence the government wanted to avoid. Like the poll tax campaign in Great Britain, the political discourse surrounding Bill 160 represents a dynamic interaction among government, media, and the public, despite the efforts of the government to exclude the public.

MEDIA COVERAGE AND PUBLIC OPINION

Until the teachers' walkout, the public was mostly silent on Bill 160. Those fighting the bill were teachers and activist parents. The walkout, occurring midway through Bill 160's legislative path, posed a dilemma for all the players.

Ryan (1991) contends that media frame their coverage of unions in one of two ways: as advocates of justice or as actors in their own self-interest. The government communications strategy for Bill 160 used the self-interest frame in its messages: "We all have to put our own personal interests aside for the sake of our students" (MEdT, 1997b). The media echoed this self-interest frame in its coverage of the walkout. The government frame, routinely used to characterize labor action as self-interested, failed to be persuasive, however, because it was not clear to the public that teachers were self-interested unionists. Moreover, many members of the public questioned government control over education and demanded more democratic processes.

The communications plan of the OTF countered the expected government and media framing in two ways. First, when the government attacked union bosses, "we gave them Eileen Lennon,[4] everyone's grade 3 teacher" (OTF, 1998, p. 25). Second, the OTF (1998) tried to shift the media frame from the special interest frame to the justice frame with the key message: "Teachers are fighting to protect publicly funded education for our students" (p. 23).

Well-reported strategic errors by the government gave credibility to the teachers' campaign against Bill 160; and early in the campaign, Premier Harris shuffled his cabinet, removing John Snobelen as Education Minister. The first defeat for the government was a decided victory for the teachers, who had targeted Snobelen. At a later date, just before the teacher walkout, the New Democratic Party leaked documents to the media, confirming that $667 million more in cuts to education would take place. The government had been denying the possibility of more cuts, and the leak weakened public trust in the government message.

Three days after the walkout began on October 27, the government applied to the court for an injunction to get the teachers back into the classroom, citing "irreparable harm" to students. Four days later, after hearing intervenor submissions from parents' groups (including the OEA and CPE), the court denied the injunction.[5] The denial of the injunction had an explosive effect on the media and the public. Not only did Justice MacPherson deny that irreparable harm was taking place, he made a strong connection between the teachers' motives and the public interest:

The teachers have never engaged in a province-wide strike. They are deeply committed to the education of their students and they have behaved in an entirely peaceful fashion. . . . When they point to serious problems in Bill 160, they say they do so in the public interest. (Ontario Court, 1997)

In interpreting the teachers' motives as advocating justice, the court decision helped to shift the media coverage away from the self-interest frame, typically applied to union actors (Ryan, 1991). The decision also contributed to a blossoming of public and grassroots parent opposition: "Before the injunction decision, parents were divided about the walkout. They were somewhat sympathetic to the teachers, although they didn't quite understand what it was about," says John Crump (1998), spokesperson for the Ottawa-based parents' group Coalition for Public Education. "After the denial [of the injunction], parents and school councils came out of the woodwork begging for information on Bill 160 and asking us, as fellow parents, to come and speak to them."

In keeping with Deacon and Golding's (1994) findings that the public and media mutually reinforce each other, the discourse now reflected a different, contested dynamic. Although the self-interest frame was still in play (parents asked to hear from other parents, not from teachers), both parents and media questioned their previous understandings of the issues at hand. Adjustments in the issue-framing can be seen in editorial coverage in the *Toronto Star*. Between September 22 and December 7, 1997, the *Star* printed 413 news stories and 19 editorials on Bill 160, far more than its competition (the *Globe and Mail* and the *Ottawa Citizen*).

The first *Toronto Star* editorial introduced themes that ran through the whole editorial sequence: *trust and power* ("Can Ontarians Trust the Word of Education Minister John Snobelen?" 1997, p. A30); *tax cuts*, suggesting the government not cut taxes; and the *power and threat of the teachers' unions*. An October 13, 1997, headline warned "Reform Education, Don't Destroy It" (p. A12); but a week later, the *Star* lashed out against the teachers with its October 22, 1997, headline "Teachers' Strike Morally Indefensible" (p. A26).

Editorials also began to suggest compromises that should be made by both sides to prevent a walkout, increasingly taking a harsher anti-teacher tone and noting teachers' self-interest and demands. When the leak about further cuts to education funding became public, the *Toronto Star* wrote that the government's credibility had been "shattered" ("Tory Credibility," 1997, p. E2). An independent poll, taken at the same time as the leak, revealed that 46 percent of Torontonians thought the teachers had been fair and reasonable, compared to 31 percent who supported the government (Ipsos-Read, 1997a).

Still, subsequent editorials continued to take a harsh view of the teachers. After the injunction ruling, which the *Toronto Star* called "surprising" ("Time for Teachers," 1997, p. A22), editorials again urged compromise.

The last editorial, published on November 7, 1997, during the walkout, made unexpected reference to the teachers having won the "battle of public opinion" against the government but urged them to call off the strike ("All Teachers Should," p. A26).

Two weeks of ensuing editorial silence ended with an editorial taking the strongest position to date against Bill 160: "Don't Pass Bill 160 without Major Surgery" (1997, p. C2). For the first time, the editorials mentioned democracy as an issue and warned of the dangers of an education system that is overly dependent on parent volunteers. The writers expressed the fear that such a system would create two unequal tiers. The final editorial referred suddenly to widespread opposition to the bill: "We all owe a debt of gratitude to the hundreds of thousands of Ontarians who created a public debate through a grassroots movement unique in modern history, one that spanned political parties, geography and religion to oppose Bill 160" ("Impact of Bill," 1997, p. A18).

Clearly, the *Toronto Star*, far from leading public opinion, had lagged behind it. As Ipsos-Reid (1997b) polling showed, by the time Bill 160 was passed, public faith that the government was "on the right track" (p. 2) had dropped to the lowest recorded point. Yet analysis of a sample of *Star* editorials indicates that the newspaper adjusted its news frame only when public opinion clearly diverged. In a not atypical fashion, the *Star* first engaged in the kind of institutional accommodation that characterizes government–media relations. Like the government, the *Star* was in a reactive mode to the challenge posed to the discourse.

EVALUATION OF GOVERNMENT STRATEGY

Although not apparent at the outset, the government's strategy for the Bill 160 campaign was flawed. Ibbitson (1998) suggested, in a post-mortem column on Bill 160, that the government had a "thin strategy" (namely, the injunction) (p. E3). When the court denied the injunction, the government had no backup plan or worst-case strategy.

Scott (1997) suggests factors that are relevant to successful (and unsuccessful) communications campaigns waged by neoliberal governments. First, advance notice of an impending campaign is a high-risk strategy. The Ontario government effectively signaled the coming changes earlier in the year in Bill 104, its previous education restructuring legislation. For the actual campaign, however, it took the opposite "blitzkrieg" approach and launched a short, 10-week campaign.

A second condition, essential to successful communications campaigns, relates to the framing of messages. With Bill 160, the denial of the court injunction gave rise to a reframing of the teachers' motives. This reframing resonated with a public who may not have been comfortable with the original frame constructed by the government (the primary definer) and repeated by the media (the secondary definer). As the OTF (1998) communications strategy points out, the government was surprised at the resonance of the teachers' messages.

Third, the Bill 160 campaign revealed a break in the ideological coherence that is necessary to any neoliberal project. The government did not adhere to its proven successful strategy of simple messages. On different occasions, the premier and the provincial treasurer introduced new messages. Without clear messages from its institutionalized sources, the media had to look beyond advocates (sources with vested political interests) to arbiters (sources with expertise who interpret political debate) for its information, allowing for more diverse interpretations of the campaign (Deacon & Golding, 1994).

Fourth, a successful communications campaign works best when one spokesperson becomes familiar to the public. The government began its campaign with John Snobelen, switched to the new education minister Dave Johnson, and then brought in the premier and treasurer Ernie Eves. Each brought different messages, as well as a new face, to the campaign.

Other factors may have been particular to this campaign. The government may have been overly confident from several earlier legislative successes, or it may have been moving "too far, too quickly" (Crump, 1998). In the days following the passage of Bill 160, Ipsos-Reid polling (1997b) found that 68 percent of Ontarians believed that the provincial government had "acted too quickly in making its changes," and 37 percent said the government was moving "much too quickly" (p. 1). These perceptions suggest that the government strategy of not backing down neglected a political interest that was stronger than its ideological interest: "Even if the government is convinced of its own rightness, there may be a stronger political interest in conciliation, to avoid a continuing parade of allegations, the creation of confusion on complex issues and the accumulation of determined enemies" (Tiffen, 1989, p. 190). The government's defense of its legislation was further flawed by the strategic errors that cost public trust. The teachers gained the visible confidence of the public when an Ontario court justice rejected the government's attempt to get an injunction against the teachers. At this point, the public rejected the government and media frames of teachers as self-interested strikers.

CONCLUSION

Bill 160 ended a year of upheaval that repositioned Ontario state–citizen relations and forced individual people across the province to come face-to-face with the everyday meaning of neoliberalism. Still, the Bill 160 debate took place within a framework established by the dominant actors. The main opposition to the bill was not ideological, monolithic, or cohesive. Oppositional voices that called for the repeal of the proposed legislation (such as the OEA) were marginalized. In brief, a number of alternative voices (the teachers' federation, P4E, and most grassroots parents' groups) espoused the message "too far, too fast"—a message that did not challenge the dominant forces behind the restructuring.

In conclusion, the Ontario government in 1997 secured "a degree of sociopolitical and cultural change" but did not gain "total hegemony" (Phillips, 1996, p. 218), because parents and the public were able to interrupt and resist the government discourse at an emergent moment in its reproduction.

NOTES

1. The word *campaign* is used in an operational public relations sense. Although the government may not have been consciously aware that this piece of legislation would have a different policy path than previous ones, the communications group within a government setting prepared a routine communications plan to complement the legislation. Thus, by its existence, a communications plan is a campaign document.

2. Ipsos-Reid (1998, February 23) syndicated polling during the Bill 160 campaign shows that education (at 55 percent) displaced health (at 28 percent) as both the top concern and the top driver of Ontario voter disapproval.

3. The five teachers' federations follow: Ontario Secondary School Teachers' Federation, Federation of Women Teachers' Associations of Ontario, Ontario Catholic Teachers Association, Ontario Public School Teachers Federation, and Association des Enseignnant/e/s de l'Ontario.

4. Eileen Lennon, an elementary school teacher, was president of the Ontario Teachers' Federation at the time of the walkout.

5. Ministry communications plans, obtained under *Freedom of Information* legislation, show that the government had an issues management plan for a teacher walkout, but this plan related only to ensuring that ministry communications work continued in the event that teachers blocked access to government buildings. The document, "Contingency Plan: Communications Support Team," did not address changing the policy path (MEdT, 1997a).

REFERENCES

All teachers should call off strike [Editorial]. (1997, November 7). *Toronto Star*, p. A26.

Bennett, W. L. (1988). *News: The politics of illusion*. New York: Longman.

Bergvall, V., & Remlinger, K. (1996). Reproduction, resistance and gender: The role of critical discourse analysis. *Discourse & Society* 7 (4), 453–479.

Blumler, J. (1990). Elections, the media and the modern publicity process. In M. Ferguson (Ed.), *Public communication: The new imperatives* (pp. 101–113). London: Macmillan.

Brennan, R. (1995, September 13). Minister plotted to "invent a crisis": Snobelen video spurs angry calls for him to resign. *Toronto Star*, p. A3.

Can Ontarians trust the word of education minister John Snobelen? [Editorial]. (1997, September 25). *Toronto Star*, p. A30.

Crump, J. (Coalition for Public Education). (1998, March). Personal interview. Ottawa.

Deacon, D., & Golding, P. (1994). *Taxation and representation: The media, political communication and the poll tax*. London: John Libbey.

Don't pass Bill 160 without major surgery [Editorial]. (1997, November 22). *Toronto Star*, p. C2.

Golding, P. (1990). Political communication and citizenship: The media and democracy in an inegalitarian social order. In M. Ferguson (Ed.), *Public communication: The new imperatives* (pp. 84–100). London: Macmillan.

Golding, P., & Elliott, P. (1979). *Making the news*. London: Longman.

Hall, S. (1988). *Thatcherism and the crisis of the left: The hard road to renewal*. London: Verso.

Hall, S., Critcher, C., Jefferson, T., Clarke, J., & Roberts, B. (1978). *Policing the crisis: Mugging, the state and law and order*. London: Macmillan.

Hartmann, P. (1975/1976). Industrial relations news in the mass media. *Industrial Relations 6* (6), 4–18.

Hofstettner, J. (1998, April). People against cuts to education. E-mail communication.

Ibbitson, J. (1997). *Promised land: Inside the Mike Harris revolution*. Scarborough, ON: Prentice Hall.

Ibbitson, J. (1998, January 10). Farewell to the whiz kids: The center of political power inside the Harris government is changing. *Ottawa Citizen*, p. E3.

Impact of Bill 160 remains to be seen [Editorial]. (1997, December 2). *Toronto Star*, p. A18.

Ipsos-Reid (Angus Reid Group). (1997a, November 4). *Pulse of Toronto poll* [published report of poll results]. Toronto.

Ipsos-Reid (Angus Reid Group). (1997b, December 16). *The Ontario political scene* [published report of poll results]. Toronto.

Ipsos-Reid. (1998, February 23). *The Ontario political scene* [published report of poll results]. Toronto.

Knight, G. (1982). Strike talk: A case study of news. *Canadian Journal of Communication 8* (2), 61–79.

Latter, J. (1998, March). (Ontario Education Alliance). Telephone interview.

Martell, G. (1998, March). (Ontario Education Alliance). Telephone interview.

Minister plotted "to invent a crisis," Snobelen video spurs angry calls for him to resign. (1995, September 13). *Toronto Star*, p. A3.

Molotch, H., & Lester, M. (1974). News as purposive behavior. *American Sociological Review 39*, 101–112.

Ontario. Ministry of Education and Training (MEdT). (1997a). Contingency plan: Communications support team (communications plan). Toronto.

Ontario. Ministry of Education and Training (MEdT). (1997b). Government critical path for Bill 106 [sic] stakeholder relations (communications plan). Toronto.

Ontario. Ministry of Education and Training (MEdT). (1997c). New legislation ensures quality education. Press release, September 22, 1997, Toronto.

Ontario. Ministry of Education and Training (MEdT). (1997d). Snobelen welcomes EIC report. Press release, September 11, 1997, Toronto.

Ontario Court (General Division). Toronto Region. (1997, November 3). Reason for judgment. Court file No. 97-cv-134721.

Ontario Institute for Studies in Education (OISE). (1996). Highlights of the 11th OISE survey of educational issues. www.oise.utoronto.ca/OISE-Survey/hilites.html.

Ontario Institute for Studies in Education (OISE). (1998). Highlights of the 1998 OISE survey. www.oise.utoronto.ca/OISE-Survey/hilites.html.

Ontario Parent Council (OPC). (1994). *Annual report,* November 1993–April 1994. www.edu.gov.on.ca/eng/general/abcs/parentco/focus.

Ontario Parent Council (OPC). (1997, October 21). Submission by the Ontario Parent Council to the Standing Committee on the Administration of Justice regarding Bill 160, *The Education Quality Improvement Act.* Toronto.

Ontario Teachers' Federation (OTF). (1998, March 4). Ontario's teachers: A case in gaining public support. Presentation to a media panel discussion sponsored by the Public Affairs Association of Canada. Toronto.

Phillips, L. (1996). Rhetoric and the spread of the discourse of Thatcherism. *Discourse & Society* 7 (2), 209–241.

Reform education, don't destroy it [Editorial]. (1997, October 13). *Toronto Star,* p. A12.

Ryan, C. (1991). *Prime time activism: Media strategies for grassroots organizing.* Boston: South End Press.

Schlesinger, P. (1990). Rethinking the sociology of journalism: Source strategies and the limits of media-centrism. In M. Ferguson (Ed.), *Public communication: The new imperatives* (pp. 61–83). London: Macmillan.

Scott, J. M. (1995). Neo-liberalism at work: Media-politics and the *Employment Contracts Act.* Unpublished Master of Arts thesis, University of Auckland, New Zealand.

Scott, J. M. (1997). Communication campaigns and the neo-liberal policy agenda. *Media, Culture & Society* 19 (2), 183–199.

Snobelen switch [Editorial]. (1997, September 25). *Toronto Star,* p. A30.

Teachers' strike morally indefensible [Editorial]. (1997, October 22), *Toronto Star,* p. A26.

Time for teachers to go back to class [Editorial]. (1997, November 4). *Toronto Star,* p. A22.

Tory credibility on schools is shattered [Editorial]. (1997, October 25). *Toronto Star,* p. E2.

Tiffen, R. (1989). *News and power.* Sydney, Australia: Allen and Unwin.

Williams, R. (1973). Base and superstructure in Marxist cultural theory. *New Left Review* 82, 3–16.

Chapter 11

The Moccasin Telegraph Goes Digital: First Nations and the Political Usage of the Internet

David Kim Juniper

> Technology is changing the equations of power, challenging the conventional channels of communication, distributing and disseminating influence in the broadest possible fashion, to the point of democratizing the channels and getting rid of the gatekeeper. . . . The technology has a mind-boggling potential to break through barriers and overcome political obstacles to educate, inform and be an agent of political change. . . . The mouse is mightier than the missile. (Lloyd Axworthy, Canadian Minister for Foreign Affairs and International Trade, 1998)

During the 1994 Zapatista "netwar," the Internet proved to be a powerful political tool, capable of reaching thousands—if not millions—of people. As the World Wide Web has grown in popularity and accessibility, First Nations peoples have realized its informational potential. Native Canadians are making their presence known. Whether the cause is political sovereignty for the Nisga'a or the rights of Mi'kmaq lobster fishers, First Nations peoples are using new communications technologies to overcome a history of political and geographical isolation. They are becoming linked to each other through web sites, discussion forums, and mailing lists. This chapter explores this new stage in Aboriginal history. More specifically, I look at how the acephalous nature of online networks creates a dynamic medium, largely free from political censorship and control, which enables First Nations peoples to forge new webs of resistance and cooperation.

Understanding the acephalous nature of the network systems that carry online communications is critical to comprehending the political implications of the Internet. The Internet has no central authority or headquarters

(Sterling, 1993). Host to millions of users involved in transnational interactions, the Internet offers a profound challenge to the state with regard
to sovereignty and information control. Attempts to exert control, in a
situation where large numbers of web sites come online every day, are
destined to fail. The impossibility of controlling this medium, however, has
not stopped states from making the effort. In 1996, the U.S. government
passed the *Communications Decency Act*, a bill proposed by U.S. Senator
James Exon. This act would have criminalized the transfer of any material
(over fax, e-mail, html, or any other digital medium) deemed "unsuitable"
for children. Fines would have ranged to U.S. $100,000, and jail sentences
would have been an option. The far-reaching nature of the vague and subjective terminology of the *Act* would have given the state the authority to
extend its power over the Internet and censor any material deemed "ob-
scene," whether or not its creators broke existing criminal laws.

Writing on the potential impact of such bills as the *Communications
Decency Act* and its successor, the *Child Online Protection Act*, Harrington
(1996) contrasted the Internet as a "marketplace of ideas" with the Clinton
administration's vision of censorship and control:

We ought to exult in the explosion of the Internet's unrestrained expression; the
passionate desire to convey ideas and expand creativity is a hundred times better
than commercial media's suffocating programs, milquetoast news or boring sound
bytes. Mr. Exon's misguided proposal would send a message to Internet users
around the world that the United States is more interested in becoming a cybercop
than fostering a global marketplace of ideas where all can speak without fear and
in the hope of bettering the human condition. (p. 159)

Studies dating back to the 1940s and 1950s focused on the importance
of control in spreading information and maintaining a structured system
or society (Arquilla & Ronfelt, 1997c). Control, it was believed, was necessary to maintain an order within which information can easily spread.

COORDINATION VERSUS CONTROL AS A PARADIGM

These control paradigms have failed, however, in the case of the Internet,
due largely to its spider-like structure; and recent research suggests a more
decentralized, flexible approach may be the best operating strategy for governing Internet communication. This approach calls for *coordination* instead of control. Instead of seeking mastery over the chaos of cyberspace,
a coordinated approach sees its nebulous, morphing nature as a fertile field
of possibilities. Such a view concentrates on merging with the network
rather than trying to control it.

A classical communication model, proposed by Maier (1967), uses the
starfish analogy as a way to look at group interactions. A central nerve

ring coordinates the functioning of the rays of a starfish. This nerve ring receives and processes data, and locomotion occurs as a result of coordinating individual responses. Thus, the individual rays become part of a higher organism. Applying the starfish analogy to group processes, Maier argued the superiority of a cooperative model over a persuasive model of communication. Making the linkage to communication behaviors, Maier said that persuasive communication (a model that involves control rather than coordination) entails taking and defending a position, listening selectively in order to refute the arguments of the other parties, dominating the discussion, reacting unfavorably to critical comments, and interacting only with selected members of the group. Persuasive communication involves, at best, a series of interpersonal interactions, in which individuals have an agenda and maintain their identities. In persuasion, the seller of the idea typically presents several options but argues in favor of one "best solution." Conflict occurs when the parties do not agree on the "best" solution. Problem-solving behaviors, on the other hand, involve other kinds of communication patterns. As participants become a part of the group dynamic, they cease to pursue individual goals; and, instead of interacting with individuals, they interact with the group. Unlike situations involving persuasion, the solution to the problem is unknown at the beginning of the communication process. Through group interaction, members of the network or group discover or invent the solution. Thus, coordination is superior to control. Returning to the analogy of the starfish, Maier says that actions by dominant rays can sometimes destroy a starfish, causing a "locking" and division of the organism.

Arquilla and Ronfelt (1997b), analysts with the American RAND Corporation, have reached similar conclusions about the functioning of the Internet. In a recent book dealing with notions of online warfare and political conflict, the analysts discuss the implications in a model that seeks to coordinate rather than to control the Internet. "Control and coordination are different," they argue, "sometimes contrary processes; indeed, the exertion of excessive control in order to avoid entropy may inhibit the looser, decentralized types of coordination that often characterize advanced forms of complex systems" (p. 148).

Combined with the speed and effectiveness of online communications, the rise of coordination as an organizational strategy has contributed to the formation of a global civil society. The Internet links this worldwide community of like-minded individuals and non-governmental organizations. Although the environmental, feminist, libertarian, and labor groups that constitute global civil society existed prior to the rise of the Internet, they remained isolated from each other by geographical distance as well as state boundaries. Also the various organizations operated each with its own structure and leadership. In cyberspace, however, the diverse groups found the means to unite into powerful, transnational collectives. These networked actors have distinguished themselves in the recent past in such campaigns as the defeat of the Multilateral Agreement on Investment (MAI), as well as the ongoing Zapatista campaign. These successes have occurred in the absence of a central leadership that could act as a "nerve ring" (referring back to the analogy of the starfish).

Although the specific agendas of each group differ, their "common interests and objectives" enable them to act without benefit of a common leader. The idea becomes the motivating force for action. Among these commonly held ideals are commitments to fight against the oppression of minorities and racism and to fight for the protection of the environment (Frederick, 1993, p. 272). These commitments and a powerful common vision displace traditional concepts of leadership and offer a means to coordinate the responses of individual members (nodes) of the network:

Such a doctrine can enable them to be "all of one mind" even if they are dispersed and devoted to different tasks. It can provide an ideational, strategic, and operational centrality that allows for tactical decentralization. It can set boundaries and provide guidelines for decisions and actions so that they do not have to resort to a hierarchy—"they know what they have to do." (Arquilla & Ronfelt, 1997d, p. 280)

HIERARCHIES GIVE WAY TO NETWORKS AND HARD POWER GIVES WAY TO SOFT POWER

The rise of the Internet as a communication medium has had revolutionary effects on existing authority structures, for this medium presents a profound challenge to fundamental notions of power. As a child of the digital, or "information," revolution, the Internet embodies many of the hallmarks of the digital age from which it sprang. Arquilla and Ronfelt (1997a) discuss the impact of what Toffler and Toffler (1980) termed the "third wave" on industrial-era institutional structures:

The information revolution, in both its technological and non-technological aspects, sets in motion forces that challenge the design of many institutions. It disrupts and erodes the hierarchies around which institutions are normally designed. It diffuses and redistributes power, often to the benefit of what may be considered weaker, smaller actors. It crosses borders and redraws the boundary of offices and responsibilities. . . . The network form is very different from the institutional form. While institutions (large ones in particular) are traditionally built around hierarchies and aim to act on their own, multi-organizational networks consist of (often small) organizations or parts of institutions that have linked together to act jointly. The information revolution favors the growth of such networks by making it possible for diverse, dispersed actors to communicate, consult, coordinate, and operate together across greater distances and on the basis of more and better information than ever before. (pp. 26–27)

In order to identify and categorize this new threat to the political and economic *status quo*, Arquilla and Ronfelt (1997a) describe network-based activism as *netwar*. Netwar, a mode involving the use of soft power in information-oriented conflicts, typically involves small, semi-independent individuals or parties acting in concert:

[Netwar is a] mode of conflict (and crime) at societal levels, involving measures short of war, in which the protagonists use—indeed, depend on using, network forms of organization, doctrine, strategy, and communication. These protagonists generally consist of dispersed, often small groups who agree to communicate, and act in an internetted manner, often without a precise central leadership or head-quarters. Decisionmaking may be deliberately decentralized and dispersed. (Arquilla & Ronfelt 1997d, p. 277)

Following a strategy espoused by the Advanced Research Projects Agency, Department of Defense, the networked activists adopt speed and flexibility as their main tactics. Through a structural design that is aceph-alous in nature, the activists negate the possibility of a "quick kill," a means by which opponents strike at leaders to disable a campaign. Enveloped in a "digital cloak," these activists rapidly spread information and undermine the credibility of their opponents while avoiding discovery and possible termination by the state. Because of their speed and skill in navigating digital space, activists in conflict with traditional hierarchical structures generally force their opponents to adopt a defensive posture.

Rather than relying on intimidation and the threat of physical force, activists involved in netwar aim to capture the hearts and minds of the receivers. In contrast to "hard" warfare, a well-implemented strategy using "soft power" allows the protagonist to choose the battlefield and vanquish the foe without ever announcing that a battle is in progress. When military analyst Szafranski (1997) talks about the aims of war, he sounds very much like Maier (1967) discussing the objectives of persuasion. Szafranski says that the object of war is to "force or encourage the enemy to make what you assert is a better choice, or to choose what *you* desire the enemy to choose" (p. 397):

Said another way, the object of war is to subdue the hostile will of the enemy. . . . If the object of war truly is to *subdue hostile will* or *to make the opponent comply with our will*, then we must consider enemies not just as systems, but as organisms with will. Likewise, if weapons are *means used to coerce an adversary's will*, then even our understanding of weapons must go beyond things, implements or tools. (p. 397; emphasis added)

Perhaps this understanding needs to include the kind of resources em-ployed in "soft power," a concept discussed extensively by political analyst Nye (1994). Nye says that soft power draws on intangible resources such as "culture, ideology, and institutions" and even "attractive ideas" (p. 138). Philosophers, as well as political leaders, have long understood the capacity of soft power to "set the political agenda and determine the framework of the debate in a way that shapes others' preferences" (p. 138). In an online essay, Canadian Foreign Minister Lloyd Axworthy (1998) discusses the nature and importance of soft power in achieving government goals:

Soft power is the art of disseminating information in such a way that desirable outcomes are achieved through persuasion rather than coercion. Because it sets the terms of the debate, soft power influences the nature of the solution. It blurs, even counters, the perception of traditional power assets, such as military force, economic might, resources, and population. Power in this context is obtained from networking and coalition-building. To wield soft power will require a mastery of information technologies to ensure that Canada has a superior knowledge base. The government will have to call on all of the resources at its disposal to manage information and to develop innovative foreign policy tools.

Axworthy (1998) continues by noting the powerful effects of soft power strategies applied at the international level. An attractive set of values and an image as a trustworthy partner encourage other countries to consider and weigh our views. In the soft power context, Canada benefits from its status as an open, industrialized society where most citizens visibly enjoy a high quality of life and protection of their human rights.

THE FORGING OF NETWORKS OF RESISTANCE: NATIVES IN CYBERSPACE

Not all Canadians enjoy the same privileges, however. First Nations peoples, the recipients of a history of neglect and racist policies on the part of the Canadian government, have become a much more visible and vocal component of global civil society, and they use the Internet to make their voices heard in international spheres. The result has been the growth of networks of resistance that include First Nations peoples in Canada, the United States, Mexico, and Australia. Other members of global civil society such as environmental, feminist, and civil rights groups have also adopted the indigenous cause.

The standoff at Esgenoopetitj in the summer and fall of 2000 and the resulting Internet campaign arising from the conflict offer a good example of contemporary uses of the Internet by First Nations peoples. Sparked by differing interpretations of the Marshall Decision[1] of 1999, the resulting conflict over Mi'kmaq lobster harvesting rights pitted two Mi'kmaq communities against non-Native fishers, the Department of Fisheries and Oceans, and the Royal Canadian Mounted Police (RCMP). Through their own efforts and those of a web of supporters, the Mi'kmaq sought to gain support for the their cause by arguing the historical basis of their grievance. By offering a mix of eyewitness accounts, as well as audio and video footage, the Mi'kmaq showed how Canada was breaking its own laws in persecuting the First Nations peoples living within its borders.

In an article posted on the web site for *Eastern Door*, a newspaper published by the Mohawk community of Kahnawake, university student Tracy Sinclair describes her experiences in Esgenoopetitj (Zemel, 2000). Present as a human rights observer, Sinclair witnessed the deliberate ramming of a Mi'kmaq fishing boat by a government launch—a scene filmed on video and later displayed on web sites. Following her arrest by the RCMP, Sinclair warned, "Screen yourself from the generous censorship, and the blatant lying of the government in their press releases and the papers. Do not tolerate the blatant violations of human rights. This all sounds so radical and far away, but it's happening at home" (Zemel, 2000). Sinclair's allusion to state censorship comes partly from her claim that her video camera, used to film the altercation, was seized by the police.

Among the many web sites dedicated to the Esgenoopetitj conflict were an ongoing series of news pages prepared by the Canadian Broadcasting Corporation (CBC), a page built on-site by Mi'kmaq students, and the home page for the Assembly of First Nations. Although not part of the Mi'kmaq online campaign per se, the ongoing online coverage of the conflict by the CBC, as well as its deeper exploration of the issue, provided an excellent source of information. In addition to written accounts, the site provided both audio and video clips, bringing the events to life for web site visitors. Detailed reflection on the issue appeared in a section entitled "Fishing Fury."[2] This part of the web site defined and discussed the relevance of the Marshall Decision of 1999 to both Esgenoopetitj and other Native communities, who could potentially become involved in future disputes over fishing rights. One of the most significant parts of the "Fishing Fury" web site is the diaries or written accounts of observers in Esgenoopetitj. One of the entries, penned by Fenton Somerville (2000), a longtime resident of Esgenoopetitj, provides an in-depth and arresting narrative of life during those months of confrontation. Among his ruminations, Somerville questions the meaning of the Canadian identity: "How can I value anything Canadian any more," he writes, "when we are treated like common criminals for a right that is recognised by the Supreme Court?" Further, he describes "the image of the non-native fisherman wearing a wig and doing a war dance on the boat," reinforcing notions of intense racism. In one of the last entries, he asserts, "This is no way for anybody to live, especially in Canada." Thus, Somerville emphasizes the discrepancy between the Canadian dream, as it were, and the reality.

The home page for the Assembly of First Nations (AFN),[3] the Ottawa-based national organization representing all of Canada's First Nations peoples, is a comprehensive resource for many of the issues facing Canada's native peoples. A section titled "Burnt Church News" includes a list of links to materials relevant to the conflict. Among these links are CBC news broadcasts, TV interviews with Native leaders, home pages for First Nations organizations, and a number of personal web pages. One of Canada's foremost indigenous voices, the AFN has the power to bring many issues into the public eye by making online resources easily accessible. The AFN sends out a quiet "call-to-arms" when it posts the telephone numbers, fax numbers, and e-mail addresses of prominent politicians such as the prime minister and the Minister for Fisheries and Oceans on the Internet. In this way, the AFN uses the Internet as an active medium, providing visitors with an immediate way to voice their concerns to those in power.

Another web site, probably conceived locally, News from Esgenoopetitj offers a direct experience of what is happening on the reserve and in Miramichi Bay. The graphics show members of the Mi'kmaq nation smiling before a Department of Fisheries and Oceans (DFO) sign and surrounded by banners declaring their freedom to fish according to traditional ways. This site also offers letters that can serve as models for those who want to write to authority figures, as well as contact information for politicians. Prominent on the page is background information on the conflict. A traditional prayer and the description of a fasting ceremony before DFO offices bring a spiritual element to coverage of the conflict. Although not so polished as the earlier sites that were discussed, the News from Esgenoopetitj offers images and voices that do not appear on the bigger web sites.

A photograph of what appears to be a barricade at Oka during the conflict of 1990 links the CBC "Fishing Fury" site to events at Esgenoopetitj and Kanehsatake. Although there was no evidence of weapons among the Mi'kmaq nor the same degree of militancy as seen in Kanehsatake in 1990, the photograph appears to suggest First Nations conflicts do not occur in isolation but rather symbolize part of a greater struggle. This same spirit of unity can be seen online as other First Nations post material, pledge allegiance, or provide online space for information about the conflicts. An example can be seen on "Tyendinaga Mohawk Territory,"[4] a comprehensive web site created and maintained by the First Nations Technical Institute in Tyendinaga. The site includes a forum where participants discuss topics that range from land claims to fry bread recipes. The forum is very large and obviously in heavy use. References to Esgenoopetitj included calls to action, questions about how best to proceed, and a request by Mi'kmaq warriors for donations of equipment such as zodiacs, binoculars, and night vision goggles. A participant in the forum had posted a link to the Aboriginal Rights Coalition,[5] an organization that included both Aboriginal people and non-Natives active in the defense of indigenous peoples in Canada. Questions posted by non-Native researchers asked about various aspects of Mohawk culture and history. The Tyendinaga discussion forum is an excellent example of the Internet as a vibrant marketplace of ideas and a dynamic space alive with social, cultural, and political discourse free from state censorship and control.

CONCLUSION

The Tyendinaga discussion forum and others like it across the Internet are bringing the Native voice to the world stage. Long silenced by both governmental action and geographical isolation, First Nations peoples are reaching around the globe to gather support. The fundamentally acephalous structure of the Internet enables wired activists to circumvent traditional media and state censorship and to tell their stories directly to members of the growing global civil society. As the strength of civil society increases with the growth of computer-mediated communication, First Nations peoples may find sympathetic allies in their struggle to achieve a more powerful voice and presence in Canadian society and to reclaim their rights. Through the new information and communication technologies, Native peoples can forge networks and access a greater pool of knowledge and support than ever before to assist in achieving these goals.

NOTES

1. For background information on the Marshall Decision, see the CBC web site at http://cbc.ca/news/indepth/fishing/marshall.html.
2. http://cbc.ca/news/indepth/fishing/index.html.
3. http://www.afn.ca.
4. http://www.tyendinaga.net.
5. http://www.home.istar.ca/~arc/.

REFERENCES

Arquilla, J., & Ronfelt, D. (1997a). Cyberwar is coming! In J. Arquilla & D. Ronfelt (Eds.), *In Athena's camp: Preparing for conflict in the information age* (pp. 23–60). Santa Monica, CA: RAND.

Arquilla, J., & Ronfelt, D. (1997b). Information, power, and grand strategy: In Athena's camp—Section 1. In J. Arquilla & D. Ronfelt (Eds.), *In Athena's camp: Preparing for conflict in the information age* (pp. 141–171). Santa Monica, CA: RAND.

Arquilla, J., & Ronfelt, D. (1997c). Looking ahead: Preparing for information-age conflict (pp. 439–501). In J. Arquilla & D. Ronfelt (Eds.), *In Athena's camp: Preparing for conflict in the information age.* Santa Monica, CA: RAND.

Arquilla, J., & Ronfelt, D. (1997d). The advent of netwar. In J. Arquilla & D. Ronfelt (Eds.), *In Athena's camp: Preparing for conflict in the information age* (pp. 275–293). Santa Monica, CA: RAND.

Axworthy, L. (1998). Canada and human security: The need for leadership. *Can-

ada. *Department of Foreign Affairs and International Trade*. http://www. dfait-maeci.gc.ca/english/foreignp/sechume.htm.

Frederick, H. (1993). *Global communications and international relations*. Belmont, CA: Wadsworth.

Harrington, J. (1996). Beware of chilling freedom of expression. In V. J. Vitanza (Ed.), *CyberReader* (pp. 157–159). Needham Heights, MA: Allyn & Bacon.

Maier, R. F. (1967). Assets and liabilities in group problem-solving: The need for an integrative function. *Psychological Review 74*, 239–249.

Nye, J. (1994). Soft power. In G. Hastedt & K. Knickrehm (Eds.), *Toward the twenty-first century: A reader in world politics* (pp. 135–141). Englewood Cliffs, NJ: Prentice-Hall.

Somerville, F. (2000, September 14). Diaries. *CBC News*. http://cbc.ca/news/ indepth/fishing/diary.html.

Sterling, B. (1993, February). *Fantasy and science fiction*. http:// www.forthnet.gr/ forthnet/isoc/short.history.of.internet.

Szafranski, R. (1997). Neocortical warfare? The acme of skill. In J. Arquilla & D. Ronfelt (Eds.), *In Athena's camp: Preparing for conflict in the information age* (pp. 395–416). Santa Monica, CA: RAND.

Toffler, A., & Toffler, H. (1980). *The third wave*. New York: William Morrow.

Zemel, K. D. (2000, October 19). Burnt church human rights observer arrested: Observer shares what she feels the media has twisted. *The Eastern Door*. http://www.easterndoor.com/deer/9-38/9-38-4.htm.

Part IV

Regional Voices, Political Issues, and Civil Society

Chapter 12

The Internet as a Space for Civic Discourse: The Case of the Unity Debate in Canada

Chantal Benoit-Barné

In North America, we have the possibility to have debates over the Internet via different newsgroups, but we destroy this incredible chance by insulting each other. The technology is there, but we don't use it properly. We have to exploit this great window of opportunities to enrich our democracy and our freedom as citizens of a nation. Please, try to be tolerant toward Sovereigntists and toward federalists. (Thomas H.,[1] participant in qc.politique)

This excerpt appears as part of a lengthy bilingual message posted on qc.politique, a Usenet electronic discussion group devoted to political issues in Québec. The author of this message draws our attention to the democratic potential of electronic discussion groups. At the same time, he suggests that, in qc.politique, the discursive practices of the participants severely compromise this potential: "Au lieu d'essayer de 'construire des ponts,' vous vous envoyez chier comme des innocents de cours d'école! Demandez-vous pas pourquoi rien ne marche au Canada et au Québec. Les gens des deux positions ne font que se hurler dessus au lieu de s'expliquer avec des termes adéquats et polis."[2] Thomas H. deplores the fact that participants in qc.politique debates are polarized along clear ideological lines—sovereigntists or federalists. They are either in favor of Québec seceding from Canada or in favor of unity. Evidence of this bipolarization includes the constant use of *us/them* language, self-identification of participants as sovereigntists or federalists, and categorization of other members based on the content of their messages. For Thomas H., these discursive practices prevent qc.politique from fulfilling its democratic potential.

Rather than accepting such assertions at face value, this chapter aims to judge their validity by determining if—and how—electronic discussion groups can contribute to the functioning of contemporary democratic societies. More specifically, this chapter will (1) describe three theoretical lenses that we can use to study the contributions of Internet technology to civic life, (2) consider how a pluralistic model of the public sphere can inform our understanding of the current functions of the Internet in our society, and (3) look at the two main ways in which electronic discussion groups presently contribute to civil society. Finally, I conclude the chapter with an example from qc.politique to illustrate how this process is unfolding in a uniquely Canadian context.

INTERNET AS SITE OF CIVIC DISCOURSE

Much scholarly debate now takes place over the alleged contribution of Internet technologies to civic life in Canada. Over the last 10 years, the Internet has become a new space for civic discourse. Increasingly, groups seeking to have their voices heard within the public realm rely on Internet technology to promote their views, to attract new supporters, to institute a network among geographically dispersed members, and to engage the citizens of Canada in discussions about their issues.

The Canadian government has followed this trend. It now relies on Internet technologies (in particular, the World Wide Web and e-mail) to distribute public information and, in some instances, to consult the citizens of Canada on issues of public interest. In the same way, many citizens have turned to the Internet to buy new goods, as well as to obtain the information they need to make sound civic judgments and to engage each other in discussions about issues of private and public interest. For them, the Internet is both a public square and a shopping mall, as much a site of civic discourse as a place of consumption.

In sum, this "civic Internet" currently functions as (1) a source of information about problems of public significance; (2) a mode of communication among and between citizens, organized coalitions, and the state; (3) a tool for public deliberation and public participation in decision making; and (4) a new action tool, allowing marginalized groups to influence public opinion and state actions. Albeit a reality, the extent and quality of its contributions to civil society and its attendant public spheres remain to be determined.

THREE THEORETICAL PERSPECTIVES

This investigation into the place of Internet technology in civic life begins with a fundamental question: How can scholars interested in the state of the contemporary public realm best study the place of Internet technology in civic life? Or, to put it differently, what are some of the assumptions these scholars make about technology when exploring the interplay between Internet technology and the public realm? Taking this question as a starting point, I turn to the growing body of research on computer-based communication.

This literature points to at least three theoretical lenses that can be used by scholars interested in the role of Internet technology (IT) in civil society. The following metaphors represent the three perspectives: IT as an expansion of the social world, IT as a filter of the communication process, and IT as a transformative force. Each metaphor relies on a unique set of assumptions, has implications for how we can study the role of IT in public life, and calls upon particular avenues of inquiry.

Internet Technology as an Expansion of the Social World (IT Extends Civic Life)

This first perspective calls our attention to the ways in which networked computer-based communication technologies, such as the Internet, increase opportunities for social interaction by creating a new type of public space. The perspective relies on the beliefs that (a) networked computer-based communication technologies create a type of public space in which our communicative interactions can take place; (b) while this new container of public life might have particular attributes, its unique characteristics do not alter significantly the nature and purpose of our communicative interactions; thus (c) mediated and unmediated communicative interactions are fundamentally comparable. The literature on virtual communities is particularly representative of this approach. The literature generally focuses on the characteristics of electronic spaces generated by the interconnectivity of the participants' computers and on the practices of those involved in these new kinds of environments in order to explain how these phenomena contribute to society (e.g., Jones, 1995, 1997).

Applied specifically to the study of civic life, this approach suggests that IT can enhance civil society by creating new electronic public spaces. This perspective focuses particularly on the possibility to interact with others who were once out of reach and to replace the vanishing public spaces of Western societies with virtual public spaces. The ultimate objective of this approach is to understand and describe how individuals (rhetors, audience members, citizens, and others) adapt to these new computer-based environments: how they establish, use, and control these virtual public spaces and how they adapt their discourse to its unique spatial-temporal characteristics. Thus, the first perspective legitimates the recourse to public sphere theories in order to define precisely the kinds of contributions electronic discussion groups can make to civic life.

Internet Technology as a Filter in the Communication Process (IT Filters Civic Life)

The second perspective focuses on the ways in which IT can enhance or weaken the state of public life by mediating our face-to-face public inter-actions and imposing conditions that can either conflict with or facilitate their unfolding. This approach relies on the assumption that face-to-face communication is the archetype of human communication. The approach suggests that, while technological mediation alters the nature of our face-to-face interactions, it does not compromise the primacy of face-to-face communication in public life or alter its fundamental characteristics. In other words, mediated reactions are but a variation of face-to-face (FtF) interaction: FtF + IT. This model presumes that one can recover the characteristics of face-to-face communication by simply stopping the use of the technology. Thus, while the previous perspective implies that unmediated and mediated forms of engagement are fundamentally comparable, this approach views mediated encounters as a subset of unmediated communication and focuses on the link between the two.

Computer-mediated communication research often adopts this second approach. These studies often contrast computer-mediated communication and face-to-face communication. Various studies have identified (1) characteristics of computer-mediated communication that may hinder the development of social relationships (see Dubrovsky, Kiesler, & Sethna, 1991; Sproull & Kiesler, 1986; Walther, 1996; Walther & Burgoon, 1992); (2) practices that users implement in order to overcome the technical restrictions of the computer medium (see Bechar-Israeli, 1995; Marvin, 1995; Park & Floyd, 1996; Wilkins, 1991); and (3) ways in which users complement their computer-mediated interactions with other forms of communication (see Reid, 1991; Rheingold, 1993).

Applied to the study of civic life, this perspective calls our attention to the fundamental attributes lost in the move from unmediated to mediated communication. Of particular interest are those attributes central to the development of a healthy civic life, such as discussions that foster the development and discovery of our commonalities and connections lasting and extensive enough to sustain a public forum. The approach also emphasizes the nature of the link between our mediated and unmediated social inter-actions; that is, ways in which users ground their mediated discursive interactions in the "real world." Studying the role of Internet technology in civic life from this perspective entails examining how citizens interact in each context (mediated and unmediated), and, on the basis of this contrast, developing arguments regarding the quality of the mediated interaction and its contribution to twenty-first-century public life.

Internet Technology as a Transformative Force (IT Transforms Civic Life)

While the two previous perspectives suggested that technological mediation does not significantly alter the principles on which our current understanding relies, this third view assumes that communication technologies transform the communication process and its participants. This approach relies on the premise that mediated interaction is not comparable to unmediated interaction; nor is it a subset of FtF. Computer-mediated interaction is something else altogether. This distinct form of interaction establishes a unique set of conditions that can alter our essential ways of doing and thinking. Contrary to the two previous approaches, which implied that the effects of technologically mediated communication are reversible, this view suggests that the changes are cumulative and permanent.

Transformation theorists, such as Havelock (1986), Heim (1993), Innis (1950, 1952), McLuhan (1962, 1965), and Ong (1971, 1982), are particularly representative of this approach. Their works describe the ontological and epistemological shifts brought about by the introduction of certain communication technologies. For instance, Ong (1982) is particularly interested in the shift from orality to literacy and from chirography to print. The alphabet, he says, moved us from a world of sound to a world of space. As a consequence, Ong believes, "Writing makes possible increasingly articulate introspectivity, opening the psyche as never before" (1982, p. 78). The written word allowed us to develop a capacity (and later, a predilection) for linear and rational thinking. Adapting this perspective to the study of the Internet technology's place in public life implies finding features of the technology that have consequences for the ways in which we interact with one another and seeing how these features can, in a more or less distant future, significantly and permanently alter our ways of communicating. In summary, the objective of the transformative approach is to use current Internet-based practices to speculate about the future of civic life.

Each of the above three perspectives (IT as extending, filtering, or transforming civic life) can shed unique light on the role of Internet technology in public life. Table 12.1 provides a summary of the assumptions underlying each perspective, the main implications of the perspective for civic life, and questions answered by research that adopts the different perspectives.

INTERNET TECHNOLOGY AS AN EXTENDER OF CIVIC LIFE: A PLURALISTIC MODEL OF THE PUBLIC SPHERE

Although one can study the role of Internet technology in civic life from any of these three perspectives, the idea of Internet technology as an ex-

Table 12.1
Three Theoretical Approaches to the Role of Information Technology in Civic
Life

	Perspective 1	Perspective 2	Perspective 3
Underlying Assumptions	• IT creates a new type of public space. • While this new space has special attributes, it does not significantly alter the nature and purpose of our discursive interactions. • Unmediated and mediated interactions are fundamentally comparable.	• Communication mediated by IT is a mere variation of FtF (it is FtF + IT). • The technological mediation filters and/or adds some basic attributes to our FtF interactions. • This filtering effect temporarily influences, but does not fundamentally alter, the nature and purpose of our FtF interactions.	• Mediated interactions are a distinct type of interaction. • This new type of interaction can transform our ways of thinking and doing. • These transformations are cumulative and permanent.
Main Implications for the Role of IT in Civic Life	• IT can replace the vanishing public spaces of twenty-first-century Western societies.	• Relying on IT to mediate our social interactions can enhance or inhibit civic life, depending on the attributes that are filtered and/or those that are added.	• Our use of IT to mediate social interactions can transform the principles of civic life on which our current understanding of the public sphere relies.
Principal Research Questions	• How do publics access, adapt, and use these virtual public spaces?	• What attributes are lost/gained in the move from FtF to mediated public interactions?	• What principles of public life are being transformed? And with what implications?

tender of civic life is particularly relevant to this discussion. This perspective indicates that electronic discussion groups are manifestations of a type of public sphere and, as such, should be taken seriously. Moreover, because this perspective posits that mediated and unmediated forms of interactions are essentially comparable, it means that we can turn to a previously established body of research on the public sphere. This body of interdisciplinary research, which is based largely on the study of unmediated interactions, aims to theorize about the characteristics of public life in democratic polity.

Traditionally, theorists have seen the public sphere as a discursive realm existing within the framework of a civil society, a place where shared meanings and opinions can be formed and debated (Habermas, 1974, 1989). Habermas' (1974) work on the bourgeois public sphere describes this sphere as a realm of public discussion independent from the sphere of private interests and the state, where "something approaching public opinion can be formed" (p. 49). Through rational deliberation of issues, social actors create shared meanings that, in turn, constitute the basis for future social interactions.

Electronic discussion groups conform to Habermas' (1974) definition in several ways. First, the groups operate in electronic spaces generated by the interconnectivity of the participants' computers. Second, the participants generate these discursive spaces from a desire to publicly deliberate on issues of shared interest. Third, through their electronic exchanges, participants construct shared meanings that can be used to guide civic actions. Finally, most electronic discussion groups are free from private and state control. In theory, this particular characteristic allows for the creation of a realm of public discussion that exists in opposition to private interests (in particular, commercial ones) and the state.

Approached as manifestations of a public sphere, electronic discussion groups gain in complexity and significance. Critics can no longer dismiss these sites as places where asocial individuals congregate in order to live parallel lives. Instead, the electronic discussion groups become sites for exercising democratic rights. In the following section, I will discuss specific theories of the public sphere in order to predict the kinds of contributions that electronic discussion groups can make to civil society.

Some believe that Habermas' (1989) unitary conception of the public sphere does not adequately describe the problems of twenty-first-century societies, characterized by conditions of increasing diversity (see Calhoun, 1992). Scholars such as Cohen (1999), Fraser (1992, 1995), Hauser (1999), and Rodger (1985) have turned to a pluralistic model of the public sphere. Their work disputes the assumption that "the proliferation of a multiplicity of competing publics is necessarily a step away from, rather than toward, greater democracy, and that a single, comprehensive public sphere is always preferable to a nexus of multiple publics" (Fraser, 1995, p. 288).

Based on a pluralistic model, we can no longer think of the public sphere as a singular megadomain with a set of definite features and functions. Rather, the sphere becomes a web of smaller domains, each with its own features and capacity, the totality of which can never be fully conceived, solidified, or studied. While the unitary model strives to consolidate discursive processes in one identifiable domain, a pluralistic model seeks to define the existing struggle among competing publics. One of the most interesting implications of the pluralistic model, relevant to the present discussion, is the idea that public spheres come in at least two types and that each type fulfills a specific and central function within modern democratic societies. In particular, Rodger (1985) believes that we ought to differentiate between the *pre-institutional* and *institutional* levels of the public sphere. These two levels reflect the two main functions of the public sphere in contemporary democratic society: (1) to foster the creation of common meaning and (2) to balance state actions through public opinion and public participation in state affairs.

According to Rodger (1985), the *pre-institutional* level refers to the space where common meaning can emerge. It is a space of vernacular discourse where social agents can openly debate, contest, and generate new identities and understandings. New social movements are particularly illustrative of this pre-institutional level. These movements are "the bearer of 'new normative principles' and provide a 'qualitatively new framework of experience' for people. They create a public space within them for argument about the 'validity claims of legitimacy and authority' and while they could have a significant role to play in changing public institutions, this is not necessarily their main function" (pp. 212–213). The major function of social movements operating at the *institutional* level of the public sphere, on the other hand, is to effect change in public institutions (Rodger, 1985). At the institutional level, public debate occurs within a previously recognized, legal, and institutionalized framework. It is a realm of official discourse. Public hearings, town hall meetings, and public participation in political processes all occur at the institutional level of the public sphere.

Rodger (1985) is not alone in arguing for a conceptual distinction between the pre-institutional and institutional levels of the public sphere. Fraser (1992), who differentiates between strong and weak publics, and Cohen (1999), who distinguishes between political and civil public spheres, advance comparable arguments. Fraser says that the deliberative practices of *weak publics* "consist exclusively in opinion formation," whereas the practices of *strong publics* "encompass both opinion formation and decision making" (p. 134). According to Cohen, *civil publics* have no decision-making power, but *political publics* have this capacity. Although their terminologies differ, Fraser and Cohen agree that scholars of the public sphere ought to distinguish between publics with decision-making powers and those involved primarily in opinion and identity formation.

By combining these concepts, we see that weak/civic publics characterize the pre-institutional public sphere, whereas strong/political publics are attached to the institutional level of the public sphere. The functions performed by the two are complementary, and both are key to a healthy democracy. In the former, citizens influence society by fostering the formation of common opinions and meanings about political, moral, and economic issues. In the latter, they participate in institutionalized spheres of debate, as a means to directly confront and impress state actions. In both, the liveliness of the discourse is the sign of a strong civil society.

Theories based on a pluralistic model of the public sphere support the conclusion that Internet technology can contribute to civil society in at least two ways. Not only can the technology constitute and mediate institutionalized public spheres, but it can also contribute to the creation of pre-institutionalized public spheres, in which social actors discursively negotiate private and collective meanings. Most electronic discussion groups are manifestations of this second type. Approached from this perspective, it becomes apparent that what citizens say and do within electronic discussion groups can have civic implications. More specifically, through their exchanges in these electronic pre-institutional public spheres, citizens are able to form, enact, and confront their differences through talk.[3] This expression of differences is the sign of a healthy civil society. Through this process, citizens assert, evaluate, and potentially reshape their taken-for-granted assumptions about the principles that govern their lives.

ARGUMENTS ABOUT A "CLEAR MAJORITY," OR WHOSE VOICE MATTERS THE MOST IN CANADA

The remainder of this chapter will consider an illustration of this process as it has unfolded in qc.politique. This process was evident in the electronic discussions that took place within qc.politique following the 1998 Canadian Supreme Court's ruling on the right of Québec to unilaterally secede from Canada.[4] When the judgment was made public on August 20, 1998, the participants in qc.politique began discussing the nature, implications, and legitimacy of the Supreme Court ruling. In these qc.politique discussions, federalists and sovereigntists articulated their assumptions about (1) who has the right to decide Québec's future, (2) who has managed to get their issues on the table for discussion within the public realm, and (3) whose voice currently matters the most within the federal system. In the following section, I focus on arguments about the meaning of a "clear majority," as advocated by various members of the electronic discussion group.

The judges ruled that both the government of Québec and the Government of Canada are obligated to negotiate a secession of Québec from Canada in the event of "a clear majority vote in Québec on a clear question." Ironically, both sovereigntists and federalists within qc.politique interpreted this ruling as a judgment in their favor. For this reason, the discussion moved to negotiating the meaning of "a clear majority." Many federalists within qc.politique read the expression as implying that sovereigntists would need more than a simple majority in order to legally secede from Canada. Consider the following comments by federalists:

Pady: La cours Supreme a nettement declare qu'une majorite CLAIRE, a une question CLAIRE etait necessaire, ce qui implique une majorite de plus de 0.01% des voix.[5]

CAT: Une bonne majorite . . . ce n'est pas 50%+1 mais plutot quelque chose comme 67%. On ne se separe pas d'une pays sans l'accord massif de la population![6]

Remy: La decision de la Cours Supreme du Canada indique assez clairement que 50%+1 ne fera pas l'affaire.[7]

For their part, sovereigntists within qc.politique argued that a simple majority is a "clear majority." They pointed to the fact that, until the 1995 referendum—the day federalists realized that 50 percent was an attainable objective—a simple majority was considered "a clear majority." In their view, the federalists' talk about a 67 percent majority was simply an attempt to change the rules of the game once a simple majority became an attainable prospect. To support their charges, sovereigntists referred to the fact that federalists had interpreted the results of the previous referendum (50.6% against sovereignty) as a "clear" expression of majority. They also argued that Newfoundland had entered the confederation via referendum in 1949 with a majority of only 52 percent. Eric's comments nicely summarize these arguments: "O.K. C'est comme ca que ca marche au Canada. Pour entrer, c'est 50%+1. Pour sortir. . . . On peut toujours rever."[8]

While debating the meaning of a "clear majority," sovereigntists and federalists also put forward their perceptions as to whose voice matters the most (sovereigntist or federalist) within a federal system. For many sovereigntists, the fact that federalists argue for a 67 percent majority indicates that all votes are not equally important within the federal system—that the vote of a federalist has more weight than the vote of a sovereigntist. Jean explains: "Pour reconnaitre la victoire du Oui, certains antidemocrates voudraient qu'il faille 2 ou 3 fois plus de Oui que de NON, donnant ainsi un poids superieur a un vote Non. C'est innacceptable et ne sera jamais accepte: au Québec . . . c'est une personne = un vote."[9] According to Claude, when federalists argue for a 67 percent majority, they promote a system that gives more weight to their own voices. Maryse C., who shares this position, asks why the vote of a federalist should weigh more than her own: "Explique-moi pourquoi le vote de William Johnson a plus de valeur que le mien."[10] In answer to her question, a sovereigntist writes: "Mais tiens, parce que William Johnson est un anglais, et les anglais on tout naturellement plus de valeur que les autres, surtout les francais!!!"[11]

Once this belief had been articulated, other participants were able to take positions, either embracing or attempting to refute and reshape this fundamental assumption about how the federalist system treats francophones.

At this moment, a discursive space opened, and within this virtual space, a debate was able to take place over federalist and sovereigntist assumptions about whose voice matters the most within the federalist system. Through electronic exchanges on the meaning of a "clear majority," the participants in qc.politique were able to assert, evaluate, and potentially reshape some of the deeply anchored assumptions that underlie the unity debate in Canada.

CONCLUSION

While the example described in this chapter is uniquely Canadian, the issues it raises are universal. The population of contemporary democratic societies is increasingly culturally diverse, and this diversity poses unique challenges to our capacity to act as a society. Thus, the kinds of exchanges found within the qc.politique discussion group require further study in order to help us to understand (1) how electronic discussion groups create spaces in which individuals from diverse ideologies and regions can discuss their common concerns, (2) the unique impact of these spaces on society, and (3) how cultural differences impress the functioning of the contemporary public sphere(s). As part of this second line of inquiry, we return to the concern expressed by Thomas H. at the beginning of this chapter regarding the effects of certain discursive practices on the civic contributions of electronic discussion groups. Thomas H. deplored the fact that, in qc.politique, the debate is polarized along clear ideological lines. He argued that these discursive practices prevent qc.politique from fulfilling its democratic potential. But in relying on a pluralistic model of the public sphere, we see that electronic discussion groups can contribute to civil society in at least two ways. They can constitute a domain of public debate that operates within the legal framework of recognized institutions. Also, more importantly, they can contribute to the creation of a realm of vernacular discourse in which social actors discursively negotiate private and collective meanings. Most electronic discussion groups are manifestations of this second function and, as such, their most significant civic contribution is to allow citizens to open up a space in which they can assert, evaluate, and potentially reshape their taken-for-granted assumptions about issues of public significance. Through this discursive process, citizens can enact, confront, and form new shared identities and understandings.

NOTES

1. The name of the participants quoted in this chapter have been changed to protect their Internet identity.

2. "Instead of trying to build bridges, you are acting like kids and insulting each other! No wonder nothing is working in Canada and Québec. People from

both sides scream at each other instead of trying to explain their position in an adequate and civilized manner."

3. Goodnight (1991) has skillfully defended the idea that controversies can have a constructive role within our society. He explains that a controversy not only puts at stake the issues for debate, but also the "rules and presumptions on who gets to talk, what counts as proof, whose language is authoritative, what reasons are recognized, which grounds are determinative, along what lines contexts are invoked, and whether penalties should be attached to making objections" (p. 6). By putting at risk these tacit rules and presumptions, a controversy forces us to reevaluate our understanding of the relationship between reason and communication. According to Goodnight, this reevaluation is positive, for it can generate new and shared ways of thinking and doing.

4. The modern Québec independence movement has promoted a secession of Québec from Canada for more than 35 years. Whether or not the province of Québec could actually leave the Federation has been the subject of heated debate. Following the *presque-oui* of the 1995 referendum, the federal government asked the Supreme Court of Canada, the highest court in the country, to consider whether Québec could unilaterally secede from Canada. The Supreme Court's judgment gave both sovereigntists and federalists some reasons to celebrate. It deemed a unilateral declaration of sovereignty unconstitutional but legitimated the secessionist project by claiming that Canada is constitutionally obligated to negotiate the secession of Québec from Canada in the case of "a clear majority vote to a clear question." The Supreme Court left the interpretation of "clear majority vote" to the governments of Québec and Canada.

5. "The Court clearly stated that a CLEAR majority to a CLEAR question was necessary, which suggests a majority of more than 0.01% of the total votes."

6. "A good majority . . . it is not 50%+1 but rather something like 67%. One cannot secede from a country without wide support of the population."

7. "The ruling of the Supreme Court of Canada indicates quite clearly that 50%+1 won't be enough."

8. "O.K. That's the way it works in Canada. To get in, it's 50%+1. To get out. . . . Dream on."

9. "In order to recognize the OUI victory, some antidemocrats would like 2 or 3 times more OUI than NON, which would give more weight to a NON vote. That's unacceptable and will never be accepted: in Québec [. . .] it's one person = one vote."

10. "Tell me why the vote of William Johnson has more value than my own . . . ?"

11. "Because William Johnson is English and the English have naturally more value than others, especially the French!!!"

REFERENCES

Bechar-Israeli, H. (1995). From <Bonehead> to <cLoNehEAd>: Nicknames, play and identity on Internet relay chat. *Journal of Computer-Mediated Communication 1* (2). http://www.usc.edu/dept/annenberg/vol1/issue2/bechar.html.

Calhoun, C. (1992). *Habermas and the public sphere*. Cambridge, MA: MIT Press.

Cohen, J. L. (1999). American civil society talk. In D. E. Eberly (Ed.), *Building a community of citizens: Civil society in the 21st century* (pp. 305–317). Lanham, MD: Rowman & Littlefield.

Dubrovsky, V., Kiesler, S., & Sethna, B. (1991). The equalization phenomenon: Status effects in computer-mediated and face-to-face decision making groups. *Human Computer Interaction 6*, 119–146.

Fraser, N. (1992). Rethinking the public sphere: A contribution to the critique of actually existing democracy. In C. Calhoun (Ed.), *Habermas and the public sphere* (pp. 119–142). Boston: MIT Press.

Fraser, N. (1995). Politics, culture, and the public sphere: Toward a postmodern conception. In L. Nicholson & S. Seidman (Eds.), *Social postmodernism: Beyond identity politics* (pp. 287–314). Cambridge: Cambridge University Press.

Goodnight, G. T. (1991). Controversy. In D. W. Parson (Ed.), *Argument in controversy*. Annandale, VA: Speech Communication Association.

Habermas, J. (1974). The public sphere: An encyclopedia article. *New German Critique 3*, 49–55.

Habermas, J. (1989). *The structural tranformation of the public sphere: An inquiry into a category of bourgeois society*. Boston: MIT Press.

Hauser, G. A. (1999). *Vernacular voices: The rhetoric of publics and public spheres*. Columbia: University of South Carolina Press.

Havelock, E. A. (1986). *The muse learns to write*. New Haven, CT: Yale University Press.

Heim, M. (1993). *The metaphysics of virtual reality*. New York: Oxford University Press.

Innis, H. A. (1950). *Empire and communications*. Oxford: Clarendon Press.

Innis, H. A. (1952). *Changing concepts of time*. Toronto: University of Toronto Press.

Jones, S. (1995). *Cybersociety: Computer-mediated communication and community*. Thousand Oaks, CA: Sage.

Jones, S. (1997). *Virtual culture: Identity and communication in cybersociety*. Thousand Oaks, CA: Sage.

Marvin, L. (1995). Spoof, spam, lurk and lag: The aesthetics of text-based virtual realities. *Journal of Computer-Mediated Communication 1* (2). http://www.ascusc.org/jcmc/vol1/issue2/marvin.html.

McLuhan, M. (1962). *The Gutenberg galaxy*. Toronto: University of Toronto Press.

McLuhan, M. (1965). *Understanding media*. New York: McGraw-Hill.

Ong, W. (1971). *Rhetoric, romance, and technology: Studies in the interaction of expression and culture*. Ithaca, NY: Cornell University Press.

Ong, W. (1982). *Orality and literacy: The technologizing of the word*. London: Methuen.

Park, M., & Floyd, K. (1996). Making friends in cyberspace. *Journal of Communication 46* (1), 80–97.

Reid, E. (1991). *Electropolis: Communication and community on Internet relay chat*. Unpublished master's thesis, University of Melbourne, Australia.

Rheingold, H. (1993). *The virtual community: Homesteading on the electronic frontier*. Reading, MA: Addison-Wesley.

Rodger, J. (1985). On the degeneration of the public sphere. *Political Studies 33*, 203–217.

Sproull, L., & Kiesler, S. (1986). Reducing social context cues: Electronic mail in organizational communication. *Management Science 32* (11), 1492–1512.

Walther, J. B. (1996). Computer-mediated communication: Impersonal, interpersonal, and hyperpersonal interaction. *Communication Research 23*, 3–43.

Walther, J. B., & Burgoon, J. K. (1992). Relational communication in computer-mediated communication. *Human Communication Research 19*, 50–88.

Wilkins, H. (1991). Computer talk: Long distance conversation by computer. *Written Communication 8* (1), 56–78.

Chapter 13

The Impossibility of Conservatism: The Discourse of New Right Ideology

Darin Barney

> The specific care of the political philosopher is political words, not political things. Thus the unique charge of political theorists is not to direct political activists but to safeguard political language. (Andrew, 1988, p. 196)

What's in a "neo-"? Writing in 1965, Canadian patriot and philosopher George Grant (1995) lamented, "The impossibility of conservatism in our era is the impossibility of Canada" (p. 81). Nearly three decades later, political economists Stephen McBride and John Shields (1993) would write that neoconservatism is "incompatible with the continued existence of Canada as we have come to know it" (p. 1). For Grant, conservatism is essential to Canada; for McBride and Shields, neoconservatism undermines Canada. Yet all three concur that the possibility of Canada as a nation, substantially distinct from the United States, relies on its embodiment of virtues that are impossible under the regime of an unfettered market and American liberalism. For Grant, these virtues are conservative; for McBride and Shields, they are social democratic. These authors can say the same thing about liberal capitalism (and Canadian nationhood), while saying opposite things about conservatism, because Grant's conservatism was not the same as the *neo*conservatism of McBride and Shields. The latter's "neo-" refers to what Grant sensed conservatism was becoming, even in 1965, when he observed that "Lockian liberalism is the conservatism of the English-speaking peoples" (p. 75).

Confused? I have not yet reached the part about Canada's history of political parties calling themselves *Liberal* and *Progressive Conservative*, ideologies that have long since ceased to correspond unambiguously to their names. In fact, the discursive terrain of Canadian partisan ideology is as formidable, shifting, and deceptive as the geographical terrain of the country itself. This chapter will explore what the rise of "new right" political parties and ideology might mean for civic discourse in Canada. I will argue that the ideology of the new right not only presents a challenge to our contemporary political conversation, but also signals a crisis of meaning in that part of our civic vocabulary where ideological designations demarcate coherent political positions. In particular, I will suggest that the discourse surrounding the rise of the new right finally drains the word *conservative* of any descriptive utility in the Canadian context.

A NEW RIGHT PARTY FOR CANADA

The new right in Canada is a multifaceted, loosely aggregated social and political movement. Its non-partisan elements include intellectual incubators such as the Fraser Institute and the Conservative Forum; media outlets such as *Alberta Report* and *BC Report* magazines; umbrella organizations such as the National Citizen's Coalition; and more directed advocacy and activist groups such as the Canadian Taxpayers Federation, REAL Women, the Campaign Life Coalition, the Canada Family Action Coalition, and the Canada West Foundation. The partisan manifestations of the new right are similarly diverse, with several parties of varying strengths and prospects emerging in a number of provinces. Included in this list are the Progressive Conservative parties that have managed to form governments in Alberta and Ontario, the Saskatchewan Party and the Liberal Party of British Columbia (the official opposition in their respective provinces, with strong prospects for eventually forming governments), the Confederation of Regions Party (a minor but notable force in New Brunswick and elsewhere in the 1990s), and a smattering of provincial Reform and Libertarian Parties in various provinces.

For the purposes of this discussion, I will limit consideration to the federal Reform/Alliance Party. On the one hand, singling out Reform/Alliance is somewhat artificial, as the party is organically linked in membership, organization, and ideology to most of the above-listed actors. On the other hand, it is Reform/Alliance whose impact on civic discourse—and political life generally—has been felt most acutely at the federal level. Also, many of the ideological elements of the new right constellation find order in the ideology of Reform/Alliance.

The rise to prominence of the Reform/Alliance Party has been well documented (Dabbs, 1997; Dobbin, 1991; Harrison, 1995; Sharpe & Braid, 1992). Conceived at an assembly in Vancouver in May 1987, the Reform Party was born at a founding convention in Winnipeg in October. At this convention, the party chose as its leader Preston Manning, a management consultant in the oil industry and son of former Social Credit Premier of Alberta Ernest Manning. Apart from the historic sense of alienation often felt by western Canadians, a number of specific events explain the impetus behind the Winnipeg convention. The founding of Reform/Alliance coincided with the unraveling of Brian Mulroney's historic electoral coalition of moderate Québécois nationalists and disgruntled western Canadian economic and political elites. The dissolution of the coalition followed closely on the heels of the 1986 Meech Lake Agreement. In the same year, Canadair-CAE Ltd. of Montreal received a large federal contract to build CF-18 military aircraft. The unhappy loser in the bidding process was Winnipeg-based Bristol Aerospace (Carty, Cross, & Young, 2000; Harrison, 1995).

Once on its feet, the party fielded 28 candidates in the 1988 federal general election but failed to secure a seat. The pivotal issue in this election was the Canada–U.S. Free Trade Agreement, proposed by the Progressive Conservative government. Reform supported the deal, which left the upstart party in the somewhat ironic position of fighting its first campaign by aligning itself with a key platform position of the very party it had risen to oppose. Entry into the House of Commons would await the victory of Deborah Grey—"a straight-talking, gospel-singing schoolteacher with strong anti-abortionist views and a political pedigree" (Harrison, 1995, p. 140). Grey won her seat in a 1989 by-election in the Alberta riding of Beaver River. Also in 1989, Reform candidate Stan Waters won a vacant Senate seat.

The general election of 1993 marked the emergence of the Reform Party as a full-fledged player on the federal scene. The party capitalized on the collapse of the Progressive Conservative vote in the West and on its exclusive status as the only federal party based in English Canada to have opposed the Charlottetown Accord. Riding a popular sentiment (54.4% of Canadians had voted against the constitutional proposal), Reform won 52 seats, all but one from west of the Manitoba-Ontario border. These figures meant that Reform had elected five times as many MPs in western Canada as the other opposition parties combined; and in so doing, Reform had become "the *de facto* parliamentary opposition west of the Ottawa River" (Laycock, 1994, p. 214). The 1997 general election saw Reform convert *de facto* into *de jure*, as the party won 60 seats, and Preston Manning became the leader of the official opposition in the House of Commons.

The news in 1997 was not all rosy. Despite the expenditure of considerable effort, the party was unable to elect a single member to a seat east of Manitoba. The party and its leaders were convinced that their lack of success was due to a split in the right-wing, anti-Liberal vote. The division occurred between ascending Reform candidates and declining Progressive Conservatives. Soon after the 1997 election, Reform leader Preston Manning began to press for a solution to the perceived vote-splitting problem.

He appealed to Progressive Conservative voters in seat-rich Ontario to consider switching allegiances and voting strategically to prevent the election of Liberal candidates by default. Quickly, Manning's overtures matured into a full-fledged strategy to "unite the right." Manning urged Reform and Progressive Conservative constituency associations not to contest each other in ridings where their combined vote might exceed that of their Liberal opponents or, alternatively, to agree to a formal amalgamation of the parties at the national level.

Despite having his invitations rebuffed by many Reform members and the federal leadership of the Progressive Conservatives, Manning pressed forward with the plan under the auspices of the United Alternative movement. The United Alternative plan ultimately garnered the support of the federal Reform caucus, gaining 60 percent of the party membership (as expressed in a June 1999 referendum). He also gained the crucial support of Progressive Conservative Premier of Alberta Ralph Klein and several high-profile members of Mike Harris' ruling Ontario Progressive Conservative Party. As a consequence, in February 1999, a United Alternative convention voted to create a new right-wing federal political party. The proposal reignited dissension within the Reform fold, and Manning threatened to resign, should the membership reject the plan for a new party.

In January 2000, delegates attended a second United Alternative convention, at which they adopted a constitution, policy declaration, and name for the new party—the Canadian Conservative-Reform Alliance Party (CCRAP). (The name was later changed to the Canadian Reform Conservative Alliance to circumvent derogatory pronunciation of the acronym.) In a March 2000 referendum, the Reform Party membership approved formal consolidation with the Alliance. Four months later, in July 2000, the Alliance selected its first leader, Stockwell Day—a former pastor, auctioneer, and Finance Minister of Alberta under the Progressive Conservative government of Ralph Klein. The founding father of both the Reform Party and the Alliance, Preston Manning placed second in the leadership contest, with Ontario Progressive Conservative strategist Tom Long placing third. Under Day's leadership, the Alliance contested the 2000 general election in each of Canada's 301 federal ridings. The party increased its national seat total to 66 (from Reform's 60) and its percentage share from 19.4 to 25.5 of the national popular vote. The Alliance retained Reform's status as official opposition in the House of Commons. Despite a massive campaign effort in Ontario, the party captured only two seats in that province and increased its popular vote from 19.1 percent to 23.5 percent. The remaining Alliance seats were all located in western Canada, 50 in British Columbia and Alberta.

NEW RIGHT IDEOLOGY IN CANADA

In the popular imagination and discourse, Preston Manning's Reform Party and its Alliance offspring are typically characterized, often dismissively, as a western party of regional protest. Canadians view Reformists as vaguely descendant from the failed tradition of Canadian prairie populism, pathologically xenophobic (particularly in relation to the Québécois), and animated by fundamentalist Christian zealotry. This interpretation is inadequate and misleading on a number of levels, as revealed in the growing body of scholarship that attempts to reckon with the nuances and complexity of the party's ideology (Barney & Laycock, 1999; Flanagan, 1995; Harrison, 1995; Jeffrey, 1999; Laycock, 1994; Patten, 1996; Sigurdson, 1994). Concentrating on official Alliance policy, I will point to the primary and enduring pillars of the party's ideology, as it moves into its period of maturity and institutionalization. These pillars include commitments to particular interpretations of liberty, equality, and democracy—which, in turn, combine to yield a principled conviction regarding the role of the state and the character of public and private life.

Liberty

Accepting his election as leader of the Alliance, Stockwell Day began his speech by proclaiming that the "Freedom Train" was about to roll forward to Ottawa, bringing with it "freedom from oppressive government." As this declaration suggests, the core of the Reform/Alliance ideology is a principled commitment to the protection of negative liberty—understood as individual freedom from formal, external constraint. This conviction manifests itself in a particular antagonism toward the state and its government. Rooted in the political theory of John Locke (1986), this interpretation of liberal ideology seeks to provide philosophical justification for strict limits on the scope of public authority (especially in economic matters). According to Locke, men unite into political communities in order to preserve their lives, liberties, and estates. Each is reducible to "the general name, property" (p. 180).

In Article 21 of its policy declaration, the Canadian Alliance commits itself to amending the *Charter of Rights and Freedoms* to include "the right to own, use and benefit from private property" (Canadian Alliance, 2000a). While common law has historically recognized this right, its inclusion in the *Charter* would constitute a radical change. More significant, however, is the anti-state commitment to roll back the expansion of public authority, which attended the growth of Canada's welfare state in the postwar era. As stated in the preamble to the policy declaration, the party seeks to ensure "minimal government intrusion in people's lives" by limiting the powers of government to "the functions essential to a modern state" (Canadian

Alliance, 2000a). Chief among these essential functions is creating "an economic climate in which businesses can thrive" (Canadian Alliance, 2000a).
Achieving this goal implies minimizing or eliminating the intervention of
public authority in market distribution of private property and goods.

The most obvious manifestation of this ideological commitment has been
the party's policy on taxation. An indispensable instrument of wealth redistribution, taxation is perhaps the most basic claim the public good
makes against the private property of individuals. It is also the primary
target of new right liberalism. This view holds that the level of taxation
necessary to sustain the welfare state is, by definition, excessive and a coercive infringement of individuals' right to dispose freely of their property.
In its platform for the 2000 federal election, the Alliance characterized
current levels of taxation as "an incredible hardship for ordinary Canadians
trying to make ends meet." In a new-age twist on an old bourgeois refrain,
Alliance promised, "By paying lower taxes you can achieve your true potential" (Canadian Alliance, 2000b). Central to the Alliance's first campaign for office was a regressive proposal to flatten income-specific taxation
to the single rate of 17 percent.[1] In effect, this proposal would have neu-
tered what remained of the welfare state in Canada. Along with this lowering of personal income tax, the 2000 election platform pledged to reduce
payroll and capital gains taxes paid by corporations, high-technology enterprises, and small businesses (Canadian Alliance, 2000b).

The liberal conception of liberty as the freedom of property holders from
state intervention in markets animates a range of Alliance policy positions
that extend beyond matters of taxation. These oft-repeated positions include the following: support for international and interprovincial free trade;
massive reductions in social spending; dismantling of regional development
agencies such as the Atlantic Canada Opportunities Agency; reduction of
employment and income security benefits; privatization and divestiture of
Crown corporations, including the Canadian Broadcasting Corporation
and VIA Rail; comprehensive deregulation (specifically of the commercial
airline industry); abandonment of the federal spending power in social policy areas; eliminating the universality of the Canada Pension Plan; de-
collectivization of agricultural marketing; and legislated requirements
regarding social spending, balanced budgets, and debt reduction. This legislation would seriously curtail the economic discretion of elected governments.

In the Alliance's relatively unreconstructed liberal economic ideology, the
chief positive role of democratic government vis-à-vis the economy is thus,
ironically, a negative one: to institutionalize the absence of the state. Such
an absence necessarily renders moot the possibility of the state acting as a
public agent of economic redistribution or as a medium through which
considerations of common welfare might moderate the extremities and in-

equities of the capitalist market. In place of the welfare state, Alliance ideology (as expressed in its policy declaration) recommends "personal responsibility, individual freedom, and independence" (Canadian Alliance, 2000a). For "those who require assistance to achieve the level of independence of which they are capable," the Alliance suggests that, rather than the state, "families, communities and non-governmental organizations are best placed to respond to individual needs on a personal basis" (Canadian Alliance, 2000a). That these agents of civil society might face resource challenges due to reductions in social spending by the state is of no concern, as Alliance tax cuts "will leave resources in the hands of those who are best able to help" (Canadian Alliance, 2000a).

Alliance ideology, however, departs from the doctrine of strict non-interference in certain areas such as civil relations and personal morality. In these areas, Alliance recommends a robust, activist role for the state— but only in certain instances. For example, Alliance principles and platform items regarding criminal justice indicate unambiguously the party's willingness to flex the muscle of the state in order to enforce its particular vision of social order. Under the rubric of establishing "clear consequences for crime and compassion for victims" (Canadian Alliance, 2000b), the Alliance advocates a range of measures, including removal of judicial discretion in sentencing, increased use of indefinite incarceration for "career criminals," registration and mandatory lifetime supervision or monitoring for certain categories of offenders, lowering the age for prosecuting youth offenders as adults to 14, enabling publication of the identity of youth and other offenders, increasing restrictions on parole eligibility, and denying prisoners the right to vote. Survey research into the opinions of Reform Party activists in the early 1990s indicated that 82 percent favored the restoration of capital punishment (Archer & Ellis, 1994)—a position endorsed publicly by Alliance leader Stockwell Day in the 2000 election campaign (Leblanc, 2000).

The party's endorsement of the above measures confirms that the Alliance's concern for minimalist state intervention in economic liberty is not matched in reticence toward state invasion of individual civil liberties. Although it may seem contradictory and illiberal, the Alliance view is completely consistent with Locke's foundational vision of the state's primary responsibility as being to protect private property (life, liberty, and estate), in this case by punishing grievously those who threaten or do it harm. This vision of justice as individuated restraint and retribution (as opposed to, for example, equity, fairness, or collective welfare) supplements the Alliance's liberal view of negative liberty. This latter vision is expressed ideologically as a principled conviction that "the rights of victims of crime must take precedence over those of criminals" (Canadian Alliance, 2000a).

The role for the state in domestic relations, as contemplated by Alliance ideology, is also less than perfectly non-interventionist. On the one hand,

Alliance principles assert a liberal doctrine of non-intervention in private domestic matters, affirming "the right and duty of parents to raise their children responsibly according to their own conscience and beliefs" and stating that "no person, government or agency has the right to interfere in the exercise of that duty except through due process of law" (Canadian Alliance, 2000a). At the same time, the Alliance is committed to using state authority to legitimize certain types of domestic relationships as constitutive of "family," while explicitly de-legitimizing others. Calling the family "the essential building block of a healthy society," Alliance principles endorse the extension of legislated benefits to "individuals related by blood, adoption or marriage" but restrict qualification in the latter category to "the exclusive union of one man and one woman" (Canadian Alliance, 2000a).[2] Given the number of entitlements (and obligations) attached to conjugal union in Canadian society, Alliance policy regarding promotion of "the family" would involve the state in an uncharacteristically high degree of prescriptive intervention in private life. For example, an Alliance government would not define gay and lesbian couples and their children (or those living in other non-traditional configurations) as "families."

Equality

The preamble to the Alliance policy declaration lists, among the party's core principles, a devotion to "true equality of citizens and provinces" (Canadian Alliance, 2000a), and its 2000 election platform pledges that an Alliance government would "treat all Canadians equally" (Canadian Alliance, 2000b). A rhetorical commitment to equality is a minimum condition for admission into legitimate political discussion in a liberal democracy. The liberal democratic tradition proposes a range of "equalities," including radical egalitarian rejection of distinction and excellence, equality before and under the law, equal opportunity, equality of rights, and material equality. Like other ideological positions in the modern liberal democratic galaxy, Alliance principles suggest support for some of these equalities and not others. The new right, for example, opposes the award of "special" status, rights, or entitlements based on the unique characteristics, needs, or situations of individuals collected in distinct groups or categories. Pledging to abolish "preferential hiring based on gender, race and ethnicity quotas," the party opposes "the use of affirmative action or any other type of discriminatory quota system" in the federal public service (Canadian Alliance, 2000b). (It is not clear whether this proposal extends to rejecting bilingualism as a qualification for advancement in the federal public sector.)[3]

The Alliance vision of equality is indicated also in its approach to Aboriginal affairs. Citing "individual freedom and equality before and under the law" as the "key principle" of the party's position, the Alliance pledges that it will "protect the democratic rights and freedoms of *individual* aboriginals," recognizing that they have "the same rights and responsibilities as all other Canadians" (Canadian Alliance, 2000a). In practical terms, this principled commitment to equality for Aboriginals translates into elimination of most aspects of the distinct status that Aboriginals have enjoyed as a group, due to their unique historical and material circumstances in Canadian society. Thus, an Alliance government would eradicate "race-based allocation of harvest rights to natural resources" (Canadian Alliance, 2000a) and end the tax exemption extended to many Aboriginals by assuring that they "pay their share of federal and provincial tax" (Canadian Alliance, 2000b), just like any other citizens.

The doctrine of equality as identical negative liberty for individuals, coupled with non-distinction for and between groups, is equally evident in the Alliance position on multiculturalism. While pledging to "uphold the freedom of individuals and families to nurture aspects of culture that are important to them," the Alliance declares "we believe that multiculturalism is a personal choice, and should not be publicly funded" (Canadian Alliance, 2000b). Thus, in the Alliance view, individuals should be free to choose and express the identities they prefer from those available in the cultural marketplace. However, the state must not support the maintenance of those identities or the public cultural practices of individuals or collectivities, as such support privileges members of some groups over others. (The Alliance view of equality, however, does not question the institutionalization of the cultural practices of the majority in matters such as state holidays tied to the Christian calendar.)

In regard to allocation of benefits among provinces, the party believes that "all Canadian provinces should be equal before and under the law, possessing equal powers to govern within their areas of constitutional authority . . . and each should have equal freedom to build the society most appropriate to its citizens" (Canadian Alliance, 2000a). The party opposes asymmetrical federalism—the doctrine perceived to be at the root of the special status historically granted to the province of Québec and denied to the western provinces. The party also opposes federal redistributive programs that favor certain regions of the country over others.

In summary, except in matters involving definitions of family and some cultural practices that favor the majority, the new right sees *equality* as identical treatment for all individuals and groups—never differentiated treatment.

Democracy

As with its forebears in the Reform Party, the Alliance expresses its commitment to "direct democracy" under the rubric of institutional and procedural reform of the Canadian electoral and parliamentary systems. Popular discourse and pundits have often placed the new right's various democratic designs under the banner of "populism," but *plebiscitarian* is probably a better term (Barney & Laycock, 1999). The animus of the new right's program for democratic reform is a perceived corruption of democratic practice, as it presently exists in Canada. Alliance supporters see the sources of this corruption as twofold.

In the first instance, the Alliance believes that old-line parties and parliamentary conventions have corrupted democratic practice by demanding strictly disciplined voting behavior by individual members of Parliament. Adherence to such codes of practice undermines the ability of elected officials to represent the will of their constituents (Laycock, 1994). To remedy this first defect, the Alliance pledges to "restore democratic accountability in the House of Commons" by increasing the frequency of free votes (i.e., stipulating that, besides those pertaining to the budget and main estimates, no vote in the House shall be considered a matter of confidence unless expressly designated as such). This new parliamentary convention would free MPs to vote the will of their constituents without partisan consequence. Other proposed reforms would include the direct election of senators, parliamentary review of senior public service and judicial appointments, and broader use of the notwithstanding clause (Canada, 1982: s.33) to override judicial decisions. By radically altering political institutions in Canada, the new right agenda for democratic reform would seriously undermine the role of political parties—including itself, of course.

The second source of democratic corruption, identified consistently by Reform/Alliance, is the perceived capture of governance by "special interests." The new right ideology defines a special interest as "any group that requests publicly provided benefits that require governments to skew market distributions of resources" (Laycock, 1994, p. 217). According to this definition, "feminist lobby groups, native organizations, organized labor, multicultural, linguistic and ethnic groups, the management of most crown corporations and state agencies, and public sector unions are special interests" (Laycock, 1994, p. 217). Advocacy organizations such as the Canadian Taxpayers' Federation, the Fraser Institute, REAL Women, the National Citizens' Coalition, and the Business Council on National Issues, on the other hand, are *not* special interests because their efforts do not demand redistribution of public resources.

In the new right imagination, special interests exert inordinate influence on bureaucrats and elected officials, whose legitimacy becomes contingent on their ability to satisfy these groups. This "tyranny of minorities" usurps the sovereignty of ordinary Canadians (Manning, 1992, p. 321). The proposed remedy for this condition is a reconstruction of democratic practice to include a variety of direct democracy instruments—often technologically mediated (see Barney, 1996). The use of these tools would de-amplify the voice of institutionalized special interests and enable the common sense of the common people to emerge and be recognized. Thus, the Alliance maintains traditional Reform Party commitments to the frequent use and recognition of instruments such as MP recall, state-sponsored referenda, and citizens' initiatives in Canadian democratic politics (Canadian Alliance, 2000a).

As mentioned above, previous research has demonstrated that the democratic elements of new right ideology are best described as *plebiscitarian*, rather than simply *populist*. Briefly, plebiscitarian democratic practices bear three definitive elements: a relative absence of institutionalized preference mediation/representation, decision-making oriented toward private calculation of personal interest (as opposed to public deliberation on collective goods), and a high degree of elite manipulation in the process of opinion registration (Barney & Laycock, 1999). Direct democracy, as designed and practiced by the Reform Party, exhibited each of these qualities, and little evidence suggests that the Alliance mutation will differ substantially. While this plebiscitarian approach to democracy makes logical sense, it also drains democratic participation of its public-spirited character and downplays the role of collective deliberation and dialogue. Thus, plebiscitarian democracy deprives civil society of a regime (i.e., a political sphere and corresponding set of civic practices) in which it might organize itself to attend to its common welfare. Plebiscitarianism thus accomplishes a profound depoliticization/privatization of public life. That it can do so in the name of increased democratic participation is the model's particular, albeit cynical, genius.

A QUESTION OF DEFINITION

Some would contest the designation of the partisan new right as an ideological phenomenon. Reflecting on his tenure as senior advisor and strategist for the Reform Party, Tom Flanagan (1995) rejects ideological characterizations of the party as "fundamentalist" or "conservative" (pp. 5–36). Instead Flanagan attributes the party's direction to the personal, non-ideological, methodical populism of Preston Manning. I would disagree. The maturing of the Reform Party into the Alliance Party and the takeover of leadership by Stockwell Day suggests that the glue binding the federal new right in Canada is something more deeply adhesive than fealty to the vision of a single individual.

In the foregoing, I have presented this glue as ideology. That is not to say that new right ideology is coherent, consistently expressed, or easy to name. Indeed, attempts to locate the thread that stitches together the various elements of the party's ideology are thwarted by the subject's complexity and the emptying of meaning from nomenclature historically applied to ideologies. Thus, for example, Harrison (1995) labels Reform ideology as *pure populism* when it comes to politics and *neoconservatism* when it comes to economics. Patten (1996) writes, "Reform's neo-liberal populism is further characterized by libertarian and socially conservative ideological commitments" (p. 96). Jeffrey (1999) prefers simply *neoconservative*. Laycock and I throw *neoconservative* around with abandon but also isolate in Reform "a distinctive ideology we call *plebiscitarianism*" (Barney & Laycock, 1999, p. 318). Sigurdson (1994) describes Manning's ideological disposition as "a distinctively postmodern conservatism" (p. 250).

In brief, if there is a consensus on how to characterize the ideology of the new right in Canada, it is roughly as follows: liberal economics, populist politics, and conservative social values, with the label *neoconservative* often offered as the discursive bag to hold these three attributes. Yet this elaboration of the contemporary new right's positions on liberty, equality, and democracy provides ample support for its designation as predominantly liberal in the classic Lockean sense; it suggests modifying the populist label to *plebiscitarian*, and finds little persuasive ground for a meaningful association of the word *conservative* with the new right in Canada.

Still, the label persists, and not without reason. As Jeffrey (1999) has shown, the lineage of the party's liberal economics are traceable to roots in parties led by Thatcher in the United Kingdom, Mulroney in Canada, and Klein in Alberta. Each of these parties carried the word *Conservative* in their names. (U.S. counterparts are the Reagan/Bush Republicans.) In the same way, Reform/Alliance leaders and members refer to themselves as *Conservatives*, although some prefer *fiscal* to *social* as an antecedent modifier. The Alliance recently added *Conservative* to its official name. The left has managed to convince many that the proper name for an ideology supportive of market capitalism is *Conservative*. However, while extant, the reasons for calling Reform/Alliance *Conservative* are ultimately not persuasive, particularly in the Canadian context.

It is commonly supposed that the label *conservatism* connotes an abstract aversion to change. Thus, Sigurdson (1994) suggests that Reform conservatism "speaks to the fear that Canadian society is changing too rapidly" in the wake of the cultural and economic dynamo of postmodernity (p. 267). However, to the extent that conservatism in the Canadian tradition has ever existed as a meaningful category, the ideology is rooted in British "Tory-ism," not American liberalism. The priorities of Canadian Tory conservatism include the following: a preference for stability over change, order and collective welfare over abstract individual liberty, a willingness to use the state to intervene in the market distribution of resources, support for nationalism, protection of hierarchy and social distinction (rather than abstract egalitarianism), and deference to duly constituted and responsible authority exercised by elites in the public interest (Ajzenstat & Smith, 1997; Horowitz, 1967; Taylor, 1982).

CONCLUSION

If the preceding discussion even remotely captures the distinctive historical attributes of Canadian conservatism, then it is difficult to refer to the ideology of the new right as *Conservative*. Indeed, the Reform/Alliance agenda precisely inverts each of the principles listed above. Individual liberty must trump the demands of social order and collective welfare. State intervention in the market must be minimized. Free trade and globalization are encouraged. Equality (as identical negative liberty for individuals) obliterates hierarchy and disallows social and political distinction (i.e., multiculturalism) or asymmetry (distinct status for Aboriginals and Québec). Plebiscitarian populism neuters elite trusteeship and shifts power back to the people. Even the argument that the new right is Conservative because its adherents value tradition over change is difficult to sustain, since Reform/Alliance proposals for institutional upheaval in the Canadian electoral and legislative systems verge on the revolutionary.

Should we label adherents as "Conservative" simply because they maintain a conception of "the family" and domestic life that might be better described as reactionary? Calling the new right *Conservative* makes sense only if that word is drained of its Canadian content and historical substance. Calling the new right *Conservative* only makes sense when, as Grant observed, it is reduced to identity with the very liberalism it has historically opposed. On a discursive terrain where unreconstructed liberalism assumes the mantle of conservatism, there is no place for the latter as a genuine, substantive ideology. Ironically, the rise of a new right liberalism that calls itself *Conservative* speaks to the final impossibility of conservatism in Canada.

NOTES

1. Article 17 of the Alliance's Policy Declaration commits the party to "a single rate of taxation" (Canadian Alliance, 2000a). The 2000 election platform promises an Alliance government would "move towards a single rate of tax on income"—moving in the first term of office from the current rates to two (a basic rate of 17 percent and a rate of 25 percent on incomes above $100,000), and presumably to a single rate in a subsequent term (Canadian Alliance, 2000b).

2. It should be noted that at the time of this writing Canadian law also defines marriage in this manner. However, it is also true that some federal benefits and entitlements are beginning to extend to same-sex couples. The evolution of this shift is slow and far from complete, but it is fair to say that even this limited extension of rights to non-heterosexual couples and alternative families is beyond the contemplation of new right ideology in Canada.

3. Article 40 of the Alliance Policy Declaration supports the need to maintain service in both official languages in "key federal institutions, such as Parliament

and the Supreme Court," which might suggest that the party contemplates relaxing this requirement in the public service more broadly. This same article stipulates that the application of bilingualism must "reflect the reality of the community served," which can only be read as a retreat from the policy of Official Bilingualism in Canada.

REFERENCES

Andrew, E. (1988). *Shylock's rights: A grammar of Lockian claims*. Toronto: University of Toronto Press.

Ajzenstat, J., & Smith, P. (Eds.). (1997). *Canada's origins: Liberal, tory or republican?* Ottawa: Carleton University Press.

Archer, K., & Ellis, F. (1994). Opinion structure of party activists: The Reform party of Canada. *Canadian Journal of Political Science 27* (2), 277–308.

Barney, D. (1996). Push-button populism: The Reform party and the real world of teledemocracy. *Canadian Journal of Communication 21* (3), 381–413.

Barney, D., & Laycock, D. (1999). Right-populists and plebiscitary politics in Canada. *Party Politics 5* (3), 317–339.

Canada. (1982). *The Constitution Act, Part II: Canadian Charter of Rights and Freedoms*. Ottawa: Minister of Supply and Services.

Canadian Alliance. (2000a, July). Policy declaration. www.canadianalliance.ca.

Canadian Alliance. (2000b, October). A time for change: An agenda of respect for all Canadians. www.canadianalliance.ca.

Carty, R. K., Cross, W., & Young, L. (2000). *Rebuilding Canadian party politics*. Vancouver: University of British Columbia Press.

Dabbs, F. (1997). *Preston Manning: The roots of reform*. Vancouver: Greystone.

Dale, S. (1999). *Lost in the suburbs: A political travelogue*. Toronto: Stoddart.

Dobbin, M. (1991). *Preston Manning and the Reform Party*. Toronto: Lorimer.

Flanagan, T. (1995). *Waiting for the wave: The Reform Party and Preston Manning*. Toronto: Stoddart.

Grant, G. (1995). *Lament for a nation: The defeat of Canadian nationalism*. Ottawa: Carleton University Press.

Harrison, T. (1995). *Of passionate intensity: Right-wing populism and the Reform Party of Canada*. Toronto: University of Toronto Press.

Horowitz, G. (1967). Conservatism, liberalism and socialism in Canada: An interpretation. In H. Thorburn (Ed.), *Party politics in Canada* (2nd ed.) (pp. 55–73). Scarborough, ON: Prentice Hall.

Ibbitson, J. (1997). *Promised land: Inside the Mike Harris revolution*. Scarborough, ON: Prentice Hall.

Jeffrey, B. (1999). *Hard right turn: The new face of neo-conservatism in Canada*. Toronto: HarperCollins.

Laycock, D. (1990). *Populism and democratic thought in the Canadian prairies, 1910–1945*. Toronto: University of Toronto Press.

Laycock, D. (1994). Reforming Canadian democracy? Institutions and ideology in the Reform party project. *Canadian Journal of Political Science 27* (2), 213–247.

Leblanc, D. (2000, July 11). Here's what Day has in store for Canada. *Globe and Mail*, p. A4.

Locke, J. (1986). *Two treatises of government*. London: Dent/Everyman.

Manning, P. (1992). *The new Canada*. Toronto: Macmillan.

McBride, S., & Shields, J. (1993). *Dismantling a nation: Canada and the new world order*. Halifax, NS: Fernwood.

Patten, S. (1996, Summer). Preston Manning's populism: Constructing the common sense of the common people. *Studies in Political Economy 50*, 95–132.

Ralph, D., Régimbald, A., & St. Amand, N. (1997). *Open for business, closed to people: Mike Harris's Ontario*. Halifax, NS: Fernwood.

Sharpe, S., & Braid, D. (1992). *Storming Babylon: Preston Manning and the rise of the Reform Party*. Toronto: Key Porter.

Sigurdson, R. (1994). Preston Manning and the politics of postmodernism in Canada. *Canadian Journal of Political Science 27* (2), 249–276.

Taylor, C. (1982). *Radical Tories: The conservative tradition in Canada*. Halifax, NS: Formac Publishing.

Walkom, T. (1997). The Harris government: Restoration or revolution? In G. White (Ed.), *The government and politics of Ontario* (5th ed.) (pp. 402–417). Toronto: University of Toronto Press.

Chapter 14

The Center-Periphery Dialectic in Cape Breton: A Discourse Analysis

Carol Corbin and Mike Hunter

Many institutions bind people together as citizens of the nation-state. In a democracy as geographically vast and as culturally diverse as Canada, vital national institutions include defense, transportation, and communication. In addition, national social programs such as publicly funded health care, employment insurance, and old age income security make this country the envy of the world, according to the United Nations.[1] In partnership with provincial governments, Canada's Parliament strives to configure the national infrastructure so as to redistribute wealth between geographic areas of plenty and those of scarcity, between the economically blessed and the economically stressed—marginalized people and regions at the periphery of prosperity.

Nonetheless, the centralized institutions of redistribution, including economic development agencies and Crown corporations, sometimes become the site of political conflict. The conflict grows out of the perception that centrally incorporated political and economic power happens at the expense of self-reliance at the periphery. Indeed, these institutions are often the proverbial pigskins of political football, to the detriment of those least able to assert themselves.

One such site of the center-periphery dialectic is Cape Breton Island, situated on Nova Scotia's east coast. Cape Breton Island is sometimes viewed as culturally, as well as geographically, distinct from the rest of the province (if not the entire country). In recent decades, the Cape Breton economy has relied heavily on federal and provincial programs such as employment insurance and social assistance, as well as intervention in the form of economic development subsidies and takeovers of industries. Despite billions of government dollars expended, Cape Bretoners continue to view their political masters at the center with resentment and suspicion. Perceiving that political and cultural institutions are concentrated in centers such as Halifax and Ottawa, and that decision-making excludes them, Cape Bretoners express a popular sentiment that they are at the periphery of power. The purpose of this chapter is to analyze the discourse related to the contesting of power between the provincial center (Halifax) and the periphery (Cape Breton), as recorded by the daily press serving Cape Breton Island. This analysis will enable us to determine to what extent the people construct their situation as marginalized and disenfranchised.

CONTEXT

For three centuries, Cape Breton Island was a vibrant center of trade and commerce—a sea link and stepping-stone connecting Europe with North American expansion (Moore, 1990). As Europeans encroached on the continent in mounting numbers, the Island evolved from its role as a staging point and supplier of resources to a trade and communication link. Meanwhile, coal mining and steel-making employed thousands. As settlements pushed westward across the continent, Cape Breton gradually lost its strategic economic prominence. During the 300 years prior to World War II, a small merchant class prospered from this colonial exploitation; but, more often than not, the general population remained largely rural and/or working class (Bitterman, 1990; Hornsby, 1990). The Euro-population consisted largely of economic refugees and their descendants. Cape Breton's heavy industries were often a battleground for colonial capitalists and a frustrated proletariat, whose ancestors had come here in search of a better life. Yet the better life, at least as signified by economic prosperity, seemed to develop further west, along with the centers of power.

Government policy papers and academic studies have made two antithetical points about Cape Breton's economic history: (1) the Island has a cultivated reliance on government and (2) economic development must grow from local initiatives. In fact, federal government policies modernized Ontario and Québec factories but ignored an existing capability to manufacture steel plates for ships in Sydney's steel mill, a policy that also pulled non-enlisted workers away from the Island (Forbes, 1986). The postwar economies elsewhere continued to grow, leaving the Island behind. Then in the 1960s, the provincial and federal governments intervened directly when private investment pulled out of the Island's two largest industries—steel-making and coal mining. This withdrawal of capital by private industry threatened thousands of jobs and contributed to the collapse of the regional economy. Antithetically, while Cape Breton relies heavily on government, experts allege that its economy can develop only through local initiatives (Enterprise Cape Breton Corporation, 2000; MacIntyre, 1998).

Despite the interdependence implicit in confederation and the explicit

dependence on government intervention and social programs, Cape Bretoners frequently raise the idea that the Island should become Canada's
eleventh province. Historian Robert Morgan notes that Cape Breton has a
long history of movements seeking independence from Halifax (MacInnis,
2000, p. 1A). One *Cape Breton Post* editorial asks, "What is it . . . that
seems to resonate so strongly with the perception that Cape Breton is ill-
treated within Nova Scotia?" The editorial answered: "Politicians will have
to take seriously [the notion of] splitting the Island away from a central
authority that is seen as unresponsive if not downright hostile to the interests of outlying regions" ("Parallels Show," 2000, p. 4). Letter after letter
in the newspapers' editorial pages expresses a general dissatisfaction with
the disparity (see Isaac, 2000; J. MacDonald, 2000; Morrison, 2000). "It's
high time we took charge of our own destiny and stopped the years of
standing in line with our hands out waiting for something to drop in them,"
writes another (Martell, 2000, p. 5).

Historically, the Canadian government has played an active role in building transportation and communication systems across the vast geographic
expanse of the country to create a national economy. In his analysis of the
role of communication in the economy of Canada, Harold Innis recognized
that communities at the frontier struggle with the central power at the
"back tier" for control over their place in time and space (Carey, 1985).
The strength of the industrial center of Canada accrues, in part, from harvesting of resources from the periphery—a hallmark of colonialism. This
practice generated two forms of dependency: (1) government ownership
and intervention (the legacy of supporting private enterprises during industrial and territorial expansion) and (2) a dependency that is "the net
effect of intervention [that] undermines the very aims" of economic policy
(Dowler, 1996, p. 333). Although labeled a "culture of dependency," the
people of the Island have struggled repeatedly to control their own decisions and futures, only to have outside forces impose decisions on them
(deRoche, 2000).

Cape Breton's center-periphery struggle plays out in many discursive theaters and on different geographic scales. Similar micro-marginalization occurs within and between Cape Breton communities, while in macro terms,
the entire Atlantic region occupies a position peripheral to the economic
and social hegemony of central Canada. The marginality of the periphery
at various levels creates a continuous site of Foucaultian struggle over "difference" and identity (see Brown, 1995; Fiske, 1998; Hall, 1980). The
power of the center to name and define Cape Breton as "dependent," "a
problem," and the "have-not" region of Canada further identifies the dominant discourse of Cape Breton as marginal, even as Cape Bretoners resist
it in their struggles for self-reliance.

SCOPE AND METHOD

In this section we explore perceptions of the distribution of power and decision making, the autonomy of small communities, and the future of communities in terms of development. We look at three issues: the construction of a casino in Sydney, the amalgamating of rural Cape Breton schools, and disputes over community development. We analyze how these struggles were discursively presented in daily newspapers in Cape Breton from 1994 to 2000.

We analyzed news items and letters to the editor related to our three topics, which appeared in the *Cape Breton Post* and the *Halifax Chronicle Herald* during the period from 1994 to 2000. We outline the general background of each issue in order to establish a context for the discourse and present perspectives of both the center and the periphery. Narratives emerge within the sets of discourses chosen for this study and we have, as often as possible, included direct expressions of the power struggle. The three topics that we selected are not unique; other contentious issues exist that, at different times and with different levels of saliency, also demonstrate how central powers imposed decisions on the periphery. They include municipal amalgamations, fisheries policy, labor relations, and transportation policy, to name a few. In each of the cases we explore, Cape Bretoners were resigned to accepting control from afar as their lot—but not without a struggle.[2] It is the struggle we wish to document.

We recognize that the provincial government and its agencies have greater expertise and more resources at their disposal to frame and present their case (e.g., through media releases and public relations professionals), compared with limitations at the periphery. On the other hand, individuals and community groups at the periphery have more freedom to express their opinions. They are less constrained by political, electoral, and employment considerations. Additionally, journalists tend to gravitate toward controversial topics, grassroots rebellion, and insubordination because conflict is "news." Knowing the power of government to both create and be at the center of news stories, journalists often take an adversarial role in writing and researching those stories. The comparative volume of rhetoric from the periphery and its emotional content ensured a large presence in the media, evident in our analysis. Nonetheless, the voices from the periphery are more likely to be muted than overstated, and however much we report the rhetoric from the periphery, inherent bias still favors the center. Hackett and Gruneau (2000) agree that when bias is present, it tends to favor the establishment over any advocacy group(s).

ISSUES

As previously noted, this section of the chapter examines three issues: the construction of a casino in Sydney, the amalgamating of rural Cape Breton schools, and disputes over community development.

Casinos

In April 1994, the government of Nova Scotia announced plans for a new framework of regulations for gambling in the province. Lotteries, bingo, video gambling machines, and casinos would be regulated and all other forms of gambling outlawed. It was argued that the building of casinos in the province would generate revenue that would ultimately result in tax breaks (MacDonald, 1994c). Liberal Premier John Savage attempted to persuade Cape Bretoners that casinos would offer substantial benefits to the province's health, social, and educational systems.[3] "The casino will create hundreds of jobs," Savage asserted (Stewart, 1994a, p. 1). The head of the provincial gaming authority agreed, "Our purpose in starting the casino is to create employment and bring in revenue" (Lichter, cited in Campbell, 1994b, p. 3). The reactions of outraged advocacy groups were echoed by public sentiment in Cape Breton, where one of the two casinos was built against the wishes of the general population ("Casinos Would," 1994).

Having "banked" on the revenue casinos would create, there was no turning back in the face of public opposition. "There's a price for not having the revenues. . . . The price for that may in fact be additional service cuts," threatened government house leader Richie Mann (cited in Jeffers, 1994, p. 1). After the enactment of the casino legislation, the premier stated, "Whether or not people approve of casinos in Cape Breton, they have to realize there is a major opportunity there, including for employment" (Savage, cited in Montgomery, 1994b, p. 3). When construction was actually under way, Savage noted, "The employment factor is the issue [to be] more focused on than anything," as opposed to problem gambling and predicted increases in crime (Savage, cited in Hayes, 1995, p. 3).

When the Sydney city council called for public hearings on the matter, the provincial finance minister Bernie Boudreau stated he would consider public hearings only if the process could not be used "to subvert the decision government has made" (Boudreau in Chambers, 1994, p. 3). The casino legislation waived public hearings under the environment act; circumvented local planning authorities, as well as the need for building permits; and resisted the need to hold plebiscites in granting liquor licenses to the casinos (Chambers, 1994). Boudreau said the legislation meant that "it is not a municipal matter" (Stewart, 1994b, p. 3). Premier Savage and Minister Boudreau were resolute in their intent to push through the legislation, regardless of opposition. Premier Savage said that "a casino for Cape Breton is a sure bet, no matter what opposition rises against the idea now." He added that such opposition "had already been heard and would no longer be considered" (MacDonald, 1994b, p. 2). Boudreau reiterated, "I respect their concerns . . . but the province as a whole has never been run by groups like these and I don't think we can allow that to start now" ("Casino Bill," 1994, p. 28).

For Sydney's elected officials, the board of trade, advocacy groups, and citizens at large, the issue was greater than just jobs and government revenues. Their focus was on perceived social costs and the fact that they were powerless to stop the provincial government from overriding local concerns. A municipal casino committee rejected a gaming facility, "concerned [it] would only take more money out of the area's fragile economy and . . . not create any new wealth" (MacInnis, 1994, p. 3). Mayor Vince MacLean said, "Sydney is saying no deal . . . unanimously." He planned to "oppose a casino by any legal means available" (Hayes, 1994b, p. 3). Although "vehemently opposed" to the casino, the municipal council was "all but powerless to overturn or change a decision already taken by their provincial overseer" (MacDonald, 1995, p. 6). The Board of Trade's president said, "over 80 percent of members said 'no' to casinos"; a board member remarked that jobs in casinos "will be jobs lost when smaller businesses and entertainment [go out of business]. We won't gain anything" (Morrison, cited in MacDonald, 1994a, p. 3).[4]

Advocacy groups such as People Against Casinos were vociferous in their opposition, predicting casinos would bring "economic disaster" to the Island ("Casinos Would," 1994, p. 3). Their premise, which ran counter to government's prediction of more jobs and increased revenues, was that legalized gambling would negatively affect a large number of poor people, draw money out of circulation in local businesses, and increase crime. The Medical Society of Nova Scotia also spoke against casinos, saying that the government did not completely calculate social and health costs. The society's president stated, "Like most Nova Scotians, the medical society understands that casinos will cause irrevocable harm to our economy and our society" (Kimball in Hayes, 1994a, p. 3).

Citizens at large were the most vocal on the casino issue, citing concerns for the social impact of a casino and for the unilateral manner in which the provincial government imposed it. "What do we want for Cape Breton?" asked one reader of the Cape Breton Post. "We must reject this quick fix . . . which will destroy what little integrity we have left" (Pilsworth, 1994, p. 5). "Gambling will financially devastate many families who are already struggling," increasing demand on "our already over burdened social agencies and charitable organizations" (George, 1994, p. 5). "Casinos just take money from us" (Webber in Montgomery, 1994a, p. 7).

One citizen asked, "Whose idea is this anyway? I have heard no public clamor . . . for such an enterprise. To the contrary, the very idea is repugnant to us" (Patterson, 1994, p. 5). "We, as citizens, have a right to say Yes or No for something which . . . will be of no value to us or our children," said another resident (Cameron, 1994, p. 5). Others stated that the casino was "disastrous" (Morrison, cited in MacDonald, 1994c, p. 1) and "the greatest threat to the Cape Breton economy since the threatened closure of the Sydney steel plant in 1967" (Stubbert, cited in Campbell, 1994a, p. 3).

Finally, sensing defeat in their efforts to stop the project, the municipal council tried to cut a deal that would make the best of a bad hand. A Sydney alderman stated, "It is with great disgust that we follow the total arrogance in the way they've shunted aside the democratic process" (MacEachern, cited in MacDonald, 1995, p. 6). Over the objections of local government, businesses, advocacy groups, the official opposition, the clergy, and the majority of the population, a casino was imposed on the people of Sydney by their political masters in Halifax.

Schools

Declining enrollment and a perceived need to equip public schools with high-technology tools led government to institute a plan to build large, centralized schools through a program called public-private partnership (P3, in the local vernacular). Private enterprises used their own capital to construct the schools, then leased them to the school boards. Government messages emphasized belt-tightening measures, efficiencies, and improved services, stating that "larger schools allow for more specialized instruction and greater program variety" (Harder, 1998, p. A4). "Full-time positions can be provided for music, gym and resource teachers. Equipment and facilities can be superior at bigger schools" ("Superschool," 1998, p. A7). From a "system point of view it makes only too much sense, inevitable sense, and it's only in the view of individual local communities on the losing end that it doesn't" ("Losing Schools," 1999, p. 4).

In some Cape Breton communities the P3 scheme was accepted as a means for replacement of run-down institutions, but others were opposed to—and suspicious of—the plan. "Don't be deceived by the words or promises," cautioned one reader of the Cape Breton Post. "The aggressive promotion of public-private partnerships reflects government irresponsibility and corporate greed" (MacInnis, J., 1999, p. 5). Citizens argued that school amalgamations, long bus rides, and profit-driven models were impractical in rural areas. One letter stated, "Replacing government-owned, community-based schools with privately-owned leased schools . . . is not a practical solution in rural areas," which lack "the population density to fit a profit-driven school model" (Yipp, 1999, p. 5). "Groups battling for their schools contend that it makes no financial or academic sense to abandon aging but still serviceable schools to construct new multi-million dollar ones" ("Losing Schools," 1999, p. 4).

When one community in central Cape Breton (Whycocomagh) learned that a proposed hour-long school bus route would result from a change to their community's existing school, they were outraged. Parents and teachers believed their children were being forced to make the journey in order to make a new P3 school in Mabou viable. Dozens of community meetings, public demonstrations, audiences with cabinet ministers and the premier, and even an advertising campaign, were to no avail. The parents' group said it believed "there is a two-tier education system in the province—one for urban areas and larger towns, and another for rural communities" (King, 2000b, p. 7). A provincially mandated school advisory group's recommendation that the Strait-Region School Board should consider the parents' concerns went unheeded. "Some public officials and representatives do not consider distance to be an issue, or the [wishes of a] 'minority' of students . . . to be important" (Machin, 1999, p. 5). Parents and school children staged a noisy protest that disrupted traffic on the trans-Canada highway near their town and vowed to continue their "battle" with the school board (King, 1999h, p. 13).

Parents in two other small communities, who learned of a proposed school closing and a one-hour commute for children, staged protests. Seeing a community without children as no community at all, indignant parents "occupied" the school, locking out administrators, teachers, and students for more than a week. Meanwhile, they demanded the intervention of the Minister of Education. "The parents had tried going through the proper channels" but lost "patience" (Rankin in King, 1999a, p. 13). Most of the community supported the protest. Local businesses closed their doors and darkened storefronts one afternoon, in an attempt to show the media and politicians what the towns might eventually look like if the school was closed. The protesters won their meeting with the Minister of Education, after which he noted that hearing their concerns and touring the school "certainly brings it into perspective. I think they have real concerns" (King, 1999b, p. 15) He said he would raise those concerns with the school board but that he had no intention of changing the decision. Threat of a court injunction brought an end to the parents' occupation of the school, but not to their fight.

During that same period (March 1–10, 1999), parents in North East Margaree, Cape Breton, briefly occupied their town's elementary school, in protest of another P3 construction scheme. Their protest was ended by a court injunction. In the coastal town of Inverness, parents and students joined hands and formed a one-kilometer human chain to express concerns that Inverness Academy (a high school less than 10 years old) would also be sacrificed to "pad enrollment figures" at the P3 high school in Mabou (Ryan, cited in King, 1999d, p. 25). Meanwhile, on the other side of the

Island, in Richmond County, parents and students were engaged in protests over the location of a proposed P3 school—a location they felt was politically motivated (because it favored one community over others) and unsuitable because it was adjacent to a former landfill site. During one protest, a grade 11 student told a reporter that parents and students were "tired of people not listening" (Samson, cited in King, 1999c, p. 10). Parents formed a lobby group and launched a court challenge of the school board's decision. Although they received some concessions, the P3 plan was implemented (King, 1999b, p. 9).

Parents in smaller communities wanted to keep schools closer to home for a variety of reasons. "Worries about larger schools [included fears of] increased violence, longer bus rides, lower parent participation, and reduced achievement for some students" (Harder, 1998, p. A4). For small communities, the "demographic realities" of school populations and concerns about viability were symbolic of the growing perception that the communities themselves were being phased out ("Losing Schools," 1999, p. 4). When the school board said that they "don't have sustainable enrollment" (King, 1999e, p.18) and that the physical structures of schools were "inadequate to offer modern education" (Proctor, 1998, p. A6), it was like saying that small and rural communities were likewise unsustainable and inadequate. The threat of school closures in favor of bussing children to a neighboring town pitted "community against community" in the competition for new facilities (King, 1999d, p. 25).

While bureaucrats championed change and efficiency, parents championed "community values" (Roach, 1999, p. 5). The debate highlighted "how painful . . . this is for rural communities that are losing the vital focus of their schools, after they have lost so much else in the relentless march of demographic change and public centralization" ("Losing Schools," 1999, p. 4). Schools help to define intensely proud communities, and loss of a school tends to entrench feelings of hopelessness and alienation from decision making, further silencing small towns and rural communities. To say bigger is better is to say that smaller is less desirable, and rural citizens emphasized that "losing a school would have a dramatic effect on the community," like making a community into a suburb (King, 1999f, p. 16; Proctor, 1999, p. A7).

The school debate was as painful for rural Cape Breton communities as the casino debate was for Sydney. Although elected school board members (trustees) and board employees were local residents, they were mandated by government to carry out its wishes, thereby placing added strain on community relations and the struggle with centralized power. "Community groups see the board as a corrupt central force that will destroy the community" (Roach, 1999, p. 5). "The board is out of touch with the people of the community [and] has turned many a community against their neighbor" (Boucher in King, 2000a, p. 19). "Meetings set up by the school board to work on the future plans . . . are not open to the public, nor are minutes kept. The majority of participants are school board employees who are not allowed to disagree openly with board policy" (Gunn, 1999, p. 5). Still, as one writer noted, the center sees the issue as an unemotional one, based on "cost effectiveness and efficiency" and views the rhetoric from the periphery as coming from "emotional reactionary tribes who do not understand the monetary pressures of the modern world" (Roach, 1999, p. 5). None of the school decisions were reversed.[5]

Community Development

Governments intervened even more directly in the Cape Breton economy[6] in the late 1960s—first the provincial (which took over the steel mill) and then the federal (which took over the coal mines). They attempted to deflect a catastrophic loss of nearly 10,000 jobs by finding new owners, or alternatively, gradually diversifying the local economy. During the 30 years that followed, billions of tax dollars were allocated in periodic attempts to either modernize or to keep the operations afloat; both Sydney Steel Corporation and Cape Breton Development Corporation became highly politicized as Cape Bretoners were forced to depend on government. That reliance grew as successive government-driven diversification efforts failed and the economy in Atlantic Canada continued to decline in favor of central and western regions. Years of continued downward economic pressure in Cape Breton (slumping coal markets, declining fish stocks, the demise of family farming, and out-migration) and continued subsidies found the local economy contingent on election promises and attacks from revolving opposition parties. Chronic high unemployment[7] resulted in characterizations of Cape Breton as "an island of beggars always asking for more money" and subsidies as a "waste" of taxpayers' money (Gallant & Desaulniers, 2000, p. 5). Cape Breton leaders asserted that Islanders needed a "hand up," not a "hand-out," but two generations of political rhetoric had been internalized by the population, who saw themselves as both dependent on—and victimized by—government largess.

Yet Cape Breton has long been regarded as the birthplace of the self-help, cooperative movement in Canada. In the 1920s and 1930s, Cape Breton cousins Reverends Moses Coady and Jimmy Tompkins mobilized fishers, coal miners, farmers, women's groups, and churches to cooperate on processing, marketing, housing, and community development efforts in Cape Breton and in eastern Nova Scotia; and the situation appeared for a time to be changing. Government policy makers began to use terms like "grassroots" and community "capacity-building" to describe development initiatives and to promulgate a more facilitative role for government. They pulled back from outright intervention. In the 1980s and 1990s, modest government investment helped to fund a number of community-based groups and strategies. These endeavors enjoyed varying degrees of success. Then in 2000, both levels of government announced changes in focus. While they continued to use the grassroots language of community cooperation, they began to back only recognized regional development agencies (RDAs). Smaller, community-based grassroots development corporations, commissions, and citizen groups lost funding and folded (Collins, 2000a).

Cape Bretoners repeatedly advanced decentralization of government as a means to improve peripheral economies by dispersing jobs, wealth, and power. They asked the provincial government to consider changes such as moving some offices from Halifax: "Sydney has the lowest number of public-sector jobs per capita in the country" ("Halifax Grows," 1999, p. 1). As long as centralization is the norm, "high-earning management positions, which control the key decisions, will be in Halifax" (MacLeod, 1999, p. 5). Decentralization would not only bring jobs but would increase the participation of rural Canada in key policy decisions (Surette, 1999). The provincial premier has said that he is committed to a more equitable distribution of influence and benefits across the province (Hamm in "Hinterlands," 2000). Nonetheless, during the first half of 2000, the provincial government introduced measures that would privatize many civil service jobs in some rural areas, thus abdicating willy-nilly any decentralization of those positions and casting doubt on their very existence (Collins, 2000b; King, 2000c).

The president of the University College of Cape Breton—itself the product of a hard fight—noted in a speech to the legislative Standing Committee on Economic Development, "The relationship between Cape Breton and mainland Nova Scotia has been characterized by a culture of colonization" (Scott, 1999, n.p.) She highlighted the "willingness of provincial politicians to buy into [the] view of Cape Breton as a 'problem,' " thus creating a climate in which "civil servants are suspicious and inclined to believe Cape Bretoners are too stupid or corrupt to make their own decisions" (Scott, 1999, n.p.).

Most of the Cape Breton discourse concerning community development reflected a feeling of disenfranchisement from decision making. Despite the rhetoric of policy makers who regularly exhorted grassroots empowerment, Cape Bretoners articulated frustration over lack of control of their destiny. In practice, Cape Bretoners are rarely permitted the luxury of self-determination, because consultation usually occurs after policy decisions have been made. Such consultations, therefore, are regarded merely as "sell jobs." Development programs devised outside the Island are met with suspicion (well-founded, according to the discourse), and this "resistance" continues to confound government and to impede progress to alleviate long-standing economic disparity.

CONCLUSION

We suggest that pressure to centralize (and sometimes to recentralize) power in metropolitan areas is in constant tension with the decision-making power and decentralization sought by rural communities. This continuous push and pull for empowerment of the periphery has become, in our estimation, an impediment to rural development. Inflexibility on the part of the center toward the needs of the periphery leads to contradictions in terms of community empowerment and community development. In one context, centralizing rhetoric takes power away from the periphery; in another context, the center expects self-determination and independent action of the periphery. The result is confusion, conflict, embittered relations, and little real development or self-determination.

It is not surprising, then, that citizens of Cape Breton have talked of seceding from Nova Scotia and forming an independent province. Cape Bretoners have had little say in their affairs, having repeatedly been directed from Halifax regarding matters that are at the very core of community viability, identity, and culture. Canadian emphasis on the mosaic of culture and the instantiation of multicultural values in the *Charter of Rights and Freedoms* have led to extensive discussions about how to protect and nurture communities or groups of people within Canada. A community's identity, like a person's identity, is formed through dialogue. Often that dialogue is one of struggle, a dialectic because "dominant groups tend to entrench their hegemony by inculcating an image of inferiority in the subjugated" (Taylor, 1994, p. 68). Yet, in order for a community to encourage active civic participation among its members, legacies of dependence and exploitation need to be replaced with reciprocity and trust (Putnam, 1993). The rhetoric of centralization tends to strengthen deeply rooted hierarchies, creating frustration and antagonism at the periphery and weakening local civic involvement by decreasing faith in the political process. By making Halifax the site of all decision-making opportunities, the provincial government says that it does not trust Cape Bretoners to know what is best for their own island. Additionally, the disregard of central powers for the views of rural constituents further erodes local pride, cultural identity, and civic initiative.

Our analysis suggests that the tensions between the political center of Nova Scotia and the peripheral areas of Cape Breton over community futures create an inconsistent relationship when it comes to development in poorer areas. As development agencies exhort local initiatives, grassroots activists see opinions dismissed and decisions ignored. Considering the chronic unemployment, high out-migration, loss of industry, and conflicting rhetoric, it is not surprising that development is a struggle in Cape Breton. Moreover, the lack of consultation and the coercive tactics used by government in these and other cases throws into question the very notion of democracy. Time and again, Cape Breton residents question whether they in fact live in a democracy. In Cape Breton, decision making has been removed from the people who are to reap the benefits or suffer the consequences of the decisions. This center-periphery dialectic is not exclusive to Cape Breton's struggle with Halifax; and these contradictions have implications for all Canadian communities, as power continues to concentrate in centralized urban areas.

NOTES

1. Findings of the 1995, 1996, and 1997 United Nations Human Development Report stated that Canada's overall quality of life makes it the best country in the world in which to live. See http://www.cio-bic.gc.ca/facts/mondocan_e.html.

2. A February 2000 survey of citizens in the Cape Breton Regional Municipality indicated that 70 percent believed they had not been well served by a 1995 amalgamation of eight smaller municipal units into one metropolitan area. Nevertheless, 54 percent believed amalgamation was "here to stay," and an even larger percentage felt powerless to change it (Camus, 2000).

3. In July 2000, the Nova Scotia Gaming Corporation reported the province's two casinos took in $84.1 million in the year ending March 31, 2000, $28.5 million in Sydney. Total gaming revenues in that year (casinos, VLTs, lottery games) were $417 million, netting the province $148.6 million ("Sydney Casino," 2000). Still, in the fiscal year beginning April 1, 2000, the government cut funding for hospitals and for public education, because of a budgetary deficit of nearly $300 million, despite five years of gaming profits ("Budget Documents," 2000).

4. This assertion was borne out in time. Several eating and drinking establishments near the casino in the downtown Sydney area did eventually go out of business (White, 2000).

5. A change of government, resulting from a provincial general election in 1999, caused a reexamination of the P3 concept, in part because of the public outcry. The new government said it would not pursue further partnerships for new school construction and it would revert to conventional methods of financing. In its first full budget, in April 2000, however, the new government promised to slash $23.7 million and 400 teachers from school boards across the province, amid predictions of classes swelling to 50 students. Yet, in a growth strategy document published in June 2000, the government recognized that it must work to provide leadership which "cuts across many lines of responsibilities . . . especially education" (Nova Scotia Economic Development, 2000).

6. The term *community development* has many connotations, but public discourse generally revolves around the state of the Cape Breton economy and our focus necessarily follows.

7. "Halifax's unemployment rate stands at . . . about a third of the Cape Breton rate" ("Cape Breton's Jobless," 1999, p. 4).

REFERENCES

Bitterman, R. (1990). Economic stratification and agrarian settlement: Middle River in the early nineteenth century. In K. Donovan (Ed.), *The Island: New perspectives on Cape Breton history 1713–1990* (pp. 71–88). Fredericton, NB: Acadiensis.

Brown, W. (1995). *States of injury: Power and freedom in late modernity.* Princeton, NJ: Princeton University Press.

Cameron, A. (1994, June 24). Sydney should stand against casino [Letter to the editor]. *Cape Breton Post*, p. 5.

Campbell, J. (1994a, August 12). Opposition to gambling enforced by western trip. *Cape Breton Post*, p. 3.

Campbell, J. (1994b, August 18). Casino bids under review. *Cape Breton Post*, p. 3.

Camus, T. (2000, June 30). Amalgamation costly concept—CB survey. *Halifax Chronicle Herald*, p. B5.

Cape Breton's jobless rate moves upward [Editorial]. (1999, November 6). *Cape Breton Post*, p. 4.

Carey, J. W. (1985). Culture, geography, and communications: The work of Harold Innis in an American context. In W. H. Melody, L. R. Salter, & P. Heyer (Eds.), *Culture, communication, and dependency: The tradition of H. A. Innis* (pp. 73–91). Norwood, NJ: Ablex.

Casino bill moves ahead. (1994, November 26). *Cape Breton Post*, p. 28.

Casinos would be economic disaster, claim opponents. (1994, August 17). *Cape Breton Post*, p. 3.

Chambers, B. (1994, November 11). Public interference won't be tolerated. *Cape Breton Post*, p. 3.

Collins, J. (2000a, July 19). New Deal Developments fears for its survival. *Cape Breton Post*, p. 27.

Collins, J. (2000b, August 23). Uncertain future upsets employees. *Cape Breton Post*, p. 10.

deRoche, C. (1999). *Culture of poverty revisited: Dependency and community economic development theory in the new world order.* Unpublished paper. University College of Cape Breton.

Dowler, K. (1996). The cultural industries policy apparatus. In M. Dorland (Ed.), *The cultural industries in Canada: Problems, policies and prospects* (pp. 328–346). Toronto: James Lorimer.

Enterprise Cape Breton Corporation. (2000, March). *Growing the new economy: Findings of the economic adjustment fund public consultation process.* Sydney, Nova Scotia.

Fiske, J. (1998). Culture, ideology, interpellation. In J. Rivkin & M. Ryan (Eds.), *Literary theory: An anthology* (pp. 305–311). Malden, MA: Blackwell.

Forbes, E. R. (1986). Consolidating disparity: The Maritimes and the industrialization of Canada during the Second World War. *Acadiensis 15* (2), 3–27.

Gallant, R., & Desaulniers, C. M. (2000, January 21). We'll share the pain if you'll share the wealth [Letter to the editor]. *Cape Breton Post*, p. 5.

George, L. (1994, June 11). Casinos threaten Cape Breton family life [Letter to the editor]. *Cape Breton Post*, p. 5.

Gunn, T. (1999, December 11). Ad campaign well supported by community [Letter to the editor]. *Cape Breton Post*, p. 5.

Hackett, R. A., & Gruneau, R. (2000). *The missing news: Filters and blind spots in Canada's press*. Ottawa: Garamond Press.

Halifax grows as remainder of province starves: ECBC head. (1999, March 6). *Cape Breton Post*, p. 1.

Hall, S. (1980). Encoding/decoding. In S. Hall, D. Hobson, A. Lowe, & P. Willis (Eds.), *Culture, media, language: Working papers in cultural studies* (pp. 128–138). London: Hutchinson.

Harder, S. (1998, August 26). Big schools worry parents. *Halifax Chronicle Herald*, p. A4.

Hayes, C. (1994a, August 26). Doctors chip in on casinos. *Cape Breton Post*, p. 3.

Hayes, C. (1994b, September 16). Council says no deal to casino plan. *Cape Breton Post*, p. 3.

Hayes, C. (1995, August 2). Premier lists benefits of Sydney casino. *Cape Breton Post*, p. 3.

Hinterlands getting nicked [Editorial]. (2000, April 19). *Cape Breton Post*, p. 4.

Hornsby, S. (1990). Scottish emigration and settlement in early nineteenth-century Cape Breton. In K. Donovan (Ed.), *The Island: New perspectives on Cape Breton history 1713–1990* (pp. 49–69). Fredericton, NB: Acadiensis.

Jeffers, A. (1994, October 24). Legislation package expected to draw fire. *Cape Breton Post*, p. 1.

Isaac, W. (2000, February 17). Deck is stacked [Letter to the editor]. *Cape Breton Post*, p. 5.

King, N. (1999a, March 2). Protesters settle in. *Cape Breton Post*, p. 13.

King, N. (1999b, March 4). Protest draws official's ire. *Cape Breton Post*, p. 15.

King, N. (1999c, March 5). Strait school board facing $2.2 million cut due to declining student enrollment. *Cape Breton Post*, p. 10.

King, N. (1999d, March 6). Parents, students join hands to make point about school. *Cape Breton Post*, p. 25.

King, N. (1999e, March 9). Sides stand firm in Judique. *Cape Breton Post*, p. 18.

King, N. (1999f, April 28). Board members under fire in public meeting. *Cape Breton Post*, p. 16.

King, N. (1999g, December 3). Marchers hit streets in protest. *Cape Breton Post*, p. 9.

King, N. (1999h, December 7). Parents accept settlement. *Cape Breton Post*, p. 13.

King, N. (2000a, January 22). School board review group told bigger isn't better. *Cape Breton Post*, p. 19.

King, N. (2000b, January 31). Residents berate school board meeting. *Cape Breton Post*, p. 7.

King, N. (2000c, June 15). Highway workers ask council for help in fight against privatization. *Cape Breton Post*, p. 25.

Losing schools a painful thing [Editorial]. (1999, March 6). *Cape Breton Post*, p. 4.

MacDonald, J. (2000, February 17). Provincehood needs hearing [Letter to the editor]. *Cape Breton Post*, p. 5.

MacDonald, T. (1994a, July 26). BoT to poll members on casino support. *Cape Breton Post*, p. 3.

MacDonald, T. (1994b, August 12). Savage says Island casino sure thing. *Cape Breton Post*, p. 2.

MacDonald, T. (1994c, September 24). We'll believe it when we see it. *Cape Breton Post*, p. 1.

MacDonald, T. (1995, January 6). Sydney Alderman will take casino protest to Halifax. *Cape Breton Post*, p. 6.

Machin, A. (1999, March 18). Long bus rides would hurt students [Letter to the editor]. *Cape Breton Post*, p. 5.

MacInnis, J. (1999, November 17). Beware privatization by stealth [Letter to the editor]. *Cape Breton Post*, p. 5.

MacInnis, S. (1994, July 15). Committee issues casino demands. *Cape Breton Post*, p. 3.

MacInnis, S. (2000, February 19). Cutting the cord. *Cape Breton Post*, p. 1A.

MacIntyre, G. A. (1998). *Perspectives on Communities*. Sydney, NS: University College of Cape Breton Press.

MacLeod, G. (1999, June 25). Halifax still covets power jobs [Letter to the editor]. *Cape Breton Post*, p. 5.

Martell, J. (2000, March 18). Separation might change island's beggar status [Letter to the editor]. *Cape Breton Post*, p. 5.

Montgomery, S. (1994a, September 12). Horror stories top petition meeting. *Cape Breton Post*, p. 7.

Montgomery, S. (1994b, December 31). Premier bets casino will benefit bars. *Cape Breton Post*, p. 3.

Moore, C. (1990). Cape Breton and the North Atlantic world in the eighteenth century. In K. Donovan (Ed.), *The Island: New perspectives on Cape Breton history 1713–1990* (pp. 31–49). Fredericton, NB: Acadiensis.

Morrison, D. B. (2000, February 28). Provincehood distracts attention from reform [Letter to the editor]. *Cape Breton Post*, p. 5.

Nova Scotia Economic Development. (2000). *Toward prosperity: Developing an economic growth strategy for Nova Scotia'a discussion paper*. Halifax: Communications Nova Scotia.

Parallels show among dissenters [Editorial]. (2000, February 19). *Cape Breton Post*, p. 4.

Patterson, P. (1994, July 30). Casino a stiletto aimed at Island's soul. *Cape Breton Post*, p. 5.

Pilsworth, D. (1994, June 17). Gambling casino out of place in Cape Breton's way of life and should not be permitted [Letter to the editor]. *Cape Breton Post*, p. 5.

Proctor, S. (1998, October 15). Truro residents want to save two schools. *Halifax Chronicle Herald*, p. A6.

Proctor, S. (1999, October 17). Brookfield plans too costly board. *Halifax Chronicle Herald*, p. A7.

Putnam, R. D. (1993). *Making democracy work: Civic traditions in modern Italy*. Princeton, NJ: Princeton University Press.

Roach, R. (1999, March 9). Perceptions clash in school standoff [Letter to the editor]. *Cape Breton Post*, p. 5.

Scott, J. T. (1999, April). *Presentation to the Standing Committee on Economic Development*. Nova Scotia House of Legislative Assembly, Halifax.

Stewart, W. (1994a, April 21). Casino coming to Cape Breton. *Cape Breton Post*, p. 1.

Stewart, W. (1994b, September 20). Decision noted by minister. *Cape Breton Post*, p. 3.

Superschool may be dead. (1998, October 17). *Halifax Chronicle Herald*, p. A7.

Surette, R. (1999, August 21). Rural agenda still a voice crying in the wilderness. *Halifax Chronicle Herald*, p. A13.

Sydney casino records $3.2 million profit. (2000, July 19). *Cape Breton Post*, p. 6.

Taylor, C. (1994). The politics of recognition. In A. Gutmann (Ed.), *Multiculturalism* (pp. 25–73). Princeton, NJ: Princeton University Press.

White, K. (2000). *A casino for Sydney: By choice or by force?* Unpublished paper, University College of Cape Breton.

Yipp, R. (1999, October 4). Profit driven school model cannot work in rural areas [Letter to the editor]. *Cape Breton Post*, p. 5.

Chapter 15

Virtually Civil: Studio XX, Feminist Voices, and Digital Technology in Canadian Civil Society

Neil Gerlach and Sheryl N. Hamilton

Civil society . . . has its splendors and its less prepossessing proclivities. These two are much more difficult to separate than state and society proved to be. The political indifference and apathy of the citizens and the state retreating on its obligation to promote the common good are civil society's unpleasant, yet legitimate children. (Bauman, 1999, p. 156)

Referring to civil society, Gramsci (1971) stated, "The State's goal is its own end, its own disappearance, in other words, the re-absorption of political society within civil society" (p. 253). Many analysts argue that in the early twenty-first century we are achieving this ideal, as western states shrink and become less interventionist within the civil sphere. This trend certainly appears true in Canada. The process of merging the political and civil spheres has, however, created a paradox, producing some of the negative effects observed by Bauman (1999). Moreover, contrary to Gramsci's expectations, the separation of civil society from political society has not produced a more progressive democratic social order. In this chapter, we acknowledge this paradox and recognize the challenges of maintaining a socially progressive civic discourse in our current neoliberal social environment. Rather than merely lamenting these developments, however, we explore another kind of "legitimate child" of this paradox: Studio XX, a Montreal women's digital technology center.[1]

Studio XX is important to study for a number of reasons. First, the studio began operation in 1995, in an environment created by advanced capitalism. Second, as a feminist cultural organization, Studio XX is trying to make a space for itself in a technological, masculine, and market-driven public domain. In carrying out its mandate, this organization intervenes in new technology practices and discourses, the great hope of many optimistic and somewhat naive reformulations of civil society. This chapter considers Studio XX as both a specific actor in Canadian civil society and as an example of broader social phenomena within current political, market, and civil environments.

In accomplishing its major purposes, this chapter reviews theoretical concepts of civil society; explores the mandate and origins of Studio XX; defines the relationship between Studio XX and the public, private, and civil sectors; and looks at how Studio XX negotiates the tensions among feminist politics, cultural organizations, and digital technology in order to produce a space in which feminist voices may be heard in Canadian civil society.

CONSIDERING CIVIL SOCIETY

Scholars who study civil society often locate the hope for its regeneration in the voluntary sector and in information technologies. Born in the heyday of the neoliberal restructuring of government in Canada, Studio XX has been influenced by recent developments in both areas. Analyzing Studio XX's experience as a voluntary organization within current Canadian civil society allows us to (1) situate a specific Canadian experience within a historical understanding of civil society; (2) bring a stronger critique of global corporate capitalism into the theorization of civil society; (3) recognize the specifically Canadian context of the state's interventionist relationship to culture as not always antithetical to the goals of civil society; (4) recognize the role of French and English as language formations and Québec as a governmental formation in Canadian civil society; and, perhaps most importantly, (5) illustrate the lived strategies and tactics employed by an alternative civil society organization in negotiating the challenges of progressive social change through cultural practice. Both the organization and members of Studio XX are what we term *virtually civil*. That is, they employ the technologies of capitalism, the state, and the civil sector to promote feminist alternatives. They refuse to be the politically indifferent and apathetic citizens that Bauman decries (1999).

Interest in the notion of civil society resurfaced in the late twentieth century, after having been largely relegated to the dustbin of history. The inspiration for this rekindling of interest was the sense that civil society as a space of non-state, non-market, social relations was absent in politically centralized countries in Europe and elsewhere.[2] This recognition resulted in a flurry of intellectual activity around the concept of civil society across a variety of disciplinary and ideological domains. Still, the concept remains murky because it is defined, used, and valued in different ways by different scholars. Nonetheless, an acceptance of certain shared attributes of civil society emerges in the literature. Gellner (1994) offers a simple, yet useful, definition:

[Civil society] is that set of diverse non-governmental institutions which is strong enough to counter balance the state and, while not preventing the state from fulfilling its role of keeper of the peace and arbitrator between major interests, can nevertheless prevent it from dominating and atomizing the rest of society. (p. 5)

According to this definition, civil society includes such organizations and institutions as reciprocal and household economies, social movements, voluntary sector organizations, and political parties (Keane, 1988b).

We suggest that most contemporary work on civil society fits into three broad streams of thought: *critical, neoliberal,* or *liberal.*[3] Each approach posits a different ideal or actual relationship among the state, civil society, and the market; and each calls for different political solutions to the problems of late modernity.

The *critical* perspective draws on traditions established by Rousseau, Hegel, and Gramsci (see discussions in Bauman, 1999; Hardt, 1995; Keane, 1988a, 1988b; Sparks, 1994; Walzer, 1993). This perspective characterizes society as having a two-part structure of civil society and the state. The ruling class empowers the state to protect its privileges and wealth, while civil society becomes the space for both resistance to, and the hegemonic manufacture of consent for, this political domination. Thus, civil society has a revolutionary potential to overcome state oppression and democratize society.[4] The critical tradition rests, we argue, on an untenable conflation of market forces into civil society. Including the market in civil society is problematic, as economic players may be at least as dangerous as state formations to progressive political movements. As well, the critical perspective assumes a conflict-ridden model of interaction between the state and progressive elements of civil society, a model that does not account for accommodations between governments and activist voluntary organizations.

Propounded by intellectuals such as Drucker (1993), Rifkin (1995), and Osborne and Gaebler (1992), the *neoliberal* tradition has a shorter historical pedigree. Unlike the critical tradition, this perspective views society as comprised of the state, the market, and civil society. The neoliberal perspective privileges the corporation and private ownership as the ideal form for all social organizations. As a result of privileging market over state, this intellectual alternative also justifies the downloading of traditionally public services onto the voluntary sector.

The neoliberal tradition recognizes that, in a period of late capitalism, we need to theorize market forces as distinct from the state and civil society. However, encouraging civil society to develop its own social economy, independent of the state and the market, results in an evacuation of all political potential and means. Under this model, market actors need not share in the responsibility for social reproduction. As well, this model effectively removes the possibility for conflict over social values and structures, because the voluntary sector adopts the same organizational ideal as the private sector. Hospitals, schools, and even the family embrace corporate goals of efficiency, productivity, and market orientation.

Current concerns relating to civil society in late capitalist economies are tied to the perception that governments are shifting the social welfare system onto the voluntary sector (e.g., Hall & Reed, 1998). Both the critical and neoliberal approaches agree that these shifts are taking place, although each places a different value on the phenomenon. Morison (2000) suggests that these change processes may be much more complex than many thinkers assume, "involving, on the one hand, a paradigmatic shift from welfarism to economic rationality and, on the other, an idea of non-state actors developing autonomy or resistance to control in a complex engagement between actors from the formal state and those from within informal networks of power beyond the state" (p. 102).

Morison's work (2000) is part of an emerging third perspective, which seeks to combine the political potential of civil society (as conceived by the critical tradition) with the neoliberal recognition of three distinct social sectors. Advocates of the *liberal* approach include Giddens (1998), Cohen and Arato (1992), Salamon (1995), and Hefner (1997).[5] Giddens suggests that the liberal model, which he labels "the third way," involves partnering between local civic actors and government to produce, protect, and enhance community infrastructure and encourage bottom-up decision making. Although called upon to provide the foundation of that infrastructure, nonprofit organizations are not expected to accomplish these tasks alone. They are to work with government and the private sector in a triad model.

We believe that this perspective on civil society most accurately describes the Canadian context, where the civil sector has always had a close relationship, through funding, with the state. The liberal approach most accurately diagnoses the current economic, political, and social conditions. As well, this more pragmatic approach allows us to explore and describe the creative social formations currently present in Canadian civil society, as the public, private, and civil sectors all struggle with the implications of a reduced welfare state, global capitalism, and counterpolitics. However, this model may place too much emphasis on partnering. While not all relations between state and civil society organizations are—or need be—characterized by conflict, it may be overly optimistic to assume that power imbalances can be contractually leveled. This emphasis on partnering privileges civil society organizations with the cultural and economic capital and social location to partner with governments and the private sector. Other alternative civil society organizations may be inadvertently excluded from the same possibilities.

We conclude this discussion by suggesting that tensions among the three sectors may be necessary to maintain a critical project, to produce exciting alternative politics, and to prevent state and market elites from using civil institutions as a modality of rule. By negotiating these tensions, Studio XX makes space for feminist voices.

MANDATE AND ORIGINS OF STUDIO XX

Three feminist activists—a sound artist, a filmmaker, and an academic—founded Studio XX in 1995 as a space where feminist artists, academics, and activists could come together to explore the implications of information technology on their lives and practices. Its mandate was to facilitate and create access by women to digital technologies through activism and art. Studio XX fulfills this mandate by sponsoring a variety of activities, including a community radio program, monthly salons, a web art festival, a bilingual web site, and technology training for women. From the outset, Studio XX's identity was fluid, emerging out of the various activities that it operated. The *Femmes Br@nchées*, for example, allowed women from a diversity of backgrounds to present reviews, art works, editorials, and performances in an informal, interactive setting. A community radio program, *The XX Files*, featured electro-acoustic artists, visiting and local artists, and information columns. "How-to" workshops for women oriented them to computers and emerging Internet technologies.

Three stages define the evolution of Studio XX: (1) establishment (1995–1997), (2) conflict and stabilization (1997–1999), and (3) development and expansion (1999 to the present). Initially, the studio operated largely on the basis of volunteer labor and donations and support from committed feminists in the city. A volunteer steering committee governed operations, with each member responsible for a particular activity. Despite well-attended events and a demand for the programming offered, leaders soon realized that continued growth and achievement of the studio meant expansion of its financial base. The studio could not continue to operate on the goodwill, financial backing, and free labor of its founders.

Characteristic of the second stage in the development of Studio XX were rapid increases in external funding (primarily from arts organizations), the creation of a board of directors, and the hiring of paid staff. The pace of change produced a climate where conflict developed over issues of vision, feminist politics, and organizational structure. This conflict not only gave the organization a reputation of being "cliquish," but also reduced membership and participation (Kearns, 2001; Studio XX, 1999). Despite significant increases in funding, Studio XX had not succeeded in establishing the necessary structures and practices to administer these funds and manage its staff effectively. Recognizing these deficiencies, Studio XX leaders implemented new policies to stabilize the structure. At the same time, the studio recognized it had to address more actively the lack of Francophone members. Despite these challenges, the organization added several new initiatives, including a web art festival featuring national and international web artists, a fully developed bilingual web site, peer-taught workshops for artists, co-productions with other arts organizations, and a community-based research project working with low-income women's groups to explore the potential of the Internet as a resource. The primary focus of activities in this period was artistic, with the arts sector as the primary base for government funding (Studio XX, 1999).

The success of stabilization efforts in the second period moved the studio into its third and current stage—development and expansion. In this period, the funding base and actual activities began to more accurately reflect the social activism and community elements of the organization's mandate (Gagnon, 2001; Kearns, 2001). Changes included an increased number of staff; fully bilingual operations;[6] clarified lines of authority between staff and volunteers, with a resulting decrease in the direct involvement of the board of directors; the reaching of a consensus on staff job descriptions; and a general "professionalization" of the organizational culture (Gagnon, 2001).

Current activities of the studio, in addition to the still successful *Femmes Br@nchées* salons and the radio program, include a much larger web art festival (Les HTMlles); artists-in-residency programs; co-productions; an active web site with both archival and current material; *Terre à terre dans le cyberespace*, which has grown from a research project into a larger program of community activism on behalf of women and women's groups (see Lelièvre, 1999); a computer laboratory offering a greatly expanded scope of workshops (from beginner to high-end web creation); ongoing professional workshops for artists; special projects such as the Science Fair Project, which offers a critical history of women scientists and inventors through web art and critical writing; and an increased network of interaction with women's groups across the country (Studio XX, 2000).

Plans for the future of the studio include its consolidation as a digital technology laboratory space for both creative and training activities; the continued expansion of its social and cultural activist work; the achievement of charity status; the consolidation of the workshops program; and the initiation of an online journal, "a kind of feminist version of *Wired* magazine" (Kearns, 2001). Other goals include better serving the Francophone community and stabilizing organizational structure and financing (Gagnon, 2001; Kearns, 2001).

Given these characteristics, we suggest that Studio XX is an interesting case study of the functioning of a grassroots, alternative civil society organization that creates a "space of social experimentation for the development of new forms of life, new types of solidarity" (Cohen & Arato, 1992, p. 38). Yet, at the same time, the studio operates within the constraints and possibilities of its relationship with the state, the private sector, and its cultural community. We consider each of these in turn.

STUDIO XX AND THE STATE

The primary relationship of Studio XX with the state has been financial. The studio was incorporated as a Québec not-for-profit corporation in 1995 at the height of government cutbacks to cultural and voluntary organizations. In part for this reason, its initial mandate was to operate exclusive of government support, as "a cautionary strategy" (Kearns, 2001). Its founding members had seen too many community-based organizations begin, prosper, and collapse due to their dependence on public funding. Instead, the studio sought to earn revenue through activities to support its costs. Tensions arose, however, between this goal and the mandate of the organization as a grassroots women's center. The "clientele" of the studio, its commitment to low-cost activities for its members, and its desire to pay fair wages rendered the private sector model of self-generated profits untenable, resulting in a turn to public funding. One of the founders, Kearns, suggests that it is currently not realistic to imagine the studio without any public funding. However, rather than viewing this dependence as a shortcoming, she says, "I am a strong advocate of public funding for the arts and community activities and believe we should be . . . supported for the work we do."

At present, the public revenue base of the studio has become more diverse, and self-generated revenues have skyrocketed in the past year; however, funds obtained from non-public sources remain a small fraction of the operating costs (Gagnon, 2001). Like other contemporary civil society organizations, the studio has felt the state's shift to an increased emphasis on reporting and accountability in administrating funding programs. Audience size and door proceeds have become the criteria for "success" of events. At the same time that the organization must enforce strict accountability, its staff must meet training needs and ensure job opportunities for those who come to the center. Interestingly, on a day-to-day basis, staff do not think that this shift has been onerous or that significant (Gagnon, 2001).

In the second period of the studio's development, staff faced the need to adapt their programming to the demands of available funding programs (Gagnon, 2001), a dilemma faced by many other civil society organizations as well. Existing close links to the artistic community and a pre-established reputation with provincial and federal arts funding agencies meant that Studio XX tended to de-emphasize the social activism component of its mandate in favor of artistic activities.[7] Funding for social activism was also more difficult to locate and secure, because no one government department or level of government controlled all of the funding (Gagnon, 2001). Furthermore, the state was less than enthusiastic in its commitment to these goals. Given the relative youth and small size of the studio, it did not have credibility with funders such as Industry Canada, whereas arts funders were more sympathetic to artist-run centers and marginal organizations. As well, government programs (with the exception of Status of Women Canada and sometimes Health Canada) rarely identified women as a priority group. The feminist mandate of the studio thus limited its access to—and relationship with—the state, outside of the arts sector.

From approximately 1999 to the present, a marked diversification has occurred in the public funding base of the studio (Gagnon, 2001). Connections with the municipal, provincial, and federal governments—through a variety of arts, culture, and training/education programs—have permitted the studio to mobilize both parts of its mandate (creative and activist) and to stabilize organizationally (Gagnon, 2001). Still, the outlook is not totally positive. Despite general increases in revenues, the studio still functions in relation to the cycles of funding programs, supports a majority of employees through short-term employment programs, and remains vulnerable to changes in state funding policy (Gagnon, 2001).

STUDIO XX AND THE PRIVATE SECTOR

The studio's relationship with the private sector has been limited from its inception. The private sector offers donations and sponsorship to civil sector organizations as a means of demonstrating a philanthropic image to the public. At the heart of this relationship, however, is charity status under the Canadian *Income Tax Act*. Studio XX has not yet sought charity status under these regulations for a number of reasons, including volunteer inaction, stricter government guidelines on who qualifies for charity status, and the political and organizational implications of charity status. An education organization targeted only at women, for example, is not eligible for charity status. This limitation would require the studio to incorporate a second organization (with its own board of directors and financial records) to focus on its educational activities and broaden its mandate to include men and women. The failure to undertake this initiative has stemmed from both a political reluctance and a lack of human resources; however, this is a current priority now that the studio is more stable. For the above reasons, Studio XX, as previously stated, has had a limited relationship with private sector organizations that offer sponsorship opportunities. Most funding has been project-specific, and the support has come from corporations with which the studio has had an exchange relationship.

This deficit has been felt particularly in terms of the studio's own technology. Ironically, the studio has found itself in the position of being an organization devoted to women and digital technology, without a sound base of operational digital technology (Gagnon, 2001). The costs of using digital technologies to provide services to women or enabling the women to gain access to the current technologies are prohibitive. As well, maintaining the technology requires sophisticated expertise. A partial solution has come in a one-time capital grant from the City of Montreal, rather than from private sponsorship by a technology company (Gagnon, 2001).

A more abstract aspect of the studio's relationship to the private sector has been the generalized circulation of neoliberal corporate models of organizational functioning. From the beginning, such practices have created a tension within the studio between feminist, grassroots politics and hierarchical (arguably masculine) forms of organizational management. While the feminist politics of the studio have not denied that power relations exist in any organization, the specific relations of power and questions related to structuring have been at issue. Also, as the studio grows and begins to move away from a marginal existence, it is professionalizing its organizational culture in a number of ways. It remains to be seen whether or not these shifts will provoke any further reappraisals of the organizational structure.

As the training workshops, in particular, become regular, self-supporting activities, their fee-for-service structure raises continual pressures. The workshops committee, staff persons, and the board of directors must balance imperatives of profit-making, controlling expenses, and fee collection with the need to offer valuable services at reasonable fees to members, to permit low-income clients to exchange volunteer hours for course tuition, and to ensure feminist pedagogy across a range of different courses, from the most basic to the most technologically advanced. Finding women instructors for some courses has been difficult, and the decision to give priority to non-fee or reduced-fee female clients over paying male clients has its costs. For example, the profits from the workshops pay the salary of the workshops coordinator. In this way, the studio is always imbricated within the structures of capitalist enterprise, even as it tries to maintain a feminist philosophy and practice. On the other hand, the studio questions the necessity to separate feminism from all forms of capitalism.

STUDIO XX AND THE CIVIL SECTOR

As a civil sector organization, Studio XX participates in larger structural processes that are changing the nature of civil society in Canada. One significant development within this context is the ongoing impact of information technology on the nature of work, general modes of interaction, networking, and communication within and outside of civil society groups. Interestingly, in 1995 when the studio was founded, it engaged in rhetorical strategies to distance itself from the "hype" of new information technologies. The studio repeatedly asserted the right of women to refuse to learn about or use Internet and digital technologies. Spokespersons argued that the option lay with the individual to determine her level of participation (if any).

While still retaining a cynical eye toward the *Wired* magazine–style hype of new technology discourses, the rhetorical strategies have shifted in recent years from maintaining the possibility of refusal toward expanding the type of use. Gone is the implicit suggestion that women could or should refuse to engage with the Internet and computers. Instead, the studio's discourse emphasizes empowerment through using these technologies in ways that are meaningful to the individual. While a feminist political perspective grounds both rhetorical strategies, the shift reflects a societal recognition of the pertinence (at least in practical terms) of these technologies. The studio can still question the social significance of these technologies, but the space to question their practical utility or existence has closed.

A second significant pattern, reflected in Studio XX's operation (as well as the larger civil sector), is the increasing reference to a body of expertise specific to the support and development of volunteer organizations. A number of consultants and firms now specialize in training volunteers, facilitating the development of boards of directors, mediating conflicts, giving legal advice, and offering professional development for staff in areas such as personnel management and fund-raising. Studio XX has accessed legal advice on the question of charity status, commissioned individual fundraisers to act on its behalf, obtained volunteer training and coaching in organizational planning, and utilized the services of a professional conflict mediator in the instance of a staff conflict. Board members and staff agree that these resources have been invaluable to the growth and organizational health of the studio.

These important social developments, evidenced in the case study of Studio XX, imply an evolution in the ability of the civil sector to become a self-sustaining third force in society. Some consultants and firms operate with public funding, some without. Typically, they offer their services on a commission or other basis, at a reduced rate. In other instances, the consulting firm absorbs the costs of the knowledge services. These practices suggest the emergence of a hybrid market/social economy designed to support volunteer organizations. Some might argue that the new way of operating reflects the neoliberal call for an independent social economy within the civil sector. We suggest, on the other hand, that it is a creative and positive example of partnering among the private, public, and civil sectors. The new mode of operating also reflects the existence of a wide variety of support networks between and among non-profit organizations in Canada. Notwithstanding competition for ever-shrinking public funds, the resulting relationships are supportive.

One final aspect to Studio XX's unique experience, which permits further reflection on the nature of civil society in Canada, is its location in Montreal, Québec. Most civil society theorists conceive of the state as a relatively unified entity with a largely coherent set of interests. Studio XX, however, has developed relationships with a municipal government of a Francophone city with a bilingual population, with a provincial government whose agenda is sovereigntist and fully opposed to that of the federal government, and a federal government concerned about combating Québec nationalism and fostering "Canadian culture." The role of the provincial government is especially important to civil society organizations, given the large number of social and (especially) cultural activities that fall under provincial authority.

Studio XX has always declared itself to be a bilingual organization, but its linguistic profile has shifted over its life as a result of direct intervention by the volunteer leadership. At its founding, the majority of volunteers and members were university-connected Anglophones. Many were functionally bilingual. In the second period of the studio's development, deliberate efforts were made to hire management personnel who were Francophone and who worked outside of the university context. Combined with a greater attention to bilingual programming, these changes have had a significant impact on membership profile. The emphasis on achieving a more balanced membership has, in turn, raised the credibility of the studio within the community and with government bodies politicized around questions of language. The organization's bilingualism has increased its appeal to municipal, provincial, and federal governments, albeit for very different reasons in each instance.

Some conclusions can be drawn from the experience of Studio XX, insights pertinent to understanding the experience of other alternative civil society organizations. The studio's links with the state are primarily financial, in part due to its limited relationship with the private sector and the relatively non-interventionist role the state plays in the mandates and operations of such organizations. Studio XX's success in obtaining public funding for creative activities of an oppositional and feminist nature suggests a general tolerance within the Canadian state for a certain amount of counterpolitical discourse. At the same time, organizations such as Studio XX have a tendency to adapt their programs to the available types of funding, thus risking their political objectives.

Tensions arise between the exploration and use of a corporate model of organization and an inability (due to political commitments and lack of stable financial resources) to function as a successful capitalist enterprise. The impact of the generalized movement within all three sectors of society toward corporatization is definitely reflected in the studio's experience. The temptation is always to move toward the apparent comfort offered by a capitalist mode of operation, and yet volunteers and staff clearly believe that such a shift would result in the rejection of the counterpolitical feminist mandate of Studio XX.

Our analysis confirms that the civil sector in Canada is emerging as a

highly significant space for social negotiation. Many of the social, economic, and political issues of the day are played out, in part, in this space.
It is a space of conflict, partnership, and most of all, negotiation of a multiplicity of voices.

NEGOTIATING THE TENSIONS: FEMINIST VOICES, ALTERNATIVE CULTURE, AND DIGITAL TECHNOLOGY

As an organization devoted to mobilizing feminist voices in the production of culture through digital technology, Studio XX lives at the intersection of a series of tensions that it must continually negotiate. The
organization struggles to be virtually civil. Its ideological positioning as a
feminist, grassroots organization puts it in opposition to other discourses
(both private and public); yet at the same time, its very existence is indebted
to its cooperative relationship with the other two sectors. While these relationships do not directly inhibit the expression of feminist voices, the
work of producing this space must be acceptable to grassroots organizations with political agendas. The political interests of the different sectors
clearly diverge and occasionally conflict, and yet mutual benefits emerge
through their institutional relations.

By intervening in the cultural domain, the studio has been able to sustain
its counterpolitical objectives; yet it has operated in novel kinds of ways
within civil society. Working with digital technologies has also placed the
studio in a relatively unusual position in relationship to the technology
industries, capitalist enterprise, cybercultural rhetoric, and the information-
knowledge economy.

Although Studio XX's experience may not be unique, it reflects a series
of trends in broader civil society. These trends call for a more complex and
nuanced theorization of the notion of civil society to account more fully
for the Canadian, early twenty-first-century experience. Specifically, any
understanding of civil society must recognize a three-part division of interests within society—specifically, the state(s), the market, and the civil sector. That said, each of these must be understood as a heterogeneous set of
institutions and relations. In Canada and elsewhere, there is rarely (if ever)
one state, one market, or one coherent entity that can be called civil society.
The student of civil society must examine each in its specificity and as a
product of ever-shifting power relations. At the same time, the three sectors,
which overlap substantially in their day-to-day functioning, cannot be discussed outside of their intersector relationships.

Current empirical research into civil society, whether in Canada or elsewhere, has emphasized issues of health and welfare over culture (e.g., Hall
& Reed, 1998; Panet & Trebilcock, 1998). Studio XX and other alternative
cultural organizations confirm that culture is a significant domain in which
social actors engage in oppositional politics. Civil society is about more

than meeting the basic needs of human beings. It is also about relationships and the contexts in which people act. Civil society scholars must be careful to account for culture and communications in their theorizations.

Dowler (1996) argues, "The innovative possibilities ascribed to Canadian cultural practices at the margin can only occur as the product of the consolidation of a relation organized by the state" (p. 335). We suggest instead that Canadian cultural organizations at the margin exist not because of the consolidation of a relation organized *by* the state, but rather because of a relation *with and against* the state. Studio XX's experience calls for the rejection of a simple model of either conflict or partnership. Instead, we suggest that a model of continual negotiation more accurately describes the current experience within this domain. Negotiation implies the willingness or need to come together for mutual gain and to identify common interests. Thus, these organizations can produce civil society, while they retain a notion of conflict that permits the continued space for progressive politics. Finally, a negotiation model recognizes that the struggle to maintain these politics is continual.

NOTES

1. It is important for us to note that both of us have been members of Studio XX from 1995 until the present. Further, Sheryl Hamilton served as the chair of the steering committee/co-president of the board of directors from 1996 to 1999. She presently continues as a volunteer, serving as a member of the Workshops Committee. The research for this paper is based on participant observation, both within the organization and at events like Femmes Br@nchées; Maid in Cyberspace; review of archival records (e.g., publicity, annual reports, financial statements, grant applications, and transcripts of events); and interviews with key personnel (in particular, Patricia Kearns, member of the board of directors and current programming coordinator, and Lise Gagnon, general manager).

2. Although the resurgence of civil society is often attributed to the fall of communist regimes in Europe, in fact interest in the idea surfaces across a variety of centralized governmental regimes, including South America and Africa. Certainly, within European scholarship, however, the collapse of European communist governments and the revolutionary movements of the late 1980s were a strong impetus to retheorize state relations.

3. We limit this discussion to the contemporary period of late capitalism in order to distinguish it from earlier divisions in the conceptualization of civil society indebted to enlightenment and Hegelian thought. From the mid-nineteenth century onward, the concept fell largely out of use in mainstream social theory; when it reemerged in the 1980s, it was employed in ways different from the period prior to the 1850s. For a good discussion of the historical evolution of the concept from the enlightenment onward, please see J. Ehrenberg (1999).

4. A recent trend in this field has been to explore the contribution of governmentality theory; however, we suggest that, with its focus on state power, governmentality rests on many of the same assumptions as the critical tradition, even

though it poses new questions about the interests of the state and the modalities of its exercise of power (for example, Rose & Miller, 1992).

5. We are reservedly labelling this approach *liberal*, in that it is liberal in its politics more than in its historical adherence to a Lockean understanding of civil society. Although there may be overlaps with classical liberal political theory, this approach arises out of an engagement with the debates between the critical and neoliberal perspectives.

6. "Le fait que les membres de l'équipe soient et francophones et anglophones et que l'on passe fluidement d'une langue à une autre est non seulement une caractéristtique du Studio XX, c'est une très grande richesse pour le Studio" (Gagnon, 2001).

7. In particular, the *Conseil des arts et des lettres du Québec* (the major Québec arts funder) and the Canada Council for the Arts (the major federal arts funding agency).

REFERENCES

Bauman, Z. (1999). *In search of politics*. Stanford, CA: Stanford University Press.

Cohen, J. L., & Arato, A. (1992). *Civil society and political theory*. Cambridge, MA: MIT Press.

Dowler, K. (1996). The cultural industries policy apparatus. In M. Dorland (Ed.), *Canadian cultural industries: Problems, policies, and prospects* (pp. 328–346). Toronto: Lorimer.

Drucker, P. (1993). *Post-capitalist society*. New York: Harper Business.

Ehrenberg, J. (1999). *Civil society: The critical history of an idea*. New York: New York University Press.

Gagnon, L. (2001). Personal interview.

Gellner, E. (1994). *Conditions of liberty: Civil society and its rivals*. London: Penguin.

Giddens, A. (1998). *The third way: The renewal of social democracy*. Malden, MA: Polity Press.

Gramsci, A. (1971). *Selections from the prison notebooks of Antonio Gramsci*. Q. Hoare & G. Nowell Smith (Eds. and Trans.). London: Lawrence & Wishart.

Hall, M., & Reed, P. (1998). Shifting the burden: How much can government download to the non-profit sector? *Canadian Public Administration 41* (1), 1–20.

Hardt, M. (1995). The withering of civil society. *Social Text 45* (14), 4, 27–44.

Hefner, R. W. (1997). Civil society: Cultural possibility of a modern ideal. *Society 34* (2), 16–27.

Keane, J. (1988a). *Democracy and civil society*. London: Verso.

Keane, J. (1988b). *Civil society and the state*. London: Verso.

Kearns, P. (2001). Personal interview.

Lelièvre, C. (1999). L'accès à internet, certainement, mais pas n'importe comment! Une analyse des besoins en technologies de communication pour les groupes de femmes à Montréal. Montreal: Studio XX.

Morison, J. (2000). The government-voluntary sector compacts: Governance, governmentality, and civil society. *Journal of Law and Society 27* (1), 98–132.

Osborne, D., & Gaebler, T. (1992). *Reinventing government: How the entrepreneurial spirit is transforming the public sector.* Reading, MA: Addison-Wesley.

Panet, P. de L., & Trebilcock, M. J. (1998). Contracting-out social services. *Canadian Public Administration 41* (1), 21–50.

Rifkin, J. (1995). *The end of work: The decline of the global labor force and the dawn of the post-market era.* New York: Tarcher/Putnam.

Rose, N., & Miller, P. (1992). Political power beyond the state: Problematics of government. *British Journal of Sociology 43* (2), 173–205.

Salamon, L. M. (1995). *Partners in public service: Government-non-profit relations in the modern welfare state.* Baltimore, MD: Johns Hopkins University Press.

Sparks, C. (1994). Civil society and information society as guarantors of progress. In S. Splichal, A. Calabrese, & C. Sparks (Eds.), *Information society and civil society* (pp. 21–49). West Lafayette, IN: Purdue University Press.

Studio XX. (1999). Annual Report. Montreal: Studio XX.

Studio XX. (2000). Annual Report. Montreal: Studio XX.

Studio XX: http://www.studioxx.org.

Walzer, M. (1993, Winter). Exclusion, injustice, and the democratic state. *Dissent*, 55–64.

Chapter 16

Law and Constitution in Canadian Civil Culture

Michael Dorland and Maurice Charland

Debates in Canada over the concepts of political and cultural identity have been long-running, agonistic ones that have weighed, often wearily, upon the constituents (or would-be constituents) of the civil culture. These constituencies include English Canadian, Québecois, new Canadians of color, First Peoples, and others with regional identifications. The locus of debate has been variable, ranging from questions of religion, the separation of church and state, education, and ethnicity, among others. The focus of the debates, however, has been on the doublet formed by the notions of "law" and "constitution," including questions such as "Whose law?" "What law?" "What's law?" and "How can we bridge the law and constitution?" This ongoing muddle has framed a major part of Canada's history since the mid-nineteenth century, if not before.

In this chapter, we argue that these questions—in particular, the bridging of law and constitution—are neither the will-o'-the-wisps they often seem, nor sinister manifestations of the long fingers of imperial interference. Rather, they stem far more concretely from insufficient understanding of the complexities of translating legal cultures from a metropolitan to a colonial context. In sum, the difficulties derive from inadequate attention paid to the "rhetorics" of law and constitution in a historical context. Briefly, our analysis of Canadian civil culture has uncovered five major rhetorical responses to questions of law and constitution, which we present in the form of visual metaphors. We use semiotic techniques to explore these metaphorical representations. First, however, we will examine the impact of colonialism on Canada's efforts to create a constitutional framework.

THE POSTCOLONIAL CONSTITUTIONAL DEFICIT

Writing on the transnationalization of the legal field, Boaventura de Sousa Santos (1995), the Portuguese sociologist of law, argues that there are a number of "passes of entry into modernity" (p. 271). For reasons of power, the "European gate" has been asymmetrical to all others. Even so, the European path—in particular, what legal scholar Pierre Legendre (1968) calls its "colonial projection"—has been little more than an exercise in the "dressage" of peoples, in the sense of training horses. This colonial exercise, which began as early as the Roman colonization of the Mediterranean, has entailed the destruction of Aboriginal cultures and the inculcation of education as the gateway to the competitive race. The legal arena became the site of often unequal struggles among the diverse interest groups in colonial societies, including struggles between traditional leaders and the new elites. The incorporation of differences in language, skin color, and race (especially in relation to slavery) posed major and lasting problems that the legal system addressed in curiously ambiguous ways (Merry, 1991).

The process of colonial imprinting included the extension of European law to North America. When one colonial power replaced another, as in the cession of New France to England in the late eighteenth century, the result was "unprecedented" major social experimentation (Kolish, 1987, p. 324). The colonial transfer involved not only the exchange of governments, but also legal and linguistic regimes, with an accompanying severing of ties with the previous legal and doctrinal systems. These major ruptures raised questions such as "What law should we follow?" "What is the law?" and "In which language should we answer such questions?" The role of translation, not unpredictably, became critical; but what is meant by *translation*? What kind of translation? Does translation answer the problems that arise in such situations?

CONSTITUTIONAL METAPHORS

Using metaphors in the form of paintings, the following discussion identifies the five most common rhetorical responses to the challenges that faced postcolonial Canada as the country coped with its constitutional deficit.

Constitution as "The King's Two Bodies"

In semiotic terms, the contrast between these two paintings (*The Death of General Wolfe* and *The Death of Montcalm*) signifies the transition from French pre-revolutionary civil law to English common law. More specifically, the oil by Benjamin West (1770) visually depicts Kantorowicz's (1989) famed analysis of the king's two bodies—the mortal and physical body of the dying general (the prince or king) and the sacred, eternal body

Benjamin West, *The Death of General Wolfe*. National Gallery of Canada, Ottawa.

François-Louis-Joseph Watteau, *The Death of Montcalm*. National Gallery of Canada, Ottawa.

of the kingdom founded in law (the laws of war in this case). Although Wolfe may be mortally afflicted in the representation, he will never actually die. As Kantorowicz notes, the duality between the private and public body extends to the concept of the kingdom itself, resulting in the establishment of an extraterritorial kingdom or "eminent domain" within the kingdom (p. 778). The continuity of this domain, which extends beyond the life of the particular prince, becomes a matter of general and public interest. Its "constitution" concerns all subjects. Kantorowicz further argues that the public domain of continuity/constitution is sacred because it is concerned with ensuring the common good through peace and justice.

In other words, the "death/non-death" of Wolfe not only signifies the passing of the French regime, but it is also a claim to extraterritoriality in the sense of establishing the legitimacy of the conquest or cession of New France to Britain. The metaphorical passing of Wolfe also represents the subordination of the Crown to a regime of law in which the common good is secured by virtue of freedom to acquire property for exchange. The French, on the other hand, conceived of the Crown as having a different role, founded not in the law of the commons but in a corporatist doctrine of political power. Under this doctrine, the king or prince becomes the head of a body of "men" united morally and politically in the *res publica* (Kantorowicz, 1989). As the head, the king "completes" the political body that derives its unity, indeed its oneness, from the codification of the law.

While both depictions (Watteau and West) show much posturing and dramatic gesturing, differences exist. A society of officers ("the social") is in the foreground of Watteau's (n.d.) chalk and wash painting. Watteau sees the constituent *corps* (in this instance, the officer corps) serving the king and dying for their country. Although marked by a systemic coherence, the corporatist organization also has a hierarchical rigidity. By way of contrast, West demonstrates a much greater awareness of the land and, to some degree, its Aboriginal inhabitants. No *speech acts* are visible in this tableau of the passing of legal regimes.

Constitution as Speech

The question of speech—as well as issues pertaining to languages spoken—would only later become a major concern of civil culture in Canada. Disproving the much-repeated allegation that French Canadians cannot appreciate the subtleties of English law and constitution (see Lemire, 1991), the members of the Lower Canadian Legislative Assembly mastered the techniques of British parliamentary practice in a remarkably short time. In the first of many such crises, the language issue came to a head in a 1793 dispute over rules respecting the tabling of bills. The English-speaking minority in the Assembly wanted English to be *the* legal language: it was after all the legal language of the Empire. The French-speaking majority wanted the Assembly's *Journal of Debates* to be published in both languages. The French also demanded that bills concerning the criminal law be tabled in English and those regarding the civil law be tabled in French. Charles Huot's (1910) painting *Esquisse de la première séance de la Chambre d'Assemblée* depicts, in compressed form, the Assembly debate over French that lasted from 1792 to 1793.

Obvious animation characterizes this scene. The body language of the orator, with his arm outstretched in the classic elocutionary gesture, suggests that something of great import is being said. The surrounding press of bodies in the Chamber—sitting, standing, milling about, leaning in closely to hang on the words of the orator—paints a scene that is almost identical to representations of the constitutional debates at the Philadelphia Convention of 1787. But differences do exist. For example, we have some idea of what was said at Philadelphia in its reasonably well-known process of self-constitution. The key documents are part of the civil culture of Americans. Only specialists in Canadian parliamentary history, however, would be able to identify the character of the debate taking place in the Huot painting. This knowledge does not reside in the general public.

Many reasons explain Canadians' ignorance of this moment of self-constitution. One of the most important may be that the language debate that took place in 1792–1793 was never resolved in *law* (i.e., in a text of law or some equivalent quasi-legal and quotable document). Rather, the end result of the debate was a code of *practices*. Because the French held the voting majority, French became the language of the Assembly and appeared in its *Journal of Debates*. The French-speaking members believed that they had satisfactorily demonstrated to the "public" that they could use their numerical weight to impose the will of the collectivity in cases of general public concern. Still, this was a limited victory for bilingualism. Not until 1867 would the kind of bilingualism adopted by the Lower Canadian Assembly become actual law in the federal Parliament and in the Québec legislature, and language issues continued to erupt well into the 1980s and beyond. For example, attempts by the Québec government in the 1970s to impose French unilaterally as the "public language" brought a virulent response from English and ethnic Québecers. In short, then, Huot's canvas represents the moment of self-constitution, although few Canadians would have any idea of the rhetorical content associated with the event.

Constitution as Administration

British North American delegates met at Québec City in October 1864, to settle the terms of confederation. Robert Harris' 1883 cartoon, which depicts this meeting, has been widely reproduced on stamps and in high school textbooks. This cartoon is probably familiar to every Canadian

Charles Huot, *Esquisse de la première séance de la Chambre d'Assemblée*. Musée du Québec.

schoolchild as *the* representation of confederation. (The subsequent oil painting was destroyed in the fire that ravaged the federal Parliament in 1916.) This interpretation of confederation is, however, deceptive, as deal-making, arm-twisting, and backroom maneuvering (involving unidentified parties) continued for another two years after the 1864 meeting.

Note the differences between Harris' and Huot's celebration of parliamentary oratory. The "Fathers of Confederation" are frozen, speechless, as if posing for one of those early photographs that required sitters not to move for 20 minutes so as not to spoil the take. But this representation is not a photograph. More likely, this cartoon sketches the partners of a law firm in some sort of meeting of sufficient importance to be worth recording. Without looking to some other source, we cannot know why this solemn, glum, or bored lot have chosen to meet. The drawing tells us next to nothing. Thus, a semiotic interpretation of this drawing requires that we look to textual representations in it. For example, MacDonald is holding a book in his right hand, his left hand rests on other texts, a delegate to the left is reading a newspaper, and books appear on the table at the bottom left of the cartoon. The *hors-textes* that frame this drawing include the traditions of legal redaction, analysis, and interpretation that both precede and follow this meeting: in short, the enormous discourse of constitutional law in the Canadian context.

The gap between Huot's and Harris' representations—between rhetoric and the texts of the law, between public speech and the silent secrecies of the text, between the place of the French language in the public realm and its place in the texts of Canadian constitutionalism—was ultimately filled by what we term the *legal-administrative* political style. Between 1864 and 1867, a legal framework appeared. Finally, there was *law* in the narrow and technical sense of the term. The civil law of Québec had undergone the first major round of what would become a series of codifications. The criminal law had been codified nationally. A significant measure of agreement had been reached on a constitutional framework for the United Canadas, which would become a Dominion on July 1, 1867. The law and the constitution were finally conjoined: let there be Canada.

Constitution as Justice

So it came to be. But Canada was a fractious and resentment-filled place, in which few agreed on anything. Disagreements persisted over the distribution of powers between the central government and provinces, the language of education, the relationship of education to religion, the site of the judiciary (i.e., London or Ottawa), and how to modify the constitution. The Canada that emerged in 1867 was top-heavy with political corruption and reliant on an extensive party system of political patronage, a dependent civil service, a supine judiciary, and complex networks of elite accommodation. Critics accused politicians and government bureaucrats of being

Robert Harris, Cartoon for "Meeting of the Delegates of British North America to Settle the Terms of Confederation, Quebec, October 1864." National Gallery of Canada, Ottawa.

bigoted and intellectually dead or dull. When matters spun out of control, there was always the army or London, where Lordships could relieve Canadians of the burdens of self-governance. In a word, Canada was not a country of justice.

In the absence of justice as a constitutive element in the civil culture, we must be satisfied with a representation of what justice might resemble. We find such a symbolic representation in Napoléon Bourassa's never-completed turn-of-the-century fresco titled *The Apotheosis of Christopher Columbus*.

For most of his life, Bourassa was predominantly a religious painter. This religious affiliation is apparent in the upper portions of the fresco, with figures lining the lintel or hovering amid clouds of glory. But a literal gap appears in the lower right, between the mythic or quasi-mythical figures on the left and historical figures standing on secular ground. The S-shaped procession begins with Jacques Cartier and ends with Macdonald, Moses-like, holding the *British North American Act*, the fifth of Canada's constitutions.

Both realms of the fresco are threaded together by a genealogy of rhetorical and legal figures, as represented by Numa (mythical founder of Rome and Roman law), Cicero (the great Tully himself), and Bartolomeo de las Cases (the sixteenth-century Dominican theologian and jurist who argued that the "Indios" of New Spain actually had souls). The secular or historical portion of the fresco literally "figures out" a genealogy of Canada's civil culture. Together with the French explorers and leading figures of the French regime, we find the Canadian "Republicans" (Papineau, Mackenzie, Baldwin, and Lafontaine) and founding figures of the American Republic (Penn, Lafayette, Washington, and Franklin). Bourassa thus depicts a lineage of the figures who encoded the rules, conduct, and procedures of "a just society," one that has successfully aligned its multicultural and plurijural heritages. The question of application, however, remains symbolically suspended in the figure of Macdonald, the law-giver and constitution-maker.

Constitution as Irony

As our concluding image shows, the question of application (i.e., turning theory into practice) is revealed as profoundly ironic. Robert Houle's 1992 *Kanata* ironizes West's *The Death of General Wolfe* by foregrounding the Rodin-like figure of the Indian who sits in ironic judgment on the promises of British liberty, law, and constitution. This native Canadian archly seems to be wondering, "Well, what do you have to say about all this shittalk now?"

Canada's elites have often deployed the rhetorical strategy of irony. However, since irony has an edge that cuts both ways, it is not just an elite

Napoléon Bourassa, The Apotheosis of Christopher Columbus. Musée du Québec.

Robert Houle, *Kanata*. National Gallery of Canada, Ottawa.

tool. Popular culture has also made extensive use of this rhetorical idiom (Hutcheon, 1988). Muecke (1970) (cited in Enos, 1996) sees situational irony as a verbal response that enables its users to cope with the general state of affairs. Thus, irony can become a point of entry to civil discourse, allowing those who have been excluded from the public sphere (e.g., women, First Peoples, and so on) to "ironize" official discourse. When the disenfranchised mock the discourse "civilly" (i.e., non-violently), official sources must live up to the manifest content of their rhetoric.

This tendency to "ironize" has extended into the legal domain. What then of constitution as irony? Never perfect, the tension between the state and the constitution remains agonistic, and irony recognizes such situational limitations. Albeit pointedly ironic at times, "civilized" rhetoric facilitates the negotiation of differences.

CONCLUSION

To conclude, six metaphors in the form of paintings have led us along a traceable path of self-constitution. This process entailed a lengthy apprenticeship in learning how to speak, followed by learning to constitute law from three different legal cultures (France, England, and the United States), and finally learning how to create an instrument for self-government (under Canadian-made conditions) from a British-imposed constitution. This is not to say that all is utopian in Canadian civil culture; however, this journey has allowed us to arrive at a better sense of the constitutional and legal challenges that face the country.

A recent study of the Supreme Court of Canada, "a minor blip on the Canadian political scene fifty years ago [and] a small and undistinguished body" (McCormick, 2000, p. 3), reveals a process of judicial self-understanding that has involved the progressive rejection of English case law, a brief but not lasting flirtation with American concepts of authority, and the move to a self-referential doctrinal body. By *self-referential*, we mean that the Court draws principally on its own previous reflections as the basis for making decisions. Second, the dramatic growth of judicial independence since the early 1980s *Charter of Rights and Freedoms* is consistent with the global expansion of judicial power, in which de Sousa Santos (1995) sees such great hopes for the future of an emerging just society. We began with a reference to the difficulties of effecting the transition from a colonial regime to a postcolonial one and the implications for self-constitution. While it may be overly optimistic to generalize from the title of Peter McCormick's recent study of the Supreme Court (*Supreme at Last*), we think it enough to be satisfied with a better sense of where we have been and how we have gotten from there to here. In the end, Canada is—in its not-so-quiet way—a very noisy place after all.

REFERENCES

de Sousa Santos, B. (1995). *Towards a new common sense: Law, science and politics in the paradigmatic transition.* New York: Routledge.

Enos, T. (Ed.). (1996). *Encyclopedia of rhetoric and composition.* New York: Garland.

Hutcheon, L. (Ed.). (1988). *Essays in Canadian irony,* vol. 1. North York: York University.

Kantorowicz, E. (1989). *Oeuvres.* Paris: Gallimard.

Kolish, E. (1987, June). The impact of the change in legal metropolis on the development of lower Canada's legal system: Judicial chaos and legal paralysis in the civil law, 1791–1838. In *Papers presented at the 1987 Canadian law in history conference*: Vol. 1 (pp. 318–358). Ottawa: Carleton University.

Legendre, P. (1968). *Histoire de l'administration de 1750 à nos jours.* Paris: Presses universitaires de France.

Lemire, M. (1991). *La vie littéraire au Québec*: Vol. 1. Sainte-Foy, QC: Presses de l'Université Laval.

McCormick, P. (2000). *Supreme at last: The evolution of the Supreme Court of Canada.* Toronto: James Lorimer.

Merry, S. (1991). Law and colonialism. *Law and Society Review 25* (4), 889–922.

Muecke D. C. (1970). *Irony.* London: Methuen.

Chapter 17

Public Sphere and Public Sphericules: Civic Discourse in Ethnic Media

Karim H. Karim

Does democracy require a public or publics? A public sphere or separate public "sphericules"? Does the proliferation of the latter, the comfort in which they can be cultivated, damage the prospect for the former? Does it not look as though the public sphere, in falling, has shattered into a scatter of globules, like mercury? The diffusion of interactive technology surely enriches the possibilities for a plurality of publics—for the development of distinct groups organized around affinity and interest. What is not clear is that the proliferation and lubrication of publics contribute to the creation of *a* public—an active democratic encounter of citizens who reach across their social and ideological differences to establish a common agenda of concern and to debate rival approaches. (Gitlin, 1998, p. 173)

Habermas' (1989) notion of the ideal public sphere implies the existence of a largely monolithic civic discourse. His model derives from eighteenth-century Europe, where enlightened upper- and middle-class white men conducted discussions about public affairs. These members of the bourgeoisie, who met regularly to converse in coffee houses, monopolized civic discourse, as did the newspapers owned by their socioeconomic classes. Despite being such a restricted locus of public discourse, the notion of public sphere has become a primary basis of discussion about the activities of civil society. It tends to be viewed as a theoretical space for democratic debate and the social structure for an open and dynamic system of mass media. The public sphere often defines the parameters within which to study the role of the media in society and politics. Even the critics of this concept bring it to the fore in their attempts to highlight its deficiencies (Calhoun, 1992; Dahlgren, 1995).

Some of the most vigorous early challenges to Habermas' ideas come from feminist writers such as Fraser (1992) and Benhabib (1992). Criticizing the exclusion of women from the idealized space of civic discourse, they propose decentered and heterogeneous models of the public sphere. Postmodernist and postcolonialist theories, which highlight the need to recognize cultural diversity in contemporary societies, suggest more inclusive alternatives. Kalantzis (1995) proposes a model of "civic pluralism" which "means that all people have access to political power, economic resources, social services, and most importantly, cultural symbols regardless of their cultural affiliations and styles" (p. 2). Her vision includes a national ethos based on the creative virtues of internal diversity; an outward-looking global perspective; a new relationship between the state and the citizen; the recognition of differences as productive resources; the state as a broker of symbolic and cultural capital; the use of media—especially new media—to provide voices for minorities; and the overlapping of multiple communities of work, interest, affiliation, gender, and ethnicity.

Bhabha (1994) suggests that marginalized immigrant minorities operate in a "third space," distinct from the hegemonic public sphere, involving the country of settlement as well as the country of origin. This space allows for a high order of creativity and cutting-edge modernity. Operating in this third space, minority intellectuals and artists (e.g., Michael Ondaatje, M. G. Vassanji, Atom Egoyan and Tu Ly, in Canada) often find themselves in the avant-garde in seeking out innovative solutions to their marginalization. Goldberg (1994) proposes the establishment of official spaces where institutions may negotiate relations between dominant and subordinate groups, thus allowing all citizens to participate in civic culture in a way denied under the concept of a monocultural public sphere.

The public sphere has not disappeared, as Gitlin (1998) seems to suggest, but remains the locus of dominant discourses that coexist with others emanating from public sphericules—the smaller loci of social interaction. While a number of groups interact in society, elites and their discourses maintain dominance (Karim, 1993). Although the various sphericules overlap with the public sphere, they also produce distinct civic discourses not often heard in hegemonic spaces like the mass media.

MULTICULTURALISM AND ETHNIC MEDIA IN CANADA

Ethnicity and language have been at the heart of Canadian political discourse for several centuries. Canada was one of the first polities to give official status to the culture of a minority group. French has had equal status with English in Parliament and the federal judiciary since the establishment of the Canadian state in 1867. By the early twentieth century, dominant discourses described the country as "bilingual and bicultural." However, this view of Canada disregarded the broader diversity of its people. Policies of assimilation remained in place with regard to citizens of non-British and non-French descent. Aboriginal cultures were disparaged and immigration by non-European peoples severely restricted in what was viewed as a "white man's country" (Ward, 1978). Little room in the mass media was conceded to ethnic minorities.

The Royal Commission on Bilingualism and Biculturalism, which traversed the land in the late 1960s, found vehement opposition from the larger non-British, non-French groups of European origins to the conception of Canada as only British and French. In response, in 1971, the federal government adopted the policy of "multiculturalism within a bilingual framework" (Harney, 1988, p. 69), which officially recognized the country's cultural diversity. This new policy led to the formation of multiculturalism programs within the bureaucracy and the availability of modest resources to support cultural pluralism, but dominant discourses steadfastly resisted the policy (Karim, 1993).

Nevertheless, the idea of multiculturalism, which has spread to many countries around the world, provides important symbolic support to the activities of minority ethnic groups in Canada. A counterdiscourse in the form of critical multiculturalism is challenging the hegemony of theories that privilege monolithic forms of civic discourse. It also questions an "encyclopedic multiculturalism" that, "with its tendency toward a multiplication of essentialist representations, leads to the 'banality of difference' and the leveling of distinctions in favor of the larger 'unity' of the nation" (Kirshenblatt-Gimblett in The Rockefeller Foundation, 1992, pp. 38–39).

Ethnic media (i.e., media that identify their readers or audiences as belonging solely or primarily to an ethnic group) have occupied a marginal place in the country. Nevertheless, they have helped various communities in the Canadian cultural landscape to achieve a visible presence and have provided a means to engage in discourse about public affairs.

Apart from occasionally buying advertising space, neither federal nor provincial governments fund ethnic media. Since an organization does not need a license to establish a print medium, hundreds of ethnic newspapers exist in Canada. Some have a distinguished history, while others disappear within months of beginning operations, only to be replaced by new publications. Among the few ethnic dailies are the *World Journal*, the Italian *Corriere Canadese*, and the Chinese-language *Ming Pao* and *Sing Tao*.

The CRTC developed an ethnic broadcasting policy within the context of federal multiculturalism in 1985 (Karim, 2001). Ethnic radio programming is present in most cities of significant size. Dissemination channels include mainstream, community, and campus stations, as well as a few 24-hour ethnic broadcasters. CHIN Radio in Toronto broadcasts in various languages, and the Chinese-language Fairchild Radio is on the air in Vancouver, Calgary, and Toronto. The availability of sub-carrier frequencies has allowed several ethnic radio stations to emerge in some cities. Ethnic television programming of varying quantity and quality is also present in most places in Canada. Free-to-air ethnic TV can be found on community cable and time slots bought on local and national channels, as well as on ethnic stations such as CFMT (Toronto) and CJNT (Montreal). Asian Television Network (South Asian), Fairchild Television (Chinese), Telelatino (Italian and Spanish), and Odyssey (Greek) are variously available through digital broadcasting satellite, cable, and Look Television technologies. The national Aboriginal Peoples' Television Network was established in 1999. Recipients of new digital licenses from the CRTC in 2000 have included a number of ethnic broadcasters.

THE DEBATE OVER ETHNIC MEDIA

Ethnic media seek to meet the specific information needs of minority readers and audiences that are not addressed by the mass media (Stoiciu, 1987). Sociologists and communication scholars have viewed these media as serving what may appear to be two contradictory purposes—to contribute to ethnic cohesion and cultural maintenance and to help minorities to integrate into the larger society (Riggins, 1992).

Whereas some observers (Kim & Kim, 1989; Lam, 1980) have challenged the viability of the latter function, other researchers (Anderson, 1984; Bancroft, 1990; Black & Leithner, 1988; Rettie, 1984; Surlin & Romanow, 1984; Svendson & Watchel, n.d.) have validated the capacity of ethnic media to serve an integrative function. Viccari (1995), a prominent Canadian ethnic media journalist, asserts that "through the ethnic media, the newcomer can learn about Canadian culture, history, social services and a multitude of other things that can help him or her understand the privileges and the responsibilities inherent in Canadian citizenship" (p. 6). However, not all ethnic media offer such information to readers or audiences: it appears that the smaller the print media publication or broadcast production, the lesser the possibility that civic discourse will appear. For example, an August 1999 analysis of programming on Rogers' multicultural channel in the Vancouver area revealed very little discussion of civic issues.

The primary goal of most ethnic media is to provide cultural and informational programming, generally unavailable in the mass media, to the respective communities. Once this goal has been met, the medium uses additional time or space for discussions about Canada-related public affairs. Ethnic radio stations such as CHIN, as well as some 24-hour stations broadcasting on sub-carrier frequencies (e.g., Rim Jhim in Vancouver), offer information on Canadian public affairs through news bulletins, feature programs, and talk shows. The ethnic television station CFMT also provides time for Canadian issues on its news programming.

Husband (1994) asserts that "we need autonomous ethnic minority media which can speak for, and to, their own community; ethnic minority media which can generate a dialogue between ethnic minority communities; and between these and dominant ethnic community audiences" (p. 15). Husband (1998) promotes the development of a multiethnic public sphere where "difference is mutually comprehensible and mutually sustainable" (p. 136). Within such an ideal, ethnic minorities have not only the right to communicate, but also "the right to be understood" (pp. 137–141). Such a multilateral model facilitates broader interaction among various communities, including the dominant public sphere and ethnic sphericules. It enables the voices of minorities to be heard in civic discourses at the public level.

CASE STUDY: SOUTH ASIAN MEDIA IN CANADA

Canadian South Asian media[1] serve a diverse set of communities that include people who have migrated directly from South Asia (India, Pakistan, Sri Lanka, Bangladesh, Nepal), their descendants, and the South Asian diaspora (from eastern and southern Africa, the Caribbean, Fiji, Europe, and Southeast and eastern Asia). According to the 1996 national census, 670,590 Canadian residents had South Asian origins (Pendakur & Hennebry, 1998). Most located in large urban centers: Toronto (359,475), Vancouver (125,350), Montreal (48,955), Calgary (27,475), Edmonton (23,615), and Ottawa-Hull (18,905). Apart from English and French, these people variously spoke Punjabi, Tamil, Hindi, Urdu, Gujerati, Bengali, or other languages.

South Asian media reflect some of this cultural and linguistic diversity. Certain magazines and television programs also attempt to meet the needs of younger members of the community, a significant proportion of whom were born in Canada. There does not exist in Canada a daily South Asian newspaper like those published in Italian. Nonetheless, the history of Punjabi-language newspapers in Vancouver dates back to 1910 (Tatla, 1991). Almost 14 percent of ethnic newspapers and magazines listed in the 1991 survey by Ethnomedia Monitor Services were South Asian. These figures confirm a high level of media activity in a group that comprises about 5 percent of the non-British, non-French population. The growth of South Asian broadcasting is reflected in the increasing reach of those operating on sub-carrier frequencies, the existence of a national South Asian broadcaster in the Asian Television Network, and the granting by the CRTC of several licenses for digital broadcasting in specific South Asian languages and formats.

The level of civic discourse varies widely in Canadian South Asian media.

Such public dialogue tends to be very limited or non-existent in print media published on a monthly or less frequent cycle and in radio and television programs broadcast on a weekly or less frequent basis. Media geared specifically toward South Asian cultural content (e.g., literary magazines or television programs on the Bollywood film industry) also contain little in the manner of civic discourse. Discussion about public affairs relating to Canadian contexts is more likely to be found in well-established weekly newspapers, published mostly in Vancouver and Toronto—the cities with the largest number of residents of South Asian origins. Most of the smaller publications tend to contain news and information on activities in their home countries or local South Asian communities.

The bulk of South Asian radio programming in Canada—disseminated through community, campus, multilingual, or commercial stations—occupies a block of time ranging from half an hour to several hours, generally on a weekly basis. The content of these programs is typically musical. The primary exceptions are 24-hour stations that run on sub-carrier frequencies: a multilingual (Rim Jhim) station based in Burnaby, B.C., and three Tamil-language stations in Toronto. These stations provide regular (usually hourly) bulletins containing local and transnational news, as well as discussions on Canadian public affairs. Rim Jhim also has weekday (evening) call-in shows on a variety of issues, including controversial topics such as family violence. The inclusion of such controversial subject matter is especially significant, given the general reluctance of South Asians to discuss these kinds of topics publicly. Dutt (1999), the host of the show and owner of the station, was the victim of vandalism when she initially produced these shows. Among members of the South Asian community, however, such reaction dissipated when women and men of various ages began to engage in on-air discussions. This turn of events indicates the power of this medium to encourage public discourse in a cultural group that had previously shunned this type of civic involvement.

The Toronto-based CFMT includes several South Asian programs on its weekly schedule: *South Asian Newsweek*, *TV Ceylon*, *Bollywood Boulevard*, *Ishtyle TV*, and *Veggie Table*. In addition to broadcasting news from South Asia (largely India), *South Asian Newsweek* also provides news and information about events in Canada. Whereas the latter tends to highlight the activities of South Asian Canadians, the one-hour program usually carries one or two news stories of general interest as well. Examples include civic discourse on social and political issues that go beyond South Asian communities. Significantly, overlap between this sphericule and the public sphere also occurs in the area of personnel: Indira Naidoo-Harris, a co-anchor of the news program, frequently appears as a newsreader on CBC radio and CBC television.

Civic discourse in Canadian South Asian media is most clearly visible in print media. The following analysis of *The Indo-Canadian Voice*, an

English-language Vancouver weekly, examines political coverage in five issues published in October and November 2000, a period leading to the November 27 federal election. South Asian media in British Columbia have a special interest in civic issues, since members of the communities are actively involved in politics at municipal, provincial, and federal levels. Ujjal Dosanjh, the premier of B.C. at the time, is of Punjabi descent, as are a number of the cabinet ministers. Herb Dhaliwal in the federal cabinet is also a British Columbian of Punjabi origins. Political coverage in the *Indo-Canadian Voice* tends to revolve around elite South Asian and non–South Asian actors, although one of the primary areas of focus is the Sikh community in Surrey (a suburb of Vancouver). This newspaper, along with the English-language *The Link* and the Punjabi-language *Indo-Canadian Times*, appears to be one of the largest-circulation South Asian publications in B.C.'s Lower Mainland.[2] The *Voice*'s owners also produce a Punjabi-language weekly called *Indo-Canadian Awaaz* in the Vancouver area.

During the period under study, the *Indo-Canadian Voice* had three sections: local and transnational news, "Bollywood" gossip, and real estate. One or two news stories dominated its front page. The front section, which ran between 48 and 56 pages, also carried humorous news items, several local news stories, half a page of letters, over two pages of editorial commentary, more than half a page on the crime beat, a consumer section on autos, a quarter-page of home improvement information, a half-page Sikh religious column, and several pages on news from abroad—all generously interspersed with advertisements of various sizes and a classified section at the end. Political and community stories, which appeared under the rubric of local news, were distributed throughout the first section. The three major political themes during this period were the federal election; activities of the provincial New Democratic Party (NDP) government, led by Ujjal Dosanjh; and the nomination battles for candidates for the yet unannounced provincial election.

The headline in the October 14 issue referred to the victory of a prominent Indo-Canadian (Dave Hayer) in a nomination race for the provincial Liberal Party. A page-three story discussed the competition between two hopefuls, including one Indo-Canadian, for the Liberal nomination for a riding held by former premier Glen Clark. The editorial commentary opened with half a page on provincial politics. The two letters to the editor addressed federal and municipal issues, respectively. Another article reported the federal cabinet's instruction to the CRTC to review its decision to deny a license for the establishment of a multilingual television station in Vancouver.[3] A local news story described the Ottawa meeting of two prominent federal ministers (Paul Martin and Jane Stewart) with the Old Age Benefits Forum, whose secretary is a Vancouver resident of South Asian origins. Another story discussed preparations for the federal election by the incumbent Canadian Alliance MP in Surrey Central, Gurmant Grewal, who is Indo-Canadian.

The main story of October 28 related to the decision of the provincial education minister (non–South Asian Penny Priddy) to end her political career; it shared the front page with a picture of Prime Minister Jean Chretien, who had visited Vancouver. The page-three article also covered Chretien's visit to Vancouver, indicating that this part of the election campaign had its "First stop, [on] Herb Dhaliwal's turf." A letter to the editor suggested that Chretien should be lobbied on the matter of financing Vancouver's transportation system; another from the provincial minister for multiculturalism (Sue Hammell) "congratulated the South Asian community" on Diwali 2000, a Hindu religious festival. One-third of the editor's commentary talked about the provincial education minister's decision to step out of politics, as discussed in a personal interview conducted in the newspaper's offices; another third described the Liberal election "circus" in Vancouver. A local story covered the continuing labor strike by city workers. Other stories discussed successful attempts by the federal Liberals to persuade prominent NDP members to run on their ticket in the election and the provincial premier's announcement of a cooperative strategy to market lumber products. This week also saw the first appearance of an advertisement by an Indo-Canadian candidate (John Nuraney) running for the federal Parliament in the Burnaby-Willingdon riding.

Coverage of two Indo-Canadian suspects in the 1985 bombing of an Air India airliner dominated the November 4 issue, reducing the space normally devoted to political coverage. The sole letter to the editor came from a non–South Asian representative of a taxi company, who complained that the "Surrey council bleeds taxis, [and the] physically challenged." More than half of the editor's commentary related to political and community activist support for Rogers' proposed multilingual television station in Vancouver. The remainder of the newspaper discussed a provincial cabinet shuffle. Herb Dhaliwal advertised his candidacy for the federal election.

Statements by federal ministers Herb Dhaliwal and Elinor Caplan on a Radio Rim Jhim talk show captured front-page coverage on November 18. Page four covered the meeting of Sheila Copps, the federal minister of Canadian Heritage, with the ethnic media in Vancouver. The only letter came from Geoff Plant, the official opposition member for the attorney general, who challenged the NDP premier on his government's treaty with the Nisga'a First Nation. The federal election campaign dominated the electoral commentary. Local coverage included publication of the electoral platform of the Natural Law Party, a marginal political group. Another local story profiled an Indo-Canadian candidate running for the Liberals in Surrey North. Additional articles spoke of the continuing community presence of Penny Priddy, the former education provincial minister, and of the decision of yet another non-South Asian provincial NDP member not to run again. Herb Dhaliwal and Don Goy (non–South Asian candidate running on the Liberal ticket in the Surrey Central riding) advertised their candidacies.

A front-page story on November 25 discussed local non–South Asian Liberal Party candidates Francesca Zumpano and Lee Rankin. The issue also had articles on Grewal, the Sikh Alliance candidate for Surrey-Central, and on two non–South Asian candidates in the Richmond riding. The latter represented the Liberal and Alliance Parties. A reduced commentary section focused entirely on the federal election, highlighting non–South Asian candidates. Two stories covered provincial issues: premier Dosanjh's maintenance of a moratorium on oil and gas development and the B.C. government's expansion of a cell-phone program aimed at protecting women from violence. A sole letter came from Dosanjh's press secretary Shari Graydon, who explained her office's policies on media access to the premier. Graydon's letter responded to the complaints of the editor of the *Indo-Canadian Voice*. This final issue, which appeared shortly before the November 27 election, featured advertisements for five South Asian and five non–South Asian candidates from various parties around southern British Columbia.

DISCUSSION

It is evident that the ethnic media studied above are not isolated from public discourses. However, as Black and Leithner (1988) conclude, it is difficult to demonstrate that ethnic media's coverage of public issues directly leads to the national integration of the immigrant community members. Nevertheless, the presence of heavy political content in the *Indo-Canadian Voice* does indicate an already-existing interest in municipal, provincial, and federal political affairs among the producers of the newspaper, some of the people on whom it reports, and its readership.

Let us now return to the questions posed earlier by Gitlin (1998). Gitlin suggests that the natural state of society is to have one public sphere, which has "shattered into a scatter of globules," and he worries that these separate public sphericules have damaged the prospect for a unitary space that he views as the proper locus of democracy. However, societies normally include several cultural groupings, and the fiction of a unitary public sphere allows elite groups to appear to represent all interests and to dominate civic discourse. In the construction of the Canadian public sphere, Aboriginal peoples and other ethnic minorities have often been occluded and their histories and politics marginalized. The involvement of Aboriginal people in key events in recent national history,[4] along with the growing demographic presence of ethnic minorities, has changed the politics of the country. The voting power of large concentrations of minority ethnic groups in constituencies such as Surrey Central becomes very significant during elections. When politicians attempt to reach these electorates in their own cultural idioms, ethnic media become key vehicles. This strategy is apparent in the content of the *Indo-Canadian Voice*, analyzed above. Politicians of various backgrounds gave interviews to—and held special press conferences for—journalists of ethnic media. They wrote letters to editors of ethnic newspapers and appeared on ethnic broadcasters' talk shows. The strength of Greater Vancouver's 46 ethnic newspapers is evident in their total circulation, which is reportedly larger than the combined figures of the city's two main English-language papers (Grescoe 1994/1995).

Let me turn to a second concern expressed by Gitlin (1998), who questions whether this proliferation of active publics will block the development of a larger public sphere with common concerns. He says that citizens will experience difficulty in reaching across "social and ideological differences to establish a common agenda of concern and to debate rival approaches" (p. 173). Yet it is clear that the *Indo-Canadian Voice* provides a space for a variety of political and social actors to present their views, despite the dominant role of this weekly's editor. The various other print, radio, and television media serving the South Asian communities in B.C.'s Lower Mainland also appear to offer the opportunity to air a number of different perspectives. Letters to newspaper editors and the call-in shows of Rim Jhim Radio allow for some feedback from readers and audiences. The latter do not appear to be disconnected from the larger society, nor do some of the ethnic media that serve them. They participate in the debates over public issues, and they engage in agendas of concern to the larger society. The coverage in the South Asian media studied above, although dominated by the activities of Punjabi Indo-Canadians, is not limited to this ethnic group.

The South Asian sphericules do, nevertheless, remain distinct from the dominant public sphere. Whereas non–South Asian politicians often engage with the South Asian sphericules, other Canadians remain largely cut off from these smaller spheres of discourse. Even though a significant number of South Asian print media organs publish in English, their distribution points are usually limited to the communities' grocery and garment stores. Apart from the English-language South Asian programming of CFMT and a few other broadcasters, the electronic content disseminated in South Asian languages on sub-carrier frequencies (requiring modified radio sets) is inaccessible to other Canadians. Therefore, the interaction between ethnic sphericules and the larger public is limited. The opinions expressed in ethnic media are rarely available to audiences other than their primary ones. The *Vancouver Sun* runs a weekly item carrying content gleaned from the ethnic press in the city, but this information often appears out of context. Thus, even though civic discourse disseminated through ethnic media may not be as fragmented as Gitlin (1998) fears, the situation is also far from Husband's (1994) ideal of the multiethnic public sphere, where a multitude of voices reach a larger audience.

NOTES

1. The information in this section is based on a research study funded by Canadian Heritage, Metropolis, and Carleton University.

2. This statement is based on the author's visual observation of the regular placing of stacks of newspapers in Vancouver-area South Asian businesses for distribution free-of-charge. Circulation figures are not audited by an external agency.

3. Although not supported by all members of ethnic minorities in the Vancouver area, this application by the communications corporation Rogers had resulted in a vigorous lobbying effort. Mobina Jaffer, a South Asian lawyer based in Vancouver and a key player in the federal Liberal Party, led the lobby. The story, which had received strong running coverage in the *Indo-Canadian Voice*, illustrates the successful engagement of ethnic sphericules with the mainstream national media (even though they remained attached to corporate media and political interests). In this case, the lobby obtained a federal cabinet response.

4. Particularly in point were the standoff at Oka, Québec, and the refusal by Elijah Harper (an Aboriginal member of the Manitoba provincial assembly) to assent to the Meech Lake Accord. Both events occurred in 1990.

REFERENCES

Anderson, G. M. (1984). Functions of the ethnic press. *Multiculturalism/e 8* (1), 29–30.

Bancroft, G. W. (1990). *The civic participation of visible minorities in Canadian society: Framework and issues for research and analysis.* Ottawa: Multiculturalism and Citizenship Canada.

Benhabib, S. (1992). Models of public space: Hannah Arendt, the liberal tradition, and Jürgen Habermas. In C. Calhoun (Ed.), *Habermas and the public sphere* (pp. 73–98). Cambridge, MA: MIT Press.

Bhabha, H. (1994). *The location of culture.* London: Routledge.

Black, J., & Leithner, C. (1987). Patterns of ethnic media consumption: A comparative examination of ethnic groupings in Toronto. *Canadian Ethnic Studies 19* (1), 21–39.

Black, J., & Leithner, C. (1988). Immigrants and political involvement in Canada: The role of the ethnic media. *Canadian Ethnic Studies 20* (1), 1–19.

Calhoun, C. (Ed.). (1992). *Habermas and the public sphere.* Cambridge, MA: MIT Press.

Dahlgren, P. (1995). *Television and the public sphere: Citizenship, democracy and the media.* London: Sage.

Dutt, S. (1999, August 18). Personal interview. Vancouver, BC.

Ethnomedia Monitor Services. (1991). *Canadian ethnic press guide.* Toronto: Andrew Machalski and Associates.

Fraser, N. (1992). Rethinking the public sphere: A critique of actually existing democracy. In C. Calhoun (Ed.), *Habermas and the public sphere* (pp. 109–142). Cambridge, MA: MIT Press.

Gitlin, T. (1998). Public sphere or public sphericules? In T. Liebes & J. Curran (Eds.), *Media, ritual and identity* (pp. 168–174). London: Routledge.

Goldberg, D. T. (1994). Introduction: Multicultural conditions. In D. T. Goldberg (Ed.), *Multiculturalism: A critical reader* (pp. 1–41). Cambridge, MA: Basil Blackwell.

Grescoe, T. (1994/1995, Winter). Hot type. *Vancouver 82–84*, 114–118.

Habermas, J. (1989). *The structural transformation of the public sphere* (Thomas Burger, Trans.). Cambridge, MA: MIT Press.

Harney, R. F. (1988, Fall). So great a heritage as ours. *Daedalus 117* (4), 51–98.

Husband, C. (1994). General introduction: Ethnicity and media democratization within the nation-state. In C. Husband (Ed.), *A richer vision: The development of ethnic minority media in western democracies* (pp. 1–19). Paris: UNESCO.

Husband, C. (1998). Differentiated citizenship and the multi-ethnic public sphere. *Journal of International Communication 5* (1 & 2), 134–148.

Kalantzis, M. (1995, April). Civic pluralism: Renewing Australia's social contract. Paper presented at the Global Cultural Diversity Conference, Sydney, Australia.

Karim, K. H. (1993). Reconstructing the multicultural community in Canada: Discursive strategies of inclusion and exclusion. *International Journal of Politics, Culture, and Society 7* (2), 189–207.

Karim, K. H. (1998). From ethnic media to global media: Transnational communication networks among diasporic communities. *Transnational Communities Working Papers Series*. Oxford, UK: University of Oxford.

Karim, K. H. (2001). Ethnic and multi-lingual broadcasting in Ottawa-Hull. Unpublished paper.

Kim, K. S., & Kim, Y. G. (1989). Who reads an ethnic newspaper, and why? *Multiculturalism/e 12* (1), 28–30.

Lam, L. (1980). The role of ethnic media for immigrants: A case study of Chinese immigrants and their media. Toronto. *Canadian Ethnic Studies 12* (1), 74–90.

Pendakur, R., & Hennebry, J. (1998). *Multicultural Canada: A demographic overview*. Ottawa: Canadian Heritage, Multiculturalism.

Rettie, N. C. (1984). Immigrant women's radio project: Theory, operation, analysis. *Currents 2* (2), 19–22.

Riggins, S. H. (1992). The media imperative: Ethnic minority survival in the age of mass communication. In S. H. Riggins (Ed.), *Ethnic minority media: An international perspective* (pp. 1–20). Newbury Park, CA: Sage.

The Rockefeller Foundation and the Aga Khan Trust for Culture. (1992). *Pluralism and its cultural expressions*. Falls Church, VA: The Rockefeller Foundation and the Aga Khan Trust for Culture.

Stoiciu, G. (1987). Les médias écrits des communautés culturelles constitutent un système particulier de communication. *Humanitas* (17), 43–45.

Surlin, S. H., & Romanow, W. I. (1984). The uses and gratification of heritage language newspapers and general Canadian mass media by five heritage language groups. *Multiculturalism/e 8* (2), 21–27.

Svendson, A., & Watchel, A. (n.d.). *The ethnic media and the promotion of social services to immigrants: An exploratory discussion*. Vancouver: Social Planning and Research, United Way of the Lower Mainland.

Tatla, D. S. (1991). The Punjabi ethnic press of North America: A selected listing. *Ethnic Forum 11*, 29–49.

Viccari, B. (1995, April). Canada's ethnic media. Paper presented to the Media and Ethnicity Symposium, organized by Canadian Journalism Foundation and International Communication Forum, Mississauga, ON.

Ward, W. P. (1978). *White Canada forever: Popular attitudes and public policies towards Orientals in British Columbia*. Montreal: McGill–Queen's University Press.

Chapter 18

Major League Sports, Civic Discourse, and the World-Class City: A Case Study of Vancouver

Mark Douglas Lowes

In March 1999, the *Globe and Mail* provided a status report on the "Technodome," a $1 billion entertainment megaproject spearheaded by Canada's famous Reichmann family ("Toronto in Danger," p. A2). Although slated to begin development in Toronto in the autumn of 1998, by the spring of 1999, the Technodome project had stalled for several months.

As planned, the Technodome would function as an entertainment and sports complex, roughly the size of Toronto's Skydome. The project would cover more than two million square feet and feature a number of spectacular entertainments, including an indoor mountain for year-round skiing, a watercourse for whitewater kayaking, a rainforest, and an enormous entertainment center with amusement rides, movie theaters, and a variety of sports facilities. Overall, the main objective of the Technodome "megaproject" was to provide what amounts to a "spectacular consumption palace," an international attraction designed to rival Disneyland and Universal Studios.

Nonetheless, the project floundered when talks broke down between Canada Lands Company (the Crown corporation in charge of the development site) and the famous Reichmann family (key promoters of the Technodome project). Frustrated by a lack of progress, the Reichmanns secretly opened talks with city officials to relocate the development to Montreal, thereby heating up the long-standing rivalry between Canada's two biggest cities for the most glamorous real estate developments. Landing the Technodome would certainly have been a coup for Montreal, which had watched Toronto thrive while it turned into a development wasteland over a period of two decades. As one member of Montreal's executive committee responsible for economic development and tourism put it, "It's about time we won one over you guys" in Toronto ("Toronto in Danger," p. A2). Despite this enthusiasm, investors were unable to secure a favorable site for the development, and plans for the Technodome project stalled in a second city ("Technodome Dead").

This case provides an excellent illustration of the increasingly prominent role that sports entertainment megaprojects play as signifiers of civic prosperity and ambition in large North American cities. The very presence of such megaprojects marks a city's arrival on the "world stage." And in a climate of relentless interurban competition for public and private investments that contribute to economic growth, many perceive spending on image-making and public relations to be as important as spending on urban infrastructure and other upgrades (Lowes, 2000). Civic leaders believe that the more their cities appear on the same stage (or in the same league) with New York, Tokyo, and Los Angeles, the stronger their chances will be of growing and prospering.

Working against this background, I explore this notion of the "world-class" city, its relationship to major league sports entertainment, and the particular genre of civic discourse that underpins the selling of a world-class city. A case study of the Molson Indy Vancouver motor sport event allows us to see the central role that such events play in a civic discourse designed to promote Vancouver as a world-class city. More specifically, I argue that the annual Molson Indy Vancouver motor sport event has become a key feature of a civic discourse in which Vancouver projects itself as a world-class city.

This discourse takes place within the broader context of the global sports entertainment industry and its seamless integration with mass media that reach global audiences. Major league sports entertainments like the Indy have become surrogates for—and mobilizers of—civic identity in Vancouver and many other North American cities. Indeed, civic officials from Montreal to Tampa Bay, Toronto to San Francisco, and Vancouver to Los Angeles have embraced the idea that major league sports teams and world-class events (including the facilities associated with these teams and events) are essential in projecting an image of sophistication and economic dynamism (Ellen & Schwartz, 2000; Lowes, 2000; Noll, 1997). As Gruneau and Whitson (1993) put the case, "The pursuit of major league (sports) franchises and 'world-class' events is now best understood as part of a larger project in which corporate and civic elites struggle to establish and maintain their cities' status in a transnational economic and cultural hierarchy" (p. 224).

Harvey (1989) argues that cities now take much more care to create a positive and high-quality image of place; they seek an architecture and forms of urban design that respond directly to this need. It appears that, for civic boosters, *image is everything*. "That they should be so pressed," Harvey writes, "is understandable, given the grim history of de-industrialization and restructuring that left most major cities in the advanced capitalist world with few options except to compete with each other, mainly as financial, consumption, and entertainment centers" (pp. 91–92).

A recurrent theme in media coverage of the Molson Indy is that the event puts the city on the world stage, promising to make Vancouver "the Monaco of North America, Canada's Monte Carlo" (Lowes, forthcoming). This allusion trades on the glitz and glamour of Europe's Monaco: the high-flying Royal Family and its Hollywood connections (through the late Grace Kelly), its palaces and mansions, posh hotels and casinos, breathtaking Mediterranean landscape. Monaco and Monte Carlo have become signifiers of a playground for globetrotting financial power players. Their annual Formula One race, the Monaco Grand Prix, is one of the most prestigious and anticipated stops on the F-1 circuit, drawing the attention of the world.

Event promoters argue that the Molson Indy carries connotations of money, power, and international chic. Televised in the spectacular harbor-front setting of False Creek, the international event showcases the European and South American stars of elite motor sport racing. "The Molson Indy Vancouver has gotten to the point where it's more than just a race. It has become a world-class event," a Tourism Vancouver official has said of the event. More importantly, the event signifies Vancouver's arrival as a world-class city: "It is Canada's Monte Carlo, pure and simple, a stunning setting where the Coast Range meets the Pacific Ocean."

Vancouver's claims to its "Monte Carlo-ness" reflect both its international pretensions and the importance of showcasing itself as a site of affluent lifestyle pursuits (Fotheringham, 1995). The latter are visible in the concentrations of art galleries, designer clothing and accessory boutiques, and "upmarket" coffee shops and restaurants that saturate the city's downtown and the False Creek area where the races take place. Motor sport racing appeals to an affluent audience, and extensive coverage of the Molson Indy gains widespread international exposure for Vancouver. International reporters and television crews typically spend several days in the city, filing stories on the race and its star personalities, but also conveying the cosmopolitan atmosphere of the city and its varied lifestyle attractions.

Vancouver's growth-oriented elites place a high value on the Molson Indy as a promotional vehicle for the world-class city. They love the "value" the event adds both to the region's *economy* and to its *image* as a world-class tourist destination. This event generates a purported $19 million in economic spin-offs (according to Tourism Vancouver and Indy officials), as well as pumping $500,000 directly into the city's tax base (Lowes, forthcoming).

Race promoters also remind Vancouverites of the promotional value of having Vancouver's scenery appear, even in the background, on television screens in an estimated 100 million homes around the affluent world. No other show in town even dreams about garnering an audience of this size, with the same global distribution potential: not the Canucks, and certainly not the British Columbia Lions of the Canadian Football League. Each year an estimated 160,000 people flood the stands during the Indy's Labor Day weekend run, including 70,000 who attend the final day of events. All of this activity helps to create 1,000-plus temporary jobs and approximately $2.4 million for local contractors, making the Molson Indy an economic contributor that few civic leaders want to lose.

Moreover, though there is little hard evidence to support claims that the presence of "world-class" sports is decisive in residential and business relocation decisions, these events do contribute to a cumulative image of the world-class city. And it is along these lines that Vancouver's political, business, and other civic boosters make the case that hosting the Molson Indy is simply a matter of economic and cultural "common sense"—that entertainment spectacles are a necessary component in efforts to gain world-class recognition and status for the city. In effect, such events function as an important vehicle for the marketing and promotion of Vancouver as a world-class city.

In this regard, I want to single out the central role of Vancouver sports media in the relentless promotion of this event (Lowes, forthcoming). For example, Vancouver's daily newspapers the *Province* and the *Sun* produce 30- to 40-page "special Indy supplements" in the week before the race. In addition to this pre-event hype, both newspapers provide exhaustive daily race coverage, culminating in complete wrap-up coverage. Local radio stations likewise contribute to these promotional efforts by airing 30-second "Eye on Indy" information spots, sometimes up to 25 times per day over the eight-week period leading to the race.

Not all members of the Vancouver community believe that such sports events bring wholly positive consequences. Critics argue that cities are better served by investing resources in areas of civic life other than major league sports events: in public services, community groups, and different kinds of urban public spaces such as parks and community recreation centers (Hulsman, 1997a; Johnson, 1999; Lowes, forthcoming). They also point to the more noxious aspects accompanying such a large-scale entertainment spectacle: the event's profound noise pollution, increased traffic around the False Creek area, the congestion of people and cars, the celebration of car culture in a city choking on smog and snarled in traffic jams. These are not the sorts of issues that contribute to the promotion of the Molson Indy event and of Vancouver as the world-class city. Their voices are lost or submerged in the "hyper-boosterism" surrounding the sports spectacle. Nowhere in the media is there a serious (or even half-hearted) engagement with the valid concerns of Indy critics.

Public investment in sports entertainment megaprojects now seems to be more influential than ever in determining the character of "world-class" civic discourse. Taken in this context, *world-class* means meeting the expectations of the affluent consumers of spectacular entertainment and leisure pursuits. The events must conform to global standards of excellence in terms of facilities (Whitson, 1999). Major league sports events are part of a larger project in which corporate and civic elites struggle to establish and maintain their cities' status in a transnational economic and cultural hierarchy. Although their ultimate objective is economic growth, major league sports megaprojects become badges of a city's stature—a sign of "arrival" on the world stage, from which other forms of growth will presumably follow (Whitson and Macintosh, 1993). In other words, spectacular events such as the Molson Indy Vancouver act as symbolic representatives of "community"—signifiers of civic prosperity and ambition. As such, they are constitutive elements in the broader promotional culture of the "world-class" city and its particular brand of civic discourse.

In his book *Promotional Culture* (1991), Andrew Wernick claims that we live amid a "vortex of promotional signs," in what amounts to an endless circulation of messages and images. Virtually every aspect of social life becomes part of a sales pitch. This is especially the case with life in the world-class city. In a world increasingly dominated by advertising and marketing, we find that consumer goods have become *the* currency of urban public life.

The sports entertainment industry, in particular, has become a significant site for the promotion and extension of commodities and styles, creating what amounts to an unprecedented global field of sources for consumer satisfaction and identity formation (Whitson & Gruneau, 1997). Yet these sources of satisfaction have become ever more closely tied to the market, to the need to find *meaning* through consumption. Through these discourses of consumption, the consumer has replaced the "citizen" as the focal point of much urban economic strategy. It is the *buying public*—in particular, the affluent buying public with tastes and interests oriented toward global markets and incomes to support these tastes—who are of paramount concern to cities with world-class aspirations. In this formulation, consumption reigns supreme; it is the motor and the ideological engine of the world-class city and the civic discourse that underpins it. And major league sports events like the Molson Indy Vancouver are constitutive features of such promotional civic discourse.

In short, urban marketing and promotion have created a new vision of world-class cities, those urban places depicted locally on television and in newspaper advertisements and situated symbolically at national and international levels. This promotional discourse has resulted in a widespread construction and display of personal identities—or expressions of "self"— on the basis of consumer preferences and "the apparent naturalness of the notion that people have common 'interests' with those who share their preferences" (Gruneau & Whitson, 1993, p. 221). This narrow conception of community is based on appeals to our collective interests as consumers. We become little more than a "community of fans," consumers sharing a fleeting entertainment experience and united by shared product preferences. Such communities, formed around acts of consumption or product loyalties (whether to the Molson Indy Vancouver sports event, the Ottawa Senators hockey franchise, or Honda cars), are not *political communities* in any meaningful sense of the term: "If we confuse these different meanings of community on a continual basis, or if political communities are effectively remade into communities of consumption and lifestyle, then surely we lose something important about the meaning and practice of public life" (pp. 219–221).

Researchers must examine the ways in which visions for urban development are framed and contested and identify the limits and possibilities for resistance. Complex and rooted deeply in belief systems and values, these visions reference instrumental places of deliberate self-aggrandizement and ambition, including sports entertainment megaprojects. In short, we need to continue to explore how efforts to shape a particular vision of a city's future draw on, as well as help to transform, understandings of democracy and citizenship in Canada. Identifying how these visions are manufactured and disseminated and how they articulate with wider political and economic processes is the first step toward understanding the nature of civic discourse and urban life in Canada in the new millennium.

REFERENCES

Ellen, I. G., & Schwartz, A. E. (2000). No easy answers: Cautionary notes for competitive cities. *The Brookings Review* 18 (3), 42–45.

Fotheringham, A. (1995). Development seeks out the water: Vancouver's face is changing and list of the top 25 Vancouver houses owned by Asian Canadians. *Financial Daily Post*, p. 15.

Gruneau, R., & Whitson, D. (1993). *Hockey night in Canada: Sport, identities, and cultural politics*. Toronto: Garamond.

Harvey, D. (1989). *The urban experience*. New York: Oxford University Press.

Hulsman, N. (1997a, Spring). The Molson Indy approach to neighbourhood park planning. *New City Magazine* 17 (3), n.p.

Hulsman, N. (1997b, Summer). Good NIMBY: Molson Indy vs. Hastings Park—the aftermath. *New City Magazine* 17 (4), n.p.

Johnson, P. (1999, March 28). Indy bid to satisfy locals stuck in pits. *Vancouver Courier*, p. 13.

Lowes, M. D. (2000). Indy dreams in the world-class city. In P. Donnelly (Ed.), *Taking sport seriously: Social issues in Canadian sport* (pp. 147–149). Toronto: Thompson Educational Publishing.

Lowes, M. D. (Forthcoming). *Indy dreams and urban nightmares: Speed merchants, spectacle, and the struggle over public space in the "world-class" city*. Toronto: University of Toronto Press.

Noll, R. G. (1997). Are stadiums worth the cost? *The Brookings Review 15* (3), 35–39.

Technodome dead: Bourque. (2000, October 17). *Montreal Gazette.* www.montrealgazette.com/news/pages/oo1017/4699666.html. Article accessed April 28, 2001.

Toronto in danger of losing Technodome project to Montreal. (1999, March 20). *Globe and Mail,* p. A2.

Wernick, A. (1991). *Promotional culture.* London: Sage.

Whitson, D. (1999). World-class leisure and consumption: Social polarization and the politics of place. In C. Andrew, P. Armstrong, & A. Lapierre (Eds.), *World class cities: Can Canada play?* (pp. 303–320). Ottawa: University of Ottawa Press.

Whitson, D., & Gruneau, R. (1997). The (real) integrated circus: Political economy, popular culture, and "major league" sport. In W. Clement (Ed.), *Understanding Canada: Building on the new Canadian political economy* (pp. 359–385). Montreal and Kingston: McGill–Queen's University Press.

Whitson, D., & Macintosh, D. (1993). Becoming a world-class city: Hallmark events and sports franchises in the growth strategies of western Canadian cities. *Sociology of Sport Journal 10,* 221–240.

Part V

Echoes from a Romanticized Past, Mythological Discourses

Chapter 19

A Truly Comic History:
Central Canadian Nationalism
and the Politics of Memory

Peter Hodgins

In the beautiful and enigmatic novel *Invisible Cities*, Italo Calvino (1974) writes of the city of Maurilia. Travelers arriving in Maurilia are invited to tour the city and then to compare what they have seen with old postcards of the city. This rite demands a specific performance from the traveler. In order to avoid disappointing the inhabitants, the traveler must praise the postcard city and cite her preference for the old city over the new. This task must be accomplished, however, with a certain delicacy. At the same time the visitor praises the old city, she must also praise the prosperity of the new city. In so doing, she must be exceedingly careful not to suggest that different cities have been born and died on the same site, each without knowing of the existence of the others. In speaking of the lost past, Calvino said: "At times even the names of the inhabitants remain the same, and their voices' accent, and also the features of the faces; but the gods who live beneath names and above places have gone off without a word and outsiders have settled in their place" (pp. 30–31).

It seems to me that Calvino (1974) has isolated a "rhetoric of nostalgia." The rhetoric of nostalgia juxtaposes the past—a golden age of simplicity, comfort, harmony, stability, and epistemological and moral certainty—against the fallen present. However, this rhetoric insists that the golden past endures as a source of identification and a repository of values and traditions, which continue to act as touchstones in a "brave new world." This felt need to preserve the past explains why the nostalgic Maurilians would so fear the intrusion of outsiders who lack these memories (Calvino, 1974, p. 31). In recent years, members of the central Canadian elite have publicly expressed the unspoken and unspeakable fears of the Maurilians.[1] Red Wilson (quoted in Foot, 1999), chairman of Bell Canada Enterprises

and founder of Historica (a charitable foundation devoted to the dissemination of knowledge of Canadian history), has registered his profound concern "about how we are transmitting the cultural heritage, inspiring pride
in the past, encouraging reasonable loyalty and fostering the development
of responsible democratic citizens" (p. A8). Similarly, A. Charles Baillie
(1997), CEO of the Toronto Dominion Bank, has argued that "we are
gripped by an appalling, abiding ignorance of each other, of our shared
past, of what has made this country great. The lessons of history are for-
gotten. . . . Our sense of common heritage, joint achievement, and shared
values is withering away. We live totally in the present, forgetting our past
and so risking our future" (p. 16).

This chapter addresses concerns related to Canada's national amnesia or
memory crisis, the many cultural histories of Canada, and the recent attempt to restore our past through the Heritage Minutes.

NATIONAL AMNESIA: THE MEMORY CRISIS

In recent years, many prominent central Canadian public intellectuals
and politicians have voiced the same lament as the corporate elite. Historians like Bliss (1992) and Granatstein (1998) have launched a campaign
to rescue "national" history from its "martyrdom" at the hands of Québec
separatists, social historians, feminists, and postcolonial critics. They believe that Canada will be able to regain its lost "national unity" in this
way. Journalists, essayists, and public figures like Robert Fulford (quoted
in Gwyn, 1996), Richard Gwyn (1996), and John Ralston Saul (1997) have
echoed these expressed concerns. Fulford, for example, laments that we are
"slowly obliterating the country's symbolic landscape" (p. 282). Saul and
Gwyn argue that when Canadians speak of the past (a rare event), they
typically claim victimization at the hands of external or internal aggressors.
As Gwyn astringently comments: "We positively scorn the greater part of
our history, not merely as dull . . . but also nowadays as an unending
chronicle of racism, sexism, homophobia, militarism, environmental-
degradation" (p. 283). This situation is exacerbated, Saul argues, by the
fact that the transmission of memory must now take place in a global
system of mediated communication, in which concern with the past and
place has given way to a concern with ubiquity and instantaneity: "The
very mass of information and sounds flying around us creates unease [and]
drives us into stubborn, ill-tempered passivity" (p. 34).

Critics place the blame for this national amnesia on many different
groups. Axworthy (1997), for example, blames the "self-inflicted assassi-
nation" of Canadian memory on provincial politicians "who preside over
education departments that have systematically cut back on history as a
core subject or who have dumped it into the mishmash they call social
studies" (p. 21). While Axworthy's remark exemplifies the traditional Ca-

nadian pastime of federal–provincial sniping, Granatstein's (1998) analysis of this crisis takes on all of the demons that populate the "angry white guy" imaginary. Granatstein (in Dorland & Charland, 2001) blames "provincial ministries of education and their bureaucrats, ethnic communities 'conned' by multiculturalism policies, boards of education, the media, university professors, university presses and the government agencies that subsidize 'unreadable books on minuscule subjects' and, of course, the federal government—in a word, pretty much everyone responsible for education" (p. 57).

The discourse of the memory crisis follows the logic of the rhetoric of nostalgia. As Tannock (1994) argues, the rhetoric of nostalgia always structures time into three moments: a golden age, a cut or a fall, and the deficient present. Furthermore, as Hutcheon (1998) points out, this golden age is always a historical inversion of the present. That is to say, the golden age is constructed in terms of utopian ideals and values that fail to materialize themselves in the present. This utopian character gives nostalgia its political character. As Moser (1999) argues, the nostalgic subject is animated by the utopian faith that she can "turn back the clock" and reconstitute the golden past. Translated into action, this assumption leads to interventions to reestablish what is imagined to be a previously existing state.

In a similar way, the discourse of the memory crisis constructs the present as a period of confusion, conflict, ambiguity, and forgetting. This lamentable state has arisen as a result of a series of "falls from grace," marked by the emergence of separatist movements in Canada, the specialization and radicalization of professional history, the bureaucratization of public education, a changing demographic makeup, and the rise of the global media and economy. Less explicit in this discourse is the belief that, at some time in the not-so-distant past, a unified Canada existed, bound together by shared national memories and values. Furthermore, this logic maintains that, within the hearts of all Canadians, a shared memory waits to be rekindled.

READING THE PAST: THE MANY HISTORIES OF CANADA

Before discussing the texts of some memorial nationalists, I would like to briefly discuss the main obstacles facing any attempt to restore a "national memory" in Canada. Canada is a "plurinational" country, whose colonial history has produced three mutually antagonistic so-called founding peoples. The first two clusters include the Aboriginal peoples and the French and the English, whose pre- and post-Confederation political and economic history has exacerbated regional tendencies. The third group of Canadians, whose numbers have greatly increased over the last century, includes an influx of non–Northern European immigrants (many of whom draw upon other histories for their projects of self-constitution). As a result, every attempt to represent an event in Canadian history entails taking a position within both a "politics of memory" and cultural politics. As Sorlin (1980) has argued, "The historical tradition defended by each group and class is . . . only an instrument for talking about the present: the conflicts that divide a society, and the goals pursued by the opposing forces are transposed in the semblance of past events" (p. 17).

To take an obvious example, historians have read the conquest and its aftermath in many different ways: the birth of a bicultural nation, the proof of the superiority of British institutions, the beginning of the end of native sovereignty over the lands west of the Appalachians, the colonization and continued subjugation of a once proud and independent *peuple*, and a simple exchange of colonial masters. To read this event in one way or the other is not only to commit oneself to a certain line of historical interpretation, but also to commit oneself to a concomitant political position on the power-saturated relationship between the various cultural groups in contemporary Canada. Viewed from this perspective, Dickinson's (1996) position seems more than tenable: "No consensual view [of Canadian history] has ever existed that could reconcile all Canadians. . . . As long as the majority in English Canada was still British and French-Canada still could be ignored, the illusion that a widely accepted common history existed could be maintained" (p. 148).

The West had been multicultural from its inception, but central Canada was slower to attract the new immigrants. Toronto did not lose its British face until after World War II, and Québec's "quiet revolution" did not occur until the 1960s. The memorial nationalist project is rooted in a nostalgia for the "old certainties and identities" of pre-1960s central Canada.

RESTORING THE PAST: "THE HERITAGE MINUTES"

In recent years, attempts to restore shared national memory in Canada have been legion. Adding to the academic discourse, numerous organizations have conducted surveys, which confirm serious gaps in the historical knowledge of the average Canadian. A group of professional historians, who broke away from the Canadian Historical Association, founded the National Organization of Historians and established a new journal suitably titled *National History*. This move responded to the perception that the Canadian Historical Association lacked a serious interest in "national history." The 1990s also witnessed the creation of an entire department in the federal government devoted to the preservation of "Canadian Heritage," while private institutions such as the Dominion Institute sprang up in hopes of rekindling the interest of Canadians in their past. Perhaps the most telling indicator of the desperation of Canada's elites to restore a national narrative is the CBC's latest (and perhaps last) megaproject—a documentary series entitled "Canada—A People's History."

The remainder of this chapter concentrates on one specific attempt to counter Canada's suspected amnesia, a series of 60-second "mini-films" called "The Heritage Minutes." In 1986, philanthropist Charles Bronfman established the CRB Foundation in order to produce these clips, which were shot on 35mm film and widely aired on Canadian television and in movie theaters. These "open-ended stories" depicted the past exploits of heroic Canadians. More recently, the production of the minutes has been incorporated into a larger project dubbed the "Historica Foundation," aimed at reconstituting a shared Canadian national memory. Board members for this project include such luminaries as Bronfman, Red Wilson (Chairman of Bell Canada Enterprises), John Cleghorn (CEO of the Royal Bank), Peter Lougheed (former premier of Alberta), Frank McKenna (former premier of New Brunswick), and Antonio Lamer (former Chief Justice of Canada).

This project is interesting because it marks the privatization of state efforts to ensure national security through the building of "national culture." Dowler (1996) explains the reasoning behind this statement. He says that the Canadian state has always been plagued by a chronic insecurity over its ability to defend its borders and to keep the various fissile elements within the federation "in line." These insecurities prompted the state to invest heavily in the creation of a national transportation and communication infrastructure. However, the creation of national networks had the unintended effect of exacerbating tendencies toward regionalism within Canada and facilitating the flow of American cultural products across wider swaths of Canadian space. To counter these tendencies, the Canadian state turned to culture. Policies aimed at fostering a "national culture" constituted a form of defense against both external and internal threats. It was hoped that these policies would secure the hearts and minds of Canadians from the lures of "continentalism," regionalism, separatism, and identity politics.

Historica's project of reviving and/or inventing national memories in order to counteract centrifugal tendencies within the Canadian federation and to ensure its continued existence clearly conforms to the logic of the cultural policy discourse described by Dowler (1996). Historica will seek to bind the country together through an interactive retelling of "the colony to nation" narrative of Canadian history, to be broadcast to television sets and computer monitors across Canada. This mythic narrative, which features the "heroic" exploits of upper-class white men, served as the backbone of the English Canadian schoolbook histories in the 1950s and 1960s. This "old foundational myth" recounted the story of a colony "triumphing over physical circumstance on its way to autonomy and maturity as a nation" (McKillop, 1999, p. 295).

While most memorial nationalists advocate such an approach (Granatstein, 1998; Saul, 1997), the strategy of "The Heritage Minutes" is much more subtle. Although the minutes depict the struggles of various groups (women, Québecois, Natives, Afro-Canadians, and Asian Canadians) to overcome social barriers, they tend to present the portraits in a way that reaffirms the foundational myth of colony to nation. That is, the minutes seek to suture potentially centrifugal elements of internal threats back into the body politic by making their actions appear part of a greater national movement toward "autonomy and maturity." One can see this suturing strategy at work, for example, in a minute titled *Nitro*. This minute details the construction of what has been mythologized in English Canadian culture as the skeleton that holds together the Canadian body politic: the Canadian Pacific Railroad. We watch as a white foreman offers a group of Chinese laborers boat fare to Canada for their wives if they dare place a bottle of nitroglycerin in a tunnel that is being excavated. One young man volunteers and advances into the tunnel. An explosion follows and a white foreman looks on impassively as he says to another: "Damn! That's the third we've lost this month. Get another volunteer."

Had the minute ended at this point, it would have been a fairly poignant depiction of the racism and brutality faced by Chinese laborers when they arrived in Canada to work on the railroad. However, in true comic fashion, the minute ends by redeeming Canada. Following the foreman's words, we are surprised to see our volunteer stagger out of the tunnel, soot-covered but still alive. Then the scene flashes to Vancouver, 50 years later, where our volunteer—now a distinguished older man dressed in a three-piece suit—sits in a comfortably appointed drawing room with grandchildren at his knee. With a photograph album on his lap, he tells the children, "I lost many friends. They say that there is one dead Chinese man for every mile of the track" (Historica, 1999). In re-presenting our volunteer as prosperous and surrounded by family, the narrative shifts the emphasis from an exploration of racism to a celebration of opportunity, reconciliation, and the willingness of Asian Canadians to sacrifice their lives to the Canadian nation-building project. Thus, conflict in the short term gives way to justice, truth, and beauty in the long run (see White, 1973). This Heritage Minute performs the dual function of integrating Asian-Canadians into the national narrative at the same time that its "all's well that ends well" conclusion expiates any lingering sense of guilt among white Anglo-Canadians about the sins of their fathers.

"The Heritage Minutes" also employ what Bakhtin (1994) calls "the hidden polemic" to ward off potential internal threats to Canada. One can see this textual strategy at work in the minute titled *Peacemaker*. The film begins with a close shot of young Native girl and her father (dressed in contemporary garb) planting a pine sapling. The dialogue runs as follows:

Father: This tree represents our people.

Girl: What kind of tree is it, dada?

Father: A tree of great peace. The Peacemaker gave the Great Laws of Peace to the Iroquois.

(Switch to a scene portraying "traditionally" dressed Native peoples brandishing war clubs and standing in front of a smoking hole in the ground.)

Father: In the dark times many years ago, Hiawatha spoke for the Peacemaker.

Hiawatha: You chiefs have brought ruin and despair to your children through war. You must fling this burning demon into the underground river to be carried away forever, Peace now . . . Peace.

(The assembled chiefs then fling their clubs into the river and the Great Tree of Peace rises and covers them.)

Father: And the power of the Great Peace drove the evil from them.

(The scene switches back to the present.)

Girl: Does the Great Peace still have power?

Father: You're here now, aren't you? (Historica, 1999)

On the face of it, this account would seem like just another garden-variety plea for peace and understanding, adorned with the stereotypical "Noble Savage" imagery. Such imagery is common in white representations of Native North American culture (Sayre, 1997). However, in the shadow of the Oka crisis and subsequent disputes over land claims, fishing rights, and self-government, the story takes on a very different meaning. "Peace-maker" is a hidden polemic directed, in general, against militant Native separatists and, in particular, against the Mohawk Warriors who faced down the Canadian army at Oka.

This hidden polemic is evident, for example, in the fact that the minutes identify the Peacemaker story as a traditional Iroquois tale. The Iroquois are a centuries-old confederacy of Native nations residing in western New York, Ontario, and Québec, and the Mohawk nation is a charter member. While non-Native Canadians might interpret this text as a generalized plea for peace, the hidden message to the Mohawk is perhaps more threatening. In essence, it may be an attempt to tell them that "You're still here, aren't you?" mainly as a result of their willingness to abjure armed resistance and work within the Canadian federation. The rather chilling message that do-ing otherwise will bring "ruin and despair to your children" reinforces this interpretation.

The minutes also use the hidden polemic to contest the claims of Québec separatism. *Les Voltigeurs de Québec*, for example, opens with a military band preparing to leave after practice. They are then called back to their seats by the band leader, who tells them in an exaggerated French accent: "We are now going to rehearse the crowning touch for the St. Jean Baptiste

Day. This score has just been composed especially for the event." The band then bumbles through a rendition of "Oh Canada!" which ends in cacophony and laughter. The band leader, with a sharp tap of his baton, remonstrates the band with the following words: "This piece deserves better and the authors are Canadian just like us" (Historica, 1999). Thus reminded of their duty to honor the composition of their fellow Canadians, the band plays the tune properly.

In addition, the film makes much of the fact that the song being rehearsed was composed for St. Jean Baptiste Day, a holiday that celebrates the Québecois nation. In creating an association between "Oh Canada" and St. Jean Baptiste Day, this minute seeks to bring St. Jean Baptiste Day (and, by extension, the centrifugal tendencies of Québec nationalism) back into the Canadian national narrative. This project of re-inscription becomes even more explicit in the use of the phrase "they are Canadian, just like us." Thus, the minute seeks to reintegrate potential fissile elements by re-identifying them with the pan-Canadian movement toward "autonomy and maturity."

Still another strategy of the minutes is to produce "Canadian identity" by highlighting cultural differences between Canadians and the all-too-similar Americans. In minutes such as *The Underground Railroad*, *Sitting Bull*, and *Jackie Robinson*, for example, the Canadian-American border acts as a haven from American racism and injustice, with the implied message that racism is an American problem to which morally superior Canadians are immune. The portrayal of Canadian heroes repelling American advances on our soil also confirms the difference between—and superiority of—the "Canadian way." *Sam Steele*, for instance, is set on the Alaska/Canada border in 1898. The minute begins with a lone prospector with a heavy American accent muttering to himself. The scene then cuts to the interior of a log cabin where the prospector sits at a table, facing a stern but impassive Mountie; another Mountie stands watch behind him. After the prospector reveals his intention to go to the Klondike, the seated Mountie tells him that he cannot wear pistols and bring gambling gear into Canada. The prospector then draws his gun and points it at the seated Mountie and shouts, "I'm an American, you can't do this to me!" The Mountie, who remains ice-calm, replies: "In that case, I'll be lenient. We'll keep the gambling gear and you'll be back in the United States by sundown." In the final scene, we watch as the mounted police escort the prospector back across the border. The prospector is muttering to himself, "Why didn't I shoot him?" (Historica, 1999).

This minute falls within a long Canadian tradition of favorably comparing our "national personality" with that of the Americans (New, 1998). In the Canadian nationalist imaginary, the so-called "average American" has most of the characteristics of our Yankee prospector: cowardly, self-aggrandizing, bombastic, individualistic, violence-prone and parochial. Our seated Mountie, on the other hand, represents the heroic virtues that this imaginary holds dear: bravery, a calm and rational demeanor, and the commitment to the protection of "peace, order and good government." Such comparisons, Makolkin (1992) argues, act as "sign systems controlling group behaviour" (p. 20). In other words, by ending the minute with a scene of the boisterous Yankee being led back to the border, this minute acts as both a celebration of so-called "Canadian values" and a prescription for future actions: like our heroic Mountie, Canadians should expel individualism, racism, greed, violence, and ignorance from the Canadian body politic.

CONCLUSION

In this chapter, I have argued that the attempt by the Historica and other elite "memory projects" to restore lost Canadian national memory and values stems less from a concern to bring to light a submerged past than to shape the present and future of Canadian public culture. To fulfill this goal, "The Heritage Minutes" have employed two opposed but related textual strategies. The first has been to contest the power of competing forms of collective belonging such as race and ethnicity and to attempt to restore the primacy, if not the monopoly, of the Canadian nation as a source of social solidarity. The second strategy has been to reanimate the threat of a marauding external "Other" in the form of the Americans in order to encourage Canadians to "rally 'round the flag." In so doing, advocates of the memory project have hoped that the forces of amnesia and fragmentation will be destroyed and Canadians can live again in unity.

Like most, I would agree with the producers of "The Heritage Minutes" that the "core Canadian values" that they identify (tolerance, the refusal of violence as a means of problem solving, the willingness to reach out to others in need, and the willingness to fight against racism, sexism, and social barriers of all kinds) are all values deserving of celebration. I would like to question, however, their assumption that Canadian public memory has been fragmented as a result of the proliferation of the countermemories of so-called internal and external threats to a unified national culture. What the elites behind this and other such projects fail to ask themselves is the potentially painful question, "Is the imminent death of Canadian national memory really only the death of their power to define Canada?" As Michael Ignatieff (1996) suggests:

[Memorial nationalists] may find it frightening that there is no longer, if there ever was, a national consensus; but all that means is that groups will no longer allow themselves to be spoken for. . . . To long nostalgically for lost consensus is actually to long for the days when everyone knew his place, when minorities let elites speak for them. Instead of fragmentation, we should call it democratization: the chaotic, fearful immensely productive logic of empowerment. (p. 48)

Do we lament fragmentation and seek the restoration of a lost Golden Age of national unity, or do we recognize cultural democratization and accept that all Canadian voices deserve to be heard and engaged (even those who tell not-so-heroic stories about Canadian history)? This will be the central question in the battle over the construction, definition, and dissemination of Canadian public memory in the twenty-first century. The future of Canada might well rest in the answers given to that question.

NOTE

The author acknowledges that funding for the research and writing of this text was provided by a doctoral fellowship from the Social Sciences and Humanities Research Council of Canada.

REFERENCES

Axworthy, T. (1997, October). Curing the historical amnesia that is killing Canada. *Canadian Speeches* 11 (6).

Baillie, A. C. (1997, October). Respecting differences to make Canada work. *Canadian Speeches*.

Bakhtin, M. M. (1994). Double-voiced discourse in Dostoevsky. In P. Morris (Ed.), *The Bakhtin reader* (pp. 102–111). London: Edward Arnold.

Bliss, M. (1992). Privatizing the mind: The sundering of Canadian history, the sundering of Canada. *Journal of Canadian Studies* 26 (4), 5–17.

Calvino, I. (1974). *Invisible cities*. Orlando, FL: Harcourt Brace.

Conlogue, R. (2000, September 19). Why do Canadians confuse this man with a car? *Globe and Mail*, p. R1.

Dickinson, J. (1996). Canadian historians—agents of unity or disunity. *Journal of Canadian Studies* 31 (2), 148–153.

Dorland, M., & Charland, M. (2001). *Peace, order and good government: Law, rhetoric and irony in the formation of Canadian civil culture*. Toronto: University of Toronto Press.

Dowler, K. (1996). The cultural industries policy apparatus. In M. Dorland (Ed.), *The cultural industries in Canada* (pp. 328–346). Toronto: Lorimer.

Foot, R. (1999, October 22). Business leaders on mission for Canadian history. *National Post*, p. A8.

Granatstein, J. (1998). *Who killed Canadian history?* Toronto: HarperCollins.

Gwyn, R. (1996). *Nationalism without walls*. Toronto: McClelland and Stewart.

Historica Foundation. (1999). Promotional materials. Toronto.

Hutcheon, L. (1998). Irony, nostalgia, and the postmodern. Department of English, University of Toronto. http://www.utlink.utoronto.ca/www/utel/criticism/HutchINP.html.

Ignatieff, M. (1996). The narcissism of minor differences. In J. Littleton (Ed.), *Clash of identities* (pp. 41–54). Toronto: Canadian Broadcasting Company.

Makolkin, A. (1992). *Name, hero, icon: Semiotics of nationalism through heroic biography*. New York: Mouton de Gruyter.

McKillop, A. B. (1999). Who killed Canadian history? A view from the trenches. *Canadian Historical Review 80*, 267–299.

Moser, W. (1999). Mélancholie et nostalgie: Affects de la Spätzeit. *Études Littéraires 31* (2), 83–102.

New, W. H. (1998). *Borderlands*. Vancouver: University of British Columbia Press.

Saul, J. R. (1997). *Reflections of a Siamese twin*. Toronto: Penguin Books.

Sayre, G. (1997). *Les sauvages Américains*. Chapel Hill: University of North Carolina Press.

Silver, A. (1999). Introduction. In J. Meisel, G. Rocher, & A. Silver (Eds.), *Si je me souviens bien: As I recall* (pp. 1–6). Montreal: Institute for Research on Public Policy.

Sorlin, P. (1980). *The film in history*. Oxford: Basil Blackwell.

Tannock, S. (1994). Nostalgia critique. *Cultural Studies 9* (3), 453–464.

White, H. (1973). *Metahistory*. Baltimore, MD: Johns Hopkins University Press.

Chapter 20

Reclaiming "Authenticity": *Cape Breton's Magazine* and the Commodification of Insularity

Jennifer M. MacLennan and G. John Moffatt

Whatever else may reasonably be said of it, Canada is a small island. Despite its being the world's second-largest nation-state in terms of land mass, the country's cultural discourse traditionally favors the perspective of the small, isolated, and insular community as the key to a vision of Canadian distinctiveness. This "islandized" perspective functions both as an authentication of a unique cultural identity and as an expression of the culture's marginalized position on the rim of a larger, more aggressive neighbor.

The island as metaphor for the national community is well represented in Canadian and Québecois literature, as in the work of Alistair MacLeod, Jack Hodgins, and Jean Poulin. However, the most pervasive expression of insularity as the lynchpin in the Canadian self-image lies in popular culture. Our magazines and newspapers—as well as our film, television, and music industries—have consistently featured Canada's island communities (Newfoundland, Cape Breton, PEI, and Vancouver Island) as sites of authenticity. These sites provide the kind of visual and verbal signals for cohesion that Canadian audiences recognize as part of their identity.

Cape Breton Island, in many respects, exemplifies the power of the island community as national point of reference. Smith's (1968) tongue-in-cheek observation that Cape Breton is the "thought-control center of Canada" has been validated in the last decade alone by the success of Cape Breton–centered films (*Margaret's Museum* and *New Waterford Girl*), novels (Ann-Marie MacDonald's *Fall On Your Knees* and Alistair MacLeod's *No Great Mischief*), television series (CBC's *Pit Pony*), and above all, music (from Rita MacNeil to the Rankins to Ashley MacIsaac). Significantly, each of the above takes the Island's past as subject and highlights some of the romantic elements from that past. The success of these films, novels, and musicians suggests that English-speaking Canadians at large are prepared to buy a romanticized version of Cape Breton's past as a legitimate expression of a pan-Canadian cultural difference within the larger North American context.

THE ISLAND AS CULTURAL METAPHOR

Our analysis focuses on the award-winning *Cape Breton's Magazine* as a representative manifesto of this approach to cultural distinctiveness. Fusing oral history with photographic portraiture in a popular format, the magazine "speaks to everyone concerned about the authentic lives of extraordinary ordinary people" (Lotz, 2000). As its editor R. Caplan (1979) notes, the Island represents "a touchstone" (p. viii) for those who wish to reclaim a sense of centeredness and tradition: "They are looking for something they might, if pressed, call 'the authentic' . . . for qualities they hope are still within themselves, for something of which they are still capable, regardless of where they now live or how they live out their lives" (p. viii). As such a touchstone, the Island not only offers a distinctive and well-defined physical space, but also a metaphorical space for the reclaiming of authenticity and tradition. Mythologically, the Island both contains the Islanders and *is contained within them*, since it puts them in touch with qualities and traditions that lie within. As cultural metaphor, Cape Breton becomes at once a place the Islanders inhabit and an essence that inhabits them.

Although the conflation of place and cultural identification is not unique to the Island, the insularity and physical separateness of Island life capture the essence of this link. As Corbin and Rolls (1996) note in their study of Cape Breton Island culture, the Islanders' sense of identity is inescapably framed by the clearly defined physical space they inhabit, a place that is conceptually, as well as geographically, distinct. Island communities are *always* marginal in the geographic sense: distinct entities, smaller, more sharply visible than the surrounding culture, they form an ideal metaphorical and mythopoeic identification for any culture threatened by overwhelming outside influences.

In *The Colony of Unrequited Dreams* (1998), Newfoundland novelist Wayne Johnston puts the following words in the mouth of his character Joey Smallwood: "For an islander, there had to be natural limits, gaps, demarcations, not just artificial ones on a map. Between us and them and here and there, there had to be a gulf" (p. 132). The physical boundaries of the Island help to preserve the values and experiences of a traditional village community, typically "a small place, tightly knit, old" (Dull, 2000, p. 5), bound by shared values, including "living close to nature, experiencing isolation, entertaining ourselves, being unpretentious, and being practical, capable people" (Rolls, 1996, p. 142). Such village values resist commodification, enabling us to "hold [a community] together and retain its identity while being bombarded by media messages—primarily American media messages—produced by different cultures in distant places" (Corbin, 1996a, p. 178).

That the Island, whose inhabitants hold the sense of place most strongly, provides a metaphor of depth and resonance for Canadian identity is not surprising. Northrop Frye (1971) once said that, for Canadians, the question of "Who am I?" is more accurately rendered as "Where is here?" (p. 22). The Island as metaphor may be a particularly attractive container for issues of Canadian cultural identity because, as Walsh (1993) notes of her fellow Newfoundlanders, Islanders "always knew who we were and where we were" (p. 5). The Island therefore offers an unmistakable, almost palpable, connection with our identity. "To cross the causeway to Cape Breton," note Corbin and Rolls (1996) "is to discover this sense of difference" (p. 14).

DISTINCTIVENESS AND SURVIVAL

Not surprisingly, the sense of distinctiveness at the heart of the Island experience, in turn, finds its expression in themes of survival. On the Island, a strong communal connection is essential to survival. *Cape Breton's Magazine* is a celebration both of that survival and of the community-building that enables it. As Caplan (1996) explains, the magazine is about "some of the strategies and techniques of survival in a tough, tough place—the voices of surviving remnants in a world under siege. The telling of stories is just one of those strategies, those accomplishments" (p. ix). But as much as communal identification is a survival strategy, it is also an inescapable product of close containment within clearly defined geographic boundaries, a containment that produces a new form of kinship described as "spatial rather than racial" (Dull, 2000, p. 5). Not surprisingly, Island life, like any kinship, is complex and contradictory. Its contradictions find expression in a series of thematic tensions between center and periphery, between singularity and community, and between eccentricity and shared values. Like Smith (1968), Corbin and Rolls (1996) capture this dichotomy of centeredness and periphery in the very title of their study of Cape Breton. Corbin (1996) explains in the Foreword:

We called this book *The Center of the World at the Edge of a Continent* because the play of contrasts it inspires seems apt for Cape Breton. How can an edge be a center? Indeed, how can Cape Breton be the center of the world? . . . We know that this place is very much the center of our world, even as the Island rests on the edge of the North American continent. (p. 7)

Like the Corbin and Rolls (1996) collection, *Cape Breton's Magazine* explores the tensions that give shape to the Island's cultural landscape. In particular, its stories feature a dynamic interplay between individual difference—whether based on ethnic heritage, national origins, religious affiliation, or simple eccentricity—and the strongly communal aspect of Island life that has enabled Islanders to forge a singular and distinct identity from the mosaic. The same relationship that binds individuals to their immediate community also exists between what Caplan (1979) describes as smaller "communities of regard" (p. viii) and the overall Island community of which they are a part. Thus, the Island as metaphor is both microcosm and macrocosm, a dynamic system in which center and periphery are continually in flux. Although composed of a mix of heritages, Cape Breton has its own character:

[Cape Breton] still has a way of doing things, a shared lore and way of speaking and regarding one another which is a people and a place. Some time between 1790 and 1900, various peoples and the place emerged as one. To say Cape Breton is to say both land *and* people. And to a Cape Bretoner there are only two places on earth: Cape Breton Island and that other place, Away. (Caplan, 1979, p. viii)

The Island identity, then, emphasizes singularity and difference even as it unites its disparate elements into a series of communities within communities. Like Canada, Cape Breton can be understood as a mosaic of smaller cultures that, taken together, constitute Island kinship and community in the "spatial" form (Dull, 2000).

ISLANDS WITHIN ISLANDS

In the three collections considered in this chapter, any number of islands within the Island emerge as focal points. Caplan (1979, 1988, 1996), for example, profiles the Scots, the Acadians, and the Mi'kmaq, whom many people would readily associate with Cape Breton. However, he also includes stories about the Poles, Ukrainians, Jews, and members of communities such as Whitney Pier and 14 Yard, created in the cities around the mines and the steel plants. Within these nested islands, it is membership in the local community that authenticates the individual. At the same time, through their toughness, their honesty, and their ability to survive and to create meaningful tales, the individuals who make up the community are the source of its authenticity.

"A Visit with Mary and Clarence Lashley" (reprinted in Caplan, 1988) is paradigmatic of the insular community's role in authenticating the individual experience, forging the community within the community or the Island within the Island. Both Clarence's account of his experience as a Barbadian immigrant in Cape Breton and Mary's portrayal of her life as an unwed mother in the area around Margaree set the stage for the subsequent enactment of authentic community in the shadow of the collieries.

The couple describe how Clarence's affection for Mary's baby brought them together, how they overcame her parents' opposition to their inter-racial marriage, and how they subsequently settled in New Waterford's 14 Yard community. Their account affirms two of the basic principles under consideration here. First, Clarence's ability to convince Mary's family that he is "a different person than they thought" (p. 125) attests to the capacity of the microcosmic Island community to see value where it lies in an in-dividual, irrespective of ethnic or national difference. Further evidence of this egalitarian spirit lies in Mary's account of Clarence's visit to her home district:

Some down Cheticamp, around Margaree, they had never seen a black man. He went down and the children used to get under the table when they'd see him coming in, but before he'd leave they were climbing all over him. He said, "Everywhere you'd look you could see a pair of eyes." (Caplan, 1988, p. 125)

The image of the omnipresent staring eyes also suggests the individual's high visibility in an Island community, where the existence of the public gaze makes anonymity difficult or impossible. Each person's actions be-come an event in the lives of others, and in this case, the children's behavior signals the Islanders' ability to overcome ignorance and prejudice in the face of individual authenticity.

The Lashleys' account of their life in 14 Yard is even more powerful testimony of the redemptive power of a community that knows and guards its boundaries, understanding how those boundaries not only distinguish it from the surrounding communities but also create cohesion within. As Clarence describes it, "In 14 Yard we lived like one family. . . . You look after one another like brother and sister. If you belonged to 14 Yard you were as safe as in God's pocket" (Caplan, 1988, p. 126). Mary explains: "That time your neighbors would run. Say a fire catch you, they'd run and take your clothes out and if you're sick they'd come and bring things" (p. 125). The story describes how the ethnically diverse (chiefly immigrant) population come together at house parties to celebrate through music and dance. "Sly Mongoose," one of the songs performed by Clarence Lashley, speaks to the power of music to create a community where people can "dance in the houses, dance in the street, dance in every open spot you get" (p. 127). (This song later found its way into Ann-Marie MacDonald's [1996] acclaimed novel *Fall On Your Knees*.)

Imagery that underscores the interdependence and self-sufficiency of the place and its inhabitants evokes this sense of insular social cohesion among the inhabitants of 14 Yard. Mary, for example, recalls vegetable gardens, goats, pigs, and poultry. Cultural brokers such as folklorist Helen Creigh-ton promote a Nova Scotian identity rooted in "the simple life," with ther-apeutic spaces to which the world-weary may turn for cultural refreshment

(McKay, 1994, pp. 214–273). Caplan (1988), however, warns against over-looking the hardship and challenges that contribute to the building of the authentic community. Clearly, the past of which 14 Yard is a part is far from utopian, and Mary Lashley, in particular, stresses the harshness of that world. She responds to Caplan's observation that theirs is "a beautiful story," with "Yea? If you've got to live it through, it's not so beautiful. It's beautiful to hear about it but it's not beautiful to live it" (p. 123). In other words, we must remember, understand, and celebrate the pain as well as the joy.

The profile of Hilda Mleczko of Glace Bay, which concludes Caplan's *Cape Breton Works* (1996), further explores the Island-within-an-Island phenomenon. A war bride from England, Hilda married into a Cape Breton mining family of Polish extraction. Her discourse reflects the degree to which she consciously synthesizes three cultural identities: English, Polish, and Cape Breton. The interview begins with a clear statement of identification with the Island: "I love Cape Breton. . . . This is my country now" (p. 291). Hilda simultaneously affirms her roots, which are "like a thumbprint. I'll be English till I die. You can't erase that" (p. 291). Nevertheless, she attempts to acquire the linguistic markers of the Island: "I tried so hard to talk like the Cape Bretoners when I came here . . . [but] it still came out English twang, so I quit" (p. 291). Similarly, her attempts to learn Polish "really cracked up my Polish family . . . the fact that I was speaking Polish with an English accent apparently was very funny" (p. 291). Hilda Mleczko's testimony not only celebrates an individual, a family, and a community, but also offers that experience as a model of tolerance. This model encourages both shared values and individuality. Hilda's narrative is replete with examples of how her Polish-Cape Breton family accommodated her and made her welcome ("even if they could only speak a few words of English, they'd switch from Polish and talk in English so that I'd feel good" [p. 284]). The newcomer's integration into an existing community also highlights the community's openness to modernity (Caplan, 1979); the society is neither "closed" nor "backward" (p. viii). Instead, the values of the insular society bring out the value within the newcomer, by providing a context for the expression and sharing of authenticity. As indicated elsewhere, Caplan (1979) attributes the success of *Cape Breton's Magazine* to this willingness to embrace the new.

At the same time, nurturing the integrity of the authentic culture takes work; it cannot be simply "put on" or imitated. Mi'kmaq fiddler Lee Cremo compares the difficulty of mastering the Cape Breton fiddling style to learning a language: "You'll never learn in one year. You have to be almost born with it. Or surrounded like where I lived. It's all Scottish" (Caplan, 1979, p. 38). Acquiring a skill, almost by osmosis, both affirms the integrity of the Scottish fiddling tradition and illustrates the ability of an insular "community within a community" to participate in the larger culture without losing its own sense of distinctiveness. The image of Cremo's own Mi'kmaq community as an island surrounded by Scots and permeated by their music serves not to make a point about the encroachment of a European culture on an Aboriginal one, but to demonstrate how a Cape Breton Mi'kmaq is able to accommodate a key element of the larger Island culture and make it his own. In so doing, Cremo affirms both his Mi'kmaq heritage and his larger Cape Breton roots. After discussing the difficulty of learning to play in the Scottish-Cape Breton style, Cremo describes this natural process of synthesis that takes place:

They don't use any kind of instrument. They just take a little piece of stick and they tap on the bottom of their sole. There's good rhythm to it. That's why I think today when I play a reel, a Scottish reel, I make it a little faster. I think it's the Micmac rhythm. . . . when I make a tune I never try to use Scottish or Micmac tunes—I think what comes is a different thing all together. (Caplan, 1979, pp. 38–39)

The two-way door between the Mi'kmaq and Scottish traditions not only validates and allows respect for both cultures, but also allows Cremo—the artist active in both communities—to find his own sound and to articulate his own authenticity before a receptive audience.

THE "REAL THING": DISTINCTIVENESS AND CULTURAL AUTHENTICITY

We have already indicated that a principal feature of an "Islandized" mythos is the creation and recognition of "authenticity," a quality that is typically—as in *Cape Breton's Magazine*—conflated with a milieu of past experience portrayed as both simpler and purer. This process is typical of what McKay (1994) has called the "commodification of innocence," which often occurs in discourse surrounding regional and national identity (pp. 73–74). Labeled "the most extensive oral history project ever undertaken on the people of Cape Breton," *Cape Breton's Magazine* is marketed as one of the vehicles through which "Cape Bretoners and all those other people who love Cape Breton, worldwide" celebrate their Island distinctiveness (Caplan, 2000b). The magazine provides the people of Cape Breton with the means to contribute to their own "history, natural history, and future" (Caplan, 1979, p. viii) and reflects a community united through bonds of social interaction, oral tradition, musical celebration, and a strong sense of family (Caplan, 2000a). In this community, we find "remnants of a bit more manageable world, evidences of a time when life was simpler and more direct. And on occasion . . . meet someone who is more than a remnant, who is, you might say, the real thing" (Caplan, 1979, p. viii).

The "real thing" referenced in *Cape Breton's Magazine* is the Island's Gaelic heritage—its language, music, and culture. References to speaking, or being spoken to, in Gaelic immediately mark individuals and their stories as participating in a cultural reality distinct from the Canadian mainstream, but central to the image of Cape Breton. In particular, two figures profiled in *Down North* (singer Hector Carmichael and storyteller Joe Neil Mac-Neil) emerge as exemplars of "the real thing"—a "corridor through which tradition passes unaltered from the distant past into our own present" (Caplan, 1979, p. 83). The bilingual format of MacNeil's lengthy tale of "Iain Mór Mac an Iasgair Mhóir" ("Big John, the Big Fisherman's Son") reflects Caplan's willingness to let the storyteller speak for himself through translator John Shaw. Significantly, MacNeil's opening remarks call attention to the fact that the stories will be told only as long as an audience exists: "You need both sides. There has to be a side that produces the sound and there has to be an ear to hear it, otherwise it doesn't register" (p. 83). In other words, preserving the voice of the last great Gaelic storyteller in Cape Breton is not by itself sufficient to capture the essence of the Island's culture; the storyteller must appear in the context of his community.

In *Down North* (1979) Caplan draws the reader's attention to the role of formal ritual in the creation of the community or, more specifically, the "community within the community." For example, the selections devoted to the Gaels include three detailed descriptions of cultural rituals or ritualized behaviors: namely, the engagement rite known as *Reiteach*; the mummering celebration of *Oidhche na Calluinn* on Christmas Eve or New Year's Eve; and the milling frolic, where handwoven cloth is "waulked" or beaten on a table to the rhythms of traditional Gaelic waulking songs. Newer songs such as Hector Carmichael's "A Milling Frolic on the North Shore" may also be sung at such events. Another article in *Down North* describes the Acadian pre-Lenten festival of *Chandeleur*.

In three of the above instances, the ritual has become extinct. Photographs accompanying "*Reiteach*: A Scottish Engagement Rite" and "*Oidhche na Calluinn*" highlight the demise of these two customs. One photograph shows the 1923 wedding of Rhoda MacDonald of Skir Dhu to Sandy Kenny Morrison of Wreck Cove, an event "said to be the product of the last formal Reitach [*sic*] on Cape Breton Island" (Caplan, 1979, p. 58). The second photograph depicts "Roderick MacLeod of Wreck Cove, the last man to wear the dried sheepskin [costume of the leader of band of mummers] on the North Shore" (p. 64). The article on *Chandeleur* begins with Marguerite Gallant of La Pointe introducing "something else they used to celebrate which they don't now" (p. 60). The milling frolic is depicted in terms of a limited revival. Thus, Caplan draws the reader's attention to the widening gulf between the Island's past and present, making the past something of an island in itself.

PRESERVING CULTURAL HISTORY

In keeping with its preservationist thrust, *Cape Breton's Magazine* offers "no news." Rather, "each issue is born old—and built to last. Rooted in Scottish, Micmac [*sic*], Acadian, and Irish traditions, *Cape Breton's Magazine* is filled with oral history, traditional tales, music and lots of photographs" (Caplan, 2000a, n.p.). The magazine is also about "love and boxing and sailing and accidents that didn't happen—it is centered on food and family and farming and fishing, coal and steel—on going away and coming back and dealing with possibilities and with what was thrown in their way" (Caplan, 1996, p. ix).

Significantly, perhaps even ironically, it is Caplan the outsider, the "Come-From-Away"—himself an island of one—who has captured the dichotomies of Island life and who, in the act of building his magazine, has authenticated both himself and the community. As the conservator of the eroding Island tradition, Caplan (1996) has come to embody the cultural heart of the Island, taking the place of those who have abdicated their cultural space, having "gone down the road or into television—or even cyber-space, leaving me with their elders at the kitchen table" (p. vii):

I sometimes see my role—recording stories in Cape Breton at the end of the 20th century—as replacing [that] generation . . . at the kitchen table or the back porch, interested and asking and being told, not in a hurry to get away, actually eager to go through an album or the old tools in the basement, photographing everything, taping, visiting the stones in a restored cemetery or the foundation of their family's first home. (p. vii)

Caplan (1988) recognizes that he is contributing to the preservation and authentication of a way of life and a tradition that are in danger of being lost:

Conversations do not just happen. They take effort, theirs and mine. Some stories are told for the first time—because I asked or because something in our being together called them up—and some are stories they've worked on for years. I am sure that it is the process of storytelling, that we are watching what may be traditional tales in the making—if only we keep talking, hearing old lines re-used and the events recreated slightly differently each time, each time, just that much more finely honed. And I'm there to tape one more step in the process, otherwise known as living together, talking, passing the time. . . . And while it would be specious to argue that "this is exactly what the speaker meant"—I do consider these true to my own experience with the speaker. (pp. vii–ix)

Caplan (1988) insists that the magazine, and the books distilled from it, belong to Cape Bretoners. They also belong to him: "[The magazine] is also a portrait of *my* Cape Breton, the rooms I was in and the people I talked with, the questions I thought to ask" (Caplan, 1979, p. vii). Through chronicling the oral history of the Island, *Cape Breton's Magazine* invites the reader to consider the voices and stories of ordinary Islanders. In doing so, the magazine contributes to the sense of community that has, for all cultures and all times in history, depended on a sense of the distinctiveness of "the people" (McKay, 1994).

CONCLUSION: PLACE AS CULTURAL FORMATION

Although other "peoples" have traditionally been defined by ethnic origins, Islanders are rendered a "people" instead by geography, by insularity and self-reliance, and finally by their "Islandized" cultural mythology. This mythology links individual to community, small communities to a larger culture, and authenticity to a layered, integrated connection to place. The anchors that hold the community in place are its traditions, its acceptance of newcomers, protection of its own, and a truly authentic example of "therapeutic space" that nurtures and reaffirms the integrity of both individual and community. Caplan (1996) explains: "I never forget that I came to Cape Breton at what felt to me as just about the end of the road. I fell in among a people who interested me and treated me well, perhaps out of habit, perhaps out of pity, perhaps because they saw value in me of which I had lost track. In any case, it sustained me long enough to focus on the place and my own possibilities in terms of the place, long enough to create *Cape Breton's Magazine*" (p. vii). The significance of Caplan's magazine and of the broader movement in Canadian popular culture of which it has stood in the vanguard attests to the ongoing need of Canadians to believe that an Islander's life is still imaginatively possible and that the Island's natural boundaries, although open and accessible to all, remain permanent, inviolate, and real.

REFERENCES

Caplan, R. (Ed.) (1979). *Down north: The book of Cape Breton's Magazine*. Cape Breton, NS: Breton Books. Reprinted 1991.

Caplan, R. (Ed.) (1988). *Cape Breton lives: A book from Cape Breton's Magazine*. St. John's, NFLD: Breakwater Books.

Caplan, R. (Ed.) (1996). *Cape Breton works: More lives from Cape Breton's Magazine*. Wreck Cove, NS: Breton Books.

Caplan, R. (2000a). Welcome to the Cape Breton catalogue. http://www.capebretonsmagazine.com/home.html. Accessed June 27, 2000.

Caplan, R. (2000b). The faces of *Cape Breton's Magazine*. http://www.capebretonsmagazine.com/faces.html. Accessed June 27, 2000.

Corbin, C. (1996a). Conversation and culture. In C. Corbin & J. A. Rolls (Eds.), *The centre of the world at the edge of a continent* (pp. 177–190). Sydney, NS: University College of Cape Breton Press.

Corbin, C. (1996b). Foreword. In C. Corbin & J. A. Rolls (Eds.), *The centre of the world at the edge of a continent* (pp. 7–9). Sydney, NS: University College of Cape Breton Press.

Corbin, C., & Rolls, J. A. (1996). Introduction. In C. Corbin & J. A. Rolls (Eds.), *The centre of the world at the edge of a continent* (pp. 11–16). Sydney, NS: University College of Cape Breton Press.

Dull, M. (2000, October). Kinship and nation in *Amelia* (1848) and *Anne of Green Gables* (1908). Paper presented at the Leiden Conference on the Rhetoric of Canadian Writing. Leiden, Netherlands.

Frye, N. (1971). *The bush garden.* Toronto: Anansi.

Johnston, W. (1998). *The colony of unrequited dreams.* Toronto: Vintage Canada.

Lotz, J. (2000). Quoted online from the *Atlantic Provinces Book Review.* http://www.capebretonsmagazine.com/cbmag.html. Accessed June 27, 2000.

MacDonald, A. (1998). *Fall on your knees.* Toronto: Vintage Canada.

McKay, I. (1994). *The quest of the folk: Antimodernism and cultural selection in twentieth-century Nova Scotia.* Montreal and Kingston: McGill–Queen's University Press.

Rolls, J. A. (1996). Once upon an island. In C. Corbin & J. A. Rolls (Eds.), *The centre of the world at the edge of a continent* (pp. 131–144). Sydney, NS: University College of Cape Breton Press.

Smith, R. (1968). Cape Breton is the thought-control centre of Canada. In A. Purdy (Ed.), *The new Romans: Candid Canadian opinions of the U.S.* (pp. 18–30). Edmonton, AB: Hurtig.

Walsh, M. (1993). A hymn to Canada. The 1993 Spry lecture, University of Toronto. Toronto: Canadian Broadcasting Corporation.

Chapter 21

Sacajawea and Her Sisters:
Images and Native Women

Gail Valaskakis

Near Sitting Bull's grave there is a bullet-ridden obelisk raised in memory of the Indian woman who accompanied Lewis and Clark on their expedition across the West. A plaque says that her name is "Sakaka-Wea, that she 'guided' the expedition to the Pacific Ocean, and that she died and was buried at Fort Manuel in South Dakota on December 20, 1812" (Duncan, 1987, p. 162). In the years since, Sacajawea has become a figure of popular culture, an Indian maiden with "more statues in her honor than any other woman in American history" (p. 162). While historians agree that her name is Sacajawea, which means "boat launcher" in her native Shoshoni, image-makers have labeled her Sakakawea, an Hidatsa word for "bird woman" (p. 163). No one knows for certain whether she died at Fort Manuel at about age 25 or lived to be an old woman on the Wind River Reservation in Wyoming (Howard, 1971, p. 192). But our image of the Bird Woman is ageless: a shapely Indian princess with perfect Caucasian features, dressed in a tight-fitting red tunic, spearing fish with a bow and arrow from a birch bark canoe suspended on a mountain-rimmed, moonlit lake.

Sacajawea is a reoccurring representation in the cultural narratives of Native and other North Americans. We imagine her as "blazing the trail" of western exploration, intriguing in the contrast of her actions and our historical images of Indians as passive extensions of the land or obstacles to its development. Her personal experience is lost to us; only pieces of the framework of her life can be drawn from the journals, diaries, and notes of those who were motivated by economic and political purpose to scout the American West between 1804 and 1806. We believe that the Hidatsas took her from her Shosoni people when she was 10 or 12 years old. At the time of the Lewis and Clark expedition, she was about 16; she was one of two "country wives" purchased by a member of the expedition named Charbonneau; and she was pregnant. Sacajawea traveled with her newborn son, supporting the mission, which would expand the prospects of colonial settlement with the panoply of her person and the amity of her languages. At the end of the expedition, she was apparently left in St. Louis when Charbonneau resumed his life as a trapper in the Southwest (Howard, 1971). This, like her experience of the land, the people in her life, and even her death, is conjecture drawn from the imagination of those who write popular history.

While Sacajawea's experience with the Lewis and Clark expedition is uncommon, our contradictory mythical memory of her is not. As a child growing up on the Lac du Flambeau reservation in Wisconsin, I remember Sacajawea. And I remember her postcard sisters that are still sold in Lac du Flambeau today, smiling Indian princesses frozen in time and deadpan women captioned "squaws" covered in baskets or beadwork, or surrounded by children. I was drawn to these postcards not because they touched some chord of displaced history of identity, but because they didn't. What was the connection between these images of princesses and squaws and my great-grandmother who lived across the road? I listened to her narratives of Chippewa struggles for empowerment until I was 18, when I went away to school and she died. I knew women whom Others called squaws and women whom we teasingly called Indian princesses. But what did these postcard representations mean in the lived experience of my great-grandmother, who was enrolled as a member of the Lac du Flambeau Band when this reservation was established, and who, at 90, bought a car and didn't speak to my father for two months because he didn't want her to get a driver's license?

IMAGINING INDIANS

Indians have always been vagrants in the historical, political, and popular impressions of the western frontier. The discourse of the Indian as noble and savage, the villain and the victim—most recently represented in the media coverage of confrontations between Indians and others over issues of land and resources—is threaded through the narratives of the dominant culture and its shifting perceptions of the western frontier as *Land of Savagery/Land of Promise* (Billington, 1981). North Americans have drawn a certain sense of identity from these images of Indians engraved on the cultural landscape, but like the narratives of the West that position them, these Indians are largely imagined and severely time-distanced. As Berkhofer (1979) writes, "For most of the past five centuries, the Indian of the imagination and ideology has been as real, perhaps more real, than the Native American of actual existence and contact" (p. 72).

In 1900, Edward S. Curtis, like other photographers and painters of the period, set out for the American West to record images of Indians. He spent 30 years and produced 40 volumes of photographs taken between 1900 and 1930, each retouched to remove any evidence of modernity. Curtis' photographs represent a "vanishing race," Indians seen through his photographer's lens "dripping dentalia and fur—the sepia kings, shot through spit and petroleum jelly, Lords of the Plains, Potentates of the Potlatch, the Last-Ofs" (Green, 1992, p. 47). His project covered the territory from the Mexican border to the Bering Straits, posing Indians who were now struggling on reservations, fighting the effects of war, disease, poverty, and cultural displacement. All this is forever erased from the fantasies contrived in almost 1,700 Curtis photographs in the Library of Congress, photographs that are reproduced and advertised today as "a rare glimpse of the nobility, passion and tradition of . . . people [who] stare out across the decades and invite you into a world that was tragically destroyed" (Brown, 1993, n.p.). Green (1992) writes about these fictive constructions suspended in the time and space of essentialist discourse:

Quit taking out your fantasies on us. Just give me one in overalls and a cowboy hat. Then we can get serious about what was happening to these people. . . . Why are we so grateful for his glorious dreams? Every Indian I know has one of them on the wall. Mine came down a long time ago. (p. 47)

Like the cultural narratives of the western frontier that sustain them, representations of Sacajawea and Curtis' photographs of real First Nations people reveal stories of conquest and its legacies told in historical fantasies that place Indians in the 1800s and erase Native histories and cultures. Imagined in North America's long gaze on the Plains Indian in the period of western settlement, Indians are folkloric figures of the teepee and war bonnet, the buffalo hunt and powwow. These are images of Native nations frozen in time and history, tribal peoples constructed in print and celluloid, silent social imaginaries without a past or a future.

Today, these cultural chronicles that absorb Indians are being rewritten by Others and challenged in the writing of Indians themselves. The new narratives and counternarratives of Indians and Others represent contradictory constructions of popular history, stories revealed in the 1992 Quincentennial titles of the Public Broadcasting Service program "Columbus and the Age of Discovery" and the Indian-made video "Surviving Columbus." In conflicting visions of dominance and survival, these emerging accounts of Natives and newcomers reconstruct the rugged individualism of Frederick Jackson Turner's imaginary American society written in 1893, and the dislocation and desolation experienced by Indians on the frontier at the turn of the twentieth century. Both narratives reveal that for newcomers, the frontier and the West have never been precisely defined and have always represented promise more than place, fantasy more than fact. But no matter how land or movement are delineated in notions of North American hinterlands or images of Indian Country, frontiers always mark social borders and margins. Our representations of the western frontier are grounded in a politics of difference that circulates in the cultural formation of both Indians and Others. McMaster (1991) writes, "It makes little sense for Indigenous people to respond to the outrageous historical fictions of the West. On the contrary, we must focus on our own perspectives" (p. 21). But if the perspectives of Natives and newcomers interface in the West, they also intertwine. The West was neither won nor lost, and the social imaginaries that circulate in representations of the West construct the identities of us all.

Today, Native North American identity and culture are entangled in an ongoing struggle over representation and appropriation—over how Indians are represented and how these representations are appropriated by Others in a political process which confines their past as it constructs their future. This struggle over who can represent whom, who can tell the stories of others—and how they should be told—involves artists, authors, and academics in a growing debate over the politics of Indianness. Indians are caught with other North Americans in a web of conflicting interests and actions, confrontations over dominant cultural and political process and the Native experience of exclusion, or stereotypical inclusion and appropriation. For Native people, this contest over the politics of difference is deeply rooted in the social imaginaries that circulate in literary, artistic, and academic and media images. These Indians of popular culture, intrinsic to our images of the western frontier, travel and transform in the action and events of our everyday lives. And in the conflicting power relations in which our communities are built, imaginary Indians construct identities with different ideologies and meanings that become central sites of cultural conflict for Indians and Others, and for Indians themselves.

PORTRAITS OF POCAHONTAS

Until recently, Others have voiced the narratives and images that represent and construct the experience of First Nations. For Indian men, there are occasional images of granite-faced Indian chiefs, sometimes named; but the dominant representation and narrative of the last century is the warrior of the western plains, the wandering Indian wearing a war bonnet or posed in warpaint, rallying his horse and ready to shoot. These archetypes of comic book Indians, who paraded and battled in hundreds of movie and pocket book westerns, outnumbered the images of their partners in primitivism, Indian women. Portrayed as fetching maidens, Indian women usually fell in love with trappers or traders or soldiers, the enemies of Indians whose identities and alliances reversed in the process of "going Native." But if visual images of Indian women seem less prevalent and more affable in popular culture, the Indian princess is an ambiguous figure that has deeper roots in North America, and her image has transformed and expanded with the development of its nation-states. In their analysis of postcards of Indian women, Albers and James (1987) point out that "if a uniform caricature [of Indian women] has existed, it has been the image of the Indian 'princess,' " and this "visual image of Indian women as 'maiden' or 'princess' has increased in popularity over time" (pp. 35, 48).

The ambiguous representations of Indian women that we associate with the western frontier have been with us since the earliest colonization of North America. The rough, earthy beauty of the Americas was initially symbolized by pairs of Indian men and women, Caribbean or Brazilian Natives framed in the exoticism of flora and fauna that depicts the bountiful resources of the continent. But by 1575, the bare-breasted, Amazonian Indian Queen took on the image of the New World. Draped in feathers and furs, carrying arrows and spears, this contradictory figure incorporated the warrior woman and the Mother-Goddess, drawing from European roots to portray the primitive challenge of America: "exotic, powerful, dangerous and beautiful" (Green, 1976, p. 702). When the colonies began to move toward independence, the Mother-Queen figure of the 1600s was transformed into the more independent Princess image of the 1700s. The statue-like figure of "liberty" or "Columbia" in flowing robes was younger, more classically European and overtly Caucasian. But armed with a spear and a peace pipe or a flag, this social imaginary wrapped in symbols of peace and power, civilization and acrimony, is equally equivocal. And this ambiguous iconography of North America incorporating the Native and the noble, which Green (1979) calls the "Pocahontas Perplex," persists in the portrayal of Indian princesses constructed to accommodate colonial experience, western expansion, and national formations.

Pocahontas is the paragon Indian princess of North American popular culture which "inspired countless works of art . . . idealizing the image of the Indian woman" (Berkhofer, 1979, p. 121). Green (1976) writes, "As a model for the national understanding of Indian women, her significance is undeniable" (p. 701). And Donnell's (1991) book entitled *Pocahontas* says on the cover, "She was a princess, a lady and a legend. Her story is the story of America." Like Sacajawea, who did not trample the wilderness or "blaze the trail" for Lewis and Clark's western expedition in 1804, but acted as an interpreter and mediator, the romantic myth of Pocahontas is constructed around her alliances with men.

In the legendary narrative of North America, fictive history constructs an imaginary Indian princess, a noble savage named Pocahontas, who saves the life of an Englishman for whom she feels a romantic attraction. Her actions bring peace between the Indians and the colonists of Jamestown, Virginia, the first permanent colony in North America. She inevitably marries a non-Indian, becomes civilized and Christian, and assimilates with the settlers.

There is, of course, a counternarrative, parts of which can be pieced together from documents of the Virginia Historical Society. The child who was nicknamed "Pocahontas," which means "playful" or "mischievous," was born in 1595, but her real name was Matoaka. Unlike the Walt Disney animated film which portrays her as a woman in her early twenties, Pocahontas was a child of 12 when she encountered Captain John Smith, who was then 27 years old. Historians disagree about whether Pocahontas saved John Smith's life, or even met him; but they agree that, in contrast to Disney's golden-haired hero, Smith was not an innocent bystander to the armed conflict that occurred between the Chickahominy Indians and the Jamestown settlers. He was known more as an Indian-fighter than the peacemaker created for the Disney film, and "his conduct may have landed his head on Powhatan's clubbing block, where Pocahontas supposedly intervened and saved his life" (Beam, 1995, p. 17). For their part, the colonists apparently identified her father, Powhatan, who was Grand Chief of a confederacy of 30 tribes, as an "emperor" or "king," and his daughter, Pocahontas, therefore became a "princess." But our knowledge of this, like the story of her life, is drawn from historical fragments and individual conjecture. Like Sacajawea, Pocahontas' experience is lost to us.

When fighting broke out in 1612 between Powhatan's confederacy and the colonists who settled on Chickahominy Indian Territory, Pocahontas was married to an Indian who was an aid to her father. No one knows how she became friendly with the Jamestown settlers and brought food to the starving colonists. But on a visit to Jamestown in 1613, she was lured aboard a ship, kidnapped, and held hostage for over a year as a safeguard against Indian attacks. During her captivity, she learned English, converted to Christianity, and was baptized "Rebecca." In 1614, John Rolfe, a widowed tobacco farmer and her religious instructor, married the 18-year-old Pocahontas, about whom he wrote, her "education has bin rude, her manners barbarous" (cited in Woodward, 1969, p. 162). Now hostage to a new persona, her role as an intermediary took her to England with her young son, Thomas, where she was presented at court as "Lady Rebecca."

Like the Indian "country wives" of trappers and traders who succeeded her, Pocahontas' mediation between Indians and Others had important political and economic implications. Her presence built a bridge between the Indians and the settlers. Strengthened by eight years of peace and the cultivation of tobacco, the Virginia colony initiated a new empire in North America. But like many Indian women who became economic and political "go-betweens," her own life was very short. She died of smallpox or tuberculosis in England in 1617, when she was 22 years old.

Pocahontas' untold story might have been the first of what became known later as "captivity narratives," populist tales that tell the exotic and arduous experiences of woman settlers who were kidnapped by Indians in books like Fanny Wiggins Kelly's nineteenth-century best-seller, *Narrative of My Captivity Among the Sioux Indians* (Reiter, 1978, p. 64). The encounter of Pocahontas and John Smith that became legend did not appear in Smith's book about his life, written in 1608. But in 1624, he wrote a second book entitled *General Historie of Virginia* (Scriba, 1995), which built the scaffold for the seventeenth-century cultural narrative of assumed friendship and harmony, cooperation, and assimilation at a time of colonial expansion. Smith's storied Pocahontas inspired the play entitled *The Indian Princess, or La Belle Sauvage*, which was performed in Philadelphia in 1808 (Black & Weidman, 1976, p. 149). This narrative of the fantasy princess has multiplied and diversified through the ensuing years of conflict between Natives and newcomers. In the modern period, Disney's historical revisionism emerges at a time of new tension between Indians and Others, over land and resources, sovereignty, and self-determination. As Fusco (1990) writes:

For me, the issue of "the other" is one of power, of a dynamic between those who impute otherness to some and those who are designated as other. So the questions I ask about otherness have to do with how others or the other are spoken of, who is speaking about them, and why have they chosen to speak of the other at the given historical moment. (p. 77)

The fairy tale of Pocahontas that absorbs or expresses the Otherness of Indians, ignores not only the presence of sovereign Indian nations and occupied Indian lands, but the spread of disease and settlement conflict that slaughtered Indians, killing "some ten million at the outside between 1492 and the 1700s" (Green, 1988, p. 31). The narrative of the fantasy princess dismisses the manifestation of Indian death in the illness that killed Pocahontas, along with the intriguing life of Matoaka, who experienced the contradictory cultural realities—and the cultural hybridity—of Pocahontas and Lady Rebecca. Like the Walt Disney film and the 50 Pocahontas products launched by Mattel toys to exploit it, Pocahontas' social imaginary is monolithic, a representation rooted in ambiguous, sexualized fantasies that construct her cultural identity. To sleep with Pocahontas would be worth "a thousand pelts," mused rock musician Neil Young (cited in Colt, 1995, p. 69).

For Indians, the counternarrative to Young's song is expressed in Jimmie Durham's (Mulvey, Snauwaet, & Durant, 1996) painting entitled *Pocahontas Underwear*, an image of blood-red panties decorated with feathers and beads, fabric and fasteners. As Dearborn (1986) writes about the sexualized images of Pocahontas:

Pocahontas' imaginative power lies in her sexuality, or, more precisely, in the promise she holds out of sexual union between a white male representative of the dominant culture and an exotic, or ethnic, woman. Her story functions as a compelling focus toward what W.E.B. Du Bois has called the "stark, ugly, painful, beautiful" fact of American life: miscegenation, or sexual relations between white men and ethnic women. (p. 99)

From the "ministering maiden" (Stedman, 1982, p. 21) image of the princess Pocahontas to her darker twin, the squaw, both the nobility and the savagery of Indian women have been defined in relation to white males—as women who rescued them, served them, married them, and who even gave up their Indian nation for them (Green, 1976). While the story of Pocahontas came to represent "the ideal merger of Native and new-comer," the image of the squaw became what Francis (1979) calls the "anti-Pocahontas," about which he writes,

Where the princess was beautiful, the squaw was ugly, even deformed. Where the princess was virtuous, the squaw was debased, immoral, a sexual convenience. Where the princess was proud, the squaw lived a squalid life of servile toil, mistreated by her men—and openly available to non-Native men. (pp. 121–122)

Adding to the indignity of this representation that devalued, defiled, and objectified Native women, the label that names the stereotype may derive from the Indian "squa" or "skwa," a word which, in some Algonkian languages, is a suffix added to build a feminine form of certain words (Herten, 1997, p. 2). But in the primal meanings that emerge in lived realities, this floating image not only moves, but merges.

As the ambiguous imaginary of Pocahontas suggests, it is the conjoined image of the princess and the squaw that is most destructive for Indian women. Dearborn (1986) remarks, "It is precisely because the Pocahontas figure is expected to embody *both* [italics in original] aspects of this image that hers is so convenient, compelling and ultimately intolerable a legend" (p. 99). The progression of these intertwined narratives that are so deeply entrenched in North America's popular culture is summarized in an excerpt from Mojica's (1991) play entitled *Princess Pocahontas and the Blue Spots*:

> Princess, Princess Amazon Queen.
> Show me your royal blood,
> Is it blue? Is it green?
> Dried and brown five centuries old,
> singed and baked and
> covered with mold?
> Princess, priestess Caribe Queen,
> What are you selling today,
> Is it corn, tobacco, beans?
> Snake oil or a beaver hat.
> Horse liniment,

You just can't beat that!
Princess, Princess, calendar girl,
Redskin temptress, Indian pearl.
Waiting by the water
For a white man to save.
She's a savage now remember—
Can't behave. (pp. 20–21)

ILLUSORY SISTERS

Populist images of the Indian princess emerge in the late 1800s as lithographs of delicate, demure Indian ladies and printed paintings of buckskin-clad maidens. Through the long North American gaze on Indian women, images shift with the vicissitudes of North American motives for marketing the West and its material and cultural products. The social imaginaries of historicized and romanticized Indian women were appropriated and propagated to accommodate the growth of immigration and industry and the interrelated expansion of railroads, mail service, and advertising.

Now, at the turn of the twentieth century, some images of Indian princesses are seeming transformations of Sacajawea in a birch bark canoe; others depict wistful princesses looking at handsome warriors, sometimes inscribed as "Hiawatha's Wedding." Indians are now relegated to reservations, but both whimsical and woeful images of women became frontier tropes that "reinforced the belief that the best Indian was the historical Indian" (Francis, 1992, p. 176). There are gold-leaf princesses on cigar boxes and the bare-breasted, primitive princesses—and sometimes squaws—promoting foods and natural medicines, like "Swamp-Root" herbal cures.

From about 1915 through the 1940s, the dominant representation of the Indian princess was the "lady in red," a maiden draped in a red tunic, wearing the requisite headband and feather, and posed with picturesque and pristine mountains, waterfalls, and moonlit lakes. These romanticized princesses that adorned calendars, advertisements, paintings, and postcards—with names like *Winona, Minnehaha, Iona,* and even *Hiawatha*—worked in consort with their male counterpart, the Indian warrior, to establish the romanticized Indian as "one of the icons of consumer society" (Francis, 1992, p. 175). Images of Indian women "garnered good will but bore no referential relationship to the goods they advertised" (Coombe, 1996, p. 213). They promoted products that were now mass-produced, including corn and peas, apples and Mazola oil, Land o' Lakes butter and Kraft foods, beer and beverages. In the move from inviting territorial expansion to enticing commercial enterprise, imaginary Indian women became the first North American "pin-up girls."

Calendar-girl princesses gazing wistfully or looking longingly appeared in a remarkable range of poses and settings. There are paddling princesses and fishing maidens, sewing princesses and maidens of the feathers or the flowers. But the most common are maidens—sometimes almost twinned—merely posed as fanciful Indian princesses amid chaste, romanticized scenery. These statue-like figures of the imagination marketed the North American West as alluring, unoccupied, and available and now open to railroad travel. Francis (1992) writes, "More than any other single aspect of White civilization, the railway transformed the world of the Indian" (p. 176). A paper parade of Indian princesses promoted settlement and tourism on Indian land that was captured or claimed, treatied or just taken, and then advertised as "1001 Switzerland's rolled into one" (Francis, 1992, p. 177). With the onslaught of settlement and tourism between 1880 and 1910, princesses urged audiences to attend Buffalo Bill's Wild West Show and the rodeos and powwows it spawned. With the mining of the West, these images of young Native women captured the imaginations of Easterners, and replicas of those posed princesses spread across the continent and the decades. After World War I, some images of Indian women took on the "flapper" fashion of the 1920s. Indian maidens appeared in the wilderness wearing long strands of corn or beads, feathered headbands, and fringed shawls, sometimes tied around their hips. They were joined by calendar princesses who were more enticing, with low necklines, net stockings, slit skirts, and outfits that were more sexually explicit.

Years earlier, regular mail service had created a new market for both calendar princesses and historicized images of Indian women. Picture postcards, which were introduced in the United States in 1873, became the common means of popular communication after the turn of the twentieth century (Smith, 1989, p. 9). Scenic views of unoccupied and rugged nature were transformed into reproductions of fantasies carrying greetings for every occasion. By the 1920s, there were travel postcards with sad-looking squaws lined up all-in-a-row, or browbeaten Indian squaws surrounded by children, or ancient Indian women heavy with beadwork. Contradicting this sense of the uncivilized, there were endless variations of picture postcards with fantasy princesses, some single-feather ladies and others wearing full war bonnets.

At the same time, Indian maidens, princesses, and "Chieftain's daughters" began to appear on a wide range of cultural products that reflected the imaginary landscape of the West. Indian princesses decorated wood-burned plaques and mirrors, puzzles and playing cards, and thermometers and ink blotters. Like the Indians in Buffalo Bill's "Wild West Show" at the turn of the twentieth century, three-dimensional maidens became the props of popular culture. Their appearance on bookends, paperweights, cups, and salt-and-pepper shakers added to the indignity. Princesses emerged as romanticized subjects in popular songs entitled "Red Wing," "Falling Star," "Laughing Water," and "Pretty Little Rainbow," and as objects of history in textbooks, children's stories, and ethnographic studies.

Princesses abounded in the popular literature that was published by the mid-1800s, when Lydia Huntley Sigourney (in Black & Weidman, 1976) wrote of Pocahontas, "A forest-child amid the flowers at play! . . . Her spirit-glance bespoke the daughter of a King," (p. 205), and Henry Wadsworth Longfellow wrote about the imaginary "Minnehaha" in his famous poem *The Song of Hiawatha*. When "dime novels" appeared, "in the tradition of Pocahontas, some of the heroines were brave Indian maidens. *Malaeska, The Indian Wife of the White Hunter* sold briskly (Reiter, 1978, p. 22). Publishing circulated the imaginary Indian women through generations of comic books and pulp magazines like *Western Story, Wild West Weekly,* and *Ranch Romances* (Pronzini, 1994). Princesses and squaws sold books like Zane Grey's *Spirit of the Border* (n.d.) or Lederer's *Manitou's Daughters* (1982) which, as part of Signet's "Indian Heritage Series," proclaimed on the cover, "proud women of a proud people—facing the white invaders of their land and their hearts." The invented social imaginaries of the Indian princess and her sisters became a staple commodity in movies and plays, paintings, and photographs that celebrated frontierism in the West.

In contrast to the representations of Indian squaws, the images of Indian princesses share one thing in common: they all look like replicas of Brooke Shields. As Sneve (1987) writes, "The models for the original paintings were not American Indian women but attractive Caucasian women who frequently besieged the artists to be allowed to pose as an Indian princess" (p. 72). These models, like children enacting powwow or Cowboys and Indians, were engaged in what Green (1988) calls "playing Indian" (p. 30). In her article entitled "The Tribe Called Wannabe," she finds that the performance of "playing Indian" is "one of the oldest and most pervasive forms of American cultural expression, indeed one of the oldest forms of affinity with American culture at the national level." And "playing Indian" situates Indian princesses in the politicized construction of North American and First Nations identity.

ENCOUNTERING PRINCESSES

Deloria writes in *Custer Died for Your Sins* (1969):

All but one person I met who claimed Indian blood claimed it on his Grandmother's side. I once did a projection backwards and discovered that evidently most tribes were entirely female for the first three hundred years of white occupation. . . . Somehow the white was linked with a noble house of gentility and culture if his grandmother was an Indian princess who ran away with an intrepid pioneer. (p. 11)

In Dearborn's (1986) words, "intermarriage seems to yoke in a rather neat fashion the concepts of ethnicity and American identity" (p. 100). If, as Deloria and Dearborn suggest, non-Natives overcome a sense of North

American alienation by being distantly related to Indians, the great-grandmothers and grandmothers who married fur traders, trappers, and settlers were caught in a maelstrom of cultural misunderstanding and conflict that produced both personal acceptance and rejection.

In the formative histories of the nation-states in North America, "there is an important Indian woman in virtually every encounter between Europeans and Indians in the New World" (Kidwell, 1992, p. 97). But the roles of wife, interpreter, mediator, and even trader, that engaged Indian women as "country wives" in the early days of the western frontier, ultimately reverted to mixed-bloods, who were in turn replaced by non-Indian women. The exclusion of Indian women from "civilized" society was built not only on the images of Indian women as workers and drudges, but Indian women as competing sexual and marriage partners. Within this context of erasure, displacement, and competition, "despite her important contributions and influence in certain areas, the Indian woman in fur-trade society was at the mercy of a social structure devised primarily to meet the needs of European males" (Van Kirk, 1980, p. 88). The long shadows of the Indian princess and her sister, the squaw, wind through Indian experience of this tenacious social structure and its cultural constructs. Braided together, these images of the primitive princess framed the voice of Indian women who performed or spoke publicly about Indian culture and living conditions in later years.

Sarah Winnemucca's autobiography, published in 1883, was one of the first books written by an Indian. But when she lectured in California, she was identified as "Princess Sarah," and the report in the *San Francisco Chronicle* referred to her "extensive and diversified matrimonial experience, the number of her white husbands being variously estimated at from three to seven" (Canfield, 1983, p. 163). Years later, Emily Pauline Johnson Tekahionwake reappropriated her imaginary sister, the princess, in performances that established her as "the voice of the Indian" (Francis, 1992, p. 114). To be heard, Pauline Johnson replaced the formal gown she wore to recite her poetry with a buckskin dress and "toured the world as the 'Indian Princess' regaling crowds with romantic tales of Native American Life" (Altitude, n.d.). Native women gained greater visibility in ethnographic studies that broke the male-focused mold of anthropology in documenting women's roles and lives, like Landes' *The Ojibway Woman* (1971) and Lurie's *Mountain Wolf Woman* (1961). But if ethnography neither analyzed nor promoted the images of the princess and the squaw, this research reflected assumptions of time-distanced, tribalized, traditional culture that were misleading.

Today, feminist writers may recognize the fragmented and contradictory representations of Indian women in the ambiguous, male-oriented images of all women. But the meaning of conflicting cultural narratives is negotiated in the historical and contemporary context of a culture's experience and political process. From the unpredictable and perplexing experience of being "country wives" that Van Kirk documents in her book *Many Tender Ties* (1980), to the "Bush Lady" of Alanis Obamsawin's poignant song of a reservation woman's painful experiences in the city, Indian women have lived emerging traces of the image that devalued and defiled Indian women in the past. And fragments of the persistent fantasy of fetching maidens have been reappropriated in the counternarratives of Indian popular culture. Like Pauline Johnson's performance, the powwow princess is a transformation of the enduring representations of Indian princesses, appropriated and redefined in hybrid expressions of contemporary Indian culture. And related to these images that continually transform and emerge, Native women experience daily struggles with identity—and with men, Indian and Other—that are neither simple nor straightforward. The economic and political presence of Native women has grown significantly since the 1960s. But battles over blood and belonging, over exclusion and reinstatement, over position and power expose the political landscape of Indian communities today. In Canada, Native women still struggle over issues of acceptance, membership, and roles related to the *Indian Act* which, until 1985, declared Native women legally non-Indian if they married a non-Indian; and their challenges to issues of male-dominated governance and policies are shared by Native American women. Across both countries, Native men and women struggle with appropriations of the western chief or warrior, and impositions of the princess or the drudge. There are also open wounds of personal abuse perpetrated by Others and by each other. And floating through these contests over reconciliation, recognition, and inclusion is the reoccurring apparition of mutual uneasiness built in representations of the past that shadow the relationships between Native women and other women who, even as they speak of Native sisters, find it difficult to bridge the distance between different lived realities and contested ideologies and to recognize themselves in the expressions of Native women.

NATIVE SISTER STORIES

Amidst yesterday's Curtis-like historical photographs and today's "Leanin' Tree" greeting card teepee princesses with longing looks and unruly hair, Mojica (1989) is moved to write, "I am not your princess—I am only willing to tell you how to make fry bread" (p. 40). The imaginary Indian princess is interwoven in the lives of Native women and their social struggles over its significance, but as Mojica's comment suggests, neither the princess nor the squaw have led to the "loss" of Indian identity or alienation from community or culture. The identity of Native North American women is simultaneously constructed in the discourses of grandmothers and mothers, daughters and others. In narratives that situate, appropriate, and transform the past, Native women take up the tales of trials and empowerment, identity, and community. Native women speak of themselves or people they know—real, memoried, or imagined—in stories that construct individual and collective identities. Erdrich (1992) reminds us, "There once were women named *Standing Strong*, *Fish Bones*, *Different Thunder*. There once was a girl named *Yellow Straps*. Imagine what it was like to pick berries with *Sky Coming Down*, to walk through a storm with *Lightning Proof*" (p. 132). And Green (1984) writes, "The taking of new names and the reshaping of old names is the essential process for becoming" (p. 7). These voices that sound nostalgic or sentimental appropriate the past in new representations of cultural continuance.

Ojibway elder Art Solomon (1990) says of his narratives, "I have borrowed this story from someone who had borrowed it from someone else who had borrowed it from someone else" (p. 132). Passed on through kinship and gossip, ceremony and social drinking, books and lectures and paintings, Indian stories are stitched to a polyvocal past as "acts encapsulated in time, 'enacted' every time they are spoken aloud or read silently" (Anzaldua, 1987, p. 67). Tales told in books like Silko's *Ceremony* (1977) and Erdrich's *Love Medicine* (1984) intertwine with the lived experience of history and heritage and everyday life. The traditional knowledge that proclaims women as "the heart of the nation," the "center of everything" is conjoined with the seemingly contradictory images of Niro's (1991) playful photographs of her own sisters, posed with captions like "Mohawks in Beehives" and "The Rebel." And spliced within the kaleidoscopic representations of contemporary Native realities that interweave the mundane, the humorous, and the prophetic are the reoccurring words of traditionalism voiced in the empowerment of Mother Earth and Grandmother Moon.

NATURAL SISTERS

Allen (1988) writes, "Native American roots of white feminism reach back beyond Sacajawea. The earliest white women on this continent were well acquainted with tribal women. They were neighbors to a number of tribes and often shared food, information, child care and health care" (p. 21). If this were ever the reality of colonial experience, it is erased in the politics and policies of populist images, which present Indian women as posed, paper-doll princesses, as homeless vagrants of the imagination. These women are alone, alienated from each other and Others in the scenic backdrops of the land and of nature which they entice Others to occupy, first as settlers, then as tourists. In the parallel representations of tribalized "real" Indians, women are equally isolated or grouped with other women, among children or the material objects of Indian culture that are valued by Others. In these historicized or exoticized worlds, there are no families, no

clans, no communities, and no kinship networks. In fact, there is no recognition of the formative social relationships that not only place Native
North Americans in relation to the land and to each other, but construct
the colonial polices of Native exclusion, assimilation, or containment. As
Carter (1997) suggests, "The contrasting representations of white and Aboriginal femininity articulated racist images that confirmed cultural difference and the need for repressive policies. Powerfully negative images of
Aboriginal women served to symbolize the shortcomings of that society"
(p. 161). But laced through the heritage of repressive policies and different
practices, there is an enduring sense of cultural continuity and Indian community, however transformed and conflictual.

Even in the current contests over power and placement, Native women
know that the narratives of the princess and the drudge have not been
experienced by women alone. Through the difference of their gendered
experience, Indian men and women are yoked together in the narratives of
cultural heritage and the lived realities of their subaltern status. And in the
traditional narratives that express identity and community, women hold a
place of empowerment. In the words of Solomon (1990), "The women is
[sic] the foundations on which nations are built. She is the heart of her
nation. If that heart is weak, the people are weak . . . the woman is the
center of everything"; and he tells us why: "The women 'were of the earth,'
they were connected to the earth mother and to the grandmother moon
whose work was to govern when all things were to be born, plants, animals,
humans" (pp. 34–35).

From a feminist perspective, this traditional Indian image of women as
close to nature is essentialized and problematic. The feminist critique is an
ideological knot tied to Western culture's project of conquering the natural
world, an undertaking articulated to frontierism, which constructs culture
and nature as oppositional. The assumption underlying this critique is that
nature is more basic than culture; but because the project of Western culture is to transform nature, culture is conceived as not only different from,
but superior to, nature. Historically, women have been characterized by
natural qualities in opposition to men; and since men, not women, are
identified with the institutional and symbolic forms of Western civilization
and cultural change, this distinction between culture and nature supports
the suppression of women. From this perspective, the physiological and
social roles, which constitute women as "the heart of the nation," support
the ideology, which constructs both the romanticized image of nature's
pristine beauty, the Indian princess, and her earthy, beast of burden sister,
the squaw. But from a Native perspective, the collective experience and
traditional teachings express conflicting representations of nature and culture. This position prompts Mohawk lawyer Patricia Montour (1992) to
tell us, "I used to shrivel when people called me a feminist. The issues that
feminism has tried to focus on are not the issues that occupy First Nations

lives." She adds, "We have to remember to respect Mother Earth. A lot of ways women are treated on this earth are reflective of the ways Mother Earth gets treated." And Allen (1988) writes, "We as feminists must be aware of our history on this continent" (p. 18).

Indian women, of course, enact the identities of the contradictory and essentializing images related to the nature/culture paradigm of the Western society. But their identities are also constructed in the circling discourse of Native traditionalism and aboriginal experience, including women's relationship to the land, to nature, and to each other. The narratives that move and multiply in transforming traditionalism and the practice of everyday life express the multivocal play of power and identity linked to the earth and the Creator. The spiritual and the natural encode the power and practice of Mohawk Clan Mothers and Ojibway Odgichidawque. In the cultural and political struggle of contested identities, the unity of culture and nature is expressed in transforming stories of Indian experience and the spiritualized land that positions its meaning.

It is the land—real and imagined, lived in heritage and current political process, and expressed in discourse—which constitutes the connection between nature and culture for Indians. And the struggle over appropriation of the discourse related to land and to nature is the struggle over land rights and treaty rights, aboriginal rights and women's rights, over New Age spiritualism and ethnographic accounts, over the words and representations of history and culture and power. Today, Native and non-Native women recognize a connection between domination of the land and domination of people on the basis of race, class, and gender. In asserting the link between ecology and feminism, eco-feminism both supports historicized images of Indians who lived on the land without disturbing it and recognizes a point of social and political connectedness between Native and non-Native women—and men. The struggle over clear-cutting forests and diverting rivers and building nuclear waste dumps sometimes expands to include Indian land rights and treaty rights, a prospect which holds the political possibility poised in plural narratives and representations that are different but allied.

FIRST NATIONS FRONTIERS

Indians are entangled in the interests of Others, and these interests are always linked to the politics of difference in which Indians themselves are absorbed. Native North American communities struggle over issues of membership, money, and cultural meaning. The expression of these battles over economic strategy and political power can be blunt and blistering. But the Native battles over different ideologies and appropriated Indian identities can only be understood in the context of common culture and history, experience, and political purpose: in shifting unities built in collective memory and the continual formation of community. It is the negotiation of relations of power—hierarchical, conflictual, and communal—expressed in contested ideology and identity, which both cuts through and knits together Indian communities in their struggle with domination and resistance. This political process, which is rooted to the western frontier, frames today's debates over traditionalism and treaty rights, representation and appropriation; and constructs the strained connectedness between Native North Americans and Others.

Green (cited in CBC *Ideas*, 1992) expresses the inevitable predicament that the image of the ministering maiden poses for communication in saying, "Once you put on the princess costume . . . you can't ever take off the princess outfit" (p. 19). And speaking on the same CBC program, Kathy Mallet tells us, "Squaw? I remember being called that word and I just kind of froze. You know, it's like somebody shot you. That's how I felt: like a bullet went right through me." These contradictory images of Indian women continue to objectify and degrade in transformations of the villain or the victim, the torturer or the sufferer; and neither the romanticized Indian princess nor the primitive squaw allows newcomers to identify First Nations as equals, as owners of this land—Indians with homes and families, jobs, and community institutions. The cultural distance of elevation or debasement that these conceptions reflect is contrary to the actual process of "one set of people in overalls displacing another set of people in overalls" (Green, 1992, p. 53), which removed Indians from their homelands and their resources as the frontier moved West. Women's voices now shatter the silence of the past, expressing real experiences and imaginary tales that challenge and recast the old narratives of dominance. But the distance built in difference continues in the current cultural and political struggles over spearfishing and hydro dams, mining and timber, land and resources. As newcomers and Natives transpose the representation of the primitive Plains warrior into the media warrior, and women press tribal governments for recognition and reform, First Nations communities struggle with the factionalism of power relations entrenched in the threats and promises of appropriated and continually constructed identities. Filmmaker Loretta Todd (1992) tells a story:

[Like Curtis] a European painter in the nineteenth century journeyed into the great plains of this continent to "record" Native people, a common occurrence of the time, born of the ethnographic. While he was painting a Native man on a horse, another Native man observed the artist's work and remarked how his painting was wrong. The artist, painting the horse from the side, had shown only two legs of the horse and one leg of the rider. The Native man reminded the artist that the horse had four legs and the rider two, which should all be shown. (p. 72)

The difference in perspective between the artist's horse and the Indian's horse is compounded, of course, through appropriation. Whether one is appropriating New Age Native spiritualism through the books of Andrews (1981), or Native culture in the film *If Only I Were an Indian* (Paskievich, 1995), or warriors and Indians as team mascots or militants, or representations of Indian princesses and squaws, the horse has only two legs. In privileging the perspective of a two-legged horse, dominant cultural narratives continue to detach and essentialize, entice and deceive in a progression of social imaginaries that not only limit First Nations' access to voice, but they blur the understanding of the pluralistic experience, which Indians and Others share.

In the images that circulate today, Sacajawea remains romanticized as the "guide" of the Lewis and Clark expedition. Her experience is impossible to retrieve. The meaning of her presence, which must have signified to Indians that this group of men, traveling with a woman and child, was not a war party, is silent in the discourse. Like the bullet holes in the obelisk that bears her name, "the monument stands, the plaque calls her the expedition's guide, and the public [including Indians] considers anything that says otherwise vandalism" (Duncan, 1987, p. 165). But like Sacajawea's contradictory social imaginaries, we are all rooted together in the construction and appropriation of images of Indians, which build different identities and enact our ideologies in an ageless western frontier.

REFERENCES

Albers, P., & James, W. (1987). Illusion and illumination: Visual images of American Indian women in the west. In S. Armitage & E. Jameson (Eds.), *The women's west* (pp. 36–50). Norman: University of Oklahoma Press.

Allen, P. G. (1988). Who is your mother? Red roots of white feminism. In R. Simonson & S. Walker (Eds.), *Multi-cultural literacy*. Saint Paul, MN: Grey Wolf Press.

Altitude Publishing Limited. *An altitude super card: Pauline Johnson.* Banff, AB.

Andrews, L. (1981). *Medicine woman.* New York: Harper and Row.

Anzaldua, G. (1987). *Borderlands/La Frontera.* San Francisco: Spinsters/Aunt Lute.

Atwood, M. (1972). *Survival: A thematic guide to Canadian literature.* Toronto: Anansi.

Beam, A. (1995, June 5). Walt Disney meets and reinvents Pocahontas. *Globe and Mail,* p. A17.

Berkhofer, R. F. Jr. (1979). *The white man's Indian.* New York: Random House.

Billington, R. A. (1981). *Land of savagery/Land of promise: The European image of the American frontier in the nineteenth century.* Norman: University of Oklahoma Press.

Black, N. B., & Weidman, B. S. (1976). *White on red.* Port Washington, NY: Kennikat Press.

Brown. (1993). Advertisement for book on Edward S. Curtis photographs. Title and place of publication unknown.

CBC *Ideas.* (1992). *Isinamowin: The white man's Indian.* Ottawa: Canadian Broadcasting Corporation.

Canfield, G. W. (1983). *Sarah Winnemucca of the northern Paiutes*. Norman: University of Oklahoma Press.

Carter, S. (1997). *Capturing women: The manipulation of cultural imagery in Canada's prairie west*. Montreal: McGill–Queen's University Press.

Colt, G. H. (1995, July). Who was Pocahontas? *Life Magazine*, 64–69.

Coombe, R. J. (1996). Embodied trademarks: Mimesis and alterity on American commercial frontiers. *Cultural Anthropology 11* (2), 202–224.

Dearborn, M. V. (1986). *Pocahontas's daughters: Gender and ethnicity in American culture*. New York: Oxford University Press.

Deloria, V. (1969). *Custer died for your sins*. New York: Avon.

Donnell, S. (1991). *Pocahontas*. New York: Berkley Books.

Duncan, D. (1987). *Out west: American journey along the Lewis and Clark trail*. New York: Viking Penguin.

Erdrich, L. (1984). *Love medicine*. New York: Henry Holt and Company.

Erdrich, L. (1992, Autumn). The names of women. *Granta 41*, 132–138.

Francis, D. (1979). *The imaginary Indian: The image of the Indian in Canadian culture*. Vancouver: Arsenal Pulp Press.

Fusco, C. (1990, Fall). Managing the other. *Lusitania 1* (3), 77–83.

Gray, Z. (n.d.). *The spirit of the border*. Akron, OH: Saalfield.

Green, R. (1976). The Pocahontas perplex: The image of the Indian woman in American vernacular culture. *The Massachusetts Review 16* (4), 698–714.

Green, R. (Ed.). (1984). *That's what she said: Contemporary poetry and fiction by Native American women*. Bloomington: University of Indiana Press.

Green, R. (1988). The tribe called Wannabee: Playing Indian in America and Europe. *Folklore 99* (1), 30–55.

Green, R. (1992). Rosebuds of the Plateau: Frank Matsura and the fainting couch aesthetic. In L. R. Lippard (Ed.), *Partial recall* (pp. 47–54). New York: The New Press.

Hall, S. (1985). Signification, representation, ideology: Althusser and the post structuralist debates. *Critical Studies in Mass Communication 2* (2), 91–114.

Hall, S. (1986). Gramsci's relevance for the study of race and ethnicity. *Journal of Communication Inquiry 10* (2), 5–27.

Hall, S. (1989). Cultural identity and cinematic representation. *Framework 36*, 68–81.

Herten, E. (1997). *Ban the "S" word*. Brussels, Belgium: KOLA. http://www.kolahq@skynet.be.

Howard, H. P. (1971). *Sacajawea*. Norman: University of Oklahoma Press.

Kidwell, C. S. (1992). Indian women as cultural mediators. *Ethnohistory 39* (2), 97–107.

Landes, R. (1971). *The Ojibway woman*. New York: W.W. Norton.

Lederer, P. J. (1982). *Manitou's daughters*. New York: New American Library.

Lurie, N. O. (1961). *Mountain wolf woman: Sister of Crashing Thunder*. Ann Arbor: University of Michigan Press.

McMaster, G. (1991). How the west was lost: An artist's perspective. In G. Young-Ing (Ed.), *Gatherings: Vol. II* (pp. 13–21). Penticton, BC: Theytus Books.

Mojica, M. (1989). An invocation/incantation to the women word-warriors for custom-made shoes. *CanadianWoman Studies/les cahiers de la femme 10* (2/3), 40.

Mojica, M. (1991). *Princess Pocahontas and the blue spots*. Toronto: Women's Press.

Montour, P. (1992). *Everywoman's almanac*. Toronto: Women's Press.

Mulvey, L., Snauwaet, D., & Durant, M. A. (1996). *Jimmie Durham*. London: Phaidon.

Niro, S. (1991). *Mohawks in beehives and the rebel*. Photographs in the collection of the Canadian Museum of Civilization, Ottawa.

Paskievich, J. (1995). *If only I were an Indian*. Zemma Productions and the National Film Board of Canada: Montreal.

Pronzini, B. (1994). The western pulps. In T. W. Knowles & J. R. Lansdale (Eds.), *Wild west show!* (pp. 92–98). New York: Wings Books.

Reiter, J. S. (1978). *The old west: The women*. Alexandria, VA: Time-Life Books.

Scriba, J. (1995). Pocahontas: A legend and a tragedy. *Milwaukee Journal*.

Silko, L. M. (1977). *Ceremony*. New York: New American Library.

Smith, J. H. (1989). *Postcard companion: The collector's reference*. Radnor, PA: Wallace-Homestead.

Sneve, V.D.H. (1987, November). Remembering Minnehaha. *Country Living*, 72–74.

Solomon, A. (1990). *Songs for the people: Teachings on the natural way*. Toronto: NC Press Limited.

Stedman, R. W. (1982). *Shadows of the Indian: Stereotypes in American culture*. Norman: University of Oklahoma Press.

Todd, L. (1992). What more do they want? In G. McMaster & L. Martin (Eds.), *Indigena* (pp. 71–80). Vancouver: Douglas and McIntyre.

Van Kirk, S. (1980). *Many tender ties. Women in fur-trade society, 1670–1870*. Winnipeg, AB: Watson and Dwyer.

Woodward, G. S. (1969). *Pocahontas*. Norman: University of Oklahoma Press.

Index

About the Editors and Contributors

ABOUT THE EDITORS

SHERRY DEVEREAUX FERGUSON holds the rank of Professor in the Communication Department, University of Ottawa, Canada. She is the author or editor of six books. Her most recent books are *Communication Planning: An Integrated Approach* (1999) and *Researching the Public Opinion Environment: Theories and Methods* (2000). A consultant to numerous government departments, she acted as a member of an advisory panel headed by the Assistant Secretary of Communications to Cabinet, Canada. This advisory panel was charged with defining curriculum needs for federal government communication officers. She has been involved for the past 12 years in the design and presentation of training workshops for federal government communication officers, and she does speech writing for Canadian politicians. In July 2000, she was co–keynote speaker at the Rochester Intercultural Conference, and she participated in the planning of the year 2000 anti-torture campaign for Amnesty International Canada. Her involvement with intercultural communication dates back to 1971, when she acted as secretary at the founding meeting of the Intercultural Communication Division of the NCA at Brown County, Indiana. She is currently program chair and president-elect of the Public Relations Division of the International Communication Association and editorial board member for the *Journal of Communication.*

LESLIE REGAN SHADE is Assistant Professor at the Department of Communication, University of Ottawa, where she teaches courses on the social and ethical aspects of ICTs. Originally from California, where she attended the University of California–San Diego and UCLA, she moved to Canada in 1987 to embark on a Ph.D. at McGill University. She has since published articles in the *Canadian Journal of Communication*, *The Information Society*, and *Ethics and Information Technology* and made contributions to *Internet Cultures*, *Virtual Genders*, and *Community Informatics*. She is the author of *Gender, Community and the Social Construction of the Internet* (2002), and co-editor of *Mediascapes* (2000) and *E-Commerce vs. E-Commons: Communications in the Public Interest* (2001).

ABOUT THE CONTRIBUTORS

DARIN BARNEY was educated at Simon Fraser University and the University of Toronto, where he trained in political theory. The author of *Prometheus Wired: The Hope for Democracy in the Age of Network Technology* (2000), he has recently completed a book entitled *The Network Society* for publication in 2002. His primary research interests are the philosophy and politics of technology. As an Assistant Professor of History and Politics at the University of New Brunswick in Saint John, Canada, he directed the Information and Communication Studies Program. In July 2001 he joined the faculty of the Department of Communication at the University of Ottawa. In winter 2002 he was the Hixon-Riggs Visiting Assistant Professor of Science, Technology, and Society at Harvey Mudd College in Claremont, California. In 2001 he received a national award, under the Canadian Legal Dimensions Initiative, for his work on digital technology and the public sphere. He is a member of the Advisory Council of the Law Commission of Canada and a director of the Canadian Communication Association.

CHANTAL BENOIT-BARNÉ is a doctoral candidate in the Department of Communication at the University of Colorado, Boulder, and a newly appointed professor at the Université de Montréal. She received her master's degree in communication studies from Emerson College, Boston, and her bachelor's degree in communication with a minor in journalism from the Université du Québec à Montréal. Her research interests lie in the intersection between the theories of public sphere(s), digital communication technologies, and rhetorical criticism. She has taught classes in Internet technologies and web site development, public speaking, and theories of argumentation. She has also worked as a part-time Internet consultant and is currently an active member of the Elab, an informal think tank and testing ground for researchers and practitioners interested in the prospects of new media technologies for civil society. As a member of this group, she is contributing to the creation of the Ecommons/Agora Electronique, a national not-for-profit online public learning network where communities and citizens can discover, develop, and exchange ideas and resources.

MAURICE CHARLAND is Associate Professor of Communication Studies at Concordia University, where he teaches rhetoric and political communication. He completed his Ph.D. in Communication at the University of Iowa in 1983. He has written a number of essays that examine Canadian political discourse in relation to rhetorical theories of constitution, judgment, and postmodernity. In 2000 he received the Charles H. Woolbert Research Award for his 1987 article, "Constitutive Rhetoric: The Case of the Peuple Québécois," published in the *Quarterly Journal of Speech*. He is presently working on a co-authored volume with Michael Dorland titled *"Peace, Order and Good Government": Law, Rhetoric and Irony in the Formation of Canadian Civil Culture* (forthcoming).

CAROL CORBIN is Associate Professor of Communication at the University College of Cape Breton, where she teaches rhetoric, mass communication, cultural studies, and postmodern theory. She received her Ph.D. in communication studies from the University of Iowa in 1992. She does research in the areas of communities and their environments—focusing in particular on how rural communities cope with changes in communication technologies, decline in industrial and resource bases, and the environment. She has edited four books related to postmodernism, Cape Breton culture, and the cod fishery, as well as three newsletters. She has published several journal articles in diverse areas, and has two books under review. She has taught in Thailand and China and lectured in Northern Ireland.

MARIE-NICOLE COSSETTE is Assistant Professor at the Department of Communication, University of Ottawa. She works in two domains of communication research: theories of communication and development communication. She has developed a pragmatic model for looking at intercultural communication in development communication, involving different contexts (such as globalization, international development, and micro-credit). Her work has been published in several journals.

MICHAEL DORLAND is Professor in the School of Journalism and Communication, Carleton University. He is the editor of *The Cultural Industries in Canada: Policies, Problems and Prospects* (1996) and author of *So Close to the State/s: The Emergence of Canadian Feature Film Policy* (1998). The present chapter is adapted from his forthcoming *"Peace, Order and Good Government": Law, Rhetoric and Irony in the Formation of Canadian Civil Culture* (co-authored with Maurice Charland).

DEREK FOSTER is a Ph.D. candidate at Carleton University's School of Journalism and Communication in the Faculty of Public Affairs and Policy Management in Ottawa, Ontario. His dissertation, "Dialogues with Difference: The Social Construction of Safe Spaces and Hot Spots," focuses on squeegee kids. He has taught courses ranging from media theory to television to Canada's place in the global village. His published articles include topics such as Internet culture, Canada Day festivities, Marshall McLuhan, William Gibson, and professional wrestling.

NEIL GERLACH is Assistant Professor of Sociology in the Department of Sociology and Anthropology at Concordia University in Montreal. He holds degrees in sociology, anthropology, law, and education and teaches in the areas of economic sociology, criminal justice, and social theory. His research interests revolve around the question of changing forms of social governance within late modernity. He is part of the "Out of Order: Courts and Social Governance in Canada" research network, which explores the changing roles of Canadian courts in the formulation of social policy. Currently he is preparing a book on the Canadian DNA data bank and its significance within criminal justice.

SHERYL N. HAMILTON is Assistant Professor in Art History and Communication Studies at McGill University in Montreal, Canada. She is a former practicing lawyer who teaches in the areas of gender and technology, interpretive methods, and law and culture. She has published articles in journals such as *Convergence: The Journal of Research into New Technologies, The Journal of Communication Inquiry, Science Communication,* and *Canadian Review of American Studies.* Her current research ("Private Persons, Public Personas: Law, Citizenship and the Ownership of Self") examines the law of appropriation of personality in Canada, with a view to its implications for social, civil, and virtual citizenship. She is currently writing a book on the history of cyberculture (*The Cybernetic Imaginary: Putting the Cyber in Cyberculture*) and working on an edited collection with Neil Gerlach. This collection, *Out of Order: Courts and Social Governance in Canada,* will explore the role of Canadian courts in making social policy.

PETER HODGINS is a doctoral student in Communications at Carleton University and Professor of Communication at the University of Ottawa. His early research was on the history of communication in colonial Canada (1600–1850). More recently, he has focused on the cultural politics of public memory in Canada—the myriad ways in which the various factions in Canadian public culture use the past to reinforce their claims to authority, status, and recognition over and against those of competing factions—as well as our changing relationship to history, memory, and heritage.

MIKE HUNTER is currently a graduate student in Communication and Culture at York/Ryerson universities. Separate careers, which have spanned more than 25 years, involved work in hotels, photography, and writing.

These interests led him to reside in six different Canadian provinces over the years. The ability to communicate well in diverse environments fostered an awareness and further interest in the value and importance of communication. His research areas include media and culture, particularly rural/ small town identity and the rural-urban dialectic. His academic association with UCCB led to three years' employment as a public relations writer. He has been a freelance writer for newspapers, magazines, and radio.

DAWN E. B. JOHNSTON is a sessional instructor and doctoral candidate in the Faculty of Communication and Culture at the University of Calgary. She holds a Master of Arts in Communications Studies from the University of Calgary and a Bachelor of Arts (Honors) in English and Women's Studies from Memorial University of Newfoundland. She has presented papers at conferences, including the Canadian Lesbian and Gay Studies Association 2000 ("Communicating Queerness in the Communications Classroom"), Canadian Communications Association 1999 ("Spatial In(queer)ies: Queer Space in Calgary"), Canadian Sociology and Anthropology Association 1999 ("Sites of Resistance and Strength: Calgary's Lesbian Spaces"), Canadian Women's Studies Association 1998 ("Queer Contemplations: The Place of Queer Theory in Contemporary Cultural Studies"), and University of Southern California Communications Conference 1998 ("Identity Bending on the Internet: A Virtual Dialogue with Susan Harris"). Her current research interests are focused on the impact of shifts in communications mediums on gay and lesbian political activism in North America. The chapter that appears in this book is part of a larger thesis entitled *Sites of Resistance, Sites of Strength: Construction and Experience of Queer Space in Calgary.*

DAVID KIM JUNIPER is an instructional web designer with Educational Media Development, Athabasca University, Alberta. He has worked as a newspaper reporter, computer consultant, and teacher. He completed his master's thesis in 2000 at the University of Northern British Columbia, where he explored the use of the Internet as a political tool by indigenous groups in Canada, the United States, and Mexico. His case study was the Zapatista rebels of Chiapas, Mexico, who used information technology to network with global civil society and triggered an information war against the Mexican government. It is his belief that the free and unfettered nature of the Internet provides indigenous nations, who have historically been oppressed and isolated by the state, the means to overcome and circumvent established channels of information and weave their own webs of resistance and cooperation.

KARIM H. KARIM is Assistant Professor at Carleton University's School of Journalism and Communication. He worked previously in the Department of Canadian Heritage as senior researcher and in the Multiculturalism Program as senior policy analyst. Dr. Karim is currently conducting research on ethnic media and public discourse. He has written journal articles and book chapters on issues of cultural diversity in the media, transnational communication flows, and the new media. He has recently published *Islamic Peril: Media and Global Violence*, and he is currently editing a forthcoming volume on diaspora and communication.

KIRSTEN KOZOLANKA is a doctoral student in the School of Journalism and Communication at Carleton University in Ottawa, Canada. A longtime education activist, she has published articles in the education journal *Our Schools/Our Selves*, on whose advisory board she sits. As a founding member of the Coalition for Public Education, she participated in the fight against education restructuring in Ontario. She has worked as a communications advisor to a leader of a federal political party and to a former Minister of Culture and Communications in the province of Ontario. She is currently employed as a communications manager in the federal government.

MARK DOUGLAS LOWES, Ph.D., is Assistant Professor in the Department of Communication at the University of Ottawa. For the past several years, he has been building a research program that is concerned with investigating the complex relationships among media, sport, and popular culture in Western societies. This research program began with an ethnographic study of sports journalism in Canada, the findings of which were published in the international *Sociology of Sport Journal*. His book *Inside The Sports Pages: Work Routines, Professional Ideologies and the Manufacture of Sports News* was published in 1999. His current research focuses on exploring the increasingly prominent role that major league sports play in the economic and cultural growth strategies of many North American cities. In addition to the chapter in this collection, the findings of this research project have been brought together in a book manuscript titled *Indy Dreams and Urban Nightmares: Speed Merchants, Spectacle, and the Struggle Over Public Space in the "World-Class" City* (forthcoming).

JENNIFER M. MacLENNAN holds a Ph.D. in rhetoric from the University of Washington and degrees in English literature from McMaster and St. Francis Xavier Universities. Her research interests include the rhetoric of Canadian identity; the rhetorical theory of Northrop Frye; rhetorical foundations of communication practice, especially teaching; and professional communication. She is co-author of *Inside Language: A Canadian Language Reader*, as well as three other textbooks and numerous papers on communication and rhetoric. She is currently D. K. Seaman Chair in

Professional and Technical Communication in the College of Engineering at the University of Saskatchewan. In addition to regular teaching and research activity, she does extensive curriculum and program development and conducts training workshops and seminars for students, faculty, and professionals.

G. JOHN MOFFATT holds a Ph.D. in Old English language and literature and an M.A. in Canadian literature from Queen's University in Kingston, Ontario. His research interests include early medieval heroic literature and folklore, in particular theories of oral composition and transmission in early medieval Britain and Ireland; Canadian literature, language, and rhetoric; Native Canadian literature; and the relationship between modernity and linguistic identity. He speaks fluent French and German, with reading knowledge of several more languages, including Old Norse/Modern Scandinavian languages, Latin, and Gaelic. He is co-author of *Inside Language: A Canadian Language Reader* and numerous papers on Canadian language and literature. He is currently a Professor of English at the University College of the Fraser Valley.

EVAN POTTER is Assistant Professor in the Department of Communications at the University of Ottawa. He has written widely on Canada's international relations, including *Trans-Atlantic Partners: Canadian Approaches to the European Union* (1999), *Economic Intelligence and National Insecurity* (1998), and *Multinationals in the Global Political Economy* (with Lorraine Eden, 1993). A forthcoming edited book will address the impact of information technology on Canadian diplomacy. He was a Reisman Fellow at the Treasury Board of Canada in 1997–1998, and he has worked in the Communications Bureau at the Canadian Department of Foreign Affairs and International Trade.

SCOTT STREINER is a senior manager in the federal public service. He worked for a decade at the Canadian Human Rights Commission, where his last position was Director of Pay Equity and Settlement Monitoring. Other areas of professional responsibility have included employment equity policy, Aboriginal self-government, and international human rights treaties. Also an academic, he has an M.A. from the Norman Paterson School of International Affairs and he is completing a Ph.D. in Political Science at Carleton University. He has published and presented academic papers on a range of human rights and related topics. His dissertation examines the revival of egalitarianism in an era of globalization.

GAIL VALASKAKIS is a former Dean of Arts and Science and Professor of Communications at Concordia University in Montreal and is currently Director of Research at the Aboriginal Healing Foundation in Ottawa. She was also a founding board member of the Montreal Native Friendship Centre, Manitou College, and Waseskun Native Half-way House. A Northern Native communications scholar, she has written on issues of First Nations representation, experience, cultural appropriation, and ethnography. The daughter of an enrolled member of the Lac du Flambeau Band of Lake Superior Chippewa, she was raised on the Lac du Flambeau reservation in Wisconsin.

www.ingramcontent.com/pod-product-compliance
Lightning Source LLC
Chambersburg PA
CBHW060145280326
41932CB00012B/1645